BODY AS LANDSCAPE,
LOVE AS INTOXICATION

ANCIENT ISRAEL AND ITS LITERATURE

Thomas C. Römer, General Editor

Editorial Board:
Susan Ackerman
Thomas B. Dozeman
Cynthia Edenburg
Shuichi Hasegawa
Konrad Schmid
Naomi A. Steinberg

Number 36

BODY AS LANDSCAPE, LOVE AS INTOXICATION

Conceptual Metaphors
in the Song of Songs

Brian P. Gault

Atlanta

Copyright © 2019 by Brian P. Gault

All rights reserved. No part of this work may be reproduced or transmitted in any form or by any means, electronic or mechanical, including photocopying and recording, or by means of any information storage or retrieval system, except as may be expressly permitted by the 1976 Copyright Act or in writing from the publisher. Requests for permission should be addressed in writing to the Rights and Permissions Office, SBL Press, 825 Houston Mill Road, Atlanta, GA 30329 USA.

Library of Congress Cataloging-in-Publication Data

Names: Gault, Brian P., author.
Title: Body as landscape, love as intoxication : conceptual metaphors in the Song of songs / by Brian P. Gault.
Description: Atlanta : SBL Press, 2019. | Series: Ancient Israel and its literature ; Number 36 | Includes bibliographical references and index.
Identifiers: LCCN 2019014657 (print) | LCCN 2019018718 (ebook) | ISBN 9781628372472 (pbk. : alk. paper) | ISBN 9780884143826 (hbk. : alk. paper)
Subjects: LCSH: Bible. Song of Solomon—Criticism, interpretation, etc.
Classification: LCC BS1485.52 .G35 2019 (print) | LCC BS1485.52 (ebook) | DDC 223/.9066—dc23
LC record available at https://lccn.loc.gov/2019014657
LC ebook record available at https://lccn.loc.gov/2019018718

Printed on acid-free paper.

To Cara:

Without your love and prayerful encouragement,
this work could not have been written.

מה־יפו דדיך אחתי כלה
מה־טבו דדיך מיין
וריח שמניך מכל־בשמים:

How beautiful is your love, my sister, my bride!
How much better is your love than wine,
And the fragrance of your perfume than any spice!

(Song of Songs 4:10)

Contents

Acknowledgments ix
Abbreviations xi

1. A Lock with No Key? Body Metaphors in the Song
   of Songs 1
   1.1. Uncertain Beginnings   2
   1.2. Allegorical Methods   8
   1.3. Reader-Response Methods   18
   1.4. Comparative Methods   23
   1.5. Summary   31

2. Missing Key: A Conceptual-Comparative Approach 33
   2.1. Terminology   34
   2.2. Theoretical Foundations   35
   2.3. Conceptual Metaphor Theory   39
   2.4. Comparative Method   43
   2.5. Summary   57

3. I Am: Poems of Self-Description 59
   3.1. The Dark-Skinned Beauty (1:5–6)   59
   3.2. A Self-Proclamation of Purity and Reward (8:8–10)   73
   3.3. Summary   87

4. Nature as Erotica: Sexual Euphemism and
   Double-Entendre 89
   4.1. The Man's Delicious Apple (2:3)   89
   4.2. A Mare among Stallions (1:9–10)   97
   4.3. Mountains of Pleasure (2:17; 4:6; 8:14)   102
   4.4. Garden of Delight (1:6; 2:15; 4:12–13, 16–5:1; 6:2,
   11; 7:13; 8:12–13)   110

	4.5. The Woman's Intoxicating Fruits (7:3a, 8–10; 8:2)	122
	4.6. Summary	135
5.	Anatomy of a Rose: Praise for the Female Body 137	
	5.1. Messengers of Love (1:15; 4:1; cf. 5:12)	138
	5.2. Large, Life-Giving Eyes (7:5)	145
	5.3. Dark, Flowing, (F)Locks (4:1c; 6:5c; 7:6; cf. 5:11b)	148
	5.4. Perfect Pair of Wooly Whites (4:2; 6:6)	157
	5.5. Sexy, Scarlet Lips (4:3a)	160
	5.6. Rouge Red Cheeks (4:3b; 6:7)	163
	5.7. Tower-Like Neck and Nose (4:4; 7:5)	168
	5.8. Passion-Provoking Breasts (4:5; 7:4; cf. 5:13b)	175
	5.9. Shapely, Superior Stomach (7:3b)	181
	5.10. Sculpted Hips/Thighs (7:2b)	185
	5.11. Miss Universe (6:4, 10; cf. 5:15b)	188
	5.12. Summary	193
6.	Outstanding among Ten Thousand: An Ode to the Male Body 195	
	6.1. Gold Standard (5:11a, 14a, 15a)	196
	6.2. Seductive Scent (5:13a)	201
	6.3. Value of Virility (5:14b)	206
	6.4. Summary	214
7.	Conclusions: Method, Metaphor, Beauty, and Unity............215	
	7.1. Methodology	216
	7.2. Metaphors	218
	7.3. Physical Beauty	219
	7.4. Literary Unity	223

Bibliography 227
Ancient Sources Index 269
Modern Authors Index 284

Acknowledgments

As the passion of the Song's lovers was fanned by family and friends, so my own acquaintance with and affections for the book of Canticles has been amplified by both scholars and students. This volume was both an individual and a cooperative effort. While the actual words are mine, this work could not have been written without the assistance of many others. First, Gordon H. Johnston (Dallas Theological Seminary) introduced me to Israel's most sublime Song and set the course for over a decade of research, culminating in the publication of this work. His continued conversation and careful review of my manuscript sharpened my ideas immensely, but his enduring friendship is valued above all.

Second, Nili S. Fox (Hebrew Union College) laid a foundation for me in comparative studies, using the archaeology of texts and material culture in the interpretation of the Hebrew Bible. She offered invaluable direction in this project from beginning to end, providing constructive criticism and valuable encouragement. Third, Samuel Greengus (Hebrew Union College) unveiled the treasures of Mesopotamian literature and culture, modeling for me the appropriate use of comparative studies in exegesis. No matter the depth of my research, he repeatedly pointed out an additional book or article that had escaped my attention. With the expert direction of these scholars, this volume was made exceptionally better.

A special thanks to Columbia Biblical Seminary for granting my sabbatical and Southeastern Baptist Theological Seminary for providing resources for my research as Visiting Scholar. The library staff at Hebrew Union College, Columbia International University, and Southeastern Seminary also played an important role in this project. I would especially like to thank Jason Schapera and Jeremy Scruggs for their help in locating works unavailable to me and Will Johnston and Sarah Cho for their research and proofreading of the manuscript.

Also, I am indebted to Thomas Römer and the other members of the editorial board of the Ancient Israel and Its Literature series for accepting this book and to Nicole Tilford at SBL Press for her graciousness throughout the production process.

Finally, I would like to express my deepest appreciation to my family for their enduring support over this long journey. To my parents and in-laws, you have taught me the ways of love (Song 8:2) through your selfless care and provision. To my daughters, Charissa and Maria, with one glance of your eyes, you have captivated my heart (Song 4:9). To my beautiful wife Cara, how much better is your love than wine (Song 1:2). Without your enduring support, faithful prayers, and constant encouragement, this work could not have been written.

Brian P. Gault
January 2019

Abbreviations

Primary Resources

1Q20	Genesis Apocryphon
1QM	War Scroll
1QS	Rule of the Community
4Q106–108	Canticles[a–c]
4Q184	Wiles of the Wicked Woman
6Q6	6QCant
11Q5	Psalms Scroll[a]
11Q10	Targum of Job
ʾAbot R. Nat.	ʾAbot de Rabbi Nathan
Ach.	Aristophanes, *Acharnians*
Aen.	Virgil, *Aeneid*
Am.	Ovid, *Amores*; [Lucian], *Amores*
Anab.	Xenophon, *Anabasis*
Ant.	Josephus, *Jewish Antiquities*
Anth. Pal.	*Anthologia Palatina*
Ars.	Ovid, *Ars amatoria*
Avod. Zar.	Avodah Zarah
Avot	Avot
b.	Babylonian Talmud
Ber.	Berakot
Bib. hist.	Diodorus, *Bibliotheca historica*
Carm.	Horace, *Odes*
CD	Damascus Document
Comm. Cant.	Origen, *Commentary on the Song*
Cult. fem.	Tertullian, *Apparel of Women*
Cyr.	Xenophon, *Cyropaedia*
De arch.	Vitruvius, *De architectura*
Deipn.	Athenaeus, *Deipnosophistae*

Descr.	Pausanias, *Description of Greece*
Ecl.	Virgil, *Eclogae*
El.	Propertius, *Elegies*; Tibullus, *Elegies*
Ep.	Jerome, *Epistles*; Martial, *Epigram*
Exod. Rab.	Exodus Rabbah
Gen. Rab.	Genesis Rabbah
Git.	Gittim
Hab. virg.	Cyprian, *Dress of Virgins*
Hag.	Hagigah
Her.	Ovid, *Heroides*
Hipp. maj.	Plato, *Greater Hippias*
Hist.	Herodotus, *Histories*
Hist. plant.	Theophrastus, *Historia plantarum*
Hul.	Hullin
Id.	Theocritus, *Idylls*
Il.	Homer, *Iliad*
In. Cant.	Hippolytus, *On Song of Songs*
Jos. Asen.	Joseph and Aseneth
Jov.	Jerome, *Adversus Jovinianum*
Ketub.	Ketubbboth
Leuc. Clit.	Achilles Tatius, *Leucippe and Clitophon*
Lib.	Apollodorus, *Library*
m.	Mishnah
Mat. med.	Dioscorides, *De materia medica*
Metam.	Ovid, *Metamorphoses*
Mon.	Tertullian, *Monogamy*
Mo'ed Qaṭ.	Mo'ed Qaṭan
Nat.	Pliny, *Natural History*
Nat. an.	Aelian, *Nature of Animals*
Naz.	Nazir
Ned.	Nedarim
Nub.	Aristophanes, *Clouds*
Num. Rab.	Numbers Rabbah
Od.	Homer, *Odyssey*
Oec.	Xenophon, *Oeconomicus*
Paed.	Clement of Alexandria, *Christ the Educator*
Parth.	Alcman, *Partheneion*
Pes.	Pesachim
Qoh. Rab.	Qoheleth Rabbah

Rem. am.	Ovid, *Remedia amoris*
Resp.	Plato, *Republic*
Rhet.	Aristotle, *Rhetoric*
Ruf.	Jerome, *Adversus Rufinum*
Sanh.	Sanhedrin
Sat.	Juvenal, *Satires*
Sens.	Theophrastus, *De sensu*
Shabb.	Shabbat
Song Rab.	Song of Songs Rabbah
Symp.	Xenophon, *Symposium*
t.	Tosefta
Taʿan.	Taʿanit
Var. hist.	Aelian, *Varia historia*
Yad.	Yadayim

Secondary Resources

AAASH	*Acta Archaeologica Academiae Scientiarum Hungaricae*
AB	Anchor Bible
AcOr	*Acta Orientalia*
AcT	*Acta Theologica*
ACW	Ancient Christian Writers
ADFU	Ausgrabungen der Deutschen Forschungsgemeinschaft in Uruk
ADPV	Abhandlungen des Deutschen Palästinavereins
AfO	*Archiv für Orientforschung*
AfOB	Archiv für Orientforschung: Beiheft
AHw	von Soden, Wolfram. *Akkadisches Handwörterbuch*. 3 vols. Wiesbaden, 1965–1981.
AIL	Ancient Israel and Its Literature
AJA	*American Journal of Archaeology*
AJP	*American Journal of Philology*
AJSL	*American Journal of Semitic Languages and Literature*
AnBib	Analecta Biblica
ANESSup	Ancient Near Eastern Studies Supplement
ANEP	Pritchard, James B., ed. *The Ancient Near East in Pictures relating to the Old Testament*. 2nd ed. Princeton: Princeton University Press, 1994.

ANET	Pritchard, James B., ed. *Ancient Near Eastern Texts relating to the Old Testament*. 3rd ed. Princeton: Princeton University Press, 1969.
ANF	Roberts, Alexander, and James Donaldson, eds. *The Ante-Nicene Fathers: Translations of the Writings of the Fathers Down to A.D. 325*. 10 vols. 1885–1887. Repr., Peabody, MA: Hendrickson, 1994.
ArBib	Aramaic Bible
AnOr	Analecta Orientalia
AOAT	Alter Orient und Altes Testament
ArOr	*Archiv Orientální*
ASJ	*Acta Sumerologica*
ASTI	*Annual of the Swedish Theological Institute*
ATD	Das Alte Testament Deutsch
AuOr	*Aula Orientalis*
ÄWb	Hannig, Rainer, ed. *Ägyptisches Wörterbuch: Mittleres Reich und zweite Zwischenzeit*. Mainz: von Zabern, 2006.
BA	*Biblical Archaeologist*
BAR	British Archaeological Reports
BASOR	*Bulletin of the American Schools of Oriental Research*
BBET	Beiträge zur biblischen Exegese und Theologie
BBR	*Bulletin for Biblical Research*
BCOTWP	Baker Commentary on Old Testament Wisdom and Psalms
BDB	Brown, Francis, S. R. Driver, and Charles A. Briggs. *A Hebrew and English Lexicon of the Old Testament*. Oxford: Clarendon, 1907.
BdH	La Bible dans l'histoire
BETL	Bibliotheca Ephemeridum Theologicarum Lovaniensium
BHQ	Biblia Hebraica Quinta
Bib	*Biblica*
BibInt	*Biblical Interpretation*
BibInt	Biblical Interpretation Series
BibOr	Biblica et Orientalia
BIE	*Bulletin de l'Institut d'Égypt*
BISNELC	Bar-Ilan Studies in Near Eastern Languages and Culture
BJS	Brown Judaic Studies
BKAT	Biblischer Kommentar, Altes Testament
BLS	Bible and Literature Series
BM	*Beth Miqra*

BN	*Biblische Notizen*
BO	*Bibliotheca Orientalis*
BRev	*Bible Review*
BSA	*Bulletin on Sumerian Agriculture*
BT	*Bible Translator*
BTCB	Brazos Theological Commentary on the Bible
BTS	Biblical Tools and Studies
BW	*The Biblical World*
BZAR	Beihefte zur Zeitschrift für altorientalische und biblische Rechtsgeschichte
BZAW	Beihefte zur Zeitschrift für die alttestamentliche Wissenschaft
CAD	Gelb, Ignace J., et al. *The Assyrian Dictionary of the Oriental Institute of the University of Chicago*. 21 vols. Chicago: Oriental Institute of the University of Chicago, 1956–2010.
CANE	Sasson, Jack M, ed. *Civilizations of the Ancient Near East*. 4 vols. New York: Scribners, 1995.
CB	Church's Bible
CBET	Contributions to Biblical Exegesis and Theology
CBQ	*Catholic Biblical Quarterly*
CBW	*Conversations with the Biblical World*
CC	Continental Commentaries
CdE	*Chronique d'Égypte*
CJ	*Classical Journal*
CM	Cuneiform Monographs
ConcC	Concordia Commentary
CRRAI	Comptes rendus de la Rencontre Assyriologique Internationale
CS	Cistercian Studies Series
CT	*Cuneiform Texts from Babylonian Tablets in the British Museum*
CUSAS	Cornell University Studies in Assyriology and Sumerology
DAIK	Deutsches Archäologisches Institut, Abteilung Kairo
DANE	Bienkowski, Piotr, and Alan Millard, ed. *Dictionary of the Ancient Near East*. Philadelphia: University of Pennsylvania Press, 2000.
DI	Sefati, Yitschak. *Love Songs in Sumerian Literature: Critical Edition of the Dumuzi-Inanna Love Songs*. BISNELC. Ramat-Gan: Bar-Ilan University, 1998.

DJD	Discoveries in the Judaean Desert
DJBA	Sokoloff, Michael. *Dictionary of Jewish Babylonian Aramaic*. Ramat-Gan: Bar-Ilan University, 2003.
DJPA	Sokoloff, Michael. *Dictionary of Jewish Palestinian Aramaic*. 3rd ed. Ramat-Gan: Bar-Ilan University, 2017.
DNWSI	Hoftijzer, Jacob, and Karen Jongeling. *Dictionary of the North-West Semitic Inscriptions*. 2 vols. Leiden: Brill, 1995.
DULAT	Olmo Lete, Gregorio del, and Joaquín Sanmartín. *A Dictionary of the Ugaritic Language in the Alphabetic Tradition*. Translated and edited by Wilfred G. E. Watson. 3rd ed. 2 vols. Leiden: Brill, 2015.
EA	El-Amarna tablets. According to the edition of Jørgen A. Knudtzon. *Die el-Amarna-Tafeln*. Leipzig, 1908–1915.
EBib	Études bibliques
ECLT	Makaryk, Irena. *Encyclopedia of Contemporary Literary Theory*. Toronto: University of Toronto Press, 1993.
EncJud	Skolnik, Fred, and Michael Berenbaum, eds. *Encyclopedia Judaica*. 2nd ed. 22 vols. Detroit: Macmillan Reference USA, 2007.
ErIsr	*Eretz Israel*
ESV	English Standard Version
EUS	European University Studies
FCB	Feminist Companion to the Bible
FCBT	Feminist Commentary on the Babylonian Talmud
FOTL	Forms of Old Testament Literature
G&H	*Gender & History*
GHb	Hannig, Rainer, ed. *Die Sprache der Pharaonen: Großes Handwörterbuch Ägyptisch-Deutsch (2800–950 v. Chr)*. Mainz: von Zabern, 2009.
GKC	Kautzsch, Emil, ed. *Gesenius' Hebrew Grammar*. Translated by Arther E. Cowley. 2nd ed. Oxford: Clarendon, 1910.
HACL	History, Archaeology, and Culture of the Levant
HALOT	Koehler, Ludwig, Walter Baumgartner, and Johann J. Stamm. *The Hebrew and Aramaic Lexicon of the Old Testament*. Translated and edited under the supervision of Mervyn E. J. Richardson. 2 vols. Leiden: Brill, 2001.
HAR	*Hebrew Annual Review*
HdO	Handbook der Orientalistik
HKAT	Handkommentar zum Alten Testament

HSCP	*Harvard Studies in Classical Philology*
HSM	Harvard Semitic Monographs
HTR	*Harvard Theological Review*
HUCA	*Hebrew Union College Annual*
IA	*Iranica Antiqua*
IB	Buttrick, G. A., et al. *Interpreter's Bible*. 12 vols. New York, 1951–1957.
IEJ	*Israel Exploration Journal*
Int	*Interpretation*
IRT	Issues in Religion and Theology
ISBL	Indiana Studies in Biblical Literature
ITQ	*Irish Theological Quarterly*
JA	*Journal Asiatique*
JAAC	*Journal of Aesthetics and Art Criticism*
JAJ	*Journal of Ancient Judaism*
JAOS	*Journal of the American Oriental Society*
JARCE	*Journal of the American Research Center in Egypt*
JBL	*Journal of Biblical Literature*
JCS	*Journal of Cuneiform Studies*
JEA	*Journal of Egyptian Archaeology*
JEMAHS	*Journal of Eastern Mediterranean Archaeology and Heritage Studies*
JJS	*Journal of Jewish Studies*
JNES	*Journal of the Near Eastern Society*
JNSL	*Journal of Northwest Semitic Languages*
Joüon	Joüon, Paul. *A Grammar of Biblical Hebrew*. Translated and revised by T. Muraoka. 2nd ed. 2 vols. Rome: Pontifical Biblical Institute, 2006.
JQR	*Jewish Quarterly Review*
JPOS	*Journal of the Palestine Oriental Society*
JPS	Jewish Publication Society
JRAS	*Journal of the Royal Asiatic Society*
JSem	*Journal for Semitics*
JSJ	*Journal for the Study of Judaism in the Persian, Hellenistic, and Roman Periods*
JSNTSup	Journal for the Study of the New Testament Supplement Series
JSP	*Journal for the Study of the Pseudepigrapha*
JSOT	*Journal for the Study of the Old Testament*

JSOTSup	Journal for the Study of the Old Testament Supplement Series
JSS	*Journal of Semitic Studies*
JTS	*Journal of Theological Studies*
JTSA	*Journal of Theology for Southern Africa*
JTamS	*Journal of Tamil Studies*
KAR	Ebeling, Erich, ed. *Keilschrifttexte aus Assur religiosen Inhalts*. Leipzig: Hinrichs, 1919–1923.
KAT	Kommentar zum Alten Testament
KTU	Dietrich, Manfried, Oswald Loretz, and Joaquín Sanmartín, eds. *Die keilalphabetischen Texte aus Ugarit*. Münster: Ugarit-Verlag, 2013.
LAI	Library of Ancient Israel
Lane	Lane, Edward W. *An Arabic-English Lexicon*. 8 vols. London: Williams & Norgate, 1863. Repr., Beirut: Libr. du Liban, 1980.
LAOS	Lepiziger Altorientalistische Studien
LCL	Loeb Classical Library
LHBOTS	Library of Hebrew Bible/Old Testament Studies
LSAWS	Linguistic Studies in Ancient West Semitic
LSJ	Liddell, Henry George, Robert Scott, and Henry Stuart Jones. *A Greek-English Lexicon*. 9th ed. with revised supplement. Oxford: Clarendon, 1996.
LXX	Septuagint
LW	Luther's Works
MdD	Drower, Ethel S., and Rudolph Macuch, eds. *Mandaic Dictionary*. Oxford: Clarendon, 1963.
MSL	*Materialien zum sumeriischen Lexikon/Materials for a Sumerian Lexicon*. 7 vols. Rome: Pontifical Biblical Institute, 1937–2004.
MSym	Melammu Symposium
MT	Masoretic Text
NEA	*Near Eastern Archaeology*
NIB	Keck, Leander E., ed. *The New Interpreter's Bible*. 12 vols. Nashville: Abingdon, 1994–2004.
NICOT	New International Commentary on the Old Testament
NIDOTTE	VanGemeren, Willem A., ed. *New International Dictionary of Old Testament Theology and Exegesis*. 5 vols. Grand Rapids: Zondervan, 1997.

NIV	New International Version
NIVAC	New International Version Application Commentary
NPNF	Schaff, Philip and Henry Wace, eds. *A Select Library of Nicene and Post-Nicene Fathers of the Christian Church.* 28 vols. in 2 series. 1886–1889. Repr., Peabody, MA: Hendrickson, 1994.
NRSV	New Revised Standard Version
OB	Old Babylonian
OBO	Orbis Biblicus et Orientalis
OBT	Overtures to Biblical Theology
OEAE	Redford, Donald, ed. *The Oxford Encyclopedia of Ancient Egypt.* 3 vols. Oxford: Oxford University Press, 2001.
OEANE	Meyers, Eric M., ed. *The Oxford Encyclopedia of Archaeology in the Near East.* 5 vols. Oxford: Oxford University Press, 1997.
OECI	Oxford Editions of Cuneiform Inscriptions
OG	Old Greek
OL	Old Latin
OLD	Glare, P. G. W., ed. *Oxford Latin Dictionary.* Oxford: Clarendon, 1982.
OLZ	*Orientalische Literaturzeitung*
OIP	Oriental Institute Publications
Or	*Orientalia* (NS)
ORA	Orientalische Religionen in der Antike
OTL	Old Testament Library
OTP	Charlesworth, James H., ed. *Old Testament Pseudepigrapha.* 2 vols. New York: Doubleday, 1983, 1985.
OTS	Old Testament Studies
Oxy.	Oxyrhynchus papyri
Parab	*Parabola*
PBS	University of Pennsylvania, Publications of the Babylonian Section
PEPP	Greene, Roland, ed. *The Princeton Encyclopedia of Poetry and Poetics.* 4th ed. Princeton: Princeton University Press, 2012.
PEQ	*Palestine Exploration Quarterly*
PG	Migne, Jacques-Paul, ed. Patrologia Graeca [= Patrologiae Cursus Completus: Series Graeca]. 161 vols. Paris: Migne, 1857–1886.

PMLA	*Periodical of the Modern Language Association*
PRSM	*Proceedings of the Royal Society of Medicine*
PTMS	Pittsburgh Theological Monograph Series
RA	*revue d'assyriologie et d'archéologie orientale*
RB	*Revue biblique*
RdE	*Revue d'égyptologie*
RevQ	*Revue de Qumrân*
RlA	Ebeling, Erich, et al., eds. *Reallexikon der Assyriologie.* Berlin: de Gruyter, 1928–.
RRJ	*Review of Rabbinic Judaism*
SAA	State Archives of Assyria
SAAS	State Archives of Assyria Studies
SAK	*Studien zur Altägyptischen Kultur*
SBLDS	Society of Biblical Literature Dissertation Series
SBS	Stuttgarter Bibelstudien
SCS	Septuagint and Cognate Studies
SHR	Studies in the History of Religions
Siphrut	Siphrut: Literature and Theology of the Hebrew Scriptures
SJOT	*Scandinavian Journal of the Old Testament*
SR	*Studies in Religion*
StBibLit	Studies in Biblical Literature (Lang)
STDJ	Studies on the Texts of the Desert of Judah
StOr	*Studia Orientalia*
SubBi	Subsidia Biblica
SVTP	Studia in Veteris Testamenti Pseudepigrapha
SyrLex	Sokoloff, Michael. *A Syriac Lexicon: A Translation from the Latin, Correction, Expansion, and Update of C. Brockelmann's Lexicon Syriacum.* Winona Lake, IN: Eisenbrauns; Piscataway, NJ: Gorgias, 2009.
TAPA	*Transactions and Proceedings of the American Philological Association*
TCL	*Textes cunéiformes*. Paris: Musées du Louvre, 1910–.
TCS	Texts from Cuneiform Sources
TDOT	Botterweck, G. Hohannes, Helmer Ringgren, Heinz-Josef Fabry, and Holger Gzella. *Theological Dictionary of the Old Testament.* Translated by John T. Willis et al. 16 vols. Grand Rapids: Eerdmans, 1974–2018.
TOTC	Tyndale Old Testament Commentary
TQ	*Theologische Quartalschrift*

TSAJ	Texte und Studien zum antiken Judentum
TynBul	*Tyndale Bulletin*
UAVA	Untersuchungen zur Assyriologie und vorderasiatischen Archäologie
UT	*Ugaritic Textbook*. Cyrus H. Gordon. Rev. ed. AnOr 38. Rome: Pontifical Biblical Institute, 1998.
UUA	Uppsala Universitetsårskrift
VA	*Varia Aegyptiaca*
VAB	Vorderasiatische Bibliothek
VAT	Vorderasiatische Abteilung Tontafel. Vorderasiatisches Museum, Berlin
VC	*Vigiliae Christianae*
VT	*Vetus Testamentum*
VTSup	Supplements to Vetus Testamentum
WÄS	Erman, Adolf, and Hermann Grapow. *Wörterbuch der ägyptischen Sprache*. 5 vols. Berlin: Akademie, 1926–1931.
WBC	Word Biblical Commentary
WesBibComp	Westminster Bible Companion
WVDOG	Wissenschaftliche Veröffentlichungen der Deutsche Orient-Gesellschaft
YJS	Yale Judaica Series
ZAW	*Zeitschrift für die alttestamentliche Wissenschaft*
ZfE	*Zeitschrift für Ethnologie*

Other Abbreviations

1cs	first-person common singular
Akk.	Akkadian
Aram.	Aramaic
fig(s).	figure(s)
frag(s).	fragment(s)
Heb.	Hebrew
ill(s).	illustration(s)
pl(s).	plate(s); plural
r.	recto
rev.	revised

1
A Lock with No Key?
Body Metaphors in the Song of Songs

No other book in the Hebrew Bible has suffered under so many different interpretations as the Song of Songs. These 117 verses have "tantalized the young, troubled the orthodox, and evaded the exegetical grasp of scholars for centuries."[1] In fact, the earliest comments on its interpretation indicate that the Song was an important yet controversial book in the second century CE. The Mishnah records R. Aqiba's famous words, "For all the ages are not worth the day on which the Song of Songs was given to Israel. All the Writings are holy, but the Song of Songs is the holy of holies" (m. Yad. 3:5).[2] Aggadat Shir Hashirim records a similar statement from Aqiba on the Song's supreme importance, "If Torah had not been given, the Song of Songs would be enough to guide the world."[3] Yet the Song's interpretation was already stirring up heated debate, implied by Aqiba's warning, "Whoever trills the Song of Songs in banquet halls and so treats it as a (love) song has no share in the world to come" (t. Sanh. 12:10; b. Sanh. 101a).[4]

For Jews and Christians, the Song of Songs has been among the most theologically significant and exegetically fruitful books of Scripture. Early bibliographies list more works on the Song than any other biblical book save Psalms, more than all Paul's epistles taken together, and the gospels.[5] However, despite centuries of prolific effort to remove the obscurity of this

---

1. Connie J. Whitesell, "Behold, Thou Art Fair, My Beloved," *Parab* 20 (1995): 92.
2. Unless otherwise noted, translations of ancient sources are my own.
3. Solomon Schechter, "Agadath Shir Hashirim," *JQR* 6 (1896): 674.
4. For further evidence of rabbinic debate, see ʾAbot R. Nat. A:4.
5. George L. Scheper, "Reformation Attitudes toward Allegory and the Song of Songs," *PMLA* 89 (1974): 556; Wilfred Cantwell Smith, *What Is Scripture? A Comparative Approach* (Minneapolis: Fortress, 1993), 22–23, 248–49 n.4.

book, the seventeenth-century Westminster clergy opined that scholars had increased rather than removed this dark cloud.[6]

In recent times, archaeological and linguistic advances have shed light on this enigmatic book, yet one aspect over which this cloud still hangs is its body metaphors. Why is the woman's hair compared to a flock of goats (Song 4:1; 6:5), her neck, nose, and breasts to a tower (4:4; 7:5; 8:10), and her belly to a heap of wheat (7:2)? Why is the man's head likened to fine gold (5:11), his cheeks to garden beds of spice (5:13), and the eyes of both lovers to doves (4:1; 5:12)? For scholar and layperson alike, the Song's body imagery is "one of the chief difficulties" in interpreting the book.[7]

Such figurative language, which both lovers employ to describe their beloved's body, has spawned countless speculation. Despite its uniqueness in the biblical corpus, there has been no comparative study of these metaphors. Therefore, this volume will analyze the Song's body imagery in light of parallels from the ancient Near East in order to shed light on its meaning. A full treatment of the Song's history of interpretation could fill volumes, but we begin with a brief survey of its uncertain beginnings as well as the three major interpretive approaches to its body metaphors as a necessary introduction to the methodology used in this study.[8]

1.1. Uncertain Beginnings

In recent years, scholars have begun to reexamine the literature of Second Temple Judaism, seeking insight into the Song's earliest interpretation.

---

6. John Downame, ed., *Annotations upon All the Books of the Old and New Testament*, 2nd ed. (London: Legatt, 1651), np.

7. Othmar Keel, *The Song of Songs*, CC (Minneapolis: Fortress, 1994), 25.

8. For a history of interpretation, see, e.g., Hans Ausloos and Bénédicte Lemmelijn, "Praising God or Singing of Love? From Theological to Erotic Allegorisation in the Interpretation of Canticles," *AcT* 30 (2010): 1–9; Michael Fishbane, *Song of Songs: The Traditional Hebrew Text with the New JPS Translation*, JPS Bible Commentary (Philadelphia: Jewish Publication Society of America, 2015), xix–xxiv, 245–310; Christian D. Ginsburg, *The Song of Songs and Coheleth* (New York: Ktav, 1970), 20–102; Ronald Hendel, "The Life of Metaphor in Song of Songs: Poetics, Canon, and the Cultural Bible," *Bib* 100 (2019): 60–83; Marvin H. Pope, *Song of Songs: A New Translation with Introduction and Commentary*, AB 7C (Garden City, NY: Doubleday, 1977), 89–229; Harold H. Rowley, "The Interpretation of the Song of Songs," in *The Servant of the Lord and Other Essays*, 2nd ed. (Oxford: Blackwell, 1965), 197–245.

1.1.1. Dead Sea Scrolls

Like most biblical books, the earliest extant evidence for the transmission of the Song of Songs is found in the Dead Sea Scrolls. Four manuscripts were found at Qumran (4Q106–4Q108, 6Q6 [4QCant^{a-c}, 6QCant]), dated by paleography from 50 BCE to 50 CE.[9] Two manuscripts differ significantly from other textual witnesses of the Song, lacking substantial segments of the canonical text: 4Q107 omits 3:6–8 and 4:4–7, while 4Q106 lacks 4:8–6:10. Peter Flint posits that these verses were omitted due to their amorous nature: "One explanation for the long glaring omission is the sensual language and erotic imagery found in much of Cant 4:8 to 6:10. Perhaps an ancient scribe or copyist wished to limit the amount of material that was no doubt controversial to some."[10] Assuming a connection between the scrolls and the site, one can easily understand how the *Yaḥad*, in its dedication to purity and adherence to the law, may have deemed metaphoric praise for the woman's breasts (4:5), an erotic dream filled with sexual euphemism (5:2–8), and a lyric portrait of the female body (6:4–7) as unfit for the righteous.[11] If Flint's theory is correct, the Song and its body metaphors were interpreted plainly by this community.

Yet, much evidence weighs against this proposal. First, abbreviating the Song to avoid erotic content does not align with internal evidence. Censorship cannot explain the omission of a platonic procession (3:6–8), and the absence of 4:4–7 in 4Q107 is hard to explain in light of its presence in 4Q106. Moreover, if such lyrics were offensive, why did the Qumran scribes leave more explicit images? 4Q106 contains two songs in which the man describes his beloved's beautiful body (4:1–5; 7:2–7), and 4Q107 includes the beginning of the first descriptive song (4:1–3) as well as a metaphor likening the female body to a sensuous, intoxicating garden (4:14–5:1).

---

9. Emanuel Tov, "Three Manuscripts (Abbreviated Texts?) of Canticles from Qumran Cave 4," *JJS* 46 (1995): 88; Tov, "Canticles," in *Qumran Cave 4.XI: Psalms to Chronicles*, ed. Eugene Ulrich et al., DJD XVI (Oxford: Clarendon, 2000), 195.

10. Peter Flint, "The Book of Canticles (Song of Songs) in the Dead Sea Scrolls," in *Perspectives on the Song of Songs*, ed. Anselm C. Hagedorn, BZAW 346 (Berlin: de Gruyter, 2005), 101. See also Pope, *Song of Songs*, 26.

11. Origen refers to a Jewish custom prohibiting one from even holding the Song scroll who had not reached a full and ripe age, while Jerome similarly cautions that the Song should be relegated to the end of one's study of Scripture (Origen, *Comm. Cant.* Prol. 1; Jerome, *Ep.* 107 [*NPNF* 2/6:194]).

In addition, Flint's theory also conflicts with erotica found in the nonbiblical scrolls. 4QWiles of the Wicked Woman uses sexually explicit images to warn against the adulterous woman (4Q184 1 12–14), Psalms Scroll[a] employs erotic euphemism to depict the pursuit of wisdom (11Q5 XXI, 11–18), and Genesis Apocryphon uses similar body imagery to describe Sarai's unparalleled physical beauty (1Q20 XX, 2–8).[12]

While many have attempted to explain the abbreviation of 4Q106–4Q108, there is not enough internal or external evidence to determine the function of these fragments or how the Song and its sensual body metaphors were viewed by the Qumran community.[13]

1.1.2. Ancient Versions

The Septuagint (LXX) translator's approach to the Song's body imagery has also been debated, from place names to repeating refrains.[14] The flashpoint in this debate is found in the first verse. While the MT opens with

---

12. Takamitsu Muraoka, "Sir. 51, 13–30: An Erotic Hymn to Wisdom?," *JSJ* 10 (1979): 175. Bernat labels 4Q184 an anti-*waṣf*, a polemical use of this traditional form. David Bernat, "Biblical *Waṣfs* Beyond Song of Songs," *JSOT* 28 (2004): 346. In Genesis Apocryphon, Hyrcanos's praise for Sarai's physical beauty appears to parallel the Song, but the generic similarities and lack of linguistic parallels weighs against dependency. Moshe Goshen-Gottstein, "Philologische Miszellen zu den Qumrantexten," *RevQ* 2 (1959): 46–48. Also, it bears greater resemblance to Hellenistic poetry, praising Sarai's wisdom without using similes as commonly found in Near Eastern love lyrics. Comparing an epigram from Philodemus, Cohen suggests that both authors hellenize the Near Eastern descriptive song. Shaye D. Cohen, "The Beauty of Flora and the Beauty of Sarai," *Helios* 8.2 (1981): 41–53.

13. For further analysis, see Brian P. Gault, "The Fragments of Canticles at Qumran: Implications and Limitations for Interpretation," *RevQ* 95 (2010): 351–71. Based on new collations of the Qumran fragments, a few scholars have recently argued for variant literary editions of the Song prior to the standardization of its canonical form. Torleif Elgvin, *The Literary Growth of the Song of Songs during the Hasmonean and Early-Herodian Periods*, CBET 89 (Leuven: Peeters, 2018); Émile Puech, "Le Cantique des Cantiques dans les Manuscrits de Qumran," *RB* 123 (2016): 29–53; Eugene Ulrich, *The Dead Sea Scrolls and the Developmental Composition of the Bible*, VTSup 169 (Leiden: Brill, 2015), 4. Although this subject is outside the scope of the present study, such debate only adds to the uncertainty over the interpretation of Canticles at Qumran.

14. Gianni Barbiero, *Song of Songs*, trans. Michael Tait, VTSup 144 (Leiden: Brill, 2004), 7; Paul Joüon, *Le Cantique des Cantiques: Commentaire philologique et exégétique* (Paris: Beauchesne, 1909), 67.

the words "your *lovemaking* [דֹּדֶיךָ] is better than wine," the LXX reads "your *breasts* [μαστοί] are better than wine" (1:2; cf. 4:10). Based on this evidence, Jean-Marie Auwers contended that the earliest Greek version (first century BCE–first century CE) rendered the Song as an allegory, while Othmar Keel argued that its eroticism is only intensified.[15]

Yet such differences between LXX Canticles and the MT are best characterized as translation errors. In the verse highlighted above, rather than revealing an interpretive motive, allegorical or sensual, the translator simply misread דֹּד "love" as דַּד "breast" (1:2).[16] Thus, whether mistaken vocalizations or confusion over place names, there is little evidence in the Greek versions favoring a specific reading of the book.[17]

Likewise, the Syriac and Latin versions of the Song also appear to be literal renderings of a Hebrew *Vorlage*, with any differences easily explained as misunderstanding or stylistic variations.[18] Unfortunately, the ancient

---

15. Jean-Marie Auwers, "Le traducteur grec a-t-il allégorisé ou érotisé le Cantique des cantiques?," in *XII Congress of the International Organization for Septuagint and Cognate Studies: Leiden, 2004*, ed. Melvin Peters, SCS 54 (Atlanta: Society of Biblical Literature, 2006), 161–68; Keel, *Song of Songs*, 5–6. On the date of LXX Canticles, see Jay Curry Treat, "Lost Keys: Text and Interpretation in Old Greek Song of Songs and Its Earliest Manuscript Witnesses" (PhD diss., University of Pennsylvania, 1996), 384; Dries De Crom, *LXX Song of Songs and Descriptive Translation Studies*, De Septuaginta Investigationes 11 (Göttingen: Vandenhoeck & Ruprecht, 2019), 304.

16. Piet B. Dirksen, "Septuagint and Peshitta in the Apparatus to Canticles in *Biblia Hebraica Quinta*," in *Sôfer Mahîr: Essays in Honour of Adrian Schenker*, ed. Yohanan A. P. Goldman, Arie van der Kooij, and Richard D. Weis, VTSup 110 (Leiden: Brill, 2006), 16, 19. For discussion of debated words and phrases, see Hans Ausloos and Bénédicte Lemmelijn, "Canticles as Allegory? Textual Criticism and Literary Criticism in Dialogue," in *Florilegium Lovaniense: Studies in Septuagint and Textual Criticism in Honour of Florentino García Martínez*, ed. Hans Ausloos, Bénédicte Lemmelijn, and Marc Vervenne, BETL 224 (Leuven: Peeters, 2008), 40–47.

17. De Crom, *LXX Song of Songs*, 304; Treat, "Lost Keys," 388–89. Treat also notes the absence of an "allegorical motive" in Aquila's translation; see Treat, "Aquila, Field, and the Song of Songs," in *Origen's Hexapla and Fragments*, ed. Alison Salvesen, TSAJ 58 (Tübingen: Mohr Siebeck, 1998), 171–74. Arguing that LXX Canticles assumes an allegorical reading based on its sacred status and cultural milieu, de Lange admits this is never explicit; see Nicholas de Lange, "From Eros to Pneuma: On the Greek Translation of Song of Songs," in *Eukarpa: Études sur la Bible et ses éxègetes en hommage à Gilles Dorival*, ed. Mireille Loubet and Didier Pralon (Paris: Cerf, 2011), 73–83.

18. Piet B. Dirksen, *General Introduction and Megilloth*, BHQ 18 (Stuttgart: Deutsche Bibelgesellschaft, 2004), 10–13. See also Bénédicte Lemmelijn, "Textual His-

versions offer no clear insight into the interpretation of the Song and its body metaphors during this early period.

1.1.3. Apocrypha and Pseudepigrapha

Finally, along with the debated evidence from the Dead Sea Scrolls, one scholar has attempted to gain additional clues into early interpretation of the Song from Jewish apocryphal and pseudepigraphal works. Wave Nunnally proposes allusions in Second Temple writings and in later rabbinic literature, demonstrating that the Song was composed and canonized earlier than modern scholars accept, with its allegorical and literal interpretation coexisting prior to Aqiba.[19]

While much of Nunnally's proposed reuse involves toponyms that can be explained as cultural knowledge or epithets that are part of the common vernacular of ancient Near Eastern love lyrics, one passage is particularly relevant to the study of the Song's body metaphors.[20] In the Syriac and Armenian translations of Joseph and Aseneth, the earliest extant versions of this work (sixth–seventh century CE), Aseneth's physical beauty is described with imagery similar to the Song:

---

tory of Canticles," in *Writings*, vol. 1C of *Textual History of the Bible*, ed. Armin Lange (Brill: Leiden, 2017), 322–26.

19. Wave E. Nunnally, "Early Jewish Interpretation, Use, and Canonization of Song of Songs," in *The History of Interpretation of Song of Songs*, ed. Paul Raabe (Downers Grove, IL: InterVarsity Press), forthcoming.

20. Nunnally relies on the epithet "my sister" in Tobit (7:16, 8:4) and Jubilees (27:14, 17), yet such familial language is attested in Near Eastern love lyrics (Nunnally, "Early Jewish Interpretation"). Westenholz refers to these parallels as "literary building blocks," which any poet could manipulate to promote imagery and realize moods. See Joan Goodnick Westenholz, "Love Lyrics from the Ancient Near East," *CANE* 4:2483. Kaplan, following Stone, offers a similar argument for reuse of the Song in 4 Ezra, suggesting that lily, dove, and sheep imagery (5:24–26), as well as a proposed syntactic parallel (4:37), indicate that an allegorical reading was present after the destruction of the Second Temple; see Jonathan Kaplan, "The Song of Songs from the Bible to the Mishnah," *HUCA* 81 (2010): 127–31; Michael Stone, "The Interpretation of Song of Songs in 4 Ezra," *JSJ* 38 (2007): 228–33. Yet Israel is described with similar faunal imagery elsewhere (Hos 14:6; Ps 74:19; Isa 59:11). Also, Stone's proposed syntactic parallel is problematic in light of an uncertain manuscript tradition. Since scholars agree that 4 Ezra was composed in Hebrew, then translated into Latin, a syntactic argument based on Latin manuscripts is tentative at best.

> Aseneth saw her face in the water. It was like the sun and her eyes (were) like a rising morning star ... and on her cheeks (there was) red like a man's blood, and her lips (were) like a rose of life coming out of its foliage ... and her neck (was) like an all-variegated cypress, and her breasts (were) like the mountains of the Most High God. (Jos. Asen. 18.9 [Burchard, OTP 2:232])

Such praise for Aseneth's physical beauty contains four possible parallels with the Song: (1) beautiful as the heavenly luminaries (6:10), (2) red-tinted cheeks and lips (4:3), (3) tall neck (4:4; 7:5), (4) and breasts pictured as mountains (2:17; 4:6; 8:14). Since Joseph, after viewing Aseneth's cosmic beautification, renamed her "City of Refuge," a spiritual portrait of Israel as God's earthly bride (19.5), Nunnally argues that this depiction of her bodily beauty indicates that the ancients allowed literal and allegorical readings of the Song to coexist.[21] However, there are a few problems with using Joseph and Aseneth to draw this conclusion.

First, as subsequent chapters will reveal, cosmic splendor, red-tinted cheeks, scarlet lips, and tall necks are common motifs of feminine beauty in ancient love lyrics, casting doubt on the uniqueness of this parallel. For example, similar depictions are attested in Egyptian and Greek love literature. Egypt's Chester Beatty Papyrus opens, "Behold, *she is like the star which appears.... Gleaming is her complexion, brilliant are her gazing eyes, sweet are her lips when they speak.... High is her neck*, resplendent are her breasts, of pure lapis lazuli is her hair, her arms surpass gold."[22] Also, Greek erotic literature commonly depicts the female breasts as apples, similar to an earlier description of Aseneth (8.5).[23]

Second, while the personification of Aseneth's breasts as mountains might suggest that the author is drawing on the Song, the value of this

---

21. Nunnally, "Early Jewish Interpretation."
22. Vincent A. Tobin, "Love Songs and the Song of the Harper," in *The Literature of Ancient Egypt: An Anthology of Stories, Instructions, Stelae, Autobiographies, and Poetry*, ed. William K. Simpson, 3rd ed. (New Haven: Yale University Press, 2003), 322–23, emphasis added. Most scholars agree that Joseph and Aseneth was composed in Greek, likely in Egypt. As a result, Christoph Burchard doubts any connection between the depiction of Aseneth and the biblical Song; see Burchard, *Gesammelte Studien zu Joseph und Aseneth*, SVTP 13 (Leiden: Brill, 1996), 307–8; Burchard, "The Text of Joseph and Aseneth Reconsidered," *JSP* 14 (2005): 89, 92–93.
23. Douglas E. Gerber, "The Female Breast in Greek Erotic Literature," *Arethusa* 11 (1978): 204.

text as comparative evidence is complicated by its uncertain transmission. Scholars continue to debate its textual history, as earlier translations preserve a longer text than later Greek copies. In 18.9, Marc Philonenko's short text stops with Aseneth's cosmic likeness, omitting the breast imagery entirely.[24] Thus, despite the above claims, extant evidence from Second Temple Judaism has produced little clear insight into how the ancients viewed the Song's body imagery. Clarity must await the midrash and commentaries of early Judaism and Christianity.

1.2. Allegorical Methods

The Song's history of interpretation, including approaches to its enigmatic body metaphors, can be divided into three major methods: (1) allegory, (2) reader-response, and (3) comparative studies. In the subsequent pages, each method will be briefly explored, illustrated by relevant examples, and concluded with a summary critique.

1.2.1. Jewish Allegories

The Song of Songs, sung and studied by Jews in every generation, is viewed as a divine love song, an allegory of God's relationship with the nation of Israel, as implied in Aqiba's words above (m. Yad. 3:5; t. Sanh. 12:10).[25] Defending this spiritual reading against modern critical sensibilities, Gerson Cohen aptly captures its basis, "The Song's very daring vocabulary best expressed, and was perhaps the only way of expressing what the Jew felt to be the holiest and loftiest dimension of religion—the bond of love between God and His people."[26] While the handful of references to

---

24. Marc Philonenko, *Joseph et Aséneth: Introduction, Texte critique, Traduction, et Notes* (Leiden: Brill, 1968), 192–93.

25. Fishbane, *Song of Songs*, xxxv; Jacob Neusner, "Divine Love in Classical Judaism," *RRJ* 17 (2014): 126–27. Though some distinguish allegory from midrash, the term is used here in its broadest sense for "any interpretation that assumes the text under analysis to mean something other than what it says" (David Stern, "Ancient Jewish Interpretation of the Song of Songs in a Comparative Context," in *Jewish Biblical Interpretation and Cultural Exchange: Comparative Exegesis in Context*, ed. Natalie Dohrmann and David Stern [Philadelphia: University of Pennsylvania Press, 2008], 87–88). Despite similarities, different types of allegory will be distinguished: Jewish, Christian, midrashic, historical, philosophical, Marian, and political.

26. Gerson D. Cohen, "The Songs of Songs and the Jewish Religious Mentality,"

the Song in the Mishnah and Tosefta shed no light on early interpretation of its body imagery, insight can be gained from the tannaitic midrashim (third century CE), Babylonian Talmud (sixth century CE), the Song of Songs Rabbah (sixth century CE), and Targum Canticles (eighth century CE).[27]

With scattered references in the tannaitic midrashim, the rabbinic sages link the Song's body metaphors with Israel's betrothal period—the exodus, Sinai theophany, and wilderness wandering—to highlight the uniqueness of Israel's beauty and the exemplarity of her God.[28]

Mekilta le-Devarim captures this in the following divine dialogue:

> Israel says, *Who is like you, O LORD, among the gods?* (Ex. 15:11). And the Holy Spirit replies, *O Happy Israel! Who is like you?* (Deut. 33:29).... Israel says, *My beloved is clear-skinned and ruddy, preeminent among ten thousand* (Song 5:10). The Holy Spirit replies and says, *How lovely are your feet in sandals, O daughter of nobles* (Song 7:2). Israel says, *Like an apple tree among the trees of the forest, so is my beloved among the young men* (Song 2:3). The Holy Spirit replies and says, *Like a lotus among thorns, so is my darling among the maidens* (Song 2:2).[29]

Similarly, the Talmud Bavli, with rare exception (b. Ber. 24a), also interprets the Song's body imagery allegorically. Israel and its members are

---

in *Studies in the Variety of Rabbinic Cultures* (New York: Jewish Publication Society, 1991), 5. Harold Fisch contends that the pressure of the Song itself, "so obviously symbolical, so rich in imaginative suggestions and reference, also so mysterious, calls out peremptorily for [this] interpretation" (*Poetry with a Purpose: Biblical Poetics and Interpretation*, ISBL [Bloomington: Indiana University Press, 1990], 96).

27. Hermann L. Strack and Günter Stemberger, *Introduction to the Talmud and Midrash*, trans. Markus Bockmuehl, 2nd ed. (Minneapolis: Fortress, 1996), 206–7; Jacob Neusner, *Song of Songs Rabbah: An Analytical Translation*, BJS 197–198, 2 vols. (Atlanta: Scholars Press, 1989), 1:ix; Philip S. Alexander, *The Targum of Canticles*, ArBib 17A (Collegeville, MN: Liturgical Press, 2003), 55; Raphael Loewe, "Apologetic Motifs in the Targum to Song of Songs," in *Biblical Motifs: Origins and Transformations*, ed. Alexander Altmann (Cambridge: Harvard University Press, 1966), 163–69.

28. Jonathan Kaplan, *My Perfect One: Typology and Early Rabbinic Interpretation of Song of Songs* (Oxford: Oxford University Press, 2015), 32–34.

29. David Zvi Hoffmann, ed., *Midrash Tannaim zum Deuteronomium* (Berlin: Itzkowski, 1908), 221. Shiʿur Qomah, a mystical portrait of the Godhead, has been dated to this period, but it is not included due to its disputed date and link to the Song (Kaplan, *My Perfect One*, 8).

personified as the woman. Commenting on her self-description (8:10), "Raba interpreted: *I am a wall* symbolizes the community of Israel; *and my breasts like the tower thereof* symbolizes synagogues and houses of study" (b. Pes. 87a). Likewise, the male portrait is linked to God, "One verse says, *His raiment was white as snow, and the hair of his head like pure wool* (Dan 7:9); and elsewhere it is written: *His locks are curled and black as a raven* (5:11)! There is no contradiction: one verse [refers to God] in session, the other in war" (b. Hag. 14a).[30] The Song of Songs Rabbah reflects the same interpretive approach, "But *my beloved* is the Holy One, blessed be He. *To his garden* refers to the world. *To the beds of spices* refers to Israel" (6:2).[31]

Foreshadowed by isolated precursors in earlier rabbinic writings, Targum Canticles inaugurated the Song's systematic historical allegory, with each poem tracing chronological events in Israel's history. This is best captured by the three descriptive songs (4:1–7; 6:4–7; 7:2–7). In all three passages, parts of the woman's body are connected to members in Israel's society, but despite similar images, the first verse of each portrait is connected to a different dispensation: the First Temple (4:1), the Second Temple (6:2), and a future time of redemption (7:2).[32]

The reading of the Song in Targum Canticles as a sequential story of Israel's history was perpetuated in medieval Judaism.[33] However, though Rashi (followed later by Rashbam and Ibn Ezra) adopted and adapted the historical allegory, his revolution of *peshat* exegesis began a progressive movement toward emphasizing the Song's plain meaning.[34]

---

30. Isidore Epstein, ed. and trans., *Hebrew-English Edition of the Babylonian Talmud*, 18 vols. (New York: Soncino, 1960–1994).

31. Neusner, *Song of Songs Rabbah*, 2:136. See also Laura Lieber, *A Vocabulary of Desire: Song of Songs in the Early Synagogue* (Leiden: Brill, 2014).

32. Alexander, *Targum*, 130, 66, 75. However, it avoids applying sexual imagery to God's relationship with Israel; see Esther M. Menn, "Thwarted Metaphors: Complicating the Language of Desire in the Targum of the Song of Songs," *JSJ* 34 (2003): 256–64.

33. From the targum to medieval Judaism, some commentators also link the female beloved to messiah, particularly in the Song's later chapters. See Maud Kozodoy, "Messianic Interpretation of the Song of Songs in Late-Medieval Iberia," in *The Hebrew Bible in Fifteenth-Century Spain: Exegesis, Literature, Philosophy and the Arts*, ed. Jonathan Decter and Arturo Prats (Leiden: Brill, 2012), 117–47.

34. Sara Japhet, "Rashi's Commentary on Song of Songs: The Revolution of Peshat and Its Aftermath," in *Mein Haus wird ein Bethaus für alle Völker genannt werden (Jes 56,7): Judentum seit der Zeit des Zweiten Tempels in Geschichte, Literatur und Kult; Festschrift für Thomas Willi zum 65. Geburtstag*, ed. Julia Männchen and Torsten Reiprich

The Karaites, a rival Jewish sect that emerged in the Islamic East in the ninth century CE, despite rejecting the authority of rabbinic tradition out of a desire to ground their beliefs in the plain sense of Scripture, also adopted an allegorical reading of the Song.[35] Yefet ben Eli, one of the earliest extant Karaite commentators, read the Song with an outlook toward his community, the Mourners for Zion, an ascetic, messianic group that settled in Jerusalem in the tenth century CE. For example, on the man's comparison of his beloved to a mare (1:9), Yefet states,

> God put a mare in the sea, and when the horses of Pharaoh beheld her, they rushed to be united to her and this was the reason for their destruction. That is why he [Solomon] compared the remnant of Israel [i.e., the Karaite Mourners for Zion] to her [this mare], because they will attract the pagan nations to them, leading to their loss.[36]

Maimonides, while never writing a commentary on the Song, changed the course of study with his philosophical allegory, viewing its lyrics as an expression of love between God and the human soul. Many of his contemporaries adopted the philosophical reading. Using medieval Aristotelian epistemology, the Song's imagery of affection between two lovers became the longing of the soul or the material intellect (human capacity to learn) for the Divine Intellect, with the goal of knowing God to the highest degree

---

(Neukirchen-Vluyn: Neukirchener Verlag, 2007), 199–219; Japhet, "Exegesis and Polemic in Rashbam's Commentary on Song of Songs," in *Jewish Biblical Interpretation and Cultural Exchange: Comparative Exegesis in Context*, ed. Natalie Dohrmann and David Stern (Philadelphia: University of Pennsylvania Press, 2008), 182–95; David A. Wacks, "Between Secular and Sacred: The Song of Songs in the Work of Abraham Ibn Ezra," in *Wine, Women and Song: Hebrew and Arabic Literature of Medieval Iberia*, ed. Michelle M. Hamilton, Sarah J. Portnoy, and David A. Wacks (Newark: de la Cuesta, 2004), 47–58.

35. Daniel Frank, "Karaite Exegesis," in *Hebrew Bible/Old Testament: History of Interpretation; The Middle Ages*, ed. Magne Sæbo (Göttingen: Vandenhoeck & Ruprecht, 2000), 1.2:110–11. Al-Qirqisânî, one of the leading Karaites of the tenth century, rejected allegory due to its inherent subjectivity, but Yefet argued that the Song's eroticism demands an allegorical reading. See Joseph Alobaidi, *The Commentary of Yefet ben Eli*, vol. 1 of *Old Jewish Commentaries on the Song of Songs*, BdH 9 (New York: Lang, 2010), 148.

36. Alobaidi, *Commentary of Yefet ben Eli*, 165–66.

possible.³⁷ On the man's comparison of his lady to an Egyptian mare (1:9), Gersonides writes,

> It is not their custom to lead them [mares] from place to place until they have been decorated.... It is clear concerning the material intellect that it cannot possibly go to the place of its desire if the man had not previously decorated himself with praiseworthy moral qualities and divested himself of the filthy garments, that is, inferior moral qualities.³⁸

While the historical allegory appears to have gone out of fashion in the seventeenth century after the rise of Rashi's *peshat* exegesis and Rambam's philosophical reading, reading the book as a divine love song continues today in contemporary Judaism.³⁹ In fact, the ArtScroll commentary merges text and symbol in its allegorical translation. Rendering שני שדיך "your two breasts" (4:5) as Israel's spiritual sustainers, Moses and Aaron, Meir Zlotowitz and Nosson Scherman opine, "The verse literally means them."⁴⁰

---

37. Mordechai Z. Cohen, *Opening the Gates of Interpretation: Maimonides' Biblical Hermeneutics in Light of His Geonic-Andalusian Heritage and Muslim Milieu* (Leiden: Brill, 2012), 208–17; Fishbane, *Song of Songs*, 276–88.

38. Levi ben Gershom, *Commentary on Song of Songs*, trans. Menachem Kellner, YJS 28 (New Haven: Yale University Press, 1998), 31.

39. Philip S. Alexander, "The Song of Songs as Historical Allegory: Notes on the Development of an Exegetical Tradition," in *Targumic and Cognate Studies: Essays in Honour of Martin McNamara*, ed. Kevin J. Cathcart and Michael Maher, JSOTSup 230 (Sheffield: Sheffield Academic, 1996), 18–19. The twentieth century witnessed the revival of historical allegory with Catholic scholars Paul Joüon and André Robert. See Joüon, *Cantique des Cantiques*; André Robert and Robert Tournay, *Le Cantique des Cantiques*, EBib (Paris: Gabalda, 1963). For two examples in contemporary Catholicism, see Edmée Kingsmill, *The Song of Songs and the Eros of God: A Study in Biblical Intertextuality* (Oxford: Oxford University Press, 2009); Ludger Schwienhorst-Schönberger, "The Song of Songs as Allegory: Methodological and Hermeneutical Considerations," in *Interpreting the Song of Songs—Literal or Allegorical*, ed. Annette Schellenberg and Ludger Schwienhorst-Schönberger, BTS 26 (Leuven: Peeters, 2016), 1–50.

40. Meir Zlotowitz and Nosson Scherman, *Song of Songs*, ArtScroll Tanach Series 26 (New York: Mesorah, 1977), lxiv.

1.2.2. Christian Allegories

Jewish rabbis were not the only ones who allegorized the Song. The earliest extant commentary was written by Hippolytus of Rome (third century CE), and though it is fragmentary, his method is clear: the Song is an allegory of Jesus's relationship with his bride, the church. On the lyric "Better are your breasts to me than wine" (1:2, LXX), Hippolytus opines, "Just as wine made the heart glad, so also the commandments of Christ make [the heart] glad. Just as infants suckle from breasts to draw out milk, so all [who] will suckle on the commandments from the law and gospel receive eternal nourishment" (*In Cant.* 3.3–4).[41]

Origen (third century CE) is considered the father of Christian allegory on the Song, though his ideas appear to be influenced by others.[42] Despite positing the Song's function as an *epithalamium* for Solomon's marriage to Pharaoh's daughter (*Comm. Cant.* Prol 1 [PG 13:61–62]), Origen pushed past the plain meaning to expound allusions to the spiritual marriage of

---

41. Yancy Smith, *The Mystery of Anointing: Hippolytus' Commentary on the Song of Songs in Social and Critical Contexts; Texts, Translations, and Comprehensive Study*, Gorgias Dissertation 62 (Piscataway, NJ: Gorgias, 2015), 444. For Jews and Christians, the Song's relationship was a framework of desire onto which they mapped the things they valued. See David M. Carr, "The Song of Songs as a Microcosm of the Canonization and Decanonization Process," in *Canonization and Decanonization*. ed. Arie van der Kooij and Karel van der Toorn, SHR 82 (Leiden: Brill, 1998), 173–80.

42. On the importance of Origen's works on the Song, see E. Ann Matter, *The Voice of My Beloved: The Song of Songs in Western Medieval Christianity* (Philadelphia: University of Pennsylvania Press, 1990), 22–48. In fact, Jerome exalted Origen's work on the Song above all else: "Origen in his other books has surpassed all other men; in the Song of Songs he has surpassed himself" (Jerome, *Ruf.* 2.14 [*NPNF* 2/3:467]). But Origen and Hippolytus were likely indebted to Jewish exegesis. See Brendan McConvery, "Hippolytus' Commentary on the Song of Songs and John 20: Intertextual Reading in Early Christianity," *ITQ* 71 (2006): 214. Reuven Kimelman and Elizabeth A. Clark argue that the writings of Origen and R. Yohanan evidence a Jewish-Christian dispute over the meaning of the Song. See Reuven Kimelman, "Rabbi Yohanan and Origen on the Song of Songs: A Third-Century Jewish-Christian Disputation," *HTR* 76 (1980): 567–95; Elizabeth A. Clark, "Origen, the Jews, and the Song of Songs: Allegory and Polemic in Christian Antiquity," in Hagedorn, *Perspectives on the Song of Songs*, 281–84. However, Stern suggests that similarities may be due to Jewish and Christian writers "independently responding to the same (or different) exegetical spurs" (Stern, "Ancient Jewish Interpretation of the Song of Songs," 103–4).

Jesus and his church. On the metaphoric depiction of the man's protective shade and sensual pleasure (2:3), Origen opined:

> She says that the Bridegroom resembles an apple tree in such a sense that she can say of herself that she *desired and sat beneath His shadow* and can affirm that *His fruit was sweet in her throat*.... When the church compares the sweetness of Christ's teaching with the sourness of heretical dogmas and their barren and unfruitful doctrine, she describes as apples the sweet and pleasant doctrines preached in the church of Christ, but as trees of the wood those that are asserted by heretics. (Origen, *Comm. Cant.* 3.71 [Lawson])[43]

Though the allegory set forth by Hippolytus and Origen was rejected by a few, such as Theodore of Mopsuestia (fifth century CE), most figures in the first few centuries of the early church adopted this view of the Song.[44] For example, on the series of similes in which the groom praises the beauty of his bride (4:1–7), patristic writers identify the parts of her body as figurative representatives of different members in the Christian church. Bede (seventh century CE) linked the maiden's dove-like eyes with the preachers who help contemplate hidden, heavenly mysteries. Ambrose of Milan (fourth century CE) identified the woman's teeth, compared to freshly washed, ready-to-be-shorn sheep, as new Christians who have laid aside their sins with the washing of baptism. Apponius (fifth–seventh centuries CE) likened her scarlet lips to the blood of martyrs and her two breasts to the nourishment of the old and new covenants.[45] Augustine (fourth–fifth centuries CE) showed a disinterest in adopting the Song's conjugal symbolism, avoiding most of its erotica. In his comments on chapter 5, he

---

43. Origen also allows for an individual referent in the Song's allegory, "This is either the Church ... or else the soul fleeing all other teachings and cleaving to the Word of God alone" (*Comm. Cant.* 3.71).

44. Theodore's view that the Song was a human love song written for Solomon's marriage to the Egyptian princess and thus unworthy a place in the canon was later condemned (among more serious charges) by the Second Council of Constantinople (Leontius of Byzantium, *Contra Nestorianos* [PG 86:1365d]).

45. Richard A. Norris Jr., ed., *The Song of Songs: Interpreted by Early Christian and Medieval Commentators*, CB 1 (Grand Rapids: Eerdmans, 2003), 154–66. For early Latin patristic writers, the Song's body imagery was used to defend the purity of the church and the special status of its virgins. See Karl Shuve, *The Song of Songs and the Fashioning of Identity in Early Latin Christianity* (Oxford: Oxford University Press, 2016), 30–34, 124–25.

omits verse 1, cites verses 2–3, and then skips to verse 9 in order to translate a scene of sexual longing into the context of baptism.[46]

Just as Judaism maintained a corporate and individual reading, Christians often intertwined the allegory of Jesus's marriage to the church with reading the Song as an expression of human longing for God. Gregory the Great (sixth century CE), in his exposition of the Song, connected this purpose to the body imagery.

> For in this book are described kisses, breasts, cheeks, limbs; and this holy language is not to be held in ridicule because of these words. Rather we are provoked to reflect on the mercy of God; for by his naming of the parts of the body, by which he calls us to love, we must be made aware of how wonderfully and mercifully he works in us.[47]

Moreover, medieval Christian scholars added an apocalyptic layer to the allegory, reading the Song in parallel with Revelation to focus on Jesus's future marriage to the church after the last judgment.[48] On the woman's dove-like eyes (1:15), Gregory of Elvira used *gematria* to link the Greek term περιστεραί "dove" to Jesus's apocalyptic epithet "Alpha and Omega" (Rev 1:8).[49] Bernard of Clairvaux, writing eighty-six sermons on thirty-five verses while avoiding most of the body metaphors (1:1–3:1), identified the bride's bringing of her groom to her mother's house (3:4, 8:2) as the future reconciliation of Israel to Jesus mediated through the church.[50] Nicholas de Lyra, possibly a convert from Judaism, combined Rashi's historical allegory with the above apocalypticism to create a historico-prophetic approach. His method is evident in his comments on the two female descriptive songs. The first (4:1–7) is described as "the spiritual

---

46. F. B. A. Asiedu, "The Song of Songs and the Ascent of the Soul: Ambrose, Augustine, and the Language of Mysticism," *VC* 55 (2001): 309–10.

47. Denys Turner, *Eros and Allegory: Medieval Exegesis of Song of Songs*, CS 156 (Kalamazoo, MI: Cistercian, 1995), 217–18. See Gregory the Great, *On Song of Songs*, trans. Mark DelCogliano, CS 244 (Collegeville, MN: Liturgical Press, 2012), 110.

48. E. Ann Matter, "The Love of the Millennium: Medieval Christian Apocalyptic and the Song of Songs," in *Scrolls of Love: Ruth and the Song of Songs*, ed. Peter S. Hawkins and Lesleigh C. Stahlberg (New York: Fordham University Press, 2006), 228.

49. Norris, *Song of Songs*, 85–86.

50. Bernard of Clairvaux, *On Song of Songs*, trans. Irene Edmonds, CS 40 (Kalamazoo, MI: Cistercian, 1980), 4:142–43.

beauty of Israel in the Old Testament," while the latter (7:2–7) is termed "the beauty of the spiritual bride in the New Testament."[51]

Although Jerome viewed the bride's locked garden (4:12–5:1) as an allusion to the Blessed Virgin (*Jov.* 1.30), Rupert of Deutz was the first to write a thorough Marian exposition of the Song, even proposing body imagery where none is evident.[52] On Solomon's couch (3:7), he explained:

> What is the couch of the true, and truly pacific, King Solomon, who made peace between us and God, if not the one in which the divine nature joined human nature to itself? And what couch is that if not your womb, O beloved of the Beloved, your virginal womb? For there the deity of the Word of God, there the Word of God confined himself and inseparably joined to himself, in unity of person, a human nature formed of your flesh.[53]

The spiritual-historical allegory reigned supreme in early Judaism and Christianity, but the emphasis of the Renaissance and Protestant Reformation on reading Scripture in its original languages caused a hermeneutical paradigm shift. However, many scholars were not able to apply these principles to their understanding of the Song of Songs.[54] For example, Martin Luther, deriding the spiritual-historical allegory of the Song as "immature and strange," devised a political allegory, suggesting that the book was Solomon's song of thanks to God for his divinely established kingdom, a prayer for its preservation and extension, and an encouragement to its citizens to maintain their trust in God in the face of trials.[55] On the woman's

---

51. Nicholas de Lyra, *The Postilla on the Song of Songs*, trans. James George Kiecker (Milwaukee: Marquette University Press, 1998), 67, 103; Karen R. Keen, "Song of Songs in the Eyes of Rashi and Nicholas of Lyra: Comparing Jewish and Christian Exegesis," *CBW* 35 (2015): 212–31. For a voluminous, modern example of Christian allegory, see Christopher W. Mitchell, *Song of Songs*, ConcC (St. Louis: Concordia, 2002).

52. Ann W. Astell, *The Song of Songs in the Middle Ages* (Ithaca, NY: Cornell University Press, 1990), 43.

53. Norris, *Song of Songs*, 151. For a modern example of Marian exegesis on Song 3:7, see Paul J. Griffiths, *Song of Songs*, BTCB (Grand Rapids: Brazos, 2011), 86.

54. For his reading of the Song as a lascivious poem unfit for the canon, John Calvin forced Sebastian Castellio to leave Geneva. See Guilielmus Baum, Edouard Cunitz, and Edouard Reuss, eds., *Ioannis Calvini Opera quae supersunt omnia* (Braunschweig: Schwentschke, 1873), 11:675.

55. Martin Luther, *Lectures on Song of Solomon*, trans. Ian Siggins, LW 15 (St.

self-depiction as "dark but beautiful" (1:5), Luther placed these words in the mouth of Israel:

> I am a state founded by God and adorned with the Word of God, yet I seem to be most wretched in appearance.... Turn your attention not to my blackness, but to the kiss which God offers me, and then you will see that I am comely and loveable.[56]

1.2.3. Critique of Allegorical Methods

As evident from the brief survey above, allegorical interpretations of the Song dominated early Judaism and Christianity, and such readings continue to play a prominent role in both communities. While these methods have been sufficiently critiqued elsewhere, there are three main arguments against using this hermeneutical model to interpret the Song's body metaphors: intent, inconsistency, and incongruence.[57]

First, there is no indication that the Song was intended to be read as an allegory. While allegories appear elsewhere in the Hebrew Bible, even depicting God's love for his people as a marriage relationship, there is always an indication of intent. Isaiah's Song of the Vineyard clearly labels Israel as the vineyard, against whom YHWH the vinedresser foretells judgment (5:1–7). The same pattern is found in historical (Judg 9:7–20) and prophetic literature (Hos 1–3; Ezek 16). Whereas these examples specify the source and target of each image, an allegorical reading of the Song's body imagery requires one to supply these details.

Second, as a result, an allegorical approach to the Song is inherently subjective and inconsistent. On the book's body imagery, advocates of this method often do not agree on the details of their interpretation. As Keel has humorously noted, "If two allegorizers ever agree on the interpretation of a verse, it is only because one has copied from the other."[58]

Louis: Concordia, 1972), 191. See also Jarrett A. Carty, "Martin Luther's Political Interpretation of the Song of Songs," *Review of Politics* 73 (2011): 449–67.

56. Luther, *Lectures on Song of Solomon*, 200.

57. For critiques of the allegorical method see, e.g., J. Cheryl Exum, *Song of Songs*, OTL (Louisville: Westminster John Knox, 2005), 73–77; Ginsburg, *Song of Songs*, 119–23; Keel, *Song of Songs*, 5–11; Harold H. Rowley, "The Interpretation of the Song of Songs," *JTS* 38 (1937): 346–48.

58. Keel, *Song of Songs*, 8.

Finally, the Song's body imagery is fundamentally incongruent with the allegory. How can the erotic portraits of the woman (4:1–7, 6:4–7, 7:2–7) and her beloved (5:10–16) be understood in a divine-human relationship? What is the meaning of the man's frequent absence (3:1–5; 5:2–8; 6:1–2) or his harem of queens, concubines, and maidens (6:8–10)? Why is the woman presented as the leading figure in their relationship?[59] While the Song's allegorical reuse has been valuable to communities, ancient and modern, the book itself "shows no clear signs of having been written to depict God's relation with His people or the soul."[60]

1.3. Reader-Response Methods

Reader-response methods approach biblical literature in terms of the values and response of readers, allowing the reader to play a role in creating meaning and significance.[61] Due to the variance of methods in this category, each reading will be explained and critiqued separately.

1.3.1. Psychological Readings

With the introduction of the social sciences into biblical studies in the mid-twentieth century, some scholars began to examine the Song from a psychological perspective.[62] Following Carl Jung's theory that every person contains a male and female element, Günter Krinetzki investigated archetypes out of which the self is constituted. The dominance of the Song's maiden was connected to the Great Mother, the primary Freudian archetype: "The 'breasts' of the girl (7:4) … promise blessed rest (1:13) and satisfaction of his tactile sensations (7:9) to the *peuer aeternus* [archetypal bisexual human psyche], and in her way bind the

---

59. Athalya Brenner, "To See is to Assume: Whose Love is Celebrated in the Song of Songs?," *BibInt* 1 (1993): 273–75.
60. David M. Carr, "Gender and the Shaping of Desire in the Song of Songs and Its Interpretation," *JBL* 119 (2000): 246.
61. Edgar McKnight, "Reader-Response Criticism," in *To Each Its Own Meaning: An Introduction to Biblical Criticisms and Their Applications*, ed. Steven McKenzie and Stephen Haynes, 2nd ed. (Louisville: Westminster John Knox, 1999), 230.
62. Pieter van der Zwan, "Psychological Approaches to Song of Songs," *JSem* 25 (2016): 660. See also van der Zwan, "Beneath the Body of the Text: Body-Images in the Song of Songs," *JSem* 26 (2017): 611–31.

groom to the bride as they remind him of the indomitable power of the 'Great Mother.'"[63]

Francis Landy also employed psychology in his rhetorical study, viewing much of the female body imagery as maternal. On the garden (4:12-16), he opines, "The Beloved as garden reconstitutes the womb, as a bountiful, fertile enclosure, irrigated and vernal. There she meets her lover, in the sexual act generating new life; they are enclosed in that womb as brother and sister, infant and mother."[64]

However, viewing the lovers' relationship through the lens of Freud's erotic desire for the archetypal mother obscures the Song's amorous imagery by adding connotations of maternal fecundity, a concept foreign to the book. In addition, this quasi-allegorical reading is subjective, reading an ancient text in light of modern psychological theory.

1.3.2. Feminist Readings

Phyllis Trible's rereading of the Song as a midrash on Gen 2–3 ("Paradise Lost Is Paradise Regained"), a reversal of the male dominance recorded elsewhere in Scripture, has inspired a generation of feminist authors.[65] Carol Meyers, building on this emphasis of gender roles, noted that the frequent use of male, military language in depiction of the female, such as her neck, nose, and breasts likened to a tower (4:4, 7:4-5, 8:10), is an unexpected reversal of conventional imagery in gender associations.[66] Thus, in contrast to the patriarchal world of ancient Israel, she posited that the

---

63. Günter Krinetzki, *Kommentar zum Hohenlied: Bildsprache und Theologische Botschaft*, BBET 16 (Frankfurt am Main: Lang, 1981), 194–95. See also Krinetzki, "Die Erotische Psychologie des Hohen Liedes," *TQ* 150 (1970): 404–16.

64. Francis Landy, *Paradoxes of Paradise: Identity and Difference in Song of Songs*, BLS 7 (Sheffield: Almond Press, 1983), 110.

65. Phyllis Trible, *God and the Rhetoric of Sexuality*, OBT (Philadelphia: Fortress, 1978), 144–65. On Trible's impact, see J. Cheryl Exum, "Developing Strategies of Feminist Criticism/Developing Strategies for Commentating the Song of Songs," in *Auguries: The Jubilee Volume of the Sheffield Department of Biblical Studies*, ed. David J. A. Clines and Stephen D. Moore, JSOTSup 269 (Sheffield: Sheffield Academic, 1998), 213; Fiona C. Black, "Looking in through the Lattice: Feminist and Other Gender-Critical Readings of the Song of Songs," in *Feminist Interpretation of the Hebrew Bible in Retrospect: Biblical Books*, ed. Susanne Scholz (Sheffield: Sheffield Phoenix, 2013), 212–15.

66. Carol Meyers, "Gender Imagery in the Song of Songs," *HAR* 10 (1987): 218.

prominence of the Song's female characters as well as the powerful military metaphors and animal figures used to depict her body indicate that the female held the primary role in private life.[67]

In contrast, renewed focus on the Song's body imagery in recent years has produced an altogether different reading of its lyric praise. Viewing the four descriptive songs (4:1–7, 6:4–7, 5:10–16, 7:2–7), Athalya Brenner suggests that the reversal in form (from head-foot to foot-head), the setting of dance, and the explicit imagery in the final poem (7:1–10) favor reading its lyrics as a female parody of the male-voiced descriptive song.[68] William Whedbee similarly explains the male portrait as a satire (5:10–16): "Is this not still another sample of rhetoric that satirically deflates the image of the male who appears as bigger-than-life … to subvert the conventional male dominance in patriarchal and royal society and to highlight and celebrate the erotic earthiness of the female dancer."[69]

Moreover, Fiona Black, detecting duplicity between the lovers' voices and bodies, questions scholars' "hermeneutic of compliment," an assumption that the Song's body metaphors must be complimentary and loving. Instead of explaining such language as exotic metaphor, she views the depictions literally, positing "grotesque" as a heuristic to encapsulate what is "playful, disconcerting, unsettling, and dangerous."[70] Thus, in light of the ill-proportioned, odd-looking, unflattering, ridiculous, even repulsive picture of the woman, Black wonders whether the Song should be considered yet another victim of patriarchy.[71]

Indeed, feminist biblical scholars have offered many valuable insights to advance the Song's interpretation, yet the above readings of the book's body imagery are beset by major weaknesses.[72] First, while many past

---

67. Meyers, "Gender Imagery," 221. See also the אשת־חיל in Prov 31:10–31.

68. Athalya Brenner, "'Come Back, Come Back the Shulammite' (Song of Songs 7.1–10): A Parody of the Waṣf Genre," in *On Humour and the Comic in the Hebrew Bible*, ed. Athalaya Brenner and Yehuda Radday, BLS 23, JSOTSup 92 (Sheffield: Almond Press, 1990), 260–61.

69. J. William Whedbee, "Paradox and Parody in the Song of Solomon: Towards a Comic Reading of the Most Sublime Song," in *A Feminist Companion to the Song of Songs*, ed. Athalaya Brenner, FCB 1 (Sheffield: Sheffield Academic, 1993), 274.

70. Fiona C. Black, *The Artifice of Love: Grotesque Bodies and the Song of Songs*, LHBOTS 392 (New York: T&T Clark, 2009), 32, 62–63.

71. Black, "Beauty or the Beast? The Grotesque Body in Song of Songs," *BibInt* 8 (2000): 318–20.

72. For a brief summary of the contributions of feminist scholarship to the Song,

scholars have noted the disparity between the role of women in the Song and their characterization in the rest of the Hebrew Bible and other Near Eastern sources, Trible's rereading of the Song as a return to Eden's egalitarian order is exaggerated. The prominence of female characters is well-known, but the Song's patriarchal environment is often ignored.[73] In opposition to Trible's claim, Ilana Pardes highlights the Song's hostile males, the watchmen (5:7-8) and brothers (1:6; 8:8-10), who appear to control the Shulammite's conduct. As in the Torah's *Sotah* ritual (Num 5:11-31), the Song's focus is placed exclusively on the girl's virginity, not the chastity of her male lover.[74]

Second, Meyers's theory that the application of masculine architectural and faunal imagery to the female indicates her primacy in private life is problematic. While such superiority may have been a reality in ancient Israel, the question centers on evidence. The Song's lack of concern with domestic activity, with no mention of the procreation or rearing of children, as well as its application of other faunal images (gazelle/doves) to both genders, renders Meyers's methodology suspect.

Third, Brenner and Whedbee's proposed parody is refreshingly original, but a comedic reading here depends more on imagination than exegesis.[75] Based on the idea that the Shulammite is dancing (7:2), Brenner posits a social situation for her portrait, assumptions that lack evidence. Also, conflict between verbal humiliation and the man's pro-

---

see Exum, *Song of Songs*, 80-81. Ginsburg was one of the first to contrast the Song's female portrait with the treatment of women in ancient Near Eastern cultures (Ginsburg, *Song of Songs*, 12-20; Pope, *Song of Songs*, 205-10). Richard S. Hess also argues that the Song also reverses the generally negative view of sexuality in the Hebrew Bible ("Song of Songs: Not Just a Dirty Book," *BRev* 21.5 [2005]: 31-34).

73. The primary feminine voice does not necessarily indicate female authorship. As Exum notes, "The sex of the author cannot be deduced from the poem.... Assuming that 'voice' offers a clue to origins fails to take adequately into account the good poet's ability to write successfully in different voices" (*Song of Songs*, 65-66).

74. Ilana Pardes, "'I Am a Wall, and My Breasts like Towers': Song of Songs and the Question of Canonization," in *Countertraditions in the Bible: A Feminist Approach* (Cambridge: Harvard University Press, 1992), 128. See also Peter Chave, "Towards a Not Too Rosy Picture of the Song of Songs," *Feminist Theology* 18 (1998): 41-53.

75. Will Kynes, "Beat Your Parodies into Swords and Your Parodied Books into Spears: A New Paradigm for Parody in the Hebrew Bible," *BibInt* 19 (2011): 297.

fessed love and longing for her (7:8–10) weighs against this imaginary construct.[76]

Finally, while her identification of the common "hermeneutic of compliment" is insightful, Black's foundational methodology and the nature of her evidence must be questioned.[77] Her "grotesque" proposal rejects any attempt to find a contextual meaning for the Song's body imagery, instead employing modern literature and linguistic theories as a heuristic model. Her method is concisely stated:

> Though ancient Near Eastern parallels might provide some clues, however, in my view it is *essentially impossible to know for certain what meaning an image was meant to convey*. Even if readers could know, their own reactions or interpretations might not necessarily gibe with these hypothesized intentions for the text. This project is not based on the insights of—or directed at—readers of former times, but rather is oriented toward readers of the present day.[78]

While Black's discussion of the Song's body imagery rightly notes the subjective nature of a criterion of common sense, she seems oblivious to the similar difficulty with her own method.[79] Without concern for contextual meaning, there is no constraint on theoretical possibilities. Such methods may bring added depth for contemporary communities; however, this study does not adopt such skepticism for finding meaning.

1.3.3. Pornographic Readings

In contrast to feminist readings, David Clines posits that the woman, rather than being portrayed as her lover's equal, is objectified by the male gaze. On its implied social context, Clines opines, "The material cause of the Song of Songs is, then, the need of a male public for erotic literature."[80]

---

76. Exum, *Song of Songs*, 231.
77. Black, *Artifice of Love*, 20.
78. Black, *Artifice of Love*, 6, emphasis added.
79. Black, *Artifice of Love*, 35–36.
80. David J. A. Clines, "Why Is There a Song of Songs and What Does It Do to You If You Read It?," in *Interested Parties: The Ideology of Writers and Readers of the Hebrew Bible*, JSOTSup 205 (Sheffield: Sheffield Academic, 1995), 100.

With his imagery of her body, the poet invites his readers to share his sight of the woman's humiliation. That is "the very stuff of pornography."[81]

Though the Song seems graphic in the context of sacred Scripture, this pornographic reading lacks awareness of comparative literature. While Roland Boer labels the Song as "one of the most erotic poems in ancient and contemporary literature," a brief perusal of love lyrics from Egypt and Mesopotamia demonstrates the Song's subtle language.[82] The Song conceals the lovers' bodies and their sexual union in metaphor. Ellen Davis contrasts the Song's delicacy with the purpose of pornography:

> The strangest thing about the descriptive poem (4:1–5) is that when we finish reading it, we have no idea what the woman looks like. But in fact, this is not unusual for love poetry and is one of the things that distinguish it from pornography. The woman's body is not a sex object.... The poet is completely involved with his subject, and we see her only as he sees her. Despite its overt physicality, there is a kind of modesty.[83]

Thus, the Song should be clearly distinguished as erotica, not pornography. Like erotica, the Song employs sexually explicit, imaginative metaphors to convey the lovers' increasingly amorous desire, evoking the same yearning in its readers, rather than satisfying such desires with repeated, pornographic displays of the sex act itself.[84]

1.4. Comparative Methods

In the early twentieth century, the archaeological rediscovery of ancient civilizations throughout the Near East produced many parallels to Israel's literature, prompting various comparative analyses with the Song.

---

81. Clines, "Why Is There a Song of Songs?," 119. See also Scott B. Noegel and Gary A. Rendsburg, *Solomon's Vineyard: Literary and Linguistic Studies in the Song of Songs*, AIL 1 (Atlanta: Society of Biblical Literature, 2009), 140–44.

82. Roland Boer, "Night Sprinkle(s): Pornography and the Song of Songs," in *Knockin' on Heaven's Door: The Bible and Popular Culture* (New York: Routledge, 1999), 57–58.

83. Ellen F. Davis, *Proverbs, Ecclesiastes, and Song of Songs*, WesBibComp (Louisville: Westminster John Knox, 2000), 263.

84. Carey Ellen Walsh, *Exquisite Desire: Religion, the Erotic, and the Song of Songs* (Minneapolis: Fortress, 2000), 42–45.

1.4.1. Greek Drama

While Origen labeled the Song a "drama" (*Comm. Cant.* Prol 1 [PG 13:61–62]) and dramatis personae were distinguished in the margins of early Greek versions (fourth–fifth centuries CE), drama theories became more prominent in the nineteenth and twentieth centuries. Advocating a two-character drama, Michael Goulder based his explanation on the girl's portrait, contending that the depiction of Solomon's queen as a dark-skinned (1:5), fuzzy-haired (4:2, 6:5, 7:6) Arabian (6:11) was an antiracial rebuttal in the postexilic Jewish intermarriage debate.[85] Yet, in addition to a lack of plot and stage directions, or any evidence for drama in Israel, Goulder's strict view of the Song's body imagery weighs against his theory.[86]

Conversely, the three-character drama, advocated most recently by Ian Provan and Petronella W. T. Stoop-van Paridon, celebrates the fidelity of a country maiden to her shepherd, even amidst pressure from Solomon and his court to join the royal harem.[87] Rather than fictional motifs for one lover, the king and shepherd are distinguished as separate characters, which often results in the maiden receiving praise from the king yet responding to her absent shepherd lover. For example, Solomon praises the Shulammite's beauty (7:2–7), expressing his sexual desire for her (7:8–10), yet her declaration of mutual possession and invitation to a tryst (7:11–14) must be addressed to her absent lover. Not present, the shepherd is added to support a preconceived storyline.[88]

---

85. Michael Goulder, *Song of Fourteen Songs*, JSOTSup 36 (Sheffield: JSOT Press, 1986), 75.

86. Duane A. Garrett and Paul R. House, *Song of Songs/Lamentations*, WBC 23B (Nashville: Nelson, 2004), 80; Lewis Sowden, "Theatre: Origins," *EncJud* 19:669. Identifying lexis, opsis, and plot as the necessary criteria for dramatic texts, Matthias Hopf contends for the "performance potential" of the Song ("The Song of Songs as a Hebrew 'Counterweight' to Hellenistic Drama" *JAJ* 8 [2017]: 208–21). However, his broad application of these categories to the Song is questionable.

87. Iain Provan, *Ecclesiastes/Song of Songs*, NIVAC (Grand Rapids: Zondervan, 2001), 246; Petronella W. T. Stoop-van Paridon, *The Song of Songs: A Philological Analysis of the Hebrew Book*, ANESSup 17 (Leuven: Peeters, 2005), 469–70.

88. Ginsburg clearly imports this character in his translation of the adjuration refrain (2:7, 3:5, 8:4), "After שתחפץ supply דוד אחר" (Ginsburg, *Song of Songs*, 143–44).

1.4.2. Syrian Seven-Day Wedding Week

At the end of the seventeenth century, Jacques Bénigne Bossuet's commentary marked a turning point in the Song's interpretation, proposing that the book reflects seven parts of Solomon's nuptials, corresponding to the Jewish hebdomadal wedding feasts.[89] Ernest Renan later noted parallels with Syrian wedding poetry and the seven-day wedding festival among Arabs in Egypt and certain localities in Syria.[90] Johann Wetzstein, Prussian consul in Damascus, subsequently published a study of Syrian peasant wedding customs, describing a seven-day festival where the bride and groom were enthroned as king and queen, *waṣf* ("descriptive") songs praising their physical beauty were sung to them, and the bride performed a war-like sword dance.[91] Based on Wetzstein's data, particularly the *waṣf* songs and dance, Karl Budde and Carl Siegfried further developed this view, linking the Song to peasant wedding songs.[92]

While such parallels will be included in our corpus of comparative data, similarities between the lyrics of nineteenth and twentieth century Syria-Palestine and the ancient Hebrew Song do not necessitate a shared nuptial setting. Only one poem in the Song speaks of a wedding (3:6–11), while many others clearly depict a premarital situation (1:6; 2:8–13; 3:4;

---

89. Jacques Benigne Bossuet, "Praefatio in Canticum Canticorum," in *Libri Salomonis, proverbia, ecclesiastes, canticum canticorum, sapientia, ecclesiasticus* (Paris: Anisson, 1693), 182–85. The wedding-week theory was later adopted by Lowth and Herder; see Robert Lowth, *Lectures on the Sacred Poetry of the Hebrews*, trans. George Gregory, 4th ed. (London: Kessinger, 1839), lect. xxx, 325; John D. Baildam, *Paradisal Love: Johann Gottfried Herder and the Song of Songs*, JSOTSup 298 (Sheffield: Sheffield Academic, 1999), 150.

90. Ernest Renan, *Le Cantique des Cantiques* (Paris: Lévy, 1860), 86.

91. Johann G. Wetzstein, "Die syrische Dreschtafel," *ZfE* 5 (1873): 287–94. Delitzsch summarized Wetzstein's work in his commentary; see Franz Delitzsch and Carl F. Keil, *Commentary on the Old Testament* (Peabody, MA: Hendrickson, 2002), 6:616–26.

92. D. Karl Budde, "Das Hohelied," in *Die Fünf Megilloth* (Leipzig: Mohr, 1898), xvi–xxi; D. Carl Siegfried, *Prediger und Hohelied*, HKAT 3/2 (Göttingen: Vandenhoeck & Ruprecht, 1898), 86–90. In the early twentieth century CE, Stephan and Saarisalo similarly recorded modern Palestinian parallels; see Stephan H. Stephan, "Modern Palestinian Parallels to the Song of Songs," *JPOS* 2 (1922): 199–223; Aapeli Saarisalo, "Songs of the Druzes," *StOr* 4 (1932): 2–144.

8:1–3, 8–10). Even in modern Palestinian marriage rites, Gustaf Dalman noted that the use of descriptive songs is by no means common.[93]

1.4.3. Mesopotamian Cult Ritual

Based on similar motifs in *KAR* 158, a Middle Assyrian song list, Theophilus Meek claimed that the Song's epithets שולמית and דודי identified West-Semitic deities (Šulmanitu/Adad), indicating that the Song was a conventionalized form of liturgies from the Tammuz-Ishtar cult, whose rites were found throughout the Mediterranean, including Israel's popular religion (Ezek 8:14).[94] Struggling to reconcile the book's nonreligious meaning with its place in the sacred canon and its consistent spiritual interpretation in early Judaism and Christianity, Helmer Ringgren similarly concluded that the Song's original sacred marriage function, forgotten by the time of its inclusion in the canon, paved the way for its transformation into a story of God's relationship with Israel.[95]

In contrast, Pirjo Lapinkivi and Martti Nissinen, eschewing the sacred-secular distinction in ancient poetry, argued that the Song belongs to a stream of tradition that, from Sumerian times, employed the sexual metaphor as an expression of the divine-human union. Thus, as part of this erotic-lyric tradition, the Song needed no transformation; it could be read as human or divine. Since performance of any poetry in Israel, whether at a festival or wedding, would hardly have been only secular in nature, the Song originally (not its current context) had a dual secular-sacred meaning.[96] Based on this conclusion, Nissinen contends that the Song's body imagery is not visual, but mystical and mythological. "In other

---

93. Gustaf H. Dalman, *Palästinischer Diwan: Als Beitrag zur Volkskunde Palästinas* (Leipzig: Hinrich, 1901), xii.

94. Erich Ebeling, *Ein Hymnen-Katalog aus Assur* (Berlin, 1923); Nathan Wasserman, *Akkadian Love Literature of the Third and Second Millennium BCE*, LAOS 4 (Weisbaden: Harrassowitz, 2016), 195–234; Theophilus J. Meek, "Canticles and the Tammuz Cult," *AJSL* 39 (1922): 2–3. See also Samuel Noah Kramer, "The Biblical 'Song of Songs' and the Sumerian Love Songs," *Expedition* 5 (1962): 25–31.

95. Helmer Ringgren, "The Marriage Metaphor in Israelite Religion," in *Ancient Israelite Religion: Essays in Honor of Frank Moore Cross*, ed. Patrick D. Miller, Paul D. Hanson, and S. Dean MacBride Jr. (Philadelphia: Fortress, 1987), 422–25.

96. Pirjo Lapinkivi, *The Sumerian Sacred Marriage in Light of Comparative Evidence*, SAAS 15 (Helsinki: Neo-Assyrian Text Corpus Project, 2004), 241; Martti Nissinen, "Song of Songs and Sacred Marriage," in *Sacred Marriages: The Divine Human*

words, the body of the beloved is not compared with the outer appearance of the items but with their meaning."[97]

Yet, many weaknesses plague this theory. First, the inclusion of a Tammuz liturgy in the sacred canon seems problematic in light of its denunciation (Ezek 8:1–18). In fact, circular reason is often employed when Sumerian, Ugaritic, and biblical poetry are interpreted as reflecting ritual practices that are partly reconstructed from the same texts.[98] Second, Sumerian and Akkadian sources attest the sacred marriage ritual from earliest time through the Hellenistic period, but there is no evidence of such literature or practice in Canaan. Third, unlike Mesopotamian texts, the Song of Songs contains no gods, no rituals, and no emphasis on human or agricultural fertility or securing a royal dynasty. Thus, reading the Song as part of an erotic-lyric tradition of divine-human union is based purely on evidence from other cultures.

Finally, the similarity of motifs and terms between Mesopotamian cult poetry and the Song of Songs does not necessitate similar function. As Harold H. Rowley noted, "How could one write a love lyric in any language if such terms [garden, vineyard, flora, and fauna] must be excluded from his vocabulary? The fact that these terms occur in relation to the Tammuz cult is no proof that they could only have relation to that cult."[99] Though Meek argued that the similarity of Canticles to modern Palestinian marriage songs is due to the fact that ancient wedding customs drew much from the sacred marriage rituals, what confirms this direction of influence?[100] Did human love songs borrow motifs from sacred marriage rites or vice versa?[101] If the ancients created their gods in their own image,

---

Sexual Metaphor from Sumer to Early Christianity, ed. Martti Nissinen and Risto Uro (Winona Lake, IN: Eisenbrauns, 2008), 173–218.

97. Nissinen, "Akkadian Rituals and Poetry of Divine Love," in *Mythology and Mythologies: Methodological Approaches to Intercultural Influences*. ed. Robert M. Whiting, MSym 2 (Helsinki: Neo-Assyrian Text Corpus Project, 2001), 126.

98. Nissinen, "Song of Songs and Sacred Marriage," 188.

99. Harold H. Rowley, "The Song of Songs: An Examination of a Recent Theory," *JRAS* 2 (1938): 265–66.

100. Meek, "Canticles and Tammuz," 8.

101. Most Sumerologists acknowledge that some of the Inanna-Dumuzi songs had a noncultic function. See Bendt Alster, "Marriage and Love in the Sumerian Love Songs," in *The Table and the Scroll: Near Eastern Studies in Honor of William H. Hallo*, ed. Mark E. Cohen, Daniel C. Snell, and David B. Weisberg (Bethesda, MA: CDL, 1993), 16–19; Jerrold Cooper, "Gendered Sexuality in Sumerian Love Poetry,"

would they not adapt human love songs to depict divine love?[102] While the enigma of the Song's body imagery and the importance of Mesopotamian comparative evidence has been aptly noted, the foundational presuppositions in this approach have not been substantiated.

1.4.4. Egyptian Love Songs

Likewise, when the litany of love lyrics from Egypt were deciphered, with four collections from the New Kingdom, similarities were recognized with Israel's most sublime Song. In his publication on the love songs in the Turin Papyrus and Papyrus Harris, Gaston Maspero notes:

> There is no one who, in reading the translation of these songs, is not struck by their resemblance with the Song of Songs. There is the same manner of indicating the heroine under the name of "sister," and the same poetic images borrowed from the voice of the swallow, and the same comparisons.... The Hebrews and Egyptians had roughly the same concept of love and thus had to speak with the same love language.[103]

In addition to parallel terms, images, themes, and motifs, the Egyptian love lyrics also contain body imagery similar to the Song. Praise for the beloved's body is dominant in two songs (nos. 31, 54), yet it also occurs in three others (nos. 3, 28, 30), as well as the later Mutirdis memorial inscription.[104] In light of these parallels, some scholars suggest that the Song's poet(s) was indirectly dependent on Egyptian lyrics.[105] In his comparative

---

in *Sumerian Gods and Their Representation*, ed. Irving Finkel and Mark Geller, CM 7 (Gröningen: Styx, 1996), 96–97.

102. On humans creating gods in their own image, see Wilfred G. Lambert, *Ancient Mesopotamian Religion and Mythology: Selected Essays*, ed. Andrew George and Takayoshi Oshima, ORA 15 (Tübingen: Mohr Siebeck, 2016), 49.

103. M. Gaston Maspero, "Les Chants d'Amour du Papyrus de Turin et du Papyrus Harris No. 500," *JA* 8 (1883): 46–47 (my translation). Adolf Erman, in his early anthology of Egyptian literature, similarly states, "The resemblance of these songs to Song of Songs will strike every reader" (Adolf Erman, *The Literature of the Ancient Egyptians: Poems, Narratives, and Manuals of Instruction from the Third and Second Millennia B.C.*, trans. Aylward M. Blackman [London: Methuen, 1927], 242–43).

104. Michael V. Fox, *The Song of Songs and the Ancient Egyptian Love Songs* (Madison: University of Wisconsin Press, 1985), 269–71.

105. Gillis Gerleman, *Ruth, Das Hohelied*, BKAT 18 (Neukirchen-Vluyn: Neukirchener Verlag, 1965), 71–72; Keel, *Song of Songs*, 4–5; Fox, *Song of Songs*, xxiv.

study, Michael Fox concludes, "As much as a thousand years separate the Israelite poem from its Egyptian counterparts. The love song genre certainly underwent many changes between its presumed Egyptian origins and the time when it reached Palestine, took root in Hebrew literature, grew in native forms, and blossomed as the Song of Songs."[106] In fact, Keel claims that the Egyptian love songs are "closer in language and mentality to the Bible's than any others in the ancient Near East," even suggesting that the *waṣf* structure is of Egyptian origin.[107]

However, at times, these scholars downplay differences between the two corpora. Egypt's love literature is a disparate collection of lyrics, with two unmarried lovers often speaking *about* their beloved, while the Song contains a more unified artistic vision, with the lovers (both in courtship and marriage) speaking *to* one another. In addition, theories of Egyptian dependence often overlook similarities with the lyrics of Mesopotamia, Ugarit, and beyond. For example, both Fox and Keel note differences in time, geography, *Sitz im Leben*, and style in the Inanna-Dumuzi love songs.[108] Yet, the influence of the Sumerian poetry upon later Akkadian and Syrian literature has been proven, and the cuneiform tablets found in Canaan demonstrate the widespread distribution of Mesopotamian texts and traditions.[109] Thus, while Egypt's love lyrics provide many parallels to the Song, "it would be unwise," as Maspero warned, "to explain these analogies as borrowings from Egypt."[110]

---

106. Fox, *Song of Songs*, 193.

107. Keel, *Song of Songs*, 4. Garrett also concludes, "The similarities are too close and too numerous to be explained as anything other than the influence of the Egyptian songs on the Israelite poem" (Garrett and House, *Song of Songs/Lamentations*, 53).

108. Fox, *Song of Songs*, 239–43; Keel, *Song of Songs*, 28–29.

109. Mesopotamian literature has been found in Canaan from the Middle Bronze Age to the Neo-Assyrian period, likely due to travel, trade, and politics. Fragments of the Gilgamesh Epic have been found throughout the Near East; cuneiform tablets were recently found at Hazor and Jerusalem. See Jeffrey H. Tigay, *The Evolution of the Gilgamesh Epic* (Philadelphia: University of Pennsylvania Press, 1982), 119–20; Wayne Horowitz, Takayoshi Oshima, and Seth L. Sanders, *Cuneiform in Canaan: The Next Generation*, 2nd ed. (University Park, PA: Eisenbrauns 2018), 4–7; Eilat Mazar et al., "A Cuneiform Tablet from the Ophel in Jerusalem," *IEJ* 60 (2010): 4–21.

110. Maspero, "Chants d'Amour," 46.

1.4.5. Shared or Universal Themes

In contrast, rather than attributing similarities exclusively to the influence of one culture, some scholars suggest that these parallels are evidence of a stream of tradition that spanned the ancient Near East.[111] Rejecting direct borrowing, Exum credited this resemblance to "a cultural milieu in which such poetry flourished."[112] Joan G. Westenholz similarly explained such parallels as the result of "literary building blocks" from which poets could draw to promote imagery and realize moods.[113]

Some have posited a broader distribution and deeper commonality, the presence of archetypal vehicles common to ancient love literature:

> Since the subject matter (love between a boy and a girl) is, of course, common to all mankind, it is not surprising that there are similarities. However, even a more detailed comparison shows that there was to some extent a common tradition within love songs that have reached us through these texts, although each particular culture retained its own individual way of handling that tradition.[114]

While similarities between the Hebrew Song and other ancient love lyrics is often credited to a shared tradition of *amore* among the cultures of the Near East, there is currently no systematic study that directly addresses this question. Thus, in addition to using comparative evidence to analyze the meaning of the Song's body metaphors, this study will also examine the relationship between the book's anatomical praise and love lyrics of other cultures. Are such motifs borrowed, shared, or universal? Jack Sasson aptly

---

111. Martti Nissinen, "Akkadian Love Poetry and the Song of Songs: A Case of Cultural Interaction," in *Zwischen Zion und Zaphon: Studien im Gedenken an den Theologen Oswald Loretz*, ed. Ludger Hiepel and Marie-Theres Wacker, AOAT 438 (Münster: Ugarit-Verlag, 2016), 154–59. See also David M. Carr, *Writing on the Tablet of the Heart: Origins of Scripture and Literature* (Oxford: Oxford University Press, 2015), 89–90.

112. Exum, *Song of Songs*, 48.

113. Westenholz, "Love Lyrics," 2483.

114. Wilfred G. E. Watson, "Some Ancient Near Eastern Parallels to the Song of Songs," in *Words Remembered, Texts Renewed: Essays in Honour of John F. A. Sawyer*, ed. Jon Davies, Graham Harvey, and Wilfred G. E. Watson, JSOTSup 195 (Sheffield: Sheffield Academic, 1995), 266. See also John B. White, *A Study of the Language of Love in the Song of Songs and Ancient Egyptian Poetry*, SBLDS 38 (Missoula, MT: Scholars Press, 1978), 153, 162.

captures the wisdom of a broad approach, "Love, the emotion, and sexuality, the physical attraction that occurs between two individuals ... are commonly shared among human beings.... To my mind those who have cast the widest nets in their search for comparisons can be just as successful in clarifying the Hebrew Song."[115]

1.5. Summary

The Song of Songs has famously been compared to "a lock whose key has been lost or a jewel beyond valuation."[116] As evident from the brief survey above, scholarship on the Song has produced a wide spectrum of ideas on the origin and function of this book and the meaning of its body metaphors.

From earliest record, the Song's uniqueness in the canon has led many to assign it a spiritual meaning—the lovers are an earthly picture of God and his people. However, whether Jewish or Christian, spiritual or historical, corporate or individual, philosophical or political, the book's body metaphors present major problems for all the allegorical methods. In addition to the foundational flaw of subjectivity, the lovers' sensual bodies defy any nonliteral readings. Thus, with the majority of modern scholars, this study begins from the premise that the Song is a skillfully woven anthology of human love lyrics, with no connection to the cult.

Nonetheless, even amid such general agreement on this theme of human love, the Song's body metaphors continue to pose problems. Reader-response methods are forced to create new details in the Song to fit these portraits of praise into their perceived storylines. Some have abandoned hope of finding contextual meaning, instead seeking to redefine the sense of these images for the benefit of their contemporary communities. Yet applicability must not overshadow authorial intent and the search for contextual meaning of the text.

---

115. Jack M. Sasson, "A Major Contribution to Song of Songs Scholarship," *JAOS* 107 (1987): 733–34.

116. Sa'adia Ga'on, "Commentary on the Song of Songs," in *Five Scrolls*, ed. Joseph Qafikh (Jerusalem: Society for the Preservation of Yemenite Manuscripts, 1962), 26. Originally written in Judeo-Arabic, Sa'adia's commentary on the Song is also preserved in Hebrew, with a similar metaphor in the opening line. See Sa'adia Ga'on, "Commentary on the Song of Songs," in *Sefer Ge'on ha-Ge'onim*, ed. Solomon A. Wertheimer (Jerusalem, 1925), 82.

While one might conclude that the key to unlock these metaphors has been forever lost, archaeological discoveries in Egypt, Mesopotamia, and Palestine have produced a treasure trove of comparative literature that may help explain the Song's enigmatic body imagery. Yet, the disparity of these sources has sidetracked scholars with the larger questions of origins and influence. In contrast, the purpose of this study is two-fold: (1) to analyze the Song's body metaphors in light of comparative evidence from the ancient Near East in order to shed light on their meaning, and (2) to examine the distribution of these enigmatic metaphors, using selected parallels from classical, medieval, and modern love literature to contribute to the continuing debate over the Song's origin and the possibility of foreign influence on the Hebrew poet. We now turn to the methodology that will govern this study.

2
Missing Key: A Conceptual-Comparative Approach

The authors of the Hebrew Bible often refer to the physical appearance (טוב/יפה) of its characters. Sarah, Rebekah, and Bathsheba are lauded as "very beautiful" (Gen 12:14; 24:16; 2 Sam 11:2), while Rachel, Joseph, and Esther are praised as "beautiful in form and appearance" (Gen 29:17; 39:6; Esth 2:7). Similarly, David is "handsome in appearance" (1 Sam 16:12), his son Absalom is "handsome, with no blemish from head to foot" (2 Sam 14:25), and his wife Abigail, as well as his daughter and granddaughter Tamar, are labeled as "beautiful" (1 Sam 25:3; 2 Sam 13:1; 14:27). Judith, Susanna, and Sarah, Tobit's wife, are depicted similarly (Jdt 8:7; Sus 2; Tob 6:12). Yet, little clue is given as to what the ancients considered beautiful.[1] The narrator briefly notes David's "ruddy tone" and "lovely eyes" (1 Sam 16:12), while Leah's "tender eyes" (Gen 29:17) serve only as a foil to Rachel's superior beauty. In contrast, the Song of Songs offers elaborate physical portraits, yet how should we interpret its enigmatic figures?

The Song's body imagery, that is, verses depicting the lovers' bodies or their members through metaphor, can be divided into three categories: (1) self-description, passages in which the woman uses figurative language to describe her own appearance (1:5–6; 8:8–10); (2) sexual euphemism, verses that use erotic double-entendre to depict the form and function of the lovers' physical bodies, with images of nature like horses (1:9–10), mountains (2:17; 4:6; 8:14), gardens/vineyards (1:6; 2:15; 4:12–13, 16–5:1; 6:2, 11; 7:13; 8:12–13), or fruit (2:3; 7:8–10; 8:1–2); (3) songs of description, lyrics in which one lover describes the other's body from head-to-toe or vice-versa. Three descriptive songs are dedicated to the woman (4:1–7;

---

1. Athalya Brenner, *Intercourse of Knowledge: On Gendering Desire and "Sexuality" in the Hebrew Bible*, BibInt 26 (Leiden: Brill, 1997), 45; Robert L. Hubbard Jr., "The Eyes Have It: Theological Reflections on Human Beauty," *Ex Auditu* 13 (1997): 61.

6:4–7; 7:2–7) and one to the man (5:10–16). Despite their differences, these four lyric portraits share the same poetic structure and are filled with similar figures of flora and fauna, architecture and agriculture.

2.1. Terminology

"Comparison is one of our most valuable sources of knowledge, the main road leading from the known to the unknown."[2] The two most common forms of literary comparison are the *simile* and *metaphor*. Although these devices overlap to a certain extent, they describe the same thing in different ways. The meaning of a simile is often clearer, either because it is more explicit or because the ground of comparison is actually stated (using *like* or *as*), while a metaphor, in contrast, is more concise and ambiguous, shifting a word or phrase from its normal use to a context where it evokes new meaning.[3] Geoffrey Leech best captured the distinction between these two devices, "Simile is an overt, and metaphor a covert comparison."[4] The Song's body imagery uses both devices, but for simplicity, *metaphor* will be used in this study as a broad, categorical term.

In his early twentieth-century work on communication theory, Ivor Richards coined labels to distinguish the different parts of the metaphor: vehicle, tenor, and ground. First, the subject from which desired attributes are derived is called the *vehicle*. In the Song, the vehicle, also known as the source domain, is one of an assortment of cultural images, flora and fauna, agriculture and architecture. Second, the object to which these attributes are ascribed is called the *tenor*. In our context, the tenor, or target domain, is the lover's body or one of its members. Third, the attribute(s) that the source and target share is called the *ground* or mapping.[5] After identifying the source and target, mainly clarifying difficult lexical terms, we will largely focus on the mapping, determining the

---

2. George. B. Caird, *The Language and Imagery of the Bible* (Philadelphia: Westminster, 1980), 144.

3. Wilfred G. E. Watson, *Classical Hebrew Poetry: A Guide to Its Techniques*, 2nd ed., JSOTSup 26 (Sheffield: Sheffield Academic, 1995), 254–55.

4. Geoffrey Leech, *A Linguistic Guide to English Poetry* (London: Longman, 1969), 156–57.

5. Ivor A. Richards, *The Philosophy of Rhetoric* (Oxford: Oxford University Press, 1936), 96–99, 117; Zoltán Kövecses, *Metaphor: A Practical Introduction* (Oxford: Oxford University Press, 2002), 4–6.

nature of the shared attribute(s). Since "metaphors hold a key to the aesthetics of the Song," we must investigate why certain images are used to depict the lovers' bodies.[6]

2.2. Theoretical Foundations

Before exploring this study's theory and method, two foundational debates need to be addressed regarding the purpose of the Song's body imagery.

2.2.1. Presentation versus Representation

First, one must determine the intended function of the Song's body metaphors: presentation or representation.[7] In other words, are two images juxtaposed to evoke the same reaction in the reader, or is the description intended to provide visual details about the lovers? Richard Soulen contends for the former function: "The writer is not concerned that his hearers be able to retell in descriptive language the particular qualities or appearance of the woman described; he is much more interested that they share his joy, awe and delight."[8]

While such figurative language is certainly an attempt by the poet to convey the overwhelming joy experienced by the lovers as they behold the physical beauty of their beloved, Soulen's dichotomy between emotion and bodily description is fallacious. As Marcia Falk rightly points out:

> By reducing the imagery in the *waṣfs* to vague evocations of ineffable feelings, Soulen deprives the relationship between tenor and vehicle of meaning.... If this were so, the poet might have chosen any beautiful thing for an image; there would hardly be a point to interpreting this particular metaphor, or any other.[9]

---

6. Robert D. Miller, "The Song of Songs: A Plea for an Aesthetic Reading," *Sacra Scripta* 10 (2012): 118.

7. These two categories are drawn from Watson, *Classical Hebrew Poetry*, 271.

8. Richard N. Soulen, "The *Waṣfs* of the Song of Songs and Hermeneutic," *JBL* 86 (1967): 189–90.

9. Marcia Falk, *Love Lyrics from the Bible: A Translation and Literary Study of the Song of Songs*, BLS 4 (Sheffield: Almond Press, 1982), 83. Falk also criticizes his evaluation of the female *waṣf* (5:10–16) as "less imaginative" (85).

In contrast, the Song's portraits of praise are presented as an itemized description, with one-to-one correspondence between the metaphors and parts of the body. A flock of goats streaming down a mountainside (4:1) is connected to the girl's hair, not her eyes; her white, matched teeth (4:2) are compared to shorn sheep, not goats.[10] Based on poetic structure, Stephen Geller notes that the bodily members are not logically interchangeable, even in a general way.[11] Thus, the images must be representational, with some objective feature(s) in common with the connected body part.

2.2.2. Function versus Form

Second, after their representational intent is confirmed, one must decide whether the common features (mapping) connecting the poet's metaphors from nature (source) to the lovers' physical bodies (target) center on function or form. Are the itemized lists and allusions to the body invoked due to a shared function, or is the connection based on a similarity of physical form? Citing Hans Walter Wolff's conclusion that parts and organs of the body mentioned in the Hebrew Bible are often substituted for their function, Keel claims that scholars are mistaken to connect the Song's body imagery to the external form of the lover's body.[12]

> In the sentences of the Song which focus on the eyes, nose, neck, etc. of the lovers through similes and metaphors, commentators ... almost always think first of their form. In the Hebrew mind, as shown in any dictionary, *'ap* "nose" is not a form but "snorting, indignation, or anger," *'ayin* "eye" is not something round or almond-shaped but a "flashing, shining," and *ṣawwār* "neck" is "pride," etc. So, with very few exceptions, the body in the Hebrew Bible is never perceived in terms of form but rather its function and dynamics.[13]

---

10. Fox, *Song of Songs*, 275.
11. Stephen A. Geller, *Parallelism in Early Biblical Poetry*, HSM 20 (Missoula, MT: Scholars Press, 1979), 35.
12. Hans Walter Wolff, *Anthropology of the Old Testament*, trans. Margaret Kohl (London: SCM, 1974), 8.
13. Othmar Keel, *Deine Blicke sind Tauben: Zur Metaphorik des Hohen Liedes*, SBS 114/115 (Stuttgart: Katholisches Bibelwerk, 1984), 27, my translation. For similar conclusions, see Silvia Schroer and Thomas Staubli, *Body Symbolism in the Bible* (Collegeville, MN: Liturgical Press, 2001), 24–27.

2. Missing Key: A Conceptual-Comparative Approach

While a functional aspect of the Song's body imagery should not be discounted, there are a host of weaknesses in Keel's theory. First, the Song contains an abundance of sensory images. As Patrick Hunt notes, "Nearly all of the Song's images start out with a *visual* referent."[14] The first female *waṣf* song in 4:1–7 is "a piece-by-piece presentation of the body of the beloved in a visual cornucopia."[15] The Song's visual emphasis is evident with the frequent use of the particle הנה (1:15–16; 2:8–9; 4:1, 7) and verbs of seeing (שזף, 1:5; ראה, 1:5; 2:14; 3:3, 11; 7:13; שקף, 6:10; חזה, 7:1; צפה, 7:5) as well as repeated references to the eyes (1:15; 4:1, 9; 6:5; 7:4).

Second, Keel's blanket appeal to the common function of anthropological terms in the Hebrew Bible to explain the Song's body imagery reverses the emphasis of his source. According to Wolff, these descriptive poems "give us the most exact information about the external characteristics of beauty.… The picture of the beloved is framed by a general impression of colour, size, strength, and sweetness. If we examine it in detail, we find that form and colour of certain features is stressed."[16] Only on the poet's comparison of the beloved's neck and nose with a tower does Wolff appeal to the function over the form of these body parts.

In fact, Keel applies Wolff's general anthropological theory throughout the Song, even in the face of contrary data. For example, on the lover's comparison of his lady's lips to a scarlet cord (4:3a), Keel appeals to the same figure in the story of Rahab (Josh 2:18), concluding that, "like Rahab's scarlet cord, the bright red lips of the beloved are an invitation to love."[17] Yet such an allusion to the conquest account is based solely on the limited use of this figure in Scripture. While Keel seems to acknowledge that the physical description of the woman's red lips depicts her attractiveness, he further argues, in light of the reference to her mouth in the parallel line (4:3b), that these two figures refer, not to external beauty but to her speech, "her ability to articulate and to awaken the longing and readiness for love."[18] In contrast, the mention

---

14. Patrick Hunt, *Poetry in the Song of Songs: A Literary Analysis*, StBibLit 96 (New York: Lang, 2008), 87.

15. Nicholas Ayo, *Sacred Marriage: Wisdom of the Song of Songs* (New York: Continuum, 1997), 183. See also Jill M. Munro, *Spikenard and Saffron: A Study in the Poetic Language of the Song of Songs*, JSOTSup 203 (Sheffield: Sheffield Academic, 1995), 126.

16. Wolff, *Anthropology of the Old Testament*, 71–72.

17. Keel, *Song of Songs*, 143.

18. Keel, *Song of Songs*, 143.

of her lip color supports a specific focus on physical form (see §5.5 for further discussion).

Third, interpreting the Song in light of other anthropological references in the Old Testament also ignores one important distinction, genre. The uniqueness of the Song must be taken into consideration. Yet Keel's concentric model (see below) prefers proximity over similar genre.[19] He argues that the primary source for understanding the Song's imagery is the Hebrew Bible itself. Next, Keel claims that the iconography of Syria-Palestine offers the most important parallels to explain the meaning of such visual imagery. Finally, if the Hebrew Bible and Syro-Palestinian culture are not enough as a reference system, only then should one look for illumination from Egypt or Mesopotamia. The figure below is a visual illustration of Keel's model for investigating the Song's imagery:

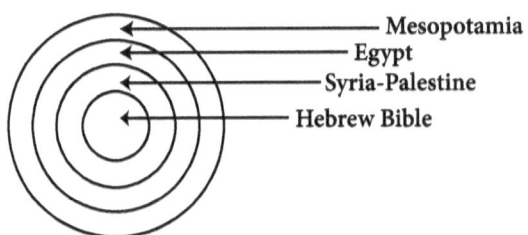

Figure 1. Keel's Concentric Model

Certainly all evidence from these geographical areas should be taken into consideration when interpreting the Song's body imagery, but the question remains whether preference should be given based on physical proximity. While such a hermeneutical progression is a good elementary guideline, is it possible that the poet(s) chose to use an image differently than other Hebrew literature, particularly in light of the Song's genre?[20]

As an illustration, let us consider the poet's image of the shepherd and shepherdess in the opening verses of the Song (1:7–8):

> [7] Tell me, O you whom my soul loves,
> Where do you pasture your sheep?

---

19. Keel, *Deine Blicke sind Tauben*, 11–30 (specifically principles 4–7).

20. For further critique of Keel's concentric approach, see Joel M. LeMon, *Yahweh's Winged Form in the Psalms*, OBO 242 (Göttingen: Vandenhoeck & Ruprecht; Fribourg: Presses Universitaires, 2010), 22–24.

Where do you cause them to lie down at noon?
Lest I be like one who wanders around,
Beside the flocks of your companions.

⁸ If you do not know, O most beautiful of women,
Follow the tracks of the sheep,
And graze your little lambs,
Beside the tents of the shepherds.

The image of a shepherd occurs frequently in the Hebrew Bible, depicting YHWH and his leaders as ones who lead, care, protect, and provide for their flock (Ps 23:1; 2 Sam 5:2; Isa 40:11; Mic 5:3).[21] Since the implication of the lovers' dialogue above is unstated, one could argue that the lady uses the standard image, seeking one to protect and care for her.

Yet, Keel's explanation of these verses violates his own principles. Rather than connecting this image to its customary biblical meaning, he rightly notes the frequency of pastoral images in ancient Near Eastern love literature as an ideal setting for lovers, particularly evident with the prototypical Sumerian lover Dumuzi.[22] Keel attempts to connect this shepherd imagery to the stories of Jacob-Rachel and Moses-Zipporah (Gen 29:9–14; Exod 2:15–22), but the settings are hardly comparable. In the biblical stories, Jacob and Moses meet their future wives in a public place amid other shepherds, while the Song's maiden appears to be proposing a tryst in nature, seeking a private rendezvous with her lover. As this example demonstrates, the Song's unique genre requires a more nuanced methodology.

2.3. Conceptual Metaphor Theory

In the late 1970s, scholars began to explore the ways in which language reflects aspects of cognition, creating the field of cognitive linguistics.

---

21. Joan G. Westenholz, "The Good Shepherd," in *Schools of Oriental Studies and the Development of Modern Historiography: Proceedings of the Fourth Annual Symposium of the Assyrian and Babylonian Intellectual Heritage Project; Held in Ravenna, Italy, October 13–17, 2001*, ed. Antonio Panaino and Andrea Piras, MSym 4 (Milan: Università di Bologna & Islao, 2004), 281–310.

22. Keel, *Song of Songs*, 51. For an example, see Yitschak Sefati, *Love Songs in Sumerian Literature: Critical Edition of the Dumuzi-Inanna Songs*, BISNELC (Ramat-Gan: Bar-Ilan University, 1998), 257–59.

Metaphor is one of the clearest illustrations of this relationship.[23] Once considered ornamental, a device of the poetic imagination and a rhetorical flourish of extraordinary language, metaphor, as George Lakoff and Mark Johnson argued in their foundational work *Metaphors We Live By*, "is pervasive in everyday life, not just in language but in thought and action."[24] With this work, conceptual metaphor theory was born. Conceptual metaphor theory is distinguished by three essential propositions: (1) metaphor is a cognitive phenomenon, not purely a lexical one; (2) metaphor should be analyzed as a mapping between two domains; (3) lexical semantics is experientially grounded.[25] This final idea that speech and thought are based in experience, deeply rooted in the body's interactions with the world, is often referred to as *embodiment* or *embodied cognition*.

2.3.1. Theoretical Basis: Universal

Based on the notion that humans employ metaphor in language because metaphor originates in a person's conceptual system, one subsequent question is whether metaphors translate across cultures. If so, are there common characteristics of this cross-cultural phenomenon? Since metaphor is based on the perception of similarities, "it is only natural that, when an analogy is obvious, it should give rise to the same metaphor in various languages."[26] Already in the eighteenth century, it was recognized that a common form of metaphor across cultures is the anthropomorphic type, those in which attributes of the body and its parts are applied to an inanimate object, or vice versa.[27] Cognitive linguists have reached a simi-

---

23. Joseph Grady, "Metaphor," in *Oxford Handbook of Cognitive Linguistics*, ed. Dirk Geeraerts and Hubert Cuyckens (Oxford: Oxford University Press, 2007), 188.

24. George Lakoff and Mark Johnson, *Metaphors We Live By* (Chicago: University of Chicago Press, 1980), 3.

25. Dirk Geeraerts, *Theories of Lexical Semantics*, Oxford Linguistics (Oxford: Oxford University Press, 2009), 204. For the most recent explanation of conceptual metaphor theory, with a summary of critiques and cogent responses, see Raymond Gibbs, *Metaphor Wars: Conceptual Metaphors in Human Life* (New York: Cambridge University Press, 2017).

26. Stephen Ullmann, *Language and Style* (New York: Barnes & Noble, 1966), 81.

27. Giambattista Vico, *New Science: Principles of the New Science Concerning the Common Nature of Nations*, trans. David Marsh, 3rd ed. (New York: Penguin, 1999), 159. See also Édouard Dhorme, *L'emploi métaphorique des noms de parties du corps en hébreu et en akkadien* (Paris: Gabalda, 1923), 2.

lar conclusion: "Since human beings all share a basic body structure, and have many common bodily experiences, it follows that different languages should have parallel conceptual metaphors across their boundaries."[28]

Furthermore, Lakoff and Johnson noted that people, regardless of culture, tend to structure less concrete concepts in terms of more concrete concepts, those more clearly delineated in our experience.[29] For example, Michele Emanatian used parallels between English and Chagga, a dialect of Tanzania, to show that the domains of eating and heat (more concrete) are preferred cross-cultural vehicles for conceptualizing sexual desire (less concrete).[30] Interestingly, the metaphor of eating occurs frequently in the Song, particularly in the book's body imagery. Whether water (4:15) or wine (1:2; 4:10; 5:1; 7:3, 10; 8:2), choice fruits (2:3; 4:13, 16; 7:14), clusters of dates (7:8–9), or a comb of honey (4:11; 5:1), the Song's poet often uses concrete images (eating) to convey abstract ideas (sexual desire).[31]

In the Song's body imagery, there are three conceptual metaphors that are nearly universal. In fact, all of the discrete figures discussed in subsequent chapters are based on these metaphors. First, the poet repeatedly returns to the BODY AS LANDSCAPE. From mountains and trees to gardens and vineyards, agricultural and architectural images are used to highlight the form and function of the lovers' bodies (1:5–6; 2:3, 16–17; 4:1–6, 12–16; 5:1, 13–15; 6:2–7, 10–12; 7:3–6, 8–10, 12–14; 8:9–10, 12–14). While Douglas Porteous suggests that such imagery originates in the Song, this conceptual metaphor, often focused on the female, is also evident in Near Eastern, classical, medieval, and modern love literature.[32] Mesopotamian, Egyptian, and Greco-Roman literature frequently portrays the beloved's

---

28. Ning Yu, "The Relationship between Metaphor, Body, and Culture," in *Body, Language, and Mind: Sociocultural Situatedness*, ed. Roslyn M. Frank et al. (Berlin: de Gruyter, 2007), 2:388.

29. Lakoff and Johnson, *Metaphors We Live By*, 112.

30. Michele Emanatian, "Metaphor and the Expression of Emotion: The Value of Cross-Cultural Perspectives," *Metaphor and Symbolic Activity* 10 (1995): 163–82.

31. Shalom M. Paul, "The Shared Legacy of Sexual Metaphors and Euphemisms in Mesopotamian and Biblical Literature," in *Sex and Gender in the Ancient Near East*, ed. Simo Parpola and Robert M. Whiting, CRRAI 47 (Helsinki: Neo-Assyrian Text Corpus Project, 2002), 295–97.

32. J. Douglas Porteous, "Bodyscape: The Body-Landscape Metaphor," *Canadian Geographer* 30 (1986): 7–11. On reading the Song through a landscape lens, see Elaine T. James, *Landscapes of the Song of Songs: Poetry and Place* (Oxford: Oxford University Press, 2017).

body with images of digging and plowing, cultivating and irrigating, while Arabic and European lyrics link her body to gardens and countrysides.[33]

Second, the Song's sensual lyrics also portray LOVE AS INTOXICATION, often mixing this conceptual metaphor with the one mentioned above. Whether produce (apples, dates, grapes) or place (vineyards, gardens), the poet regularly returns to love's inebriating effects (1:2; 2:3; 4:10, 12–5:1; 7:8–10; 8:2, 12–13). Finally, the poet steadily shows THE OBJECT OF LOVE AS A VALUABLE OBJECT. From prominent cities and cosmic luminaries to precious metals and majestic horses, the lovers often laud one another with emblems of excellence (1:9; 5:11, 14–15; 6:4, 10). Comparative evidence for these conceptual metaphors will be discussed in subsequent chapters.

2.3.2. Theoretical Basis: Cultural

However, conceptual metaphor theory (and this study of the Song's body imagery) is not based purely on the universal nature of bodily experience. Metaphor is shaped both by the body and culture. "Bodies are not culture-free objects, because all aspects of embodied experience are shaped by cultural processes."[34] As Zouheir Maalej and Ning Yu similarly state, "The experiential basis of conceptual metaphors is both bodily and cultural. Our mind is embodied in such a way that our conceptual systems draw largely upon the peculiarities of our body and the specifics of our physi-

---

33. Ulrike Steinert, "Concepts of the Female Body in Mesopotamian Gynecological Texts," in *The Comparable Body: Analogy and Metaphor in Ancient Mesopotamian, Egyptian, and Greco-Roman Medicine*, ed. John Z. Wee, Studies in Ancient Medicine 49 (Leiden: Brill, 2017), 275–357; Julia M. Asher-Greve, "The Essential Body: Mesopotamian Conceptions of the Gendered Body," *G&H* 9 (1997): 447; Joan G. Westenholz, "Metaphorical Language in the Poetry of Love in the Ancient Near East," in *La circulation des biens, des personnes et des idées dans le Proche-Orient ancien*, ed. Dominique Charpin and Francis Joannès (Paris: Recherche sur les civilisations, 1992), 382; Helen King, "Sowing the Field: Greek and Roman Sexology," in *Sexual Knowledge, Sexual Science: The History of Attitudes to Sexology*, ed. Roy Porter and Mikulas Teich (New York: Cambridge University Press, 1994), 38; Manuel Jinbachian, "The Genre of Love Poetry in Song of Songs and the Pre-Islamic Arabian Odes," *BT* 48 (1997): 136; Page duBois, *Sowing the Body: Psychoanalysis and Ancient Representations of Women*, Women in Culture and Society (Chicago: University of Chicago Press, 1988), 65–85.

34. Raymond Gibbs, *Embodiment and Cognitive Science* (Cambridge: Cambridge University Press, 2005), 13. See also Ning Yu, "Metaphor from Body and Culture" in *The Cambridge Handbook of Metaphor and Thought*, ed. Raymond Gibbs (Cambridge: Cambridge University Press, 2008), 259.

cal and cultural environment."³⁵ For example, in her study of metaphor in biblical wisdom literature, Nicole Tilford concludes:

> The concept of wisdom in ancient Israel was influenced by universal *and* cultural factors.... Biblical metaphors do not develop exclusively from biology *or* culture. Metaphorical meaning develops out a biological interaction with one's environment, and that environment includes not only the natural world but also the society to which one belongs.³⁶

In other words, "our cognitive world is constituted by culturally specific variations on universal (or more general) themes."³⁷

Therefore, this study of the Song's body imagery will explore the extent of universal themes as well as culturally specific variations. As detailed in the subsequent chapters, our analysis shows that the poet often relies on widely shared or nearly universal mappings between the source (*agriculture and architectural images*) and target domains (*lovers' bodies*). Yet these shared motifs are often adopted and adapted to their cultural conventions. As Shaye Cohen comments, "Love and love poetry are eternal and universal, but each culture appreciates love and writes love poetry in its own fashion."³⁸ Now, let's examine the method used in this study.

2.4. Comparative Method

Though most commentators address the Song's body imagery, a clear methodology has often been lacking. For example, on determining the representational import of a specific metaphor and to which sense(s) the poet is appealing, Fox opines, "There is no objective way of applying this principle; only the reader's aesthetic sensitivity can decide the pertinence of this or that association."³⁹ Falk is more hopeful, yet ultimately lacking: "The metaphors in the Song express a sophisticated poetic sensi-

---

35. Zouheir Maalej and Ning Yu, "Introduction," in *Embodiment via Body Parts: Studies from Various Languages and Cultures*, ed. Zouheir Maalej and Ning Yu (Amsterdam: Benjamins, 2011), 13.
36. Nicole L. Tilford, *Sensing World, Sensing Wisdom: The Cognitive Foundations of Biblical Metaphor*, AIL 31 (Atlanta: SBL Press, 2017), 22–23, emphasis original.
37. Chris Sinha, "The Cost of Renovating the Property: A Reply to Marina Rokova," *Cognitive Linguistics* 13 (2002): 272.
38. Cohen, "Beauty of Flora and the Beauty of Sarai," 49.
39. Fox, *Song of Songs*, 277.

bility which, although foreign to us today, can be made accessible through critical analysis. The process is simply one of proper visualization—taking the right focus or perspective, making explicit the implicit context, filling in the unverbalized details."[40] Indeed, interpreting poetic images relies heavily on the reader's aesthetic sensibilities, but Falk's method of "proper visualization" provides no objective criteria or constraint.

"Biblical literature is rich in metaphor. But the precise import of its graphic allusions can sometimes be recovered only in the light of comparative data, both textual and artefactual."[41] Thus, the methodology followed in this comparative study is based on William Hallo and Lawson Younger's contextual approach.[42] Against the early trend toward "parallelomania," this method stresses the need to explore similarities and differences between biblical and Near Eastern cultures.[43] "Our interpretive competence is ultimately commensurate with our grasp of the culture and language of a work's era of composition.... The more we know about both literary and cultural context, the greater our chance of yielding an unambiguous result."[44]

The steps outlined below are adapted from Zacharias Kotzé's cognitive linguistic methodology for the study of metaphor in the Hebrew Bible, in addition to Younger's synthesis of the contextual method.[45] First, a translation of each verse in the selected corpus will be given, seeking to clarify any difficult lexical terms or syntactical constructions. Second, the source and target of the metaphor will be clearly identified. Third, similar imag-

---

40. Falk, *Love Lyrics*, 84.

41. William W. Hallo, "Compare and Contrast: The Contextual Approach to Biblical Literature," in *The Bible in the Light of Cuneiform Literature*. ed. William W. Hallo, Bruce W. Jones, and Gerald L. Mattingly, Scripture in Context 3 (New York: Mellen, 1990), 7.

42. William W. Hallo, "Biblical History in Its Near Eastern Setting: The Contextual Approach," in *Scripture in Context: Essays on the Comparative Method*, ed. Carl Evans, William W. Hallo, and John B. White, PTMS 34 (Pittsburgh: Pickwick, 1980), 1–26; K. Lawson Younger Jr., "The Contextual Method," in *The Context of Scripture*, ed. William W. Hallo and K. Lawson Younger Jr. (Leiden: Brill, 2000), 3:xxxv–xlii.

43. Samuel Sandmel, "Parallelomania," *JBL* 81 (1962): 1–13.

44. David Aaron, *Biblical Ambiguities: Metaphor, Semantics, and Divine Imagery* (Leiden: Brill, 2001), 118.

45. Zacharias Kotzé, "A Cognitive Linguistic Methodology for the Study of Metaphor in the Hebrew Bible," *JNSL* 31 (2005): 107–17; Younger, "Contextual Method," xxxv–xlii. For a similar methodological approach in comparative study, see LeMon, *Yahweh's Winged Form in the Psalms*, 24.

ery from other ancient Near Eastern cultures will be located. The corpus of material considered will primarily include literature and iconography from Syria-Palestine, Egypt, and Mesopotamia, though later comparative evidence will also be included to determine distribution.[46] Parallels are usually sought within the same genre, but our search will not be limited to love lyrics, as a metaphor can supersede genre.

Fourth, attributes that may connect the source and target will be posited. Fifth, each option will be evaluated on linguistic, geographical, chronological, cultural, and contextual grounds (not necessarily in this order), considering both similarities and differences between the biblical and ancient Near Eastern material.[47] Finally, more likely parallels will be used to clarify the possible meaning of the Song's body imagery. These steps are concisely stated below:

1. *Translate* specified verse(s) from the Song
2. *Identify* source and target
3. *Locate* similar imagery elsewhere in the ancient Near East
4. *Posit* potential shared attributes (mapping)
5. *Evaluate* options based on language, geography, time, culture, and context
6. *Clarify* possible meaning of the Song's imagery

2.4.1. Borrowed, Shared, or Universal?

Since the nineteenth- and twentieth-century discoveries of ancient civilizations in Mesopotamia, Egypt, and the Levant, scholars have sought to explain the enigmas in the Bible with parallels in literature and iconography from these related cultures and vice versa. Yet, as mentioned above,

---

46. The necessity of incorporating textual and iconographic evidence in comparative study is confirmed by Izaak J. de Hulster, "Illuminating Images: A Historical Position and Method for Iconographic Exegesis," in *Iconography and Biblical Studies: Proceedings of the Iconography Sessions at the Joint EABS/SBL Conference, 22–26 July 2007, Vienna, Austria*, ed. Izaak J. de Hulster and Rüdiger Schmitt, AOAT 361 (Münster: Ugarit-Verlag, 2009), 139.

47. Younger's caveat is vital, "A parallel that is closer to the biblical material in language, geographic proximity, time, and culture is a stronger parallel than one that is removed from the biblical material along one or more of these lines. That does not mean that a parallel further removed is not relevant evidence. There may be circumstances that strengthen its relevance" ("Contextual Method," xxxvii).

the best method of comparative study "recognizes that the literature of the ancient Near East was produced not only out of a particular culture but also out of a larger literary tradition and that comparison with other literature that is similar ... reveals certain aspects of a text that might remain hidden."[48]

Connections between the cultures of the Near East are numerous. From earliest historical record, the Near East was home to several political entities, from Sumer, Akkad, Assyria, and Babylonia to Syria, Anatolia, Canaan, and Egypt. Textual and visual evidence preserved from these civilizations reveal a multitude of *political connections* between them. For example, the Black Obelisk of Shalmaneser III shows the Israelite king Jehu presenting tribute before the Assyrian ruler. Similarly, the Amarna archive contains diplomatic correspondence between Egypt's pharaoh and various rulers in Syria and Canaan.[49] Second, excavations in the region attest to repeated *military clashes* between these cultures, such as the Assyrian siege ramp and weaponry found at Lachish.[50]

Third, archaeological remains also imply *commercial contact*, especially when imported goods are found in domestic settings with no evidence of destruction or foreign occupation.[51] Finally, *literary contact* between these cultures is evident from the littering of nonnative texts found at various sites. For example, fragments of cuneiform texts have been found throughout Canaan, such as the Gilgamesh epic at Megiddo or the recent fragments at Jerusalem and Hazor.[52]

However, comparative methods also raise the further question of influence. How should these literary parallels be explained? Was the Song's poet aware of and dependent on literature from other cultures? If so, how is such influence detected? In *The Golden Bough*, James Frazer notes the difficulty of this question, "To sift out the elements of culture which a race

---

48. Younger, "Contextual Method," xxxvii.

49. William L. Moran, *The Amarna Letters* (Baltimore: Johns Hopkins University Press, 1992).

50. David Ussishkin, *The Renewed Archaeological Excavations at Lachish (1973–1994)* (Tel Aviv: Emery and Claire Yass Publications in Archaeology, 2004), 2:695–764.

51. Benjamin J. Noonan, "Did Nehemiah Own Tyrian Goods? Trade Between Judea and Phoenicia During the Achaemenid Period," *JBL* 130 (2011): 281–98.

52. Albrecht Goetze and Selim J. Levy, "Fragment of the Gilgamesh Epic from Megiddo," *Atiqot* 2 (1959): 121–28; Mazar, "Cuneiform Tablet from the Ophel in Jerusalem," 4–21; Wayne Horowitz and Takayoshi Oshima, "Hazor 16: Another Administrative Docket from Hazor," *IEJ* 60 (2010): 129–32.

has independently evolved and to distinguish them accurately from those which it has derived from other races is a task of extreme difficulty and delicacy, which promises to occupy students of man for a long time to come."[53] Since "empirical studies of conceptual metaphors have revealed that some of them are potentially universal, others widespread, and still others culture-specific," we will analyze the Song's body imagery on this three-fold spectrum: *borrowed, shared,* or *universal*.[54]

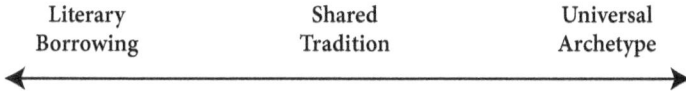

| Literary Borrowing | Shared Tradition | Universal Archetype |

Concluding the methodological process outlined above, each image will be placed on this spectrum, exploring the source of its derivation and possible channels of transmission. Thus, the sum of evidence for the Song's body imagery may provide data concerning its source(s) of influence.

2.4.1.1. Literary Borrowing

On the left end of the spectrum, *literary borrowing* refers to the inclusion of a story, motif, or image traceable to another piece of literature. Whether or not it was conscious, the author was dependent on another source. Among the few who have written explicitly enough to formulate criteria, William Albright warned, "Even when story motifs can be found in different contiguous lands, it is not safe to assume original relationship or borrowing *except where the motif is complex, forming a pattern.*"[55]

For example, in two well-known, well-worn debates over suspected borrowing, some scholars argue that similarities in subject and sequence

---

53. James G. Frazer, *The Golden Bough: A Study in Magic and Religion*, 3rd ed. (London: Macmillan, 1913), 7.1:vii.

54. Yu, "Metaphor from Body and Culture," 248. See also Meir Malul, *The Comparative Method in Ancient Near Eastern and Biblical Legal Studies*, AOAT 277 (Kevelaer: Butzon & Bercker; Neukirchen-Vluyn: Neukirchener Verlag, 1990), 13–19; Grady, "Metaphor," 204.

55. William Albright, *From the Stone Age to Christianity: Monotheism and the Historical Process*, 2nd ed. (New York: Doubleday, 1957), 67 (emphasis added). See also Joseph R. Kelly, "Identifying Literary Allusions: Theory and the Criterion of Shared Language," in *Subtle Citation, Allusion, and Translation in the Hebrew Bible*, ed. Ziony Zevit (Sheffield: Equinox, 2017), 22–40.

between the Babylonian (Enuma Elish) and biblical creation accounts as well as between Deuteronomy and other Near Eastern treaties (Hittite and Assyrian) point to the dependency of the scriptural writers.[56]

In addition to shared complexity, another factor that increases the probability that a motif or image was borrowed is *the volume of similarities and differences*: the fewer differences and more similarities, the more plausible the claim of dependency. The most commonly cited biblical passage involving literary borrowing is the Sayings of the Wise (Prov 22:17–23:11).[57] In fact, parallels between these verses and the Egyptian Instruction of Amenemope are such that many scholars choose to emend the MT in at least one place (22:20). The parallels are too numerous, specific, and sequenced to be reasonably ascribed to anything other than literary dependence.[58] Both texts include thirty sayings (22:21; §30, 27.7), a common purpose (22:21; Prol. 1.5–6), call to hearers (22:17–18; §1, 3.9–10), and many shared topics: respect for the poor (22:22–23; §2, 4.4–5), avoid an angry man (22:24–25; §3, 5.10–11), don't move a boundary stone (22:28; §6, 7.12), reward for a worthy worker (22:29; §30, 27.16–17), etiquette at the royal table (23:1–3; §23, 23.13–18), and the transitory nature of wealth (23:4–8; §7, 9.10–10.5).

---

56. On Genesis, see Hermann Gunkel, "The Influence of Babylonian Mythology upon the Biblical Creation Story," in *Creation in the Old Testament*, ed. Bernard Anderson, IRT (Philadelphia: Fortress, 1984), 25–52; Alexander Heidel, *The Babylonian Genesis*, 2nd ed. (Chicago: University of Chicago Press, 1963). For an opposing view, see Wilfred G. Lambert, "A New Look at the Babylonian Background of Genesis," *JTS* 16 (1965): 287–300. On Deuteronomy, see Moshe Weinfeld, "Traces of Assyrian Treaty Formulae in Deuteronomy," *Bib* 46 (1965): 417–27; Bernard M. Levinson, "Esarhaddon's Succession Treaty as the Source for the Canon Formula in Deuteronomy 13:1," *JAOS* 130 (2010): 337–47. For an opposing view, Kenneth A. Kitchen and Paul J. N. Lawrence, *Treaty, Law and Covenant in the Ancient Near East* (Wiesbaden: Harrassowitz, 2012), 3:250–61.

57. Michael V. Fox, *Proverbs 10–31*, AB 18B (New Haven: Yale University Press, 2009), 753–69; Bruce K. Waltke, *The Book of Proverbs: Chapters 15–31*, NICOT (Grand Rapids: Eerdmans, 2005), 217–20; John A. Emerton, "The Teaching of Amenemope and Proverbs xxii 17–xxiv 22: Further Reflections on a Long-Standing Problem," *VT* 51 (2001): 431–65. For an opposing voice, see John Ruffle, "The Teaching of Amenemope and Its Connection with the Book of Proverbs," *TynBul* 28 (1977): 29–68.

58. Michael V. Fox, "From Amenemope to Proverbs: Editorial Art in Proverbs 22,17–23,11," *ZAW* 126 (2014): 76–91. For example, Fox notes the striking way that Amenemope 9.19 and 10.4–5 are spliced together in Prov 23:5 (*Proverbs 10–31*, 755).

A third factor that may indicate dependency is the inclusion of a *unique cultural element*.⁵⁹ For example, two phrases are used consistently in the exodus narratives to characterize YHWH as divine warrior, יד חזקה "mighty hand" (Exod 3:19; 13:16; Deut 6:21; 7:8; 9:26) and זרוע נטויה "outstretched arm" (Exod 6:6). At times, these phrases occur in parallel (Deut 4:34; 5:15; 7:19; 11:2; 26:8; cf. Ezek 20:33–34). As James Hoffmeier notes, the frequent mention and depiction of Pharaoh's strong arm in Egyptian texts and reliefs, beginning in the Twelfth Dynasty but reaching a zenith in the New Kingdom (see also EA 286–288), suggests that the biblical writer appropriated these terms as a polemic to describe YHWH's victory over the Egyptian gods and their semidivine royal appointees.⁶⁰

Another example of this type may be found within the Song itself. The final chapter opens with the girl's wish for greater intimacy with her lover (8:1–2). While many scholars classify these verses as a song of yearning, the form and content better parallel the Egyptian wish song.⁶¹ In the Cairo Love Songs, a series of seven wishes portray the boy's desire to be intimate with his beloved. He wishes that he were her maidservant, attending to her constantly and seeing her naked body; her laundryman, touching her clothes and rubbing himself with them; or her mirror, gazing at her as she unwittingly gazes at him.⁶² The Hebrew wish song not only expresses the same theme as the Egyptian examples, but also reflects the same structure. In the first line, the maiden expresses a wish that her beloved was someone with whom she could enjoy closer contact, her baby brother (8:1a). In the following lines, she muses how this would allow unhindered access to him, allowing her to kiss him in public (8:1b) and enjoy intimacy with him privately in her mother's house (8:2).⁶³ The absence of the wish song in other Near Eastern love lyrics suggests that this form derives from Egypt.

---

59. Malul similarly notes the importance of unique parallels (Malul, *Comparative Method*, 93–97). See Hosea's allusion to an Assyrian royal title, מלך ירב (5:13; 10:6).

60. James K. Hoffmeier, "The Arm of God Versus the Arm of Pharaoh," *Bib* 67 (1986): 378–87. See also Brent A. Strawn, "'With a Strong Hand and an Outstretched Arm': On the Meaning(s) of the Exodus Tradition(s)," in *Iconographic Exegesis of the Hebrew Bible/Old Testament*, ed. Izaak J. de Hulster, Brent A. Strawn, and Ryan P. Bonfiglio (Göttingen: Vandenhoeck & Ruprecht, 2015), 115.

61. As a song of yearning, see Roland E. Murphy, *Wisdom Literature: Job, Proverbs, Ruth, Canticles, Ecclesiastes, Esther*, FOTL (Grand Rapids: Eerdmans, 1981), 121.

62. Fox, *Song of Songs*, 37–42 (no. 21a–g).

63. Fox argues that Song 8:1–4 centers on social recognition of the relationship, but this does not explain the girl's focus on intimacy (*Song of Songs*, 282).

Other circumstantial evidence may also increase the probability of dependency, such as demonstrating that an author could have been familiar with literature from a foreign culture in light of established channels of transmission or in light of other usage of the same source in works by the same author or in the same period.[64]

2.4.1.2. Shared Tradition

Next, in the center of the spectrum, *shared tradition* refers to a symbol, motif, or tradition that appears in numerous cultures, without being universal. In recent years, this concept of common ground shared between the cultures of the ancient world has been labeled with various terms: conceptual milieu, common *Wortfeld*, cultural codes, or cognitive environment.[65] For love lyrics, Westenholz and Nathan Wasserman similarly posit a common Near Eastern pool of stock phrases, which any poet could employ for their purpose.[66]

For example, the male lover's use of familial terms to refer to his bride (4:9–10, 12; 5:1) is attested in various parts of the Semitic world. The terms *brother* and *sister* often appear as epithets of affection, both in the Inanna-Dumuzi love songs from Sumer and more than half of the preserved Egyptian love lyrics.[67] Elsewhere in Mesopotamia, both *KAR* 158 (vii:13) and Moshe Held's faithful lover dialogue employ *mārum* "son" in an amorous context, while at Ugarit, the goddess Anat similarly uses familial terms in her attempt to seduce Aqhat (*KTU* 1.18 i.23–24).[68]

---

64. For similar criteria in intertextual comparative studies, see Christopher B. Hays, "Echoes of the Ancient Near East? Intextuality and the Comparative Study of the Old Testament," in *Word Leaps the Gap: Essays on Scripture and Theology in Honor of Richard B. Hays,* ed. J. Ross Wagner, C. Kavin Rowe, and A. Katherine Grieb (Grand Rapids: Eerdmans, 2008), 20–43.

65. Daniel Boyarin, *Intertextuality and the Reading of the Mishnah*, ISBL (Bloomington, IN: Indiana University Press, 1990), 12; Michael Fishbane, *Biblical Interpretation in Ancient Israel* (Oxford: Oxford University Press, 1985), 288; J. Richard Middleton, *The Liberating Image: The Imago Dei in Genesis 1* (Grand Rapids: Brazos, 2005), 64; John H. Walton, *Ancient Near Eastern Thought and the Old Testament: Introducing the Conceptual World of the Hebrew Bible,* 2nd ed. (Grand Rapids: Baker, 2018), 11.

66. Westenholz, "Love Lyrics," 2483; Wasserman, *Akkadian Love Literature*, 137. See also Nissinen, "Akkadian Love Poetry and the Song of Songs," 148.

67. Sefati, *Love Songs,* 77, 81–82; Fox, *Song of Songs,* 8.

68. Moshe Held, "A Faithful Lover in an Old Babylonian Dialogue," *JCS* 15 (1961):

Another feature shared across the cultures of the Near East is the *waṣf* poetic form, a lyric portrait in which one lover praises the beauty of his/her beloved's body in sequential fashion.[69] Similar to the Song's four *waṣfs* (4:1–7; 5:10–16; 6:4–7; 7:2–7), Egypt's Chester Beatty Papyrus opens with a boy's praise for his beloved, moving from her eyes to her thighs, while the Assyrian lyrics of Nabû and Tashmetu contain a broken portrait of the goddess, lauding her thighs, ankles, and heels.[70]

However, a clear methodology for identifying when a concept was part of the shared tradition of the ancient Near East has been lacking. John Walton even lauds the benefit of this less stringent method:

> When comparative studies are done at the cognitive environment level, trying to understand how people thought about themselves and their world, a broader methodology can be used.... When we see evidence in the biblical text of a three-tiered cosmos, we have only to ask, "Does the concept of a three-tiered cosmos exist in the ancient Near East?" Once it is ascertained that it does, our task becomes to try to identify how Israel's perception of the cosmos might have been the same or different from what we find (ubiquitously) elsewhere. We need not figure out how Israel got such a concept or from whom they would have "borrowed" it. Borrowing is not the issue, so methodology does not have to address that. Likewise, this need not concern whose ideas are derivative. There is simply common ground across the cognitive environment of the cultures of the ancient world.[71]

6, i:14. A similar use of *mārum* and *mārtum* occurs in two recently published Old Babylonian literary texts. See Andrew R. George, *Babylonian Literary Texts in the Schøyen Collection*, CUSAS 10 (Bethesda, MD: CDL, 2009), 52, 58.

69. For a discussion of the *waṣf* in biblical and Near Eastern sources, see Wolfram Herrmann, "Gedanken zur Geschichte des altorientalischen Beschreibungsliedes," *ZAW* 75 (1963): 176–96; George Schwab, "*Waṣf*" in *Dictionary of the Old Testament: Wisdom, Poetry, and Writings*, ed. Tremper Longman III and Peter Enns (Downers Grove, IL: InterVarsity Press, 2008), 835–42.

70. Fox, *Song of Songs*, 52; Martti Nissinen, "Love Lyrics of Nabû and Tašmetu: An Assyrian Song of Songs?," in *"Und Mose schrieb dieses Lied auf": Studien zum Alten Testament und zum Alten Orient; Festschrift für Oswald Loretz zur Vollendung seines 70. Lebensjahres mit Beiträgen von Freunden, Schülern und Kollegen*, ed. Manfried Dietrich and Ingo Kottsieper, AOAT 250 (Münster: Ugarit-Verlag, 1998), 589 r.5–8. Although later Hellenistic portraits contain an inventory of body parts, Cohen rightly notes that they lack the detailed descriptions of beauty (Cohen, "Beauty of Flora and the Beauty of Sarai," 50).

71. Walton, *Ancient Near Eastern Thought*, 10.

Though unstated, distribution certainly plays a central role in this category designation. The more widespread and numerous the occurrence of a symbol or motif, the less likely the parallel resulted from literary borrowing, and the greater the likelihood that the image was part of a shared cultural tradition.

For example, scholars have noted that biblical laws contain many parallels to known legal codes from elsewhere in the ancient Near East. Though David Wright claims that the biblical author of the Covenant Code (Exod 21:1–22:19) used and revised laws from Hammurabi, the numerous parallels with other ancient Near Eastern law codes, such as the Laws of Eshnunna, the Middle Assyrian Laws, and the Hittite Laws suggest a more widespread legal tradition.[72] In their work, Raymond Westbrook and Bruce Wells conclude that the best approach is "to see the law codes as part of an intellectual tradition, part oral and part written, that spread by diffusion from Mesopotamia, following the path taken by cuneiform legal documents, while continuing in practice to interact with the law, both local and drawn from the underlying common legal tradition."[73]

---

72. David P. Wright, *Inventing God's Law: How the Covenant Code of the Bible Used and Revised the Laws of Hammurabi* (Oxford: Oxford University Press, 2009). Other scholars have questioned Wright's reliance on thematic connections as well as problematic ordering and details. For more on this debate, see Bruce Wells, "The Covenant Code and Near Eastern Legal Traditions," *Maarav* 13 (2006): 85–118.

73. Raymond Westbrook and Bruce Wells, *Everyday Law in Biblical Israel: An Introduction* (Louisville: Westminster John Knox, 2009), 24. For other theories of a shared legal tradition, see Samuel Greengus, *Laws in the Bible and in Early Rabbinic Collections: The Legal Legacy of the Ancient Near East* (Eugene, OR: Wipf & Stock, 2011), 1–9; Julius Morgenstern, "The Book of the Covenant: Part II," *HUCA* 7 (1930): 93 n. 103. Although the legal documents drafted in Akkadian at Alalakh and Hazor, including the two recently discovered fragments, show that a written tradition was present in Syria-Palestine by the early second millennium BCE, the incomplete and random character of the legal corpora, both in the Bible and the cuneiform sources, as well as low literacy rates and a comparable oral tradition of omens, suggests that this legal tradition may have been primarily oral, not written. See Raymond Westbrook, "What Is the Covenant Code?," in *Theory and Method in Biblical and Cuneiform Law*, ed. Bernard Levinson, JSOTSup 181 (Sheffield: Sheffield Academic, 1994), 21; Samuel Greengus, "Some Issues Relating to the Comparability of Laws and the Coherence of the Legal Tradition," in Levinson, *Theory and Method*, 80.

2.4.1.3. Universal Archetype

Finally, on the right end of the spectrum, an *archetype* is an image, motif, event, or character rooted in the universal elements of human experience, recurring both in literature and life, with widespread distribution in geography and chronology.[74]

Lauriat Lane concisely summarizes the two hallmark features of an archetype: universality over time and a basis in the literature of the past.[75] Though long separated from its source, archetypal literary criticism combined facets of Frazer's comparative anthropology and Jungian psychoanalysis and applied them to the study of literature. Gilbert Murray, father of archetypal criticism, described an archetype as "a great unconscious solidarity and continuity, lasting from age to age, among all the children of the poets, both the makers and callers-forth, both the artists and audiences."[76] Maud Bodkin further elucidated Murray's idea:

> I use the term "archetypal pattern" to refer to that within us which ... leaps in response to the effective presentation in poetry of an ancient theme.... In poetry, we may identify themes having a particular form or pattern which persists amid variation from age to age, and which corresponds to a pattern or configuration of emotional tendencies in the minds of those who are stirred by the theme.[77]

Archetypal criticism became popular in the 1950–1960s with the work of literary critic Northrup Frye, who first applied this theory to biblical studies. "One of the first things I noticed about literature was the stability of its structural units: The fact that certain themes, situations, and character types ... have persisted with very little change from Aristophanes to our own time. I have used 'archetype' to describe these building blocks."[78] Therefore, "archetypes are recurrent images and motifs that keep appearing in literature and life that touch us powerfully, both consciously and

---

74. Norman Friedman and Richard Sugg, "Archetypes," *PEPP*, 76–79.
75. Lauriat Lane Jr., "The Literary Archetype: Some Reconsiderations," *JAAC* 13 (1954): 231.
76. Gilbert Murray, *Classical Tradition in Poetry* (London: Milford, 1927), 237.
77. Maud Bodkin, *Archetypal Patterns in Poetry: Psychological Studies of Imagination* (London: Oxford University Press, 1934), 4.
78. Northrup Frye, *The Great Code: The Bible as Literature* (New York: Harcourt Brace Jovanovich, 1981), 48.

unconsciously."[79] While interest in archetypes has waned in recent years, the genre and method of this study, centered on the commonality of human experience, aligns well with this approach.[80]

Similar to shared tradition, distribution is also a key to this category designation. However, in addition to widespread and numerous occurrences of a particular motif, an archetype is better explained as a commonality of human existence, shared by various cultures over time with no demonstrable contact. As Alvin Lee emphasized, "Archetypal criticism focuses on the generic, recurring and conventional elements in literature that cannot be explained as matters of historical influence or tradition."[81] While archetypes are among the building blocks of many biblical authors, for no book is this truer than the Song of Songs. What is more universal and elemental to human experience, regardless of culture, than sensual love between a man and woman? In his history of love songs, Ted Gioia notes the frequent (undetected) use of archetypal expressions:

> Though researchers in local musical customs have rarely focused on universals, preferring to champion (but seldom explicitly) the view that each culture's songs are incommensurable and inextricably embedded in local practices and traditions, the careful student of love songs is struck by the exact opposite phenomenon—namely, that the people who created these songs seem to be consulting the same playbook, *even to the extent of drawing on similar comparisons and metaphors*, and describing almost identical emotional states.[82]

For example, an archetype that recurs in love lyrics regardless of time and culture is the undisturbed love motif, the desire of lovers for privacy to

---

79. Leland Ryken, *How to Read the Bible as Literature* (Grand Rapids: Zondervan, 1984), 143.

80. As Friedman and Sugg note, "Archetypal criticism has proved better suited than some other critical approaches for certain kinds of poetry.... Such art generally aspires to express heightened experiences and relies on archetypal poetics to achieve its effects" ("Archetypes," 77).

81. Alvin A. Lee, "Archetypal Criticism," *ECLT*, 3.

82. Ted Gioia, *Love Songs: The Hidden History* (New York: Oxford University Press, 2015), 181, emphasis added. White similarly states, "It is not surprising that specific topoi be common to both Hebrew and Egyptian love literature. The fragrances, sight of the love partners, embracing and kissing, friends and enemies of the lovers, and even specific parallels ... denote the Song's participation in the world of human love expression" (White, *Song of Songs*, 162).

indulge their passions. Whether an invitation to a tryst in nature (1:7-8, 16-17; 2:10-13; 4:16; 7:11-13; 8:14) or behind the doors of a bedroom chamber (1:4; 3:4; 5:2-8; 8:1-2), the Song of Songs depicts recurring attempts at sexual union in peaceful seclusion.[83]

The Inanna-Dumuzi love songs from Sumer reflect a similar amorous desire, whether in Dumuzi's own house (DI D:7-18), among the trees of the garden (DI F[1]), or a rendezvous at the Ekur, the sacred house of Enlil (DI F:1-28). In one poem, Dumuzi offers to teach Inanna "women's lies" (i.e., deceitful words whereby she would justify her tarrying to her mother), so that they would be able to make love together all night (DI H). The same desire for privacy is evident in the love lyrics of Nabû and Tashmetu, as Tashmetu washes and adorns her body that she may go to the garden with Nabû "alone."[84] In Egypt's love lyrics and the Tamil love poems from India, this archetypal theme is evident in the Alba motif, when a girl is awakened after a night of love and complains of the disturbance of her bliss and the separation that daybreak brings.[85]

Moreover, in the Nikkal Hymn from Ugarit, the motif of undisturbed love may be implicit in the characterization of the Kothirāt, those responsible for Aqhat's conception (*KTU* 1.17 ii.24-47), as "ones who go down among the nut ['*rgz*] trees" (*KTU* 1.24 40-45), a striking parallel to the Song's mention of the lovers' tryst in the "garden of nut trees" (גנת אגוז, 6:11-12).[86] The Song's garden metaphor as well as the motif of "going down to the garden" will be discussed further in chapter 4.

However, this archetypal theme of lovers seeking privacy to indulge their passions is not limited to the ancient Near East. The undisturbed love motif is also found in the erotic lyrics of Greece and Rome as well as later Renaissance and English love poetry. In Homer's *Odyssey*, Odysseus's sexual encounter with Calypso, before departing from her island,

---

83. Though traditionally rendered as an admonition not to stir up love prematurely, the contextual and thematic continuity of the adjuration refrain (2:7, 3:5, 8:4), as well as the Song's literary structure, genre parallels, and grammar also favor understanding this passage as a warning against disturbing lovers indulging their passions. See Brian P. Gault, "A 'Do Not Disturb' Sign? Reexamining the Adjuration Refrain in Song of Songs," *JSOT* 36 (2011): 93-104.

84. Nissinen, "Nabû and Tašmetu," 618-19.

85. Fox, *Song of Songs*, 23; Abraham Mariaselvam, *The Song of Songs and Ancient Tamil Love Poems*, AnBib 118 (Rome: Pontifical Biblical Institute, 1989), 227-28.

86. On the potential link between Hebrew אגוז and Ugaritic '*rgz*, see Pope, *Song of Songs*, 574-79.

happened in the innermost recess of the hollow cave. Then, upon returning to his wife Penelope, the goddess Athena stopped time itself so that the two could make love under the cloak of a divinely prolonged night (*Od.* 5.225–227; 23.239–259). Meleager, employing the above-mentioned motif, laments the disturbance of love, "Morning star, enemy to lovers, why have you come so soon to my bed, just as I am being warmed by dear Demo's flesh?" (*Anth. Pal.* 5.172 [Paton]). Propertius, the Latin poet and friend of Ovid and Virgil, also includes this theme as he dreams of his dead mistress and their secret rendezvous:

> Have you so soon forgotten our escapades in the sleepless Subura and my window-sill worn away by nightly guile? How oft by that window did I let down a rope to you and dangle in mid-air, descending hand over hand to embrace you? Oft at the crossways we made love, and breast on breast warmed with our passion the road beneath. (Propertius, *El.* 4.7.15–20 [Goold])

Furthermore, the Italian poet Dante wove the undisturbed love motif into his wishful longings for Beatrice, his distant object of desire, dreaming of lovemaking in an idyllic, secluded setting (2.28–30).[87] This theme is also common in medieval Occitan poetry and medieval and modern Romance languages. For Christopher Marlowe, the sixteenth-century CE English poet, peaceful privacy is implied from the opening line of "The Passionate Shepherd to His Love," as the shepherd invites his beloved to become his wife and enjoy a perfect life on a secluded hillside, in perpetual spring, surrounded by peaceful country life.[88] Andrew Marvell also plays on this archetypal theme in his poem "To His Coy Mistress": "The grave's a fine and private place, but none, I think, do there embrace."[89] Finally, the American poet James Whitcomb Riley employs this motif when he pictures the darkening of night, then rhetorically asks, "But what care we for light above, if light of love is here?"[90]

---

87. Robert Durling and Ronald Martinez, *Time and the Crystal: Studies in Dante's Rime Petrose* (Berkeley: University of California Press, 1990), 282–83.

88. Roma Gill, ed., *The Complete Works of Christopher Marlowe* (Oxford: Clarendon, 1987), 1:212–15.

89. Christopher Ricks, ed., *The Oxford Book of English Verse* (Oxford: Oxford University Press, 1999), 186.

90. James Whitcomb Riley, *The Complete Poetical Works of James Whitcomb Riley* (Bloomington: Indiana University Press, 1993), 177.

Moreover, the motif of undisturbed love is only one archetypal theme found in the Song. Other examples include feelings of lovesickness (2:5; 5:8), spring as the time for lovers (2:10–13), nature as the place for lovemaking (1:17; 4:12–5:1; 6:2–3, 11–12; 7:12–14), and physical love compared to the plucking of fruit and flora (2:3; 4:12–5:1, 4–5; 7:8–14).[91] Many of these are common motifs shared across time and space.

2.5. Summary

Chana Bloch labeled the Song as "one of the most enigmatic books in the Bible, far more obscure than a reader of English might suppose."[92] Though many problems may go undetected by its casual reader, the obscurity of the Song's body imagery is readily apparent. Even among scholars, these figures have been labeled "bizarre," "grotesque," "comical," and "puzzling."[93] But as Hendrik Viviers notes, "Language is never innocent; it is an act that wants to accomplish something. This most certainly applies to the body-talk in the Song of Songs, even though at first glance, owing to the Song's lyrical and playful nature, one is tempted to conclude otherwise."[94] But what was this "body-talk" supposed to accomplish? As demonstrated by the Song's history of interpretation surveyed in the previous chapter, the foreign nature of these images has spawned a host of speculation. Resting on the premise that the Song is an edited collection of human love lyrics, with no cultic connection, the following study will approach the book's body imagery as a portrait of beauty intended to depict aspects of the lovers' lovely form and its function.

---

91. R. Rothaus Caston, "Love as Illness: Poets and Philosophers on Romantic Love," *CJ* 101 (2006): 271–98; Gioia, *Love Songs*, 131; Joanne Scurlock, "Medicine and Healing Magic," in *Women in the Ancient Near East: A Sourcebook*, ed. Mark Chavala (New York: Routledge, 2014), 106. As John Atkins notes, "One of the most universal of all sex metaphors is that of plucking flowers" (John Atkins, *Sex in Literature* [London: Calder, 1978], 3:222–25).

92. Chana Bloch, "Translating Eros," in *Scrolls of Love: Ruth and the Song of Songs*, ed. Peter S. Hawkins and Lesleigh Cushing Stahlberg (New York: Fordham University Press, 2006), 153.

93. Black, "Beauty or the Beast," 303–4; Moses H. Segal, "The Song of Songs," *VT* 12 (1962): 480; Soulen, "*Waṣfs* of the Song of Songs," 185.

94. Hendrik Viviers, "The Rhetoricity of the 'Body' in the Song of Songs," in *Rhetorical Criticism and the Bible*, ed. Stanley Porter and Dennis Stamps, JSNTSup 295 (Sheffield: Sheffield Academic, 2002), 239.

Based on the conceptual foundation of metaphor in universal themes and culturally specific variations, as well as the numerous connections between Near Eastern civilizations, this study will rely on comparative literature and iconography to help elucidate meaning. Considering both similarities and differences, parallels will be evaluated on linguistic, geographic, chronological, cultural, and contextual grounds. Based on these conclusions, each image will be placed on a relationship spectrum, in hopes of ascertaining the probable source of the image's derivation and possible channels of transmission. Cumulative evidence may also indicate whether the Song's poet was influenced more by the literature and culture of one geographic region over another. More importantly, understanding the meaning of the Song's body imagery may shed greater light on the perception of beauty in ancient Israel.

3
I Am: Poems of Self-Description

As mentioned in the previous chapter, the Song's body imagery can be divided into three categories: (1) self-description, (2) sexual euphemism, and (3) songs of description. In this chapter, we explore two poems of self-description in which the lady uses metaphoric language to describe her own appearance (1:5–6, 8:8–10). Often viewed as an *inclusio* for the book, these verses are linked by social setting, with the brothers functioning as guardians for their sister.[1] We first examine the dark-skinned beauty.

3.1. The Dark-Skinned Beauty (1:5–6)

שחורה אני ונאוה	[5] I am dark but lovely,
בנות ירושלם	O daughters of Jerusalem,
כאהלי קדר	[dark] like the tents of Qedar,
כיריעות שלמה:	[lovely] like the tapestries of Solomon.
אל־תראוני שאני שחרחרת	[6] Do not stare at me because I am too dark,[2]
ששזפתני השמש	for the sun has burned me.
בני אמי נחרו־בי	My mother's sons burned with anger at me;
שמני נטרה את־הכרמים	they made me keeper of the vineyards,
כרמי שלי לא נטרתי:	my own vineyard, I have not kept.

The chapter title is adapted from Athalya Brenner's work on female self-description, *I Am ... Biblical Women Tell Their Own Stories* (Minneapolis: Fortress, 2005).

1. On this *inclusio*, see M. Timothea Elliott, *The Literary Unity of the Canticle*, EUS 23 (New York: Lang, 1989), 201.

2. שחרחרת is a *hapax legomemon* whose reduplication likely stresses intensity. The poet may have used this unique form for its alliteration—נחרו, 1:6c (Noegel and Rendsburg, *Solomon's Vineyard*, 73). Dianne Bergant suggests that the alliteration and repetition of the *s* sounds in 1:6 reflects the sizzling of the sun; see Dianne Bergant, *The Song of Songs*, Berit Olam (Collegeville, MN: Liturgical Press, 2001), 14–15.

Source: Tents of Qedar, Tapestries of Solomon
Target: Maiden's Skin
Mapping: Darkness, Beauty

3.1.1. Comparative Evidence

The source and target in Song 1:5–6 are clear enough, exemplifying the BODY AS LANDSCAPE metaphor, yet the precise meaning of the comparison is heavily debated among scholars, particularly due to racial and gender concerns. In the Hebrew Bible, the aesthetic perception of skin color centers on two verses (Lam 4:7–8), with several other supplemental passages (1 Sam 16:12, 17:42; Job 30:28–30; Song 5:10). First, in his dirge over Jerusalem's destruction, the author of Lamentations contrasts Judah's former luxury with its current poverty (4:7–8):

> Her nobles were whiter [זכו] than snow,
> lighter [צחו] than milk.
> Their bodies were more ruddy [אדמו] than pearls,
> their beards were like lapis lazuli.
> Now their face is blacker than soot [חשך משחור];
> they are not recognized in the street;
> Their skin has shrunk over their bones,
> it has become dry as wood.

The past-present juxtaposition here is highlighted by the shift in colors, from vibrant white and red to dull black.[3] Though זכה often refers to purity or brightness (Job 9:30; 15:15) and צחח seems to imply luminosity or clarity (Isa 18:4; 32:4), the concepts of brightness and whiteness are closely related. The comparison with snow and milk, both known for their white color (Isa 1:18), as well as the contrast with blackness, suggests that צחח/זכה describe the nobles' fair skin prior to Judah's defeat. While the limited use of these terms prohibits defining their exact semantic range, Brenner posits that they function as an equivalent to לבן, particularly when associated with שלג and חלב.[4] These terms (זכו/צחו) may also have been used for their poetic effect, repeating the similar z/ṣ and k/ḥ sounds.

---

3. Adele Berlin, *Lamentations*, OTL (Louisville: Westminster John Knox, 2002), 103–4.

4. Athalya Brenner, *Colour Terms in the Old Testament*, JSOTSup 21 (Sheffield: JSOT Press, 1982), 29–30. While the white/black contrast seems evident from the

Though it is unclear from Lamentations whether their dark skin should be attributed to famine or the sun beating down as they scavenge for food, Job's self-portrait of his sad state pictures his malnourished, disease-ridden body as dark. "I walk about blackened [קדר] but not by the sun.... My skin blackens [שחר] and peels; my bones are scorched from the heat" (30:28–30; see also Lam 5:10). In sum, these passages suggest that fair skin and a ruddy complexion were desirable—a sign of health, youth, and well-being—while dark skin was associated with poverty and disease.

This degradation of dark skin and elevation of a fair complexion continues in extrabiblical Jewish literature. In his wisdom sayings, Sirach states, "A woman's wickedness changes her appearance, and darkens [יקדיר] her face like that of a bear" (Sir 25:17).[5] In a *waṣf* song for Sarai in Genesis Apocryphon, Pharaoh's emissary Hyrcanos praises her beauty, ending with this climax, "How beautiful is all her whiteness [לבנהא]!" (1Q20 XX, 2–8).[6] On this account of the couple in Egypt, the rabbis wondered why Abram, after so many years of marriage, noticed his wife's beauty anew (Gen 12:11). In response, R. Azariah suggested that Sarai's fair skin was highlighted against the Egyptians' darker color, "But now we are going into a place in which the people are ugly and swarthy" (Gen. Rab. 40:4).

---

context, another question involves the relationship between the adjectives צח "white, shining" and אדמו "ruddy." This same collocation is found later in the Song, as the girl praises her lover's appearance, "My beloved is radiant [צח] and ruddy [אדום]" (5:10). But how can skin be both fair and ruddy? Since אדמוני "ruddy" is elsewhere applied to David (1 Sam 16:12, 17:42), particularly his youthful look, this adjective appears to describe a healthy, youthful complexion, what Brenner terms "pinkish," or "peaches and cream." See Brenner, "My Beloved Is Fair and Ruddy: On Song of Songs 5:10–11," *BM* 89 (1982): 168–73; Brenner, *Intercourse of Knowledge*, 47. A parallel also may be seen in the Arabic root *šqr*. When applied to human skin, Lane defines the term as "a clear ruddy complexion with the outer skin inclining to white or having a red or ruddy tinge over a white or fair complexion" (Lane, 1581). Similarly, Gerber notes that whiteness and redness were "standard terms of praise for the complexion of Greek women" (Gerber, "Female Breast," 203).

5. Solomon Schechter, "A Further Fragment of Ben Sira: Prefatory Note," *JQR* 12 (1900): 464; Pancratius C. Beentjes, *The Book of Ben Sira in Hebrew: A Text Edition of All Extant Hebrew Manuscripts and a Synopsis of All Parallel Hebrew Ben Sira Texts*, VTSup 68 (Leiden: Brill, 1997), 86.

6. Joseph Fitzmyer, *The Genesis Apocryphon of Qumran Cave 1 (1Q20)*, 3rd ed., BibOr 18b (Rome: Pontifical Biblical Institute, 2004), 101; Daniel A. Machiela, *The Dead Sea Genesis Apocryphon: A New Text and Translation with Introduction and Special Treatment of Columns 13–17*, STDJ 79 (Leiden: Brill, 2009), 74.

A similar sentiment is evident in the Jewish legal code concerning vows. A situation is posited where a man vows not to marry a certain ugly woman who turns out to be beautiful, or a black girl who turns out to be white, or a short one who turns out to be tall (m. Ned. 9:10). These antitheses confirm that dark skin was undesirable in Jewish culture.

Such a contrast is further illustrated by two rabbinic tales. First, a midrash on Song 1:5–6 tells of a Cushite servant who thought her master would divorce his wife and marry her because he saw his wife's hands dirty. Her friend pointed out her obvious lack of reason: "If concerning his wife, who is most precious to him, you say that because he saw her hands dirty one time, he wants to divorce her, you, who are entirely dirty, scorched from the day of your birth, how much the more so!" (Song Rab. 1:6.2).[7] Likewise, the Talmud Bavli records how R. Mani interceded for a friend who was unhappy in his marriage. When his friend's wife became beautiful and enslaved him, R. Mani returned the woman to her original "black" state (b. Taʿan. 23b).[8] Targum Canticles, as well as Christian patristic writers, also assume this distinction in their allegorical exegesis, connecting blackness to sin and beauty to repentance and redemption.[9]

In fact, the portrait of fair skin as the epitome of feminine beauty is widespread throughout the ancient and classical world. In Egypt, this cultural ideal appears evident in literature and iconography. In the clearest example of a *waṣf* song in Egyptian love lyrics, the boy praises his beloved's beauty as "shining, precious, white of skin [*wbḫt inw*] … long of neck, white of breast [*wbḫt qbyt*]."[10] Since a later stanza reveals that the boy only saw his beloved stroll by, the girl's description likely conforms to an Egyptian ideal of beauty rather than detailing an intimate glimpse. Furthermore, in painting and reliefs, Egyptian women are consistently depicted with lighter skin than men. Gay Robins posits that this artistic device may reflect the tendency for women to be occupied indoors yet admits there is likely a deeper significance.[11] She notes that the representation of men and

---

7. Neusner, *Song of Songs Rabbah*, 100.

8. Tal Ilan, *Massekhet Taʿanit: Text, Translation and Commentary*, FCBT 2/9 (Tübingen: Mohr Siebeck, 2007), 226–30. However, Ilan believes Song 1:5–6 contains no such contrast between darkness and beauty.

9. Alexander, *Targum*, 81–82; Norris, *Song of Songs*, 40–45.

10. The Egyptian *wbḫ* often means "clear, shining" (*GHb* 202; *WÄS* 1:295–96), but its connection to the skin and breasts likely depicts the girl's fair complexion.

11. Gay Robins, "Gender Roles," *OEAE* 2:14.

women is idealistic. The ideal for women is youthful beauty, always a slim figure and never any negative quality—age, sickness, or deformity.[12] Thus, a woman's light skin may reflect reality, but the nature of Egyptian art suggests that fairness was an ideal of beauty.

Greco-Roman literature and art attest a similar light-dark color distinction.[13] Homer (eighth century BCE) repeatedly used the epithet λευκώλενος "white-armed" of Hera, Andromache, Helen, Arete, Nausicaa, and various female attendants.[14] As the *Iliad* opens, Achilles gathers the people of Troy in the wake of its divine attack, "for so had the goddess, white-armed Hera, put it in his heart" (*Il.* 1.55–56 [Murray]). In the *Odyssey*, Athena enhanced the appearance of Penelope, making her taller and "whiter than fresh-cut ivory" (*Od.* 18.195–96 [Murray]).[15] In Greek vase painting, black figure vases depict male figures as dark and females figures as light, a convention that appears even earlier in the Minoan palace painting.[16] Theocritus illustrates the cultural disdain for dark-skinned women in praise for his Levantine beauty, "Charming Bombyca, everyone else calls you Syrian, thin and sun-scorched; I alone call you the color of honey" (*Id.* 10.27–28 [Hopkinson]).[17]

The Latin elegists also lauded the "white" (*candida*), "snow-white," or "milk-white" (*lacteola*) face, arms, neck, breasts, and legs of their women (or young boys), and they mocked the deep ruddy tan of peasant women whose color betrayed their regular exposure to the sun.[18] About his beloved's fair face, Propertius (first century BCE) exclaims, "Lilies are not

---

12. Robins, *Women in Ancient Egypt*, rev. ed. (London: British Museum, 2008), 180–81. Ethnic depiction is also standardized: Nubians as black, Asiatics as yellow.

13. Karl Jax, *Die Weibliche Schönheit in der Griechischen Dichtung* (Innsbruck: Wagner, 1933), 46, 79.

14. LSJ, s.v. "λευκώλενος."

15. Manuel Fernández-Galiano, Joseph Russo, and Alfred Heubeck, *A Commentary on Homer's Odyssey* (Oxford: Oxford University Press, 1993), 3:62.

16. John D. Beazley and Bernard Ashmole, *Greek Sculpture and Painting: To the End of the Hellenistic Period* (Cambridge: Cambridge University Press, 1932), 6–7; Robert S. Folsom, *Attic Black Figured Pottery* (Park Ridge, NJ: Noyes, 1975), 12.

17. See also Philodemus, *Anth. Pal.* 5.132; Virgil, *Ecl.* 10.37–41.

18. For praise of white breasts, see Ovid, *Her.* 16.251–252; on snowy necks, cheeks, and shoulders, see Horace, *Carm.* 2.4.4; Ovid, *Her.* 20.120; Catullus, *Poems*, 64.65. On the white skin of young boys, see Virgil, *Ecl.* 2.17–18. Thanks to Adam Kamesar for alerting me to these Greek and Latin lexical terms and conceptual parallels.

whiter than my mistress" (*El.* 2.3.10 [Goold]). In his *Ars amatoria*, Ovid (first century BCE) explains,

> White is a shameful colour in a sailor; swarthy should he be, both from the sea-waves and from heaven's beams; shameful too in a husbandman, who ever beneath the sky turns up the ground with curved ploughshare and heavy harrows. Thou too who seekest the prize of Pallas' garland art shamed if thy body be white. But let every lover be pale; this is the lover's hue. (*Ars.* 1.723–729 [Goold])

Through the Middle Ages and into modern times, across a wide chronological and geographic spectrum, extant literature and art reflect the view that a woman's light skin is beautiful and dark skin is considered ugly.[19] Manuel Jinbachian details examples from Arabian odes in the two centuries preceding Islam's rise in which a female lover's complexion is praised as "white," compared to the color of an egg.[20] Bernart de Ventadorn, a prominent troubadour of Middle Age Europe, similarly sang, "Her body is beautiful and pleasing and white beneath her clothes. I say this only out of my imagination."[21] Moreover, among the early twentieth-century Arabs in Syria-Palestine, Dalman records antagonistic lyric exchanges between groups labeled as "brown" and "white" women, while Stephan H. Stephan notes the frequent epithet "fair/white one," with the girl or her members being compared to light-colored objects such as ivory, crystal, or a lighted candle.[22] One lyric implies a contempt for dark-skinned girls, "O darkest one, how often I was blamed for (loving) you! But the more they blamed me, the more my passion for you increased."[23]

---

19. David M. Goldenberg, *The Curse of Ham: Race and Slavery in Early Judaism, Christianity, and Islam* (Princeton: Princeton University Press, 2003), 90.

20. Jinbachian, "Arabian Odes," 126–27. For praise of white breasts, see also E. Powys Mathers, ed., *The Book of the Thousand Nights and One Night* (New York: Routledge, 1986), 1:486, 593.

21. Leslie T. Topsfield, *Troubadours and Love* (New York: Cambridge University Press, 1975), 36.

22. Dalman, *Palästinischer Diwan*, 200–201, 250–51, 297–98; Stephan, "Modern Palestinian Parallels," 218, 220, 232, 237, 249, 254, 271. See also Saarisalo, "Songs of the Druzes," 13, 15, 50; Sven Linder, *Palästinische Volksgesänge*, UUA 5 (Uppsula: Lundequistska, 1952), 83.

23. Stephan, "Modern Palestinian Parallels," 205.

Sonnet 130, one of William Shakespeare's classic poems, similarly employs the black-white antithesis in a satire on the perfect portrait of beauty, well-known from the lyrics of antiquity and his contemporaries. Instead of exaggerating the object of his affections, praising her bright eyes, brilliant red lips, golden hair, snow-white breasts, and pale skin, Shakespeare admits the truth about his beloved's appearance (e.g., dark skin) but claims that she is as lovely as any woman whose beauty is falsely presented.[24]

Similarly, Edwin Long's *Babylonian Marriage Market* (1875), combining the classical accounts with Victorian tastes, visually portrays a Mesopotamian woman on the auctioneer's block, whose pale complexion is highlighted by the dark-skinned slave next to her and the girls in line behind her whose color grow gradually darker. Although his subject is derived from Herodotus, Long's depiction of beauty closely reflects Victorian ideals.[25] Finally, based on an analysis of modern scholarship on Greco-Roman literature, Etruscan paintings, and European, Aztec, Egyptian, Chinese, and Japanese art, as well as his personal study of over fifty modern societies, anthropologist Peter Frost concludes that this data reveals a consistent worldwide association of fairness with femininity.[26]

While the elevation of fair skin as the epitome of female beauty is widespread across geography and time, this perception is not as clearly present in the literature of Mesopotamia. In fact, Wilfred Lambert argues that one image from the divine love lyrics depicts the opposite portrait—dark as beautiful. In his overwhelming desire for Ishtar, Marduk exclaims, "She was white, like a gecko; her skin was burnt [*naqlât*] like a pot."[27] Despite

---

24. For a summary of the debated identity of Shakespeare's Dark Lady, see Samuel Schoenbaum, "Shakespeare's Dark Lady: A Question of Identity," in *Shakespeare's Styles: Essays in Honour of Kenneth Muir*, ed. Philip Edwards, Inga-Stina Ewbank, and G. K. Hunter (Cambridge: Cambridge University Press, 2004), 221–39. See also "Nut-Brown Maid," in Thomas Percy, *Reliques of Ancient English Poetry* (New York: Dutton, 1910), 1:303–14.

25. Zainab Bahrani, *Women of Babylon: Gender and Representation in Mesopotamia* (New York: Routledge, 2001), 172.

26. Peter Frost, "Human Skin Color: A Possible Relationship between Its Sexual Dimorphism and Its Social Perception," *Perspectives in Biology and Medicine* 32 (1988): 39, 49. A modern example would be Snow White, with "skin as white as snow." See Jacob Grimm and Wilhelm Grimm, *The Original Folk and Fairy Tales of the Brothers Grimm* (Princeton: Princeton University Press, 2014), 1:170.

27. Wilfred G. Lambert, "The Problem of Love Lyrics," in *Unity and Diversity: Essays in the History, Literature and Religion of the Ancient Near East*, ed. Hans Goed-

his uncertainty over the reading *naqlât*, Lambert suggests that this love lyric presents dark skin as the Mesopotamian mark of female beauty, to which he compares Song 1:5.[28] Yet, the term *naqlât* can be read as *naglat*.[29] While *CAD* takes the meaning of *nagalu* as uncertain, its connection to stars and sheep suggests brightness.[30] So even here the parallelism is best seen as synonymous, stressing Ishtar's light appearance.

In contrast to the evidence above, which consistently depicts fair skin as the embodiment of feminine beauty, from antiquity to modern times, the Tamil love songs from ancient India present an opposing perspective.[31] In his comparative study, Abraham Mariaselvam records numerous lyrics in which the female lover is praised for her dark complexion. One man lauds his beloved's appearance, "You, young and pretty maid, with a dark body like the tender shoots that sprout in the rainy season."[32] From a host of examples, Mariaselvam concludes that a dark brown complexion was admired in Tamil culture. Yet, in his zeal to show comparability with the Song, other pertinent passages from the Hebrew Bible (e.g., Lam 4:7–8) are overlooked, and Tamil culture is imported back into Israel, "The Hebrew idea of female beauty is perfect when the complexion is dark with sheen."[33] While the Tamil concept of feminine beauty clearly differed from other Near Eastern cultures, Mariaselvam's proposed connection to the Song is questionable, especially considering India's distance from Israel.

---

icke and J. J. M. Roberts (Baltimore: Johns Hopkins University Press, 1975), 120 (B:15–16).

28. Lambert, "Devotion: The Languages of Religion and Love," in *Figurative Language in the Ancient Near East*, ed. Murray Mindlin, Markham J. Geller, and John E. Wansbrough (London: University of London School of Oriental and African Studies, 1987), 34.

29. *CAD* 11.1:107.

30. In the Sumerian lyrics, Dumuzi also uses adjectives of brightness (*mul-mul*) for his beloved (Sefati, *Love Songs*, 81, 136, 145). An elevation of fair skin may also be implicit in Ludingira's depiction of his mother as "a perfect ivory figurine." See Jean Nougayrol, "Signalement Lyrique," *Ugaritica* 5 (1968): 315 (26).

31. Tamil anthologies date between the second century BCE and second century CE. See V. I. Subramoniam, "The Dating of Sangam," in *Proceedings of the Third International Conference Seminar of Tamil Studies, Paris—July 1970* (Pondicherry: Institut Français d'Indologie, 1973), 83.

32. Mariaselvam, *Ancient Tamil Love Poems*, 301. Mariaselvam offers nearly twenty examples of the epithet Māayōḷ, "a girl of dark complexion" (160).

33. Mariaselvam, *Ancient Tamil Love Poems*, 193.

The widespread nature of fair-skinned beauty, from ancient Egypt to Greece and Rome, from medieval Europe to the modern Far East, might initially suggest that this image is a universal archetype. Yet, the contrasting portrait of beauty in the Tamil lyrics as well as the modern quest for a golden tan in Western culture suggests that this body metaphor is better regarded as a shared cultural ideal.[34] This perception of skin color, while shared across the ancient Near East, does not stem from a universal element of human experience, but rather it is based on a culturally defined view of beauty and well-being. So how does this comparative evidence affect our understanding of Song 1:5–6?

3.1.2. Meaning in the Song

This poem (1:5–6) is delineated from previous and subsequent lyrics by recipient, topic, and tone. The woman does not directly address her lover, either as a king in a royal setting (1:2–4) or a shepherd in nature (1:7–8), but rather, she directs her speech to the daughters of Jerusalem. Instead of asking for a private rendezvous with her lover, using words of passion, she describes her own physical appearance. The main issue here centers on the comparisons in the first verse (1:5). What is the connection between the adjectives שחורה "dark" and נאוה "lovely," and how are they related to the "tents of Qedar" and "tapestries of Solomon"? There are three options: the maiden compares herself to (1) two objects that are dark *and* lovely (Qedar/Solomon), (2) two objects known to be dark (Qedar/Salmah), or (3) one object that is dark (Qedar) and another that is lovely (Solomon).

In the first option, the maiden is declaring her self-assured beauty, even against current cultural norms.[35] Adopting this approach, Falk opines

---

34. The cultural perception of dark skin began to change after the Industrial Revolution. With more people working inside, dark skin was no longer a sign of lower status but a sign of leisure, time to spare soaking in the sun. This trend is evident in the comments of designer Coco Chanel, "The 1929 girl must be tanned. A golden tan is the index of chic" (*Vogue* 22 [June 1929], 100). A preindustrial perspective is still evident in Asia, where South Indian women use turmeric to lighten their skin and ladies in the Far East use umbrellas to shield themselves from the sun.

35. F. W. Dobbs-Allsopp, "'I Am Black *and* Beautiful': The Song, Cixous, and *Écriture Féminine*," in *Engaging the Bible in a Gendered World: An Introduction to Feminist Biblical Interpretation in Honor of Katherine Doob Sakenfeld*, ed. Linda Day and Carolyn Pressler (Louisville: Westminster John Knox, 2006), 129–30; Exum, *Song of Songs*, 105; Keel, *Song of Songs*, 46; Pope, *Song of Songs*, 307.

that the woman's assertion of her blackness is positive, not apologetic, a statement of self-affirmation and pride, "I am black and for that reason I am beautiful."[36] Thus, the two adjectives are read together, "dark *and* beautiful," while the subsequent sources are viewed as iconic items known for their dark beauty. In favor of this theory, the male lover frequently extols the beauty of his beloved in the Song (1:8–10, 15; 2:10, 13–14; 4:1–7; 5:2; 6:4–7, 9; 7:2–7), often referring to her as "most beautiful among women" (1:8; 5:9; 6:1, 9–10). As Cheryl Exum notes, the language of the Song is praise and delight, not disparagement and apology. If one assumes literary unity, one should expect an expression of pride in 1:5–6 as well.[37]

However, there are numerous problems weighing against this theory. First, contrary to Exum, the internal evidence does not support a unified self-portrait of the Song's female character. While the man consistently praises his beloved's beauty, one exchange between the lovers hints at her less-than-confident self-esteem. In the opening verse of chapter 2, the woman refers to herself as a "crocus of Sharon, a lotus of the valleys" (2:1).

While scholars continue to debate the scientific species of these flowers, it appears that the maiden is characterizing herself as ordinary, common, and less than desirable.[38] This seems implicit in her lover's response, as he elevates her above all others, "a lotus among thorns" (2:2). Also, when the lover later expresses his desire to the gaze at her beauty (7:1), the beloved responds with a question of disbelief, "Why would you gaze at the Shulammite?"[39] Therefore, an apologetic, self-deprecating comment would not be altogether dissonant with the woman's other remarks concerning her physical appearance.

Moreover, the immediate context and above comparative evidence imply that a fair complexion was prized among women in Jewish culture. In fact, the lover later lauds the ivory tone of his lady (7:5). If she instructs others not to look at her because of her tan skin (1:6), it is hard to avoid the conclusion that there is something negative or less desirable about her dark color.[40] As a result, some have resorted to semantic gymnastics

---

36. Falk, *Love Lyrics*, 110.
37. J. Cheryl Exum, "Asseverative 'al in Canticles 1,6," *Bib* 62 (1981): 418–19.
38. On the identity of the שׁוּשָׁן, see the analysis of the woman's breasts in §5.8.
39. The identity of the speaker is problematic. Perhaps, the lover employs plural verbs for intensity, a substitution (of grammatical forms) found elsewhere (1:2).
40. The adjective שְׁחוֹרָה "dark," at times rendered as "black," is not a reference to ethnicity (contra Goulder), but rather the darkening effect of overexposure to the sun's

and questionable parallels to avoid this conclusion. Exum, based on Ugaritic grammar, initially rendered the particle אל as an asserative, inviting the gaze of others ("look at me"), though she has since admitted the lack of evidence for such a reading.[41] Mitchell Dahood suggested rendering ראה as "to envy," importing intentionality into this verb of seeing, and thus, transforming the negative into a positive.[42] Other scholars render אל־תראוני (1:6) as "pay no mind" to divert the visual focus and temper a negative connotation.[43] However, these suggestions cannot avoid the clear focus on the woman's anxiety about her appearance.[44]

Proponents also suggest that the "tents of Qedar" and "tapestries of Solomon" (1:5) were both known for their color *and* beauty, despite a lack of evidence. While Qedar is mentioned in biblical and cuneiform sources, little is known about this place. In the Hebrew Bible, Qedar is listed as Ishmael's son (Gen 25:13; 1 Chr 1:29) as well as a land in the

---

rays (Brenner, *Colour Terms*, 98). Without accepting his identification of the Song's maiden as Pharaoh's daughter, see Victor Sasson, "King Solomon and the Dark Lady in the Song of Songs," *VT* 39 (1989): 412-14.

41. Exum, "Asseverative *'al* in Canticles 1:6," 416-19; Exum, *Song of Songs*, 103. For further critique, see Takamitsu Muraoka, *Emphatic Words and Structures in Biblical Hebrew* (Jerusalem: Magnes, 1985), 123-24.

42. Mitchell Dahood, *Psalms I (1-50)*, AB 16 (New York: Doubleday NY, 1966), 302.

43. Exum, *Song of Songs*, 97; Fox, *Song of Songs*, 102.

44. Pope and Keel connect the woman's dark skin with the exotic, "totally other" nature of the black goddess, a common cult image in antiquity. Yet such a parallel is governed more by their proposed cultic background than anything in the Song itself (Keel, *Song of Songs*, 47-49; Pope, *Song of Songs*, 307-18). From a personal name on an early Hebrew seal, Lubetski posits that שחרחרת (1:6) combines the color "black" with the Egyptian theophoric element Horus, thus producing a positive view of the woman's dark skin, implying "she is regal, even divine." Yet this view is problematic. First, Lubetski relies heavily on the Masoretic vocalization different from other quinqueconsonantal color terms (אדמדם "red," ירקרק "yellow-green," Lev 13:49). For a *hapax legomenon*, misvocalization seems equally, if not more, plausible. Second, Lubetski imports his proposed meaning for the above personal name onto a generic noun. This is especially problematic as Hebrew theophoric elements usually indicate an elative, with no positive or negative connotation (שלהבתיה "blazing flame," Song 8:6; [מ]הומת יהוה "intense terror," 1 Sam 5:11 in 4Q51 [4QSam[a]]). Thus, his conclusion that this term alludes to the woman's royalty, possibly referring to the Egyptian princess, is entirely conjecture. See Meir Lubetski, "A Tale of a Seal," in *Shlomo: Studies in Epigraphy, Iconography, History and Archaeology in Honor of Shlomo Moussaieff*, ed. Robert Deutsch (Tel-Aviv: Archaeological Center, 2003), 91-96.

region of Arabia, at the end of the known world to the east (Jer 2:10, 49:28). The Qedarites are described as nomadic pastoralists (Isa 42:11), known for their archery skill (Isa 21:17) and large flocks of sheep and goats (Isa 60:7; Ezek 27:21). Assyrian and Neo-Babylonian sources refer to the inhabitants of the Syro-Arabian desert, including the people of Qedar, as ones who raise camels and sheep, living in tents and unfortified temporary camps, moving from place to place with their flocks and raiding the permanent settlements in the regions adjacent to the desert.[45] The "tents of Qedar" are mentioned elsewhere in Scripture (Isa 21:16; Jer 49:28–29; Ps 120:5), but these occurrences are formulaic, offering no additional insights. While no indication is given, either in biblical or extrabiblical sources, concerning the color of the Qedarite tents, the associated verbal root קדר "to be dark" could imply that these nomads were known for their dark tents. Yet, this conclusion is based in part on a custom of modern-day Arab bedouins.[46]

Some further posit that such dark tents of black goat hair would surely have been lovely. Marvin Pope quotes William Thomson's cultural work, "Even black tents, when new and pitched among bushes of liveliest green, have a very comely appearance, especially when both are bathed in a flood of evening's golden light."[47] Yet, the original context of this quote exposes Thomson's own struggle with interpreting the Song's metaphor:

> A group of their [Arabs] tents spreads along the base of the hills on our left. If those of Kedar were no more attractive than these of Abu el Aswad, the Bride in the "Song of Songs" has fallen upon a lame comparison for her charms. Ay; but observe, it is she that is black, not the tents of Kedar, perhaps; not the curtains of Solomon, certainly. These may have been extremely beautiful.[48]

Similar to the lack of evidence supporting the visual beauty of the "tents of Qedar," the precise referent of the "tapestries of Solomon" is also unknown. Since the overwhelming majority of the occurrences of יריעה in

---

45. Israel Ephʻal, *The Ancient Arabs: Nomads on the Borders of the Fertile Crescent Ninth–Fifth Centuries B.C.* (Leiden: Brill, 1982), 5.

46. For a modern example, see Jacob Klein et al., "Song of Songs" [Hebrew], in *Megilloth* (Tel-Aviv: Davidson Atai, 1994), 28. The root קדר could also reflect the skin color of the people themselves (*HALOT*, s.v. "קדר").

47. Pope, *Song of Songs*, 320.

48. William M. Thomson, *The Land and the Book* (New York: Harper, 1859), 251.

the Hebrew Bible (forty of forty-eight) describe the construction of Israel's tabernacle in the wilderness, the Song may refer to the cultic tent that housed the ark prior to Solomon's temple, or perhaps the opulent furnishings of Solomon's royal palace (1 Kgs 7:1–12). Regardless, any connection to Solomon connotes luxury, wealth, and beauty, as the iconic splendor of Israel's golden era is clear from the biblical narratives. Yet, proponents of this view suggest that Solomon's tapestries were not only beautiful but also made of dark animal skins. As Exum concludes, "Solomon's tents, which would surely be beautiful, could also be imagined as made of black goats' skins."[49] While this hypothesis is possible, it is based on speculation rather than any solid textual or material evidence.

Finally, this position lacks any rationale for the woman's lengthy explanation of her tanned skin in the following verse (1:6). If her dark color is not negative, then why does she need to explain what made her dark? Even Exum notes this problem, "The anger of the woman's brothers is perplexing. It seems to have no role except to get the woman into the vineyards."[50] Yet, the maiden's final statement regarding her inability to care for her vineyard, likely a euphemism for her own body, indicates that she is offering a self-conscious defense of her dark physical appearance.

In the second option, the woman focuses solely on her dark skin, describing its color (1:5) and cause (1:6). The adjective נאוה "lovely" is parenthetical, and the two subsequent comparisons are considered synonymous. This position is illustrated by Fox's rendering: "Black I am—but lovely—O girls of Jerusalem, like tents of Kedar, (like) curtains of Salmah."[51] In light of the synonymous nature of אהל "tent" and יריעה "tent curtain," often found in parallel (2 Sam 7:2; Isa 54:2; Jer 4:20; 10:20; 49:29; Hab 3:7), proponents suggest revocalizing שלמה from "Solomon" to "Salmah," another nomadic Arabian tribe. Fox explains, "The tents of these tribes serve as an image for blackness, not loveliness.... The next verse shows that she is now concerned mainly with her swarthiness, and the comparisons in v. 5b are meant to make that point."[52]

However, this position also contains numerous weaknesses. The above emendation, which first appeared in the late nineteenth-century work of Wellhausen, is entirely conjectural, as the extant versions unanimously

---

49. Exum, *Song of Songs*, 105.
50. Exum, *Song of Songs*, 105.
51. Fox, *Song of Songs*, 100. See also Pope, *Song of Songs*, 320.
52. Fox, *Song of Songs*, 102.

support the Masoretic reading.[53] Also, while the tribe of Salmah does appear in numerous sources, the information known about this nomadic group is very limited.[54] The "Salmu" are mentioned by the Nabateans in their inscriptions as allies.[55] Rabbinic literature often connects this group with the Kenites, interchanging the two terms or listing them among other Arab peoples.[56] Yet, despite the lack of evidence that Salmah was known for its dark-skinned tents, this view is widely cited and commonly accepted, based purely on the poetic parallelism.[57]

While this option creates a tighter parallel between the two lines, the adjective נאוה "lovely" is minimized and any connection to the prior context is lost. If the focus is squarely on the woman's dark skin, why mention her beauty, even parenthetically?[58] Also, a mention of Solomon would suggest royal splendor and beauty but also link to the book's title as well as the setting in the previous poem (1:2–4). Thus, Fox's opinion that the parallelism could be improved is not sufficient to reject the MT.[59] These views rightly sense a tension between "dark" and "lovely," especially in light of comparative evidence for the low esteem of dark skin. Yet, this tension has caused scholars to highlight one adjective and disregard the other. To some, the maiden's words are a self-confident assertion of beauty, ignoring her self-conscious explanation in the following verse (1:6); to others, she

---

53. Julius Wellhausen, *Prolegomena to the History of Israel* (Edinburgh: Black, 1885), 218.

54. In his work on Nabatean personal names, Abraham Negev notes the occurrence of שלם in North Arabia, suggesting it was "apparently the name of an Arab tribe," but offers no further information about this group. See Abraham Negev, *Personal Names in the Nabatean Realm*, Qedem 32 (Jerusalem: Hebrew University Press, 1991), 159.

55. Aryeh Kasher, *Jews, Idumaeans, and Ancient Arabs: Relations of the Jews in Eretz-Israel with the Nations of the Frontier and the Desert during the Hellenistic and Roman Era (332 BCE–70 CE)*, TSAJ 18 (Tübingen: Mohr, 1988), 8. Stephanos von Byzanz, a sixth-century Greek grammarian known for his geographical treatise, theorizes that the Salamians "peaceful ones" may have been given this name after their alliance with the Nabateans (*Ethnica*, 550:12–13).

56. Ernst Axel Knauf, *Ismael: Untersuchungen zur Geschichte Palästinas und Nordarabiens im 1. Jahtausend v. Chr.*, ADPV 7 (Weisbaden: Harrassowitz, 1985), 107.

57. Fox, *Song of Songs*, 102; Gerleman, *Hohelied*, 100; Pope, *Song of Songs*, 320; Robert and Tournay, *Cantique des Cantiques*, 71.

58. Fox, *Song of Songs*, 102.

59. Exum, *Song of Songs*, 104.

offers a self-conscious defense of her darkness, with a brief, parenthetical aside about her beauty (1:5).

In contrast, a third option suggests that the woman's description combines self-confidence and self-consciousness. In light of the elevation of fair skin as a sign of beauty and well-being in the Hebrew Bible, extrabiblical Jewish literature, and other cultures in the ancient, classical, medieval, and modern world, these adjectives are best explained as contrastive, "dark but lovely." Yet, rather than emending the comparisons or speculating about their associations, the parallelism is best explained as distributive, dark like the tents of Qedar, lovely like the tapestries of Solomon.[60] In this structure, "the non-parallel line contains an element of each of the other lines so that the bonding is more powerful than usual."[61]

Yet, tension remains between the woman's assertion of beauty and her defense of her dark skin. How can one explain such dissonance? Although the comparative evidence suggests a culturally conditioned perspective of fair skin as beautiful, these verses also contain a universal element. No matter how self-confident a person may feel about their own appearance, they will often become self-conscious under the gaze of others. They may think of themselves as beautiful, but when they are compared to the cultural ideal, they become self-conscious about their imperfections. This aligns well with the woman's other self-deprecating comments (2:1; 7:1).

Therefore, this passage is not a statement on race. As Abraham Melamed rightly warns, readers must not look at the Bible through the eyes of later generations whose culture and values are different. We must always beware of reading Scripture through a modern lens, not allowing today's issues to shape our understanding of ancient texts.[62]

3.2. A Self-Proclamation of Purity and Reward (8:8–10)

| אחות לנו קטנה | [8] We have a young sister, |
| ושדים אין לה | and she has no breasts. |

---

60. Fishbane, *Song of Songs*, 34; Ginsburg, *Song of Songs*, 132–34; Tremper Longman, *Song of Songs*, NICOT (Grand Rapids: Eerdmans, 2001), 95–99.

61. Watson, *Classical Hebrew Poetry*, 181.

62. Abraham Melamed, *The Image of the Black in Jewish Culture* (London: Curzon, 2003), 59. For a contrasting example, see Robert K. Wabyanga, "Songs of Songs 1:5–7: An Africana Reading," *JTSA* 150 (2014): 128–47.

מה־נעשה לאחתנו	What shall we do for our sister,
ביום שידבר־בה:	on the day that she is spoken for?
אם־חומה היא	⁹ If she is a wall,
נבנה עליה טירת כסף	we will build on it a parapet of silver.
ואם־דלת היא	If she is a door,
נצור עליה לוח ארז:	we will encase it with a plank of cedar.
אני חומה	¹⁰ I was a wall,
ושדי כמגדלות	and my breasts were like towers.
אז הייתי בעיניו	Then, I became in his eyes
כמוצאת שלום:	as one who finds peace.

Source: Wall, Door, Towers
Target: Woman's Body, Breasts
Mapping: Purity, Reward

These verses are extremely difficult to interpret, with numerous questions in nearly every line. As Hans-Peter Müller aptly concluded, "This short dialogue has resisted every attempt at explanation."[63] For this reason, Ringgren labeled this unit as "one of the darkest parts of the Song."[64] Yet, rather than the Song's numerous *hapax legomena*, the *crux interpretum* here involves the architectural imagery of a wall and a door.

Scholars have interpreted these figures in one of two ways: (1) the images are antithetic, contrasting an impenetrable wall, picturing purity, with an accessible door, portraying promiscuity, or (2) they are synonymous, dual depictions of chastity. Another question relates to the results. Will these premarital conditions lead to reinforcement, reward, or both? Many offer an opinion, but few consult comparative evidence in the Song or the love lyrics of surrounding cultures.[65]

---

63. Hans-Peter Müller, "Das Hohelied," in *Das Hohelied, Klagelieder, Das Buch Ester*, 4th rev. ed., ATD 16.2 (Göttingen: Vandenhoeck & Ruprecht, 1992), 86, my translation. In his recent work, Fishbane similarly categorized the meaning of both images as "ambiguous" (*Song of Songs*, 214).

64. Helmer Ringgren, "Das Hohe Lied," in *Das Hohe Lied, Klagelieder, Das Buch Esther*, ATD 16.2 (Göttingen: Vandenhoeck & Ruprecht, 1958), 35, my translation.

65. Hicks points to the metaphorical use of architectural openings in Near Eastern literature, and Tawil refers to decorative doors and battlements in Mesopotamia, but they omit imagery from love lyrics. See R. Lansing Hicks, "The Door of Love," in *Love and Death in the Ancient Near East*, ed. John H. Marks and Robert M. Good

3. I Am: Poems of Self-Description   75

In the ancient Near East, walls were upright structures erected to enclose, divide, support, or protect—a major part of the overall fortification system for cities.⁶⁶ In the Hebrew Bible, חומה, the common term used to refer to this object, most often describes the wall of a city or building (1 Kgs 3:1; Lam 2:7). In Song 5:7, it describes the station of the city guards. Yet, this term can be employed figuratively for any dividing barrier. For example, Nabal's servants described David's men as a "wall," shielding them from harm (1 Sam 25:16), while YHWH promised to be a "wall of fire" in protection of Jerusalem (Zech 2:9). A similar image occurs earlier in the Song, although an Aramaic term (כתל) is used. In 2:8–17, the lover comes for his beloved but is stopped outside the wall of her home. Peering through the window, he calls for her to join him on a romantic romp in nature. Symbolizing their separation, the lover can issue an invitation from outside the wall, but he must await her response.

Similarly, the term דלת "door" often describes a structure that prohibits entry into a city or building (Deut 3:5; Eccl 12:4). It also can be an object of protection, as in the story of Lot and Sodom's would-be rapists (Gen 10:19), or it can symbolize separation, as in the aftermath of Tamar's humiliation by Amnon (2 Sam 13:16–19). Ezekiel 38:11 employs these terms in synonymous parallelism, warning Gog against its desire to invade the defenseless, "those living without a חומה, ones who lack bars and דלתים." Yet doors not only restrain but also enable access. Thus, the question in Song 8:9 is whether the "door" is a figure of restraint or access to the beloved. Does it symbolize her purity or promiscuity?

One clue is found in the use of door imagery in Song 5:2–8, though the term דלת is not present. The lover comes for his beloved but is rebuffed by a locked door. He is separated, knocking and calling to her. Initially unwilling to open for her lover, when the maiden rises and fumbles with the door's bolt, her lover is gone. Here, the door is an obstacle and barrier that both lovers are seeking to overcome.⁶⁷

Thus, the Song's earlier imagery, with both objects used as obstacles to the lovers' union (2:9, 5:2), as well as the example of Ezek 38:11, sug-

---

(Guilford, CT: Four Quarters, 1987), 153; Hayim Tawil, "Two Biblical Architectural Images in Light of Cuneiform Sources (Lexicographical Note X)." *BASOR* 341 (2006): 40–50.

66. Keith Schoville, "חומה," *NIDOTTE* 2:49–50.

67. Elaine T. James, "Battle of the Sexes: Gender and the City in Song of Songs," *JSOT* 42 (2017): 105. See also Lawrence Stager, "Key Passages," *ErIsr* 27 (2003): 240.

gest that the wall (חומה) and door (דלת) in Song 8:9 could be synonymous images of chastity through inaccessibility, rather than a contrast between purity and promiscuity.[68] Since most scholars agree that the wall signifies purity, the following comparative study will focus primarily on the door imagery.[69] For the meaning of Song 8:9, as well as the larger unit (8:8–10), דלת occupies an important position.

3.2.1. Comparative Evidence

Whether Near Eastern or classical love lyrics, the door frequently functions as an archetypical symbol of entry and exclusion. In Egypt, the door is an obstacle, separating lovers and preventing their access to one another. In Papyrus Chester Beatty, the boy laments that the girl's door is closed to him. The door (ṯr) is personified and urged not to obstruct the boy's desire for entry. He calls for a carpenter,

> that he may fashion for us a bolt of reeds [qꜣr n(y) is(w)],
> a door of foliage(?) [ṯr n(y) [d]ꜣisy].
> Then at any time the brother can come
> and find her house open
> and find a bed spread with fine linen,
> and a pretty little maidservant too.[70]

Later, the young boy bemoans the girl's intentional exclusion, leaving him outside the door with no invitation to enter.[71] In Papyrus Harris, a frustrated lover stands outside, wishing he could be his beloved's doorkeeper, even if it meant incurring her wrath. At least such a position would garner her attention and gain him access past the closed door.[72]

---

68. Yakov Eidelkind has argued that גל נעול (4:12), based on the use of גל/גלא in rabbinic literature, is best rendered "locked door," again picturing the lover waiting at the door, unable to enter until invited by his beloved; see Yakov Eidelkind, "Two Notes on Song 4:12," *Babel und Bibel* 3 (2006): 222–24. On the Song's affinity with Rabbinic Hebrew, see F. W. Dobbs-Allsopp, "Late Linguistic Features in Song of Songs," in Hagedorn, *Perspectives on the Song of Songs*, 27–77.

69. 'In DI Y, Inanna's parents use similar imagery to invite Dumuzi to enjoy his new bride, "Destroy our parapet … exert yourself exceedingly!" (Sefati, *Love Songs*, 274).

70. Fox, *Song of Songs*, 75–76.

71. Fox, *Song of Songs*, 75.

72. Fox, *Song of Songs*, 14.

Likewise, door imagery is also found in Mesopotamian love lyrics, particularly the sacred marriage ritual of "opening the door" (*é gál.lu*). In a poem about his wedding to Inanna (DI C¹), Dumuzi arrives at his bride's home on the appointed day, calling for her to open to him, but he is forced to wait outside. Only after Inanna had listened to her mother's counsel and properly adorned herself does she open the door for her groom.[73] Though Samuel Greengus points out that these lyrics depict a cultic ritual, both he and Thorkild Jacobsen believe that this religious rite was likely patterned after Mesopotamian marital practice. The groom would bring gifts to his bride's paternal home, calling for her to open the door and escort him to their bedroom, where the couple would consummate their marriage.[74] In support for such a practice, *Enki and Ninhursag* details Enki's arrival at Uttu's door. Bearing marriage gifts, he calls for her to open to him, followed by the couple's union.[75] Yet, door imagery is not limited to cultic rites. Jeremy Black also points to this figure in a courtship poem. Ishtar imagines inviting her lover into her parent's house to spend the night. In her heightened emotion, she apostrophizes the door and its bolt, wishing they would not prevent her lover's entry but admit him freely.[76]

In Greco-Roman love lyrics, the door is increasingly prominent, particularly in poems labeled *exclusus amator* "locked-out lover" or παρακλαυσίθυρον, a lament "beside the closed door." Howard Canter summarizes the frequency and features of this literary motif:

> Whether one reads classical comedy, elegy, epigram, or lyric, he becomes familiar with the conventional figure of the *exclusus amator*. He finds

---

73. Thorkild Jacobsen, *The Harps That Once...: Sumerian Poetry in Translation* (New Haven: Yale University Press, 1987), 19–23.

74. Samuel Greengus, "Old Babylonian Marriage Ceremonies and Rites," *JCS* 20 (1966): 62; Greengus, "The Old Babylonian Marriage Contract," *JAOS* 89 (1969): 523; Thorkild Jacobsen, "Religious Drama in Ancient Mesopotamia," in Goedicke and Roberts, *Unity and Diversity*, 65. On marital practices, see Alster, "Marriage and Love," 15–27.

75. Jacobsen, *Harps*, 197–200.

76. Jeremy A. Black, "Babylonian Ballads: A New Genre," *JAOS* 103 (1983): 30. In PBS XII 52, Inanna's parents similarly implore their son-in-law to open the door, to come enjoy his new bride; see Bendt Alster, "Sumerian Love Songs," *RA* 79 (1985): 132. Nathan Wasserman points to a similar motif in an Old Babylonian incantation, written for one "alienated like a barrier" ("Piercing the Eyes: An Old Babylonian Love Incantation and the Preparation of Kohl," *BO* 72 [2015]: 602).

also that the early love-affair is often associated with the favorite's house-door, around which eager admirers throng. The door, usually obdurate and unyielding, is now apostrophized, now flattered, now treated with violence.... By way of variation, he may sing a lover's serenade—technically known as a παρακλαυσίθυρον, a woeful ballad to the door which separates him from the object of his affection.[77]

For example, Asclepiades (third century BCE) tells of one lover, on a long wintry night, pacing back and forth outside his beloved's door, drenched by rain, smitten by desire for her (*Anth. Pal.* 5.189). Poseidippos (fourth century BCE) describes another begging for his darling to open to him, having fought thugs and thieves to get there (*Anth. Pal.* 5.213). In the same vein, Rufinus asks his beloved, "For how long, Prodice, will I wail by your door? Until when will your hard heart be deaf to my pleading?" (Rufinus, *Anth. Pal.* 5.103 [Paton]).

This literary theme is also prominent among the Latin elegists. Tibullus (first century BCE) laments separation from his beloved Delia, who is now married and closely guarded:

> For a cruel watch has been set upon my girl,
> and the door is shut and bolted hard against me.
> Door of a stubborn master, may the rain lash thee,
> and bolts flying at Jupiter's command make thee their mark.
> Door, now yield to my complaining and open only unto me.
> (*El.* 1.2.5–9 [Postgate])

Similarly, Propertius (first century CE) personifies the girl's door, which complains of her many separated suitors and records their desperate pleas for entry (*El.* 1.16), while Ovid (first century CE) suggests flattering the girl and the doorpost, as well as bribing the doorkeeper to gain access (*Ars.* 2.523–534).

Though not as common, door imagery is also found in love literature outside the Near Eastern and classical worlds. In an ancient Tamil lyric, a locked door (as well as her mother's restful embrace) prevented the girl

---

77. Howard V. Canter, "The Paraclausithyron as a Literary Theme," *AJP* 41 (1920): 355–57. Copley notes this motif in Italian literature prior to the Greeks. See Frank Copley, *Exclusus Amator: A Study in Latin Love Poetry* (Baltimore: American Philological Society, 1956), 28.

from meeting her lover for an evening tryst.⁷⁸ Shakespeare also employed this literary symbol in his poetry. In *Cymbeline*, Cloten sought to win the heart of the princess, regaling her with music, but her door remained closed, symbolizing her faithfulness to a former love (2.3.35–38). The door is similarly depicted as an obstacle to Troilus's passion for Cressida, "I stalk about her door like a strange soul upon the Stygian banks.... Give me swift transport to these fields where I may wallow in the lily beds" (*Troilus and Cressida* 3.2.7). Thomas Campion, a contemporary of Shakespeare, also utilized this image. In "Sweet, Exclude Me Not," the lover pleads with his beloved before her closed door to anticipate their wedding night, concluding with the refrain, "Here's the way, bar not the door" (6).⁷⁹ The late eighteenth-century Scot Robert Burns, in his poem "Open the Door to Me," similarly depicts a rejected lover, standing out in the cold, pleading to be with his beloved.⁸⁰ Surprisingly, the door is also an image in the lyrics of twentieth-century Arab bedouins:

> O, my gazelle, how did they remove you from me?
> They separated us and accustomed you to be far from me.
> The watchman shut the door on me and went away,
> Saying to me, "I'll not open it for you before morning."
> O, mistress of the fair ones, pray, open it for me,
> And let me sleep only this night at your house!⁸¹

Finally, in his historical survey of the love song, after noting the presence of this motif in Egyptian and Greco-Roman lyrics, Gioia adds examples from nineteenth-century Native American literature and modern popular music by the Rolling Stones ("Can't You Hear Me Knockin'"), Bob Dylan ("Temporary Like Achilles"), and Steve Earle ("More Than I Can Do").⁸²

The preceding survey of biblical and extrabiblical literature has shown that the door is an archetypal symbol of entry and exclusion, likely due to

---

78. Attipat K. Ramanujan, ed. and trans., *The Interior Landscape: Love Poems from a Classical Tamil Anthology* (Bloomington: Indiana University Press, 1967), 77.
79. David Lindley, *Thomas Campion*, Medieval and Renaissance Authors 7 (Leiden: Brill, 1986), 23.
80. Robert Chambers, ed., *The Life and Works of Robert Burns* (Edinburgh: Chambers, 1856), 285.
81. Stephan, "Modern Palestinian Parallels," 254.
82. Gioia, *Love Songs*, 22, 183; "The song delivered outside a closed door ... will recur in many different guises in the later evolution of love lyrics" (33).

its practical function. However, at times, cultures have adapted the imagery of the door, adding unique features to this near-universal symbol. In Mesopotamia, the bride's opening of the door formally concluded cultic and cultural marriage ceremonies. In Greece and Rome, the door was personified and decorated with garlands, receiving sorrowful songs from separated lovers. Thus, on the spectrum of relationships, this image fits best between shared and universal, combining human experience and shared tradition with cultural innovation. Yet since these cultures often adopted this symbol and adapted it to their conventions, the meaning of the Song's door imagery must center on context. Is this symbol of separation between lovers, evident in the Song's earlier imagery (2:9; 4:12; 5:2), also the best explanation for the architectural imagery in 8:8–10? And how does this imagery fit with the context?

3.2.2. Meaning in the Song

Before analyzing the BODY AS LANDSCAPE metaphor in Song 8:8–10 in light of the previous comparative evidence, two background issues must be considered: speaker and setting. Both of these factors play an important role in determining the meaning of this passage. First, the surrounding lyrics are spoken by the woman, but this unit opens with an unidentified speaker (8:8–9). Various options have been posited. While the man refers to his beloved as "sister" elsewhere (4:9–5:2), the plural possessive "our" and his consistent praise for her large breasts (4:5; 7:8–9) imply a different speaker here. Robert Gordis posits that a group of suitors lament the girl's immaturity, but this theory results in unknown characters speaking about breaking down her defenses, one they deemed too young for marriage.[83] Duane Garrett suggests that these verses are a dialogue between the woman and the daughters of Jerusalem, the only speaker besides the lovers. In his view, the "little sister" is merely a vehicle to allow for the woman's self-proclamation of purity.[84] While Garrett is correct that the בנות ירושלם function as a literary foil in the Song to help express the maiden's feelings, such a lengthy exchange seems out of character for this third party, as well as "curious and wholly unanticipated" at this point in the

---

83. Robert Gordis, *Song of Songs: A Study, Modern Translation, and Commentary* (New York: Jewish Theological Seminary of America, 1954), 97. See also Hicks, "Door of Love," 154.

84. Garrett and House, *Song of Songs/Lamentations*, 259.

Song.⁸⁵ Landy and Exum similarly posit that this unit is spoken by the woman, with the "little sister" (real or hypothetical) used to highlight the beloved's purity.⁸⁶ Although this preserves the continuity of speaker, to what end? Not only is a new character introduced, but an outward focus in 8:8-9 does not match the woman's sole concern for herself, her lover, or their relationship. Thus, a different speaker is most likely in these verses.

Implied by the phrase "on the day she is spoken for" (8:8), the best theory is that the girl's brothers are speaking about her future betrothal.⁸⁷ Whether the brothers speak from the past or their words are repeated by the woman is immaterial. Betrothal was the first stage in forging a marital relationship, a promised viewed as binding as the marriage itself (Hos 2:21; Deut 20:7). In the Hebrew Bible, brothers often take responsibility for protecting their sisters, particularly in matters of sex and marriage. Simeon and Levi slaughtered Shechem (Gen 34:25-29), and Absalom murdered Amnon (2 Sam 13:23-33) over the defilement of their sister. Laban similarly played a prominent role in the betrothal of Rebekah (Gen 24:50). This "flashback" fits perfectly with the woman's earlier reference to her brothers (1:5-6). In both passages, which form an *inclusio* in the book, the brothers function as guardians, exercising control over their sister.⁸⁸

Having established the speaker and setting, the meaning of the two architectural images can be examined. Virginity was valuable in the Near East and in ancient Israel, evident in both the monetary penalty for violating a virgin (Exod 22:16-17) and the legal process for a bride whose purity was suspect (Deut 22:13-21).⁸⁹ Therefore, some commentators understand these figures as a contrast between purity and promiscuity.⁹⁰ If the

---

85. J. Cheryl Exum, "The Little Sister and Solomon's Vineyard: Song of Songs 8:8-12 as a Lover's Dialogue," in *Seeking Out the Wisdom of the Ancients: Essays Offered to Honor Michael V. Fox on the Occasion of His Sixty-Fifth Birthday*, ed. Ron L. Troxel, Kevin G. Friebel, and Dennis R. Magary (Winona Lake, IN: Eisenbrauns, 2005), 277.

86. Landy, *Paradoxes of Paradise*, 160; Exum, *Song of Songs*, 256-57.

87. Using the same collocation (דבר + ב), David sent messengers to woo Abigail and take her as his wife (1 Sam 25:39). Ezekiel also connects the growth of a girl's breasts to her readiness for marriage (16:7-8).

88. Elliott, *Literary Unity of the Canticle*, 201. A similar role is depicted in the laws of Hammurabi (§184) and Middle Assyrian laws (§48) (*ANET*, 174, 84).

89. Marten Stol, *Women in the Ancient Near East* (Berlin: de Gruyter, 2016), 260.

90. Falk, *Love Lyrics*, 132; Richard Hess, *Song of Songs*, BCOTWP (Grand Rapids: Baker, 2005), 243-44; Hicks, "Door of Love," 153-58; Roland E. Murphy, *Song of Songs: A Commentary*, Hermeneia (Minneapolis: Fortress, 1990), 199.

girl is chaste (wall), she will be rewarded; but if she is loose (door), she will be secured. Yet, promiscuity is not in focus anywhere in the Song. As Keel humorously concludes, "This thesis would be tempting—if only it did not have to ignore the text."[91]

In contrast, the structure and content of this passage (8:9) suggest a different interpretation. Rather than forming an antithesis, the brothers' two poetic metaphors are best explained as a "totally parallel couplet, in form, content, and meaning."[92]

אם־חומה היא נבנה עליה טירת כסף	If she is a wall, we will build on it a parapet of silver,
ואם־דלת היא נצור עליה לוח ארז	If she is a door, we will encase it with a cedar plank.

Structurally, the type and order of elements is exactly repeated: conditional particle (אם), architectural term (חומה/דלת), third-person feminine singular pronoun (היא), first-person common plural verb of building (נבנה/נצור), preposition + third-person feminine singular suffix (עליה), objects of fortification (טירת/לוח) and reward (כסף/ארז).[93]

In such parallelism, which is common to Hebrew poetry, the B-line is best read in light of the A-line. As James Kugel summarily states, "B typically reinforces A by backing it up, going it one better, amplifying, embellishing, and so forth."[94] Therefore, following the defensive image of a wall, the door may be best understood synonymously, as an obstacle with the primary purpose of exclusion.

Yet, poetic structure must be evaluated in conjunction with content. Beginning with the A-line, the wall is certainly a figure of the girl's purity through inaccessibility. Both בנה "to build" and טירת "parapet" are construction terms, the latter referring to a camp protected by a circular wall (Num 31:10). Yet since silver was the basis of Israel's monetary system,

---

91. Keel, *Song of Songs*, 278.
92. Keel, *Song of Songs*, 278.
93. While the construction אם ... ואם often conveys contrast (GKC §162b), this is not always the case. In Prov 25:21, the sage says, "If [אם] your enemy is hungry, give him bread to eat; [ואם] if he is thirsty, give him water to drink" (Waltke, *Proverbs 15–31*, 330). For additional examples of this construction, see Job 9:19; Mal 1:6.
94. James Kugel, "Some Thoughts on Future Research into Biblical Style: Addenda to *The Idea of Biblical Poetry*," *JSOT* 28 (1984): 108.

the silver parapet contributes an added element, financial reward.⁹⁵ For example, Exum reasons, "Building a tier decorated in silver upon a wall might be a measure to strengthen it, but the use of silver suggests that the edifice is for show."⁹⁶ Thus, combining architecture with precious metals suggests a dual metaphor, reinforcement *and* reward. Hayim Tawil records numerous examples from the Neo-Assyrian royal inscriptions of Sennacherib and Esarhaddon that describe defensive battlements in Assyria that were ornamented with precious metals for beautification.⁹⁷

However, the *crux* centers on the meaning of נצור עליה לוח ארז and its relations to the preceding line. First, the root and nuance of the main verb have stirred much debate. Since צור "to bind, enclose" is most often used in the context of an offensive siege (2 Sam 11:1) rather than defensive fortification, Exum has posited that this verb is more likely from יצר "to fashion, shape."⁹⁸ However, the evidence for this by-form is scant, with debated occurrences connected to casting metal (Exod 32:4; 1 Kgs 7:15). While צור does describe the encircling of a person or city, the intent of such an action is dependent on the context. For example, the psalmist uses this verb to describe God's intimate acquaintance with his ways, "You hem me in, behind and before," something that elicits an exclamation of praise (Ps 139:5, 14). Therefore, in Song 8:9, צור likely depicts the fastening of additional wood. But for what purpose?

Furthermore, the construction materials also raise questions. The term לוח "board, plank" twice occurs in the context of construction (Exod 27:8; Ezek 27:5), but it is more often used to describe a piece of wood or stone for engraving.⁹⁹ It is commonly connected to the tablets of stone on which God inscribed the torah at Sinai (Exod 31:18; 32:15; 34:1; Deut 9:9; 1 Kgs 8:9). Nonetheless, is this plank added for strength or decoration? In the Hebrew Bible, ארז "cedar" is used as a symbol of strength (Ps 29:5; Job 40:17).¹⁰⁰ Yet cedar is also invoked for its immense height (2 Kgs 19:23;

---

95. Philip J. King and Lawrence E. Stager, *Life in Biblical Israel* (Louisville: Westminster John Knox, 2001), 195.
96. Exum, *Song of Songs*, 258.
97. Tawil, "Two Biblical Architectural Images," 42.
98. Exum, *Song of Songs*, 244.
99. *HALOT*, s.v. "לוח"; *DNWSI*, s.v. "lwḥ²"; *DULAT*, s.v. "lḥ"; *CAD*, "lēʾu," 9:157.
100. Hicks posits two others examples, Ezek 17:23 and Ps 80:11 (Hicks, "Door of Love," 157). Yet repeated references to stature in Ezek 17:22–24 suggests that the "majesty" (אדיר) of the cedar relates to its height, and the imagery of mountains in Ps 80:11 favors rendering the divine name as superlative, "the highest cedars."

Ps 92:13; Ezek 31:3–5; Amos 2:9) as well as its choice nature as a luxury import (2 Sam 5:11; 2 Kgs 6:18; Isa 9:10; Jer 22:7, 14–15).

Cedar as a symbol of stature and superiority is also evident elsewhere in the Song. In the opening chapter, the lovers describe nature as their bedroom, with lush grass as their couch and the towering cedars as their rooftop (1:17). Later, the woman compares her lover to Lebanon and its choice cedars to illustrate his superior excellence (5:15). The only other pairing of silver and cedar in the Hebrew Bible highlights their prevalence in the golden era of Solomon (1 Kgs 10:27).[101] Thus, the choice of cedar cannot be entirely explained as an attempt to provide protection. As Exum notes, "To panel [the door] with cedar wood would be a costly way to reinforce it but a most impressive form of ornamentation."[102] Thus, the combination of construction terms with items of luxury favors a dual meaning for these metaphors. If the girl proves to be pure, pictured by two symbols of separation (wall/door), then her brothers will respond with both reinforcement (parapet/planks) and reward (silver/cedar). But why?

Again, the betrothal setting is key. Since an engaged couple was practically married, outside sexual relations were prohibited.[103] In fact, Near Eastern law treated a married and betrothed woman equally—violation results in death (Deut 22:13–27).[104] Therefore, the brothers' desire to intervene "on the day she is spoken for" fulfills a twofold purpose: (1) to

---

101. Sargon's march to the cedar forest and silver mountain marks these items as desirable. See Hans Hirsch, "Die Inschriften der Könige von Agade," *AfO* 20 (1963): 38.

102. Exum, *Song of Songs*, 258. Exum suggests that the silver and cedar were to make the girl more attractive to future suitors, but this does not align with the setting. If the brothers' actions are in response to her betrothal, why attract more suitors? Elaine T. James ("A City Who Surrenders: Song 8:8–10," *VT* 67 [2017]: 456) argues that these metaphors (8:9) are best understood as a siege motif, rendering טירת as "encampment." But her suggestion that they connote the "luxurious quality of this encounter" fails to explain the literal or symbolic meaning of an "encampment of silver."

103. While Scripture prohibits a fiancée from having sex with other men, later Jewish law also forbid such relations between a betrothed couple: "Praised are you, Lord our God, King of the Universe, who sanctified us by your commandments and commanded us concerning incestuous relations and has forbidden us those who are (merely) betrothed but has permitted us those who are married" (b. Ketub. 7b). Yet in Judea, a groom was allowed to stay alone with his bride, prior to marriage, "that he might become aroused by her," but if he did, he could not complain after marriage that his wife had lost her virginity. See Étan Levine, *Marital Relations in Ancient Judaism*, BZAR 10 (Wiesbaden: Harrassowitz, 2009), 178–81.

104. Stol, *Women in the Ancient Near East*, 261.

reward the girl's past purity and (2) to reinforce her future fidelity through betrothal until marriage.

In 8:10, the beloved now responds to her brothers' past promises (8:8–9). She adopts their architectural metaphor to affirm her purity, adding the symbol of towers. This figure implies maturity and security. In contrast to her past immaturity (8:8), her breasts are now well-developed. But she rejects her brothers' promised protection. She needs no fortification, for she is an impregnable fortress with flanking towers. She can protect herself and ensure her own fidelity until marriage without any outside help.

However, "any interpretation of the obscure ending to this verse [8:10] must be tentative."[105] There are many ambiguities, but the center of the debate is the final phrase כמוצאת שלום. The verb may either be a *hiphil* participle from יצא "to bring" or a *qal* participle from מצא "to find." In light of the concentration of military imagery, Exum suggests that this final line depicts a city's surrender, an offer or acceptance of the terms of peace: "[She is] like a beautiful, fortified city offering peace, that is, surrendering to him."[106] Thus, the door is not an image of separation but invitation. Though grammatically possible, this interpretation goes against both internal and external evidence. First, Exum's proposal is based largely on inference. In Song 8:10, the woman does not compare herself to a city with open doors. Curiously, there is no mention of doors at all. If the above synonymous reading is correct, the woman may be treating the architectural metaphors together in her self-declaration of purity: "I am a wall, and my breasts are like towers" (8:10).

Second, this interpretation misses the dual nature of the imagery in 8:9–10. Instead of an abrupt shift from the brothers' promise of reward to the beloved's offer of peace, the dialogical nature of these verses favors a response to the brothers' offer. Adopting her brothers' own words, the maiden affirms her purity but rejects their promised fortification and reward. As a walled city flanked with large towers, she needs no further protection. But she also refuses their luxurious gifts. Like a city that has found peace, the maiden finds her reward in the person of her lover![107] As Tremper Longman aptly states, "שלום has a rich connotation, not only including the absence of strife but also denoting fulfillment, wholeness,

---

105. Bergant, *Song of Songs*, 102.
106. Exum, "Little Sister and Solomon's Vineyard," 272.
107. Lacking a referent, the phrase "in his eyes" is best read as a metonymy.

satisfaction, and contentment."[108] The multivalence of this term combines the military imagery with the beloved's repeated desire for satisfaction.

Finally, the motif of seeking and finding, which recurs throughout the Song, finds its fulfillment here (8:10). As many scholars note, the Song contains a pattern of cycles, beginning with separation and desire and concluding with union and fulfillment (1:2–2:7; 2:8–17; 3:1–5; 3:6–5:1; 5:2–7:10; 7:11–8:4).[109] Each unit except the last opens with the lovers apart and a sense of excited tension, and each closes on a note of tranquility, with the lovers together again. The "seek and find" motif is especially evident in the passages containing architectural imagery (2:8–17; 4:12–5:1; 5:2–7). Just as the woman invites her beloved to find satisfaction in the sensual delights of her locked garden (4:12–5:1), the one who has kept herself pure, separate from amorous advances, now finds her satisfaction in her lover.

While many scholars view these verses (8:8–10) as part of an epilogue, with no connection to the rest of the book or even anticlimactic after the dramatic paean to love in 8:6–7, the interpretation outlined above connects both to the immediate context as well as the larger lyric collection.[110] First, these verses illustrate the woman's preceding statement on the invaluable nature of love, "If a man offered all the wealth of his house to buy love, the offer would be utterly despised" (8:7). The value of love is beyond all possessions. Exemplifying this idea, the maiden rejects the reward of her brothers for the satisfaction she finds in her lover (8:10).

Second, her self-proclamation of reward employs similar terms from the chapter's opening poem, though with an opposite focus. In 8:1–2, the girl wishes that her lover was like a brother, to whom she could publicly show affection and privately satisfy with her breasts. In 8:10, however, the woman, with her tower-like breasts, does not give but finds satisfaction in her lover. Therefore, in contrast to Landy's conclusion that any clear, culturally defined meaning for these metaphors has been lost, the

---

108. Longman, *Song of Songs*, 218. On multivalence in metaphor, see Joseph Lam, "Metaphor in Ugaritic Literary Texts," *JNES* 78 (2019): 41–44.

109. Robert Alter, "The Song of Songs: An Ode to Intimacy," *BRev* 18.4 (2002): 26; Bergant, *Song of Songs*, 33; David A. Dorsey, "Literary Structuring in the Song of Songs," *JSOT* 46 (1990): 92; Elliott, *Literary Unity of the Canticle*, 40–41.

110. On these verses as an epilogue, see Exum, "Little Sister and Solomon's Vineyard," 270. As Murphy clearly states, "These verses introduce a vignette that has no obvious connection with the immediate context" (Murphy, *Song of Songs*, 198).

previous comparative evidence and textual analysis suggest that this architectural imagery, commonly found in Near Eastern and classical love literature, is employed by the female lover in order to proclaim her own purity and reward.[111]

3.3. Summary

In these two poems of self-description, the beloved describes the form and function of her body using widely shared images, variations of the BODY AS LANDSCAPE conceptual metaphor. First, the maiden laments her dark skin, like the tents of Qedar, yet lauds her own beauty, like the tapestries of Solomon (1:5–6). Although this link between self-deprecation and self-exaltation has raised many questions, the universality of human insecurity offers a key. Though self-confident about her appearance, she shows her self-consciousness under the gaze of others, particularly in comparison with the cultural ideal of beauty.

Second, her brothers describe their sister with dual, synonymous, architectural metaphors: If she proves to be pure, pictured by symbols of separation (wall/door), they will respond to her betrothal with both reinforcement (parapet/planks) and reward (silver/cedar). In reply, the maiden rejects their protection, proclaiming her inaccessibility like a wall with fortress towers, and she also refuses their reward, finding her satisfaction in the person of her lover (8:8–10). The longing of both lovers to satisfy their sensual desires in their beloved is further expanded in the next chapter. Now we turn to the Song's metaphors drawn from nature.

---

111. Landy, *Paradoxes of Paradise*, 160.

4
Nature as Erotica:
Sexual Euphemism and Double Entendre

In the Song, there is hardly a thought, feeling, or movement that is not likened to a plant or living creature, as the couple look at each other with one eye and the world of nature with the other.[1] Filled with erotic euphemism and double entendre, the poet employs flora and fauna to depict the form and function of the lovers' physical bodies. Whether mountains or trees, gardens or vineyards, animals or agriculture, the man and woman consider their beloved's body as a place of private pleasures, a source of sexual delights.

4.1. The Man's Delicious Apple (2:3)

כתפוח בעצי היער	2:3 Like an apple tree amid the forest trees,
כן דודי בין הבנים	so is my lover among the young men;
בצלו חמדתי וישבתי	in whose shade, I yearn to sit,
ופריו מתוק לחכי:	and whose fruit is sweet to my palate.

Source: Apple Tree
Target: Man's Body
Mapping: Sexual/Sensual Pleasure

This verse presents the lady's response to her lover's praise in the preceding lines (2:1–2). Having likened herself to a simple meadow flower, an image of mediocrity, her lover turns this self-deprecation into adoration. If she is a meadow flower, he says, all other women are thorn bushes (2:2). As in their earlier exchange (1:15–16), she employs a "mirroring dynamic,"

---

1. Fishbane, *Song of Songs*, xxvi; Daniel Grossberg, "Humanity, Nature, and Love in Song of Songs," *Int* 59 (2005): 233.

using similar wording and imagery in her corresponding tribute to her man.² In comparison with other young men, her lover stands out like a fruit tree in an uncultivated forest. The syntactic parallels are evident visually in the diagram below (2:2–3a):

כשושנה בין החוחים כן רעיתי בין הבנות
כתפוח בעצי היער כן דודי בין הבנים

> Like a crocus among the thorns, so is my dear among the young women.
> Like an apple tree amid the forest trees, so is my lover among the young men.

However, the woman continues her praise, expanding on the agricultural metaphor. Not only is her lover a rare commodity, superior to other young men, but she also praises his protection and pleasures. In the Hebrew Bible, צל "shade" is used literally to describe shelter from the sun (Isa 4:6; Jonah 4:6), but also metaphorically as a picture of protection (Ps 17:8; Hos 14:8).³ Like a traveler seeking shade and shelter from the midday heat, the beloved yearns for the rest and refuge of her lover.

In addition to seeking his protection, the lady also desires to taste her lover's fruit. With this image, the woman tantalizes the reader, using a double entendre to praise her lover while leaving those listening to figure out her meaning. Renita Weems aptly notes the allusive nature of this metaphor: "Exactly what was sweet to the [woman's] taste? An apple from the apple tree, or was it some part of her beloved's body? It is obviously something for the two of them to know—and the rest of us to find out."⁴ To help explain the meaning of this image, we must explore the identity of the תפוח and why this tree is used to describe the male lover.

Outside of its frequent use in proper names (Josh 15:53), תפוח occurs six times in the Bible, twice outside the Song (Prov 25:11; Joel 1:12). The minimal information gleaned from these references caused Harold Moldenke and Alma Moldenke to label this fruit "one of the most perplexing problems of biblical botany."⁵ In the Song, the תפוח is often found in the

---

2. Elliott, *Literary Unity of the Canticle*, 246–51.
3. Her desire plays on her identity: צל/חבצלת (Fishbane, *Song of Songs*, 58).
4. Renita J. Weems, "Song of Songs," *NIB* 5:389. "The language is elusive, holding its treasures in secret for the lovers" (Trible, *God and the Rhetoric of Sexuality*, 145).
5. Harold N. Moldenke and Alma L. Moldenke, *Plants of the Bible* (Waltham, MA: Chronica Botanica, 1952), 185.

context of lovemaking. When the man brings his beloved into the "house of wine," intending to make love to her, she asks for this fruit to refresh herself (2:5). Later, in his longing to enjoy his beloved's sexual pleasures, the man compares her breath to the scent of the תפוח (7:9). Finally, in the Song's last chapter, the woman identifies this tree as the amorous setting under which her lover was conceived, as well as the place she had aroused him (8:5). Thus, the תפוח was an idyllic setting for love (8:5), whose fruit was sweet (2:3), fragrant (7:9), and refreshing for lovers (2:5).

Apple is the identification given by most scholars and scientists, but it is not the only possibility.[6] Targum Canticles connects תפוח to אתרוגא ("citron"), while Falk suggests that this fruit may be a quince.[7] Yet, these alternatives fail to satisfy one vital criterion, sweet taste. Moldenke and Moldenke reject the apple as nonnative to Palestine, concluding that only the apricot meets all the above criteria.[8] While the apricot is possible, the apple should not be ruled out. As Daniel Zohary and Maria Hopf point out, several dozen carbonized apples found at Kadesh Barnea (tenth century BCE) suggest that apples were cultivated in Palestine at an early period.[9] Nonetheless, rather than rehash arguments over etymology or scientific classification, we will approach this problem from a different perspective, aiming to use comparative evidence to ascertain the meaning of such vegetal imagery and determine the direction of its diffusion.

4.1.1. Comparative Evidence

Fruit imagery is one of the most universal sexual metaphors, and the apple is commonly employed in this vein.[10] In many ancient cultures, the apple was viewed as an aphrodisiac, whose consumption would stir sexual excitement and enhance fertility. In Enki and Ninhursag, apples were among

---

6. Lexicons: *HALOT*, s.v. "תַּפּוּחַ I"; BDB, s.v. "תַּפּוּחַ I"; Scholars: Exum, *Song of Songs*, 114; Ginsburg, *Song of Songs*, 142; Gordis, *Song of Songs*, 50; Hess, *Song of Songs*, 77; Keel, *Song of Songs*, 82; Pope, *Song of Songs*, 371–72; Scientists: Michael Zohary, *Plants of the Bible* (New York: Cambridge University Press, 1982), 70; Yehuda Feliks, *Fruit Trees in the Bible and Talmudic Literature* (Jerusalem: Mass, 1994), 139–42.

7. Alexander, *Targum*, 97–98; Falk, *Love Lyrics*, 115.

8. Moldenke and Moldenke, *Plants of the Bible*, 187–88.

9. Daniel Zohary and Maria Hopf, *Domestication of Plants in the Old World*, 3rd ed. (Oxford: Oxford University Press, 2000), 174.

10. Atkins, *Sex in Literature*, 3:222; Paul, "Shared Legacy," 490–91.

the fruits that Enki presented to Uttu before he copulated with her.[11] One Mesopotamian incantation identified Inanna, the goddess *amour*, as "she who loves apples and pomegranates," and it prescribed that the desired woman should suck the juice of these fruits, after which she would come to her suitor to make love.[12] In Sumer's love songs, Inanna's breasts are twice described as "apples," the object of her lover's desire.[13]

The apple was regarded similarly in Hellenistic culture. In the Atalanta myth, Aphrodite, the goddess of love commonly depicted holding this fruit, gave Hippomenes three apples to aid in his race against Atalanta. Whenever her speed left him behind, he threw an apple in front of her, which she could not resist stopping to pick up, allowing him to win the race and her hand in marriage (Apollodorus, *Lib.* 3.9.2; Theocritus, *Id.* 3.40–42). Apples were also considered gifts given between lovers, at times inscribed with special messages (Theocritus, *Id.* 3.10–11; Propertius, *El.* 1.3.24; Catullus, *Poems* 65.19–24; Ovid, *Am.* 21.103–128).[14] In Virgil's *Eclogues* (first century BCE), Galatea threw apples at Damoetas as a demonstration of her love: "Galatea pelts me with an apple, then runs off to the willows—and hopes I saw her first" (*Ecl.* 3.64–65 [Fairclough]). In addition, Greco-Roman writers, from the time of Aristophanes (fourth century BCE), employ the apple as a metaphor for the female breasts, likely due to its erotic symbolism.[15] The amorous nature of this emblem is aptly captured in Sappho's comparison (sixth century BCE) of a bride to an apple ripening on the top branch, out of the harvesters' reach (frag. 105a).[16]

The apple motif continued in medieval and modern Hebrew and Arabic poetry. One lyric connected to Ibn Rashiq (eleventh century CE) reads, "I took an apple from a fair maid's hand; she plucked it fresh as the freshness of her body. It resembled the smoothness of her breasts, the fragrance of her breath, the savor of her mouth, the ruddy glow of her

---

11. Jacobsen, *Harps*, 199; Bendt Alster, "Manchester Tammuz," *ASJ* 14 (1992): 18.

12. Robert D. Biggs, *ŠÀ.ZI.GA: Ancient Mesopotamian Potency Incantations*, TCS 2 (Locust Valley, NY: Augustin, 1967), 70 (1–10), 74 (4–5).

13. Alster, "Marriage and Love," 15, 20.

14. This practice may stem from a myth in which goddess Earth caused apple trees to spring up as her gift at the wedding of Zeus and Hera. See Christopher Faraone, *Ancient Greek Love Magic* (Cambridge: Harvard University Press, 1999), 70.

15. Benjamin O. Foster, "Notes on the Symbolism of the Apple in Classical Antiquity," *HSCP* 10 (1899): 54; Gerber, "Female Breast," 208.

16. See also Antony R. Littlewood, "The Symbolism of the Apple in Greek and Roman Literature," *HSCP* 72 (1968): 147–81.

cheeks."[17] Likewise, Dalman and Stephan note this motif in Arab bedouin lyrics as a food fed to lovers and a metaphor for the beloved's red cheeks and sensual breasts.[18] Applying this metaphor to a modern context, Chaim Bialik tells how young Talmud students, after a long day of study, would escape to the hills, the place "where rosy girls and ruddy apples grow."[19]

However, the apple motif is present not only in ancient and modern cultures from the Near East but also in a few examples from Western literature. Amid images of spring, Robert Campbell, a nineteenth-century British major and poet, tells of lovers picking apples from garden trees to throw at one another.[20] Yet, the most vivid use of this figure is found in Keats's "Sharing Eve's Apple." The entire poem is filled with sexual puns, but the final lines employ the apple in a request for sexual liaison, "There's a sigh for yes, and a sigh for no, and a sigh for 'I can't bear it!' O what can be done, shall we stay or run? O cut the sweet apple and share it!"[21] As further support for its enduring nature, Pope refers to two twentieth-century songs that incorporate the apple motif.[22]

Due to its frequent appearance in amorous lyrics, Nissinen labeled the apple "a common aphrodisiac everywhere in the eastern Mediterranean."[23] Westenholz also classified the apple motif as a literary building block shared by the cultures of the ancient Near East, listing examples from Sumerian, Akkadian, and Egyptian literature.[24] Yet, this conclusion is unconvincing, especially with a closer look at the evidence from Egypt. Although the apple (*dph*) is attested once in a New Kingdom list of offerings, love lyrics from Egypt consistently connect different fruits to love, particularly the mandrake and persea.[25] Persea, once likened to the beloved's breasts,

---

17. Yehudah Ratzaby, "A Motif in Hebrew Love Poetry: In Praise of the Apple," *Ariel* 40 (1976): 17. See Immanuel Löw, *Die flora der Juden* (Leipzig: Löwit, 1924), 219.
18. Dalman, *Palästinischer Diwan*, 101, 179; Stephan, "Modern Palestinian Parallels," 201, 214, 218, 221, 237.
19. Chaim N. Bialik, *Shirot Bialik*, ed. Steven Jacobs (Columbus: Alpha, 1987), 56.
20. Robert C. Campbell, "Sonnet," *The Germ* 1 (1850): 68.
21. Elizabeth Cook, ed., *John Keats: The Major Works* (Oxford: Oxford University Press, 2001), 169.
22. Pope, *Song of Songs*, 372. In American popular culture, the apple's link with sexuality was evident in its use as the icon for the sitcom *Desperate Housewives*.
23. Nissinen, "Nabû and Tašmetu," 613.
24. Westenholz, "Love Lyrics," 2482.
25. For the occurrence of the apple, see James Breasted, *Ancient Records of Egypt* (Urbana: University of Illinois Press, 2001), 4:301; James Hoch, *Semitic Words in Egyp-*

are carried by the beloved as she journeys to meet her man in the "love garden" (*ddt*).²⁶ The fruit *rrmt*, identified by Egyptologists as the mandragora (*GHb*, "rrmt," 504), is compared to the girl's skin and breasts and associated with the boy's wish for his beloved's sexual pleasures.²⁷

Therefore, the motif of apple as love fruit, while attested in many cultures from antiquity to modern times, is not a commonality of human experience or even entirely shared throughout the Near East. Rather, its presence was impacted by culture. Its wide attestation may be due to a common connection of seed-bearing fruits to fertility, a view that may have continued in later scientific cultures as a frozen icon.²⁸

Nonetheless, one significant difference between the above examples of the apple motif and its presence in the Hebrew Song is the associated gender. In most instances, the apple is connected to the woman, depicting her beautiful cheeks and breasts as images of sensuality or an aphrodisiac used to seduce the woman as the man's object of desire. On the other hand, Song 2:3 applies this motif to the man. He is likened to an apple tree, whose relaxing shelter and refreshing pleasures are desired by his beloved.²⁹ For this reason, the closest parallel to the Song's imagery and best aid in explaining its complex meaning is found in Mesopotamia.

In the Sumerian love songs, some of which reflect the amorous lives of ordinary people in the secular sphere, the male lover is often compared to an apple tree.³⁰ For example, one of the Inanna-Dumuzi lyrics (DI E)

---

tian Texts of the New Kingdom and Third Intermediate Period (Princeton: Princeton University Press, 1994), 377.

26. Fox, *Song of Songs*, 15, 44.

27. Fox, *Song of Songs*, 9, 37, 347. On the identity of the *rrmt*, see Renate Germer, *Handbuch der altägyptischen Heilpflanzen*, Philippika 21 (Wiesbaden: Harrassowitz, 2008), 294; Ludwig Keimer, "La baie qui fait aimer, Mandragora officinarum L," *BIE* 32 (1951): 351; Philippe Derchain, "Le Lotus, la mandragore, et le perséa," *CdE* 50 (1975): 86.

28. As McCartney concludes, "It seems clear, therefore, that fertility was symbolized by growths with several or many seeds and that it was because the apple was so popular that it gained first place among fruits in 'the office and affairs of love'" (Eugene Stock McCartney, "How the Apple Became a Token of Love," *TAPA* 56 [1925]: 81). Littlewood supports this thesis that the apple's pips symbolized fecundity (Littlewood, "Symbolism of the Apple in Greek and Roman Literature," 179–80).

29. Garrett notes the link between apples and sexuality in Greek lyrics but misses the parallel in Mesopotamia (Garrett and House, *Song of Songs/Lamentations*, 149).

30. Alster, "Marriage and Love," 16–17; Thorkild Jacobsen, *Treasures of Darkness: A History of Mesopotamian Religion* (New Haven: Yale University Press, 1976), 27.

portrays the woman as a fertile garden, watered by the fruitful overflow of her lover. As Jacobsen notes, the apple tree is likely employed as an erotic euphemism for the man's *membrum virile*, "In the garden of deep shade, bending down his neck, my darling of his mother, my one who fills the grain in their furrows with beauty, it is the lettuce he watered, my apple tree [*giš ḫašḫur*] bearing fruit at its top, it is the garden he watered."[31]

Similar to Song 2:3, the lover in Mesopotamian lyrics is also lauded for his sweet pleasures and protective shade. In one Sumerian song (DI B), after the woman responds to her lover's sexual proposition by requesting an oath of fidelity, she concludes with this variant refrain of praise, "My blossoming one, my blossoming one, sweet is your allure! My blossoming garden of apple-trees, sweet is your allure!"[32] In a later Akkadian lyric, the beloved longs for the sexual delights of her absent lover, "Where is my loved one? He is so dear. And does he bear his fruit?... Like apples of the ripening period, filled with joy is the bed [of my lover]."[33] Protection and pleasure are also found in a hymn for the Sumerian king Shulgi, "You are a sweet sight, like a fertile *mes*-tree, laden with colorful fruit.... You are a pleasant shade like a cedar, a seed, growing on the Ḫasur-mountain."[34]

Whether the Greek μῆλον, the Sumerian/Akkadian *ḫašḫuru*, or the Hebrew תפוח, botanical identification is tentative in ancient languages.[35]

---

31. Alster, "Marriage and Love," 21. Sefati connects all the agricultural imagery (garden and apple tree) in this poem to Dumuzi (Sefati, *Love Songs*, 166–67). In Mesopotamia, a man's sexual charms are described as fruit to be plucked and eaten. See Nissinen, "Nabû and Tašmetu," 591 (r.20); Andrew R. George, *The Epic of Gilgamesh: Introduction, Critical Edition, and Cuneiform Texts* (Oxford: Oxford University Press, 2003), 618 (VI.7–9).

32. Sefati, *Love Songs*, 130:27–28; Sefati, "An Oath of Chastity in a Sumerian Love Song (SRT 31)?," in *Bar-Ilan Studies in Assyriology: Dedicated to Pinhas Artzi*, ed. Jacob Klein (Ramat-Gan: Bar-Ilan University, 1990), 53. The iconic nature of the apple is also implied in one OB lyric, "To sing (the praise) of Mami is sweeter than the *ḫananābu* fruit and (even) the apple" (*CT* 15 1.1.5).

33. Wasserman, *Akkadian Love Literature*, 106. See also Benjamin R. Foster, *Before the Muses: An Anthology of Akkadian Literature*, 3rd ed. (Bethesda, MD: CDL, 2005), 165.

34. Jacob Klein, *Three Šulgi Hymns*, BISNELC (Ramat-Gan: Bar-Ilan University Press, 1981), 72–75 (33–35).

35. For the uncertain meaning of μῆλον, see Foster, "Symbolism of the Apple," 40. In contrast, most Assyriologists identify *ḫašḫuru* as "apple." See *CAD*, "ḫašḫuru," 6:139–40; *AHw* 1, s.v. "ḫašḫuru"; Alster, "Marriage and Love," 20; Miguel Civil, "Studies on Early Dynastic Lexicography III," *Or* 56 (1987): 241. Etymologically, *ḫašḫuru/*

Yet, in contrast to the well-attested motif of "apple" as love fruit, the above unique parallels suggest that the Song's depiction of the lover as an apple tree has an erotic nuance, which likely stems from Mesopotamia and may have followed the apple's diffusion from the east.[36]

4.1.2. Meaning in the Song

Although the above comparative evidence has long been known, some scholars simply ignore these literary parallels or minimize the erotic nature of this image in order to downplay the sensuous nature of the Song. In her defense of the Song as an allegory, Edmée Kingsmill surveys the amorous connotation of the apple in Near Eastern and classical literature but attempts to fit this figure into her interpretive construct. Linking תפוח "apple" to פוח "to breathe" and רוח "spirit" by similarity in sound and meaning, she concludes, "The apple evidently does symbolize love, but in the Song it is the love which brings a person to prayer, and to the experience of dwelling in the shade of the spirit, and of tasting the sweetness of the spirit's fruit."[37] Munro interprets the Song plainly but softens the tone of this image, "[The apple tree] becomes an appropriate image for her lover, who with masculine chivalry and fatherly tenderness, shelters his young bride (2:3cd).... The sweet fruit of the tree is presumably a modest reference to the tenderness of the youth's embrace."[38]

In contrast, the Mesopotamian parallels suggest that the lover's likeness to an apple tree with sweet-tasting fruit is an erotic image of sexual pleasure. In this vein, Landy opines that Song 2:3 is a poetic depiction of

---

ḫinzūru is connected to the Syriac ḥazzurā "apple" (*SyrLex*, s.v. "ܚܙܘܪܐ"), the term used by the Peshitta in Song 2:3. Archaeologically, the apple is the only fruit described in textual sources and found in situ dried and kept on strings See Nicholas Postgate, "Notes on Fruit in the Cuneiform Sources," *BSA* 3 (1987): 119. For a contrary opinion, see Ignace J. Gelb, "Sumerian and Akkadian Words for 'String of Fruit,'" in *Zikir Šumim: Assyriological Studies Presented to F. R. Kraus on the Occasion of His Seventieth Birthday*, ed. Govert van Driel (Leiden: Brill, 1982), 67–82.

36. The apple's wild ancestor originated in central Asia before spreading eastward. See Robert N. Spengler et al., "Arboreal Crops on the Medieval Silk Road: Archaeobotanical Studies at Tashbulak," *PLoS ONE* 13 (2018): 10.

37. Kingsmill, *Song of Songs and the Eros of God*, 238–39.

38. Munro, *Spikenard and Saffron*, 83. See also G. Lloyd Carr, *Song of Solomon*, TOTC 17 (Downers Grove, IL: InterVarsity Press, 1984), 90; Murphy, *Song of Songs*, 136.

oral sex, "The apple-tree symbolizes the Lover, the male sexual function in the poem: erect and delectable."[39] While the Inanna-Dumuzi lyric favors this idea, the other parallels are general metaphors for the man's sexual charms. Thus, the maiden's desire to taste her lover's delicious apple does not demand an anatomical referent. In fact, the Song's poet repeatedly employs the eating/drinking metaphor as a symbol of lovemaking (2:4, 16; 4:11; 6:2–3; 7:3, 7–9; 8:2; see also 6:11–12; 7:12–13). In the closest parallel, the lady portrays her own body as a garden of choice fruits, inviting her lover to consume its produce (4:16). Both illustrating the BODY AS LANDSCAPE metaphor, the woman's garden is a metaphor for her delicious delights, and the man's sweet-tasting fruit (2:3) is an image of his sexual charms, bringing his beloved joy in love. Gesenius captures its essence, calling the image *Bild für den Liebesgenuss*, "a picture of sexual pleasure."[40]

4.2. A Mare among Stallions (1:9–10)

לססתי ברכבי פרעה	1:9 To a mare[41] amid Pharaoh's stallions,
דמיתיך רעיתי:	I compare you, my dear.
נאוו לחייך בתרים	1:10 Your cheeks are lovely with bangles,[42]
צוארך בחרוזים:	your neck with strings of beads.[43]

Source: Egyptian Mare

---

39. Francis Landy, "Song of Songs and the Garden of Eden," *JBL* 98 (1979): 526.

40. Wilhelm Gesenius, *Hebräisches und Aramäisches Handwörterbuch über das Alte Testament*, ed. Herbert Donner, 18th ed. (Berlin: Springer, 2013), 1078.

41. The feminine סְסָתִי is without parallel in the Hebrew Bible. The *hiriq-yod* ending is best explained, not as a 1cs suffix, but an archaic genitive construct ending (GKC §90l; Joüon §93l). Perhaps this form was used for its rhythmic similarity to דמיתיך רעיתי in the next line. For a parallel, see Lam 1:1, רבתי בגוים שרתי במדינות.

42. From Hebrew (Esth 2:12–15; 1QS VI, 11; CD XIV, 11) and cognate literature (Akk. *turru(m)* "string, band"; Aram. תּוֹרָא "line, border"), תּוֹר may describe a *row* of ornaments hanging from a headdress or *circular* earrings against the lady's cheek. The prevalence of large earrings in Near Eastern iconography and archaeology favors the latter. In Egypt, festive scenes depict female musicians and dancers wearing large earrings covering part of the cheek (*ANEP*, 208–9, 410). See also K. Rachel Maxwell-Hyslop, *Western Asiatic Jewelry* (London: Methuen, 1971) for material finds from Ur (pl. 3), Wilayah/Ashur (figs. 16–17), Troy (fig. 32), Ajjul (pl. E, 79–83), Al-Minah (pl. 213a), Marlik (pl. 148), and Persia (pls. 257–58).

43. The term חרוזים, a *hapax legomenon*, is glossed based on cognates from both Aramaic (*DJPA*, s.v. "חרוז") and Arabic (Lane, "خَرَزَ," 721).

Target: Woman's Cheeks/Neck, Beauty
Mapping: Unique Distinction, Physical Decoration, Sexual Attraction

The foreign nature of this image, comparing a woman to a horse, has spawned a host of different views among modern scholars. While Goulder concludes that no lady, regardless of culture or era, would ever regard this comparison as a compliment, the man's consistent praise for his beloved's beauty suggests that this image was intended as flattery.[44] But in what sense? What are the attributes that underlie this metaphor?

Although סוסה "mare" occurs only here (1:9), סוס "horse" and רכב "chariot" are found frequently in the Hebrew Bible, often in combination amid a military context. In Israel's early victory hymns, YHWH defeats the chariotry of his enemies (Exod 15:4, Judg 5:28). In addition to military might, horse and chariot are linked to royalty, an icon of wealth (1 Kgs 10:26–29) used in procession before a king (1 Kgs 1:5; 2 Kgs 5:9). Finally, horses are also employed as an image of sexual virility (Jer 5:8; Ezek 23:2).

Thus, following these categories, there are three interpretive options for the meaning of the Song's equine metaphor: (1) unique distinction, (2) beautiful decoration, and (3) sexual allure. Since each one is integrally connected to and dependent on comparative evidence, it is impossible to examine the literary parallels separately from the Song's own imagery.

Horses are also invoked in the love literature of other Mediterranean cultures. However, one must carefully note the attribute(s) highlighted by each comparison. For example, in Egyptian love literature, the horse is compared to the lover, rather than the beloved. Papyrus Chester Beatty reads, "If you would come [to your sister swiftly,] like a royal horse, the choicest of a thousand among all the steeds, the foremost of the stables."[45] In Mesopotamia, Shulgi similarly praises himself as "a horse, waving its tail on the highway … a stallion of Šakan, eager to race."[46] As many have noted, the emphasis of these lyrics on the speed of the lover's coming, present elsewhere in the Song (2:8–9, 8:14), is foreign to this context (1:9–10).[47]

Greco-Roman poets also employ horses in their amorous lyrics. Anacreon (sixth century BCE) compares his beloved to a Thracian filly, who grazes in the meadow and frolics to her heart's content, not ready

---

44. Goulder, *Fourteen Songs*, 17. See also Weems, "Song of Songs," 403.
45. Fox, *Song of Songs*, 66.
46. Klein, *Three Šulgi Hymns*, 189 (A 17–18).
47. Fox, *Song of Songs*, 105; Gerleman, *Hohelied*, 106–7.

to be reined or ridden (frag. 417). Horace (first century BCE) similarly likens Lyde to an unbroken filly, which gambols in the field yet shies from physical touch, not yet ripe for marriage (*Carm.* 3.11.9–12). Despite the common citation of these lyrics in connection with Song 1:9, the theme of the lady's readiness for love, a motif found later in the Song (4:8; 5:2–3; 8:8), is out of place in this context. The subsequent verses (1:10–11) focus on the beloved's beauty and rich adornment.

In addition, Greco-Roman authors also appeal to this animal as an iconic image of grace and beauty. Alcman, one of the earliest Greek poets (seventh century BCE), describes the "preeminent" Hagesichora as "a well-knit steed of ringing hoof that overcomes in the race" (*Parth.* 1.44–57 [Campbell]). Theocritus utilizes this motif to praise the superior beauty of Helen of Troy, "As a tall cypress rises high to adorn some fertile field or garden, or as a Thracian horse adorns its chariot, just so is rosy Helen the ornament of Sparta" (*Id.* 18.30–31 [Hopkinson]). Thus, Ringgren explains the mare as a picture of the lady's "outstanding physical perfection."[48]

In Song 1:9–10, the theme of the maiden's beauty, while clearly stated in the latter verse, may also be implied and illustrated in the former description, "a mare among Pharaoh's chariots" (1:9). A brief examination of iconography depicting cavalry horses and chariots on pottery and reliefs in Sumerian, Egyptian, and Assyrian as well as Greek, Roman, and Scythian art collections reveals a strong preference for stallions.[49] Mary Littauer and Joost Crouwell similarly note that chariot teams in the ancient Near East "are consistently depicted as stallions."[50] Thus, the maiden's likeness to an Egyptian mare may have been intended to stress her unique distinction, playing on the OBJECT OF LOVE IS A VALUABLE OBJECT metaphor. Just as a mare would be a rarity among the stallions of Pharaoh's army, so also this woman was a gem in the eyes of her lover. This theme is also found

---

48. Ringgren, "Hohe Lied," 9.

49. Deborah Cantrell, *The Horsemen of Israel: Horses and Chariotry in Monarchic Israel*, HACL 1 (Winona Lake, IN: Eisenbrauns, 2011), 24; Tamás Dezső, "The Reconstruction of the Neo-Assyrian Army as Depicted on the Assyrian Palace Reliefs, 745–612 BC," *AAASH* 57 (2006): 122; Oscar White Muscarella, *The Catalogue of Ivories from Hasanlu, Iran* (Philadelphia: University Museum, 1980), 162; Yigael Yadin, *The Scroll of the War of the Sons of Light against the Sons of Darkness* (Oxford: Oxford University Press, 1962), 182. However, Aelian (first century CE) disagrees, suggesting that mares were more suitable for chariotry (*Nat. an.* 6.48).

50. Mary A. Littauer and Joost H. Crouwell, "Ancient Iranian Horse Helmets?," *IA* 19 (1984): 47.

twice later in the Song, as the man describes his beloved as "a lotus among thorns" (2:2) and "unique, the special daughter of her mother" (6:8–9).

Second, the subsequent description of the lady's beautiful ornaments and beads (1:10–11) has led some to see the mapping of this metaphor as their physical decoration.[51] Meek posits that this comparison (1:9) would have been high praise in the East, "where both horses and women were excessively adorned."[52] In support of this notion, Pharaoh's horses are often depicted in Egyptian artwork with extravagant trappings.[53] Later in the Song, the beauty and allure of the maiden's physical ornamentation is described by the man as "captivating my heart" (4:9).

Finally, in light of the preference for male horses in chariot teams, Pope suggests an added significance for the Song's equine metaphor. He concluded that the juxtaposition of a single mare and a plurality of stallions requires only a modicum of what is called "horse sense" to appreciate the thrust of the comparison.[54] He posits that sending a mare in the midst of stallions would have caused great sexual stir and excitement. In favor of this meaning, Amenemhab, an Egyptian officer in the army of Thutmose III, tells how the prince of Qadesh sent a quick-footed mare into the lines of Pharaoh's army, hoping that the presence of this female would wreak havoc among the Egyptian stallions.[55] In his *Histories*, Herodotus tells how Darius's servant Oebares similarly employed a mare to ensure that his master would become king. When the chosen six men had mounted their horses, the first one whose horse neighed after daybreak would win the kingdom. The night prior, Oebares tethered a mare in the suburbs, the favorite of Darius's stallion, and then led his master's horse around the mare several times before allowing them to come together. The next morn-

---

51. Fox, *Song of Songs*, 105; Gordis, *Song of Songs*, 48; Murphy, *Song of Songs*, 132; Stoop-van Paridon, *Song of Songs*, 71–72.

52. Theophilus J. Meek, "Song of Songs," *IB* 5:107. For a parallel, see Saarisalo, "Songs of the Druzes," 23.

53. For examples, see the decorated chariots of Tutankhamen (*ANEP* 190, 318), Thutmose IV (316), Seti I (322–23), and Ramses III (345). The decoration of chariot horses was not unique to Egypt, evident from Assyrian reliefs of Shalmaneser III (365), Sennacherib (374), and Ashurnasirpal (184).

54. Marvin H. Pope, "A Mare in Pharaoh's Chariotry," *BASOR* 200 (1970): 59. In Greek literature, Blondell notes, "Horse taming is a frequent image in erotic contexts, with the *parthenos* portrayed as an unbroken filly running free" (Ruby Blondell, *Helen of Troy: Beauty, Myth, Devastation* [Oxford: Oxford University Press, 2013], 12).

55. Breasted, *Ancient Records of Egypt*, 2:589.

ing, Darius's horse, when it neared the spot where the mare was tethered the previous night, sprang forward and neighed (*Hist.* 3.85–86).[56]

While the stated meaning of the maiden's physical decoration (1:10) is almost universally accepted, there is considerable debate about the relevance of the above historical illustrations. Though commonly cited, some still reject such an implied meaning. Roland Murphy argues that the context (1:10–11) limits the basis of comparison to the girl's ornamental beauty, not her sexual appeal.[57] Yet are beauty and sexual allure mutually exclusive? In fact, there is a consistent pattern in the Song in which the man's visual observation and praise of his beloved's beauty produces sexual allure and a desire to be intimate with her (4:1–6; 7:1–10). Perhaps, the best parallel is 6:4–7, where the lover calls his beloved "beautiful," but before he can detail her beauty, he is overcome, "Turn your eyes away from me, for they overwhelm me" (6:5), likely describing his sexual desire.

Second, Garrett contends that if such a meaning was intended, it is odd that the poet does not develop it at all.[58] Yet, such is the case for most of the images found in the Song, especially erotic double entendre. Are the mountains of pleasure (2:17; 4:6; 8:14) a place of private refuge for lovers or an amorous metaphor for the maiden's breasts? Is the garden (4:12–5:1) a physical place where lovers rendezvous or an erotic image of her body? The poet relies on the reader, based on their shared cultural knowledge, to supply the meaning for many of the metaphors. At times, there is also a sense of multivalence, as certain imagery conveys numerous qualities.

Third, Garrett further labels Pope's historical explanation as "misleading."[59] Yet, this idea of sexual attraction in Song 1:9 is not a modern invention. In fact, it is frequently noted in rabbinic literature, often connected to the drowning of the Egyptian chariot horses in the Red Sea (Exod 14:23; 15:1). According to the Song of Songs Rabbah, "Since the Israelites were like a mare and the wicked Egyptians like males in heat, 'they ran after them until they sunk down in the sea.'"[60] In 'Abot de Rabbi Nathan, it is not the Israelites but YHWH himself who appears as a mare

---

56. For this reason, Cantrell suggests that geldings may have been used more than stallions to avoid the problem of sexual allure (Cantrell, *Horsemen of Israel*, 26).

57. Murphy, *Song of Songs*, 131. See also Fox, *Song of Songs*, 105.

58. Garrett and House, *Song of Songs/Lamentations*, 144.

59. Garrett, "Song of Songs," in *Zondervan Illustrated Bible Background Commentary*, ed. John H. Walton (Grand Rapids: Zondervan, 2009), 5:522.

60. Neusner, *Song of Songs Rabbah*, 1.9 ii.2. See also Exod. Rab. 23:14.

to draw Pharaoh's horses into the sea, "Rabbi Joshua ben Korḥah says, 'When Pharaoh came into the sea, he came on a stallion, and the Holy One, blessed be He, revealed Himself to it on a mare', as it is said, 'To My mare amongst Pharaoh's chariots (Cant 1:9)'" (A:27). Thus, the implication of sexual allure can be traced back as far as rabbinic Judaism.

In sum, the man's comparison of his beloved to an Egyptian mare may relate to her unique distinction, her beautiful decoration, and/or her sexual attraction.[61] First, the description of the woman's ornaments and beads (1:10), combined with the extant reliefs of decorated Egyptian chariots, confirm that this metaphor involves physical adornment. As an Egyptian mare was adorned with beautiful ornaments, so also the man's beloved wore bangles and strings of beads. With this cultural image, the Song's poet relies on the reader's knowledge, at least assuming the biblical portrait of Egypt as a place of wealth and source of fine horses (1 Kgs 10:28–29).

In addition, the Song's mare metaphor may also depict the maiden as unique and desirable. While Pope suggests that the earliest interpreters must have been aware that Egyptians used male horses for war and were familiar with the *ruse de geurre* at Qadesh, male horses were used in war throughout the Mediterranean, and the effect of a mare among stallions could be attributed to common sense.[62] Therefore, combining shared tradition and poetic genius, the man proclaims that like a mare among Pharaoh's war horses his lady's unique "beauty and sensuality are overwhelming and irresistible, so that if their love was a battlefield, she would definitely be the victor."[63]

4.3. Mountains of Pleasure (2:17; 4:6; 8:14)

עד שיפוח היום	2:17 Until the day breathes
ונסו הצללים	and the shadows flee,
סב דמה־לך דודי לצבי	turn,[64] my lover, be like a gazelle

---

61. Thöne recognizes the mare's decoration, but overreads the metaphor as domination. See Yvonne S. Thöne, "Female Humanimality: Animal Imagery in Song of Songs and Ancient Near Eastern Iconography," *JSem* 25 (2016): 405.

62. Pope, *Song of Songs*, 339.

63. Danilo Verde and Pierre Van Hecke, "The Belligerent Woman in Song 1,9," *Bib* 98 (2017): 217.

64. The woman's words contain an apparent contradiction, telling her lover to "turn" (2:17) and "flee" (8:14) yet inviting him to enjoy her pleasures. Evident in the

או לעפר האילים	or a young stag
על־הרי בתר:	on the cleft mountains!
עד שיפוח היום	⁴:⁶ Until the day breathes
ונסו הצללים	and the shadows flee,
אלך לי אל־הר המור	I will go to the mountain of myrrh
ואל־גבעת הלבונה:	and the hill of frankincense!
ברח | דודי	⁸:¹⁴ Flee, my lover,
ודמה־לך לצבי	be like a gazelle
או לעפר האילים	or a young stag
על הרי בשמים:	on the mountains of spices!

Source: Mountains
Target: Woman's Breasts
Mapping: Size/Shape and Seclusion

These three verses are connected both by shared metaphor and function. In their immediate context, these lyrics act as a variant refrain, closing their respective units (2:8–17; 4:1–7; 8:5–14). Yet each verse shares certain features with the other lyrics: 2:17 and 4:6 open with the same temporal setting; 2:17 and 8:14 issue an invitation to the male lover, likened to a gazelle or stag; and all three name mountains as the desired destination. But what is the meaning of such imagery? In contrast to previous examples, we will begin with a thorough analysis of the Song's verses, to help identify the referent of this mountain metaphor. Then, a brief survey of comparative evidence will compare and contrast the use of such imagery with biblical and extrabiblical sources.

4.3.1. Meaning in the Song

Both 2:17 and 4:6 open with an enigmatic temporal phrase עד שיפוח היום ונסו הצללים "Until the day breathes and the shadows flee," which may refer to either morning or evening. Suggesting that the woman requests her lover to leave before nightfall, Keel compares the phrase רוח היום (Gen 3:8), the

---

parallels between 2:17 and 8:14, the Song contains a paradoxical pattern of sending away and calling for one's lover as a prelude to their union (Exum, *Song of Songs*, 133). In 8:14, playing on a similar sound, the man pictures himself among "friends" (חברים), but she calls for him alone to "flee" (ברח) to her mountains (Hess, *Song of Songs*, 249).

afternoon hours when a breeze blows in off the sea, as well as ינטו צללי־ערב (Jer 6:4; Ps 102:12), the lengthening of evening shadows.[65] Yet, since the shadows of the day do not flee as the sun sets but stretch out, it seems better to understand the setting as morning, when the day comes to life, the sun chases away the night, and lovers cease their amorous activity.[66]

Moreover, in 2:17 and 8:14, the male lover is pictured as a gazelle or stag romping on the mountains. These animals are often found in an amorous context in the Song, whether as a symbol of the man (2:9; 2:17; 8:14), a witness invoked against disturbing lovers (2:7; 3:5), or a symbol of the woman's breasts (4:5, 7:4; see also Prov 5:19). In biblical and extrabiblical sources, the gazelle appears as an icon of speed. Some of David's mighty men are compared to a gazelle, stressing extraordinary quickness (2 Sam 2:18; 1 Chr 12:9). Similarly, in Egypt's Chester Beatty Papyrus, the girl wishes, "If only you would come to (your) sister swiftly, like a gazelle bounding over the desert."[67] Yet, in this context, the stag is likely employed for the power of its erotic desire. Robert Biggs notes the frequent invocation of this animal in Mesopotamian sexual potency incantations.[68]

By mentioning the gazelle/stag and mountains (2:17), the Song's poet creates an *inclusio*, returning to the imagery of the lover's coming (2:8–9). Yet here the man is not merely bounding over the mountains but is invited to romp on them. Each verse describes the desired destination differently. Verses 4:6 and 8:14 connect the mountains to various spices. As Franz Delitzsch notes, these mountains cannot be literal places, as myrrh and frankincense are not indigenous to Palestine.[69] In the Song, spices are an erotic symbol connected to the maiden's body, often in the context of lovemaking (1:13; 4:14–5:5). While such natural imagery may be a general picture of the woman's body, the immediate context suggests a more specific referent. In 4:1–5, the man sequentially details the beauty of his beloved's body. Reaching her breasts (4:5), his emotions are overwhelmed, and he stops, declaring his intention to spend the night enjoying

---

65. Keel, *Song of Songs*, 115.
66. Fox, *Song of Songs*, 115.
67. Fox, *Song of Songs*, 66. See also Nissinen, "Nabû and Tašmetu," 589.
68. Biggs, *ŠÀ.ZI.GA*, 21 (15–16), 24 (4–9), 26 (3–8, 11).
69. Keil and Delitzsch, *Commentary on the Old Testament*, 6:554. Chaim Rabin connects the spices to South Arabian trade but misses the symbolic connection to the maiden's body ("The Song of Songs and Tamil Poetry," *SR* 3 [1973]: 213–14).

her pleasures.⁷⁰ In addition, there are numerous references to the maiden's breasts preceding the final refrain (8:1–2, 8–10). Thus, these phrases are best explained as a figurative invitation (8:14) and intention (4:6) for the man to enjoy her delight-filled peaks. Visual similarities further support this identification.

While scholars agree with this reading for the final two occurrences of the Song's mountain imagery (4:6; 8:14), debate exists over הרי בתר (2:17). Even the ancient versions are divided in their rendering of this phrase: "mountains of ravines" (LXX), "mountains of Bether," a village southwest of Jerusalem (Aquila, Symmachus, Jerome), or "fragrant mountains" (Theodotion, Peshitta). Keel adopts the final option, connecting בתר to an Indian spice known in Greek as μαλάβαθρον, but it seems likely that Theodotion and the Syriac translators rendered הרי בתר (2:17) in light of הרי בשמים (8:14).⁷¹ Thus, in light of the link between spices and the maiden's body, the references to her breasts in the context, and parallels between 2:17, 4:6, and 8:14, the primary meaning of this imagery is best explained as a double-entendre for her "cleft [בתר] mountains," a clever twist on the BODY AS LANDSCAPE metaphor. In 2:17 and 8:14, the woman responds to her lover's desire for time alone (2:10–13; 8:13), while 4:6 records the man's acceptance of her invitation to romp on her mountains of pleasure.

4.3.2. Comparative Evidence

Mountains (הר) and hills (גבעה), a word pair occurring in parallel over thirty-five times in the Hebrew Bible, may be a physical phenomenon or metaphoric symbol. Their remote and rugged terrain, where fugitives hide and armies flee (Judg 6:2; 1 Sam 14:22), can depict a place of seclusion (Ps 11:1) or in contrast, a site of scattering (Jer 50:6). As a natural barrier and physical boundary (Josh 15:9–11), a mountain's visual immensity provides a benchmark for enormity as well as an image of permanence (Isa 54:10) and an obstacle of insurmountable proportion (Zech 4:7).

In contrast to the frequency of mountain imagery, שד "breast" is used only twenty-four times in the entire Hebrew Bible, with one-third of its occurrences found in the Song. This maternal organ of nourishment symbolizes comfort, security, and provision (Gen 49:25; Job 3:12;

---

70. Sarah Zhang, *I, You, and the Word 'God': Finding Meaning in the Song of Songs*, Siphrut 20 (Winona Lake, IN: Eisenbrauns, 2016), 37.

71. Keel, *Song of Songs*, 115–17.

Ps 22:10; Lam 4:3; Isa 60:16; 66:11), while its absence signifies a lack of safety and mourning (Job 24:9; Isa 32:12; Hos 9:14). It also designates stages of physical maturity, from a nursing infant (Isa 28:19; Joel 2:16) to a girl whose breast development marks her readiness for love (Ezek 16:7; Song 8:8–10). Finally, שד can be a symbol of sexuality, picturing Israel's adultery (Ezek 23:3, 21; Hos 2:4) or praising a woman's physical beauty and the sexual satisfaction she brings to her lover. The majority of occurrences in the Song fits this latter category (1:13; 4:5; 7:4, 9; 8:2). In contrast to the Song's food metaphors, breasts likened to large clusters of dates (7:9) or pomegranates filled with wine (8:1–2), the natural imagery in this variant refrain plays on the visual similarities between the maiden's breasts and the size and rugged terrain of a mountain. However, in light of the man's request for intimate time alone with his lover in the preceding verses (2:10–13; 8:13), this figure also pictures the mountains as a private place for passion, not unlike the undisturbed love motif expressed elsewhere in the Song (1:4, 7–8, 16–17; 2:7; 3:4–5; 4:16; 5:2–8; 7:11–13; 8:1–4).

In addition to the biblical evidence, material finds from Syria-Palestine may also support this literal view of the Song's mountain imagery. In the last two centuries, over eight hundred female pillar figurines have been found in Judah, most dating to the eighth–seventh centuries BCE, whose hallmark feature is their large breasts.[72] Two main ideas have been suggested to explain their function in Judean society.

First, many scholars believe that these figurines reflect pluralistic worship in ancient Israel. In light of the Kuntillet ʿAjrud inscription to "YHWH and his Asherah," some suggest that these are symbols of a goddess. For example, Judith Hadley posits that these figurines might be smaller copies of wooden pillars set up in the Jerusalem temple and other sites dedicated to the worship of Asherah (1 Kgs 14:23; 2 Kgs 23:6).[73] Not rejecting a religious purpose, others propose a socio-political function. Ryan Byrne concludes that the proliferation of pillar figurines amidst the constant

---

72. Raz Kletter, *The Judean Pillar-Figurines and the Archaeology of Asherah*, BAR 636 (Oxford: Tempus Reparatum, 1996), 83. Half were found in Jerusalem.

73. Judith M. Hadley, *The Cult of Asherah in Ancient Israel and Judah* (New York: Cambridge University Press, 2000), 205. Keel and Uehlinger also identify these as images of Asherah, based on their similarity to a scarab from Lachish with a goddess holding her breasts. See Othmar Keel and Christoph Uehlinger, *Gods, Goddesses, and Images of God*, trans. Thomas H. Trapp (Minneapolis: Fortress, 1998), 333–36.

threat of Assyrian invasion highlights a pressing interest in maternity and infant viability in eighth–seventh century Judah.[74]

Though not mutually exclusive, another function is often overlooked. As "a visual metaphor, which shows in seeable and touchable form that which is most desired," these figurines may also reflect a perception of feminine beauty.[75] In contrast to its crudely formed body, the heads of some figurines were artistically molded, with great attention paid to the eyes and hair.[76] Perhaps her exaggerated bosom shows a preference for large breasts. On its hand position, Alexander Pruss concludes, "This gesture is most probably one emphasizing the appeal of the depicted."[77] From these figurines, concern for fertility has been adequately stressed, yet the implications for female beauty have gone mainly unnoticed.

Mesopotamian culture contains a few possible parallels in which the size or pleasure of a woman's breasts is highlighted, though their context is often uncertain. In a Sumero-Akkadian hymn, Nanâ is described as having "heavy breasts" [*tu-la-a kub-bu-ta-ku*], though this attribute is given no further explanation.[78] Ruth Opificus, in her analysis of Old Babylonian terracotta reliefs, similarly connects the large breasts of the *Brustbildgöttin* to Inanna-Ishtar, the goddess of love, based on similar jewelry and ornamentation.[79] The closest evidence from Mesopotamia is found in two texts from the Ur III–Old Babylonian period. Inanna employs a similar metaphor in

---

74. Ryan Byrne, "Lie Back and Think of Judah: The Reproductive Politics of Pillar Figurines," *NEA* 67 (2004): 148–49. While state sponsorship and mass production favor a sociopolitical function, the apparently intentional breakage of many figurines supports a religious connection. Though some argue that the consistent fracture of the pillar-figurines at the neck corresponds to a structurally weak point, the evidence from Tel en-Nasbeh suggests otherwise. Of 120 figurines, most were broken at the neck, including those of solid form. See Ziony Zevit, *The Religions of Ancient Israel: A Synthesis of Parallactic Approaches* (London: Continuum, 2001), 272.

75. Tikva Frymer-Kensky, *In the Wake of the Goddesses* (New York: Free Press, 1992), 159. Urs Winters suggested these figurines were domestic icons that helped eroticize the house (*Frau und Göttin: Exegetische und ikonographitche Studien zum weiblichen Gottesbild im Alten Israel und in dessen Umwelt*, OBO 53 [Fribourg: Universitätsverlag; Göttingen: Vandenhoeck & Ruprecht, 1983], 131).

76. Kletter, *Judean Pillar-Figurines*, 50.

77. Alexander Pruss, "The Use of Nude Female Figurines," in Parpola and Whiting, *Sex and Gender*, 544.

78. Erica Reiner, "A Sumero-Akkadian Hymn of Nanâ," *JNES* 33 (1974): 233.

79. Ruth Opificius, *Das altbabylonische Terrakotareliefs*, UAVA 2 (Berlin: de Gruyter, 1961), 203.

one of the Shulgi hymns, "You are fit to dance on my pure breast like a lapis lazuli calf."[80] As in the Song, the man is likened to a bovine and invited to romp on his beloved's breasts. But the clearest example of breasts pictured as mountains is found in Westenholz's "Forgotten Love Song":

> O by the crown of our head, the rings of our ears
> *the mountain of our shoulders, and the charms of our chest*
> the bracelet with date spadix charms of our wrists
> the belt hung with (lapis lazuli) frog charms of our waist
> reach forth with your left hand and stroke our vulva
> play with our breasts; enter, I have opened (my) thighs.[81]

More than the above examples from Mesopotamia, the size and shape of a woman's breasts are highlighted in Indian love lyrics, from the early *akam* (inner world) poems to later anthologies. In his comparative work, Mariaselvam records numerous examples from early Tamil lyrics in which the beloved's breasts are depicted as prominent, budding, or bulging.[82]

Such imagery is also found in medieval Indian poetry. Govárdhana, a twelfth-century lyricist from Bengal, writes, "Do cover up your breasts—those mountains that block the road—that are impossible to by-pass."[83] Aruṇakiri, the fourteenth-century poet who initiated a renaissance of classical Tamil poetry, similarly states, "Two tusks of black elephants are those mountainous breasts, sparkling with gold chains."[84]

---

80. A similar phrase is found in Dumuzi's Dream, "I am the one who dances on the holy knees, the holy knees of Inanna" (Jacobsen, *Harps*, 40–41, 43). In light of the parallels, Klein renders both phrases the same way, viewing DU8 in Šulgi X as a phonetic writing of DU10 "knees" instead of *gaba* "breasts." For these different readings, see Bendt Alster, *Dumuzi's Dream: Aspects of Oral Poetry in Sumerian Myth*, Mesopotamia 1 (Cophenhagen: Akademisk, 1972), 118; Klein, *Three Šulgi Hymns*, 153.

81. Joan G. Westenholz, "A Forgotten Love Song," in *Language, Literature, and History: Philological and Historical Studies Presented to Erica Reiner*, ed. Francesca Rochberg-Halton (New Haven: American Oriental Society, 1987), 423. See also Wasserman, *Akkadian Love Literature*, 259–60. Mountains are also the place Inanna goes to gain her erotic skills; see Samuel N. Kramer, "BM 23631: Bread for Enlil, Sex for Inanna," *Or* 54 (1985): 122–27.

82. Mariaselvam, *Ancient Tamil Love Poems*, 198–99, 293.

83. Govárdhana, *Seven Hundred Elegant Verses*, trans. Friedhelm Hardy, Clay Sanskrit Library (New York: New York University Press, 2009), 27.

84. Kamil Zvelebil, *The Smile of Murugan on Tamil Literature of South India* (Leiden: Brill, 1973), 243.

Based on these examples from antiquity, combined with an obsession with breast size in contemporary Western culture, one may be tempted to classify the Song's mountain metaphor as a commonality of human experience. Yet, Greek, Egyptian, Renaissance, and early American culture provide contrary evidence. In light of the frequent reference to breasts in Hellenistic literature, the lack of emphasis on size is surprising. In his analysis of the female breast in Greek erotic literature, Douglas Gerber concludes, "The most striking conclusion ... is the total absence of any preference being shown for large breasts. Whereas in our present age the ample bosom is an object of worship in the eyes of many, in Greco-Roman culture, the emphasis was on smallness, firmness, and roundness."[85] Martial depicts the perfect breast as not overflowing the hand (*Ep.* 14.134), while Ovid, in his prescription for falling out of love advises imagining one's lover as unattractive, "Take care, if her large breasts offend your eyes. No dress does that deformity disguise" (*Rem. am.* 337 [Mozley]).

Large breasts are also absent in Egyptian literature and iconography. Despite numerous references to the female breast in Egypt's love lyrics, size is never stressed.[86] While Egyptian women are often depicted in a tight-fitting sheath dress, displaying every curve and placing an emphasis on her sexuality, the female breast is consistently depicted as petite. A contrast in size is highlighted in a painting from the tomb of Ramesses IX, in which a woman is depicted between two men, each in a profile posture. The male member is abnormally large while the female breasts are small.[87]

The elevation of small breasts as an ideal of feminine beauty is also evident in Europe until the mid-eighteenth century and more recently in the United States. The desire for petite, firm breasts is supported by the countless medical formulas, such as this advice from the Renaissance French handbook *Bastiment des receptes*, "To make small breasts remain in that state and to reduce the size of large ones, take the main viscera of a hare, mince them and mix with an equal part of ordinary honey. Apply this as

---

85. Gerber, "Female Breast," 208. See also Jax, *Weibliche Schönheit*, 63, 116 n. 362.

86. In Egypt's love lyrics, the girl's breasts are praised for their fairness and compared to fruits known as aphrodisiacs (Tobin, "Love Songs," 309, 319, 323).

87. Lise Manniche, *Sexual Life in Ancient Egypt* (New York, Methuen: 1987), 34. See also Dorothea Arnold and James P. Allen, eds., *Royal Women of Amarna: Images of Beauty from Ancient Egypt* (New York: Metropolitan Museum of Art, 1996), fig. 21.

a poultice to the breasts and surrounding areas."[88] A nineteenth-century French medical historian likened his own culture's ideal to the Greeks, "We learn from Juvenal and Martial that, like ourselves, the Greeks detested pendant and bulky breasts, the signs of beauty being elevation, smallness, and regularity of contour."[89] In her history of the corset, Steele points to a 1928 book for art students in the United States that describes the epitome of feminine beauty: muscularly fit, slim waist, and rounded hips, adding "breasts were flattened with tight brassieres."[90]

Thus, the Song's mountain imagery in this variant refrain (2:17; 4:6; 8:14) is best understood as a combination of visual and olfactory symbols depicting the maiden's breasts as a private place of pleasure. In 2:17 and 8:14, the woman responds to her lover's request for time alone (2:10–13, 8:13), inviting him to find seclusion and sensual satisfaction by romping on her "mountains." In 4:6, having detailed the delightful sights of her physical beauty, the man reaches her breasts and stops. Overcome with emotion, he declares his intention to indulge his passions in her sexual pleasures. Though such desires are common to human experience, "aesthetics are never neutral, universal, or independent of cultural and historical context."[91] Thus, the likeness of the lady's breasts to mountains is best classified as part of a culturally defined ideal of beauty. Since this metaphor is found in other cultures which favored larger breasts yet absent from those which viewed petite breasts as desirable, the Song's mountain imagery may indicate a preference for large breasts in Israel's society, though isolating cultural ideals with limited evidence is difficult.

4.4. Garden of Delight (1:6; 2:15; 4:12–13, 16–5:1; 6:2, 11; 7:13; 8:12–13)

אל־תראוני שאני שחרחרת	1:6 Do not stare at me because I am too dark,
ששזפתני השמש	for the sun has burned me.
בני אמי נחרו־בי	My mother's sons burned with anger at me;
שמני נטרה את־הכרמים	they made me keeper of the vineyards,

---

88. Augustin Cabanes, *Erotikon: Being an Illustrated Treasury of Scientific Marvels of Human Sexuality* (New York: Book Awards, 1966), 151–52.

89. George M. Gould and Walter L. Pyle, *Anomalies and Curiosities of Medicine* (London: Saunders, 1901), 759.

90. Valerie Steele, *The Corset: A Cultural History* (New Haven: Yale University Press, 2003), 154.

91. Janice Boddy, "Body: Female, Egypt and Sudan," *Encyclopedia of Women and Islamic Cultures: Family, Body, Sexuality, and Health* 3:34.

4. Nature as Erotica

my own vineyard, I have not kept.	כרמי שלי לא נטרתי:
²:¹⁵ Catch us foxes,	אחזו-לנו שועלים
little foxes,	שועלים קטנים
that ruin the vineyards,	מחבלים כרמים
for our vineyards are in blossom.	וכרמינו סמדר:
⁴:¹² A locked garden is my sister, [my] bride,	גן | נעול אחתי כלה
a locked door,⁹² a sealed-up spring	גל נעול מעין חתום:
⁴:¹³ Your fields⁹³ are a pleasure garden:	שלחיך פרדס
pomegranates with delicious fruits,	רמונים עם פרי מגדים
henna with nard,	כפרים עם-נרדים:
⁴:¹⁶ Awake, O north wind, come, south wind,	עורי צפון ובואי תימן
blow on my garden that its scent may spread.	הפיחי גני יזלו בשמיו
let my lover enter his garden,	יבא דודי לגנו
and devour its delicious fruits.	ויאכל פרי מגדיו:
⁵:¹ I have come to my garden, my sister, [my] bride,	באתי לגני אחתי כלה
I have plucked my myrrh with my spice,	אריתי מורי עם-בשמי
I have eaten my honey with my honeycomb,	אכלתי יערי עם-דבשי
I have drunk my wine with my milk.	שתיתי ייני עם-חלבי
Eat, O friends,	אכלו רעים
drink and be drunk, O lovers.	שתו ושכרו דודים:
⁶:² My lover has gone down to his garden,	דודי ירד לגנו
to the beds of spice,	לערוגות הבשם
to graze in the gardens,	לרעות בגנים
and gather lotuses.⁹⁴	וללקט שושנים:
⁶:¹¹ I went down to the nut grove,	אל-גנת אגוז ירדתי
to see the blooms of the valley,	לראות באבי הנחל
to see if the vine had budded,	לראות הפרחה הגפן
[if] the pomegranates had bloomed.	הנצו הרמנים:
⁷:¹³ Let us go early to the vineyards	נשכימה לכרמים

---

92. Eidelkind, "Two Notes on Song 4:12," 222–24.
93. Since שלחיך "shoots" does not make sense equated to a garden, the term is best explained as a metonymy for an irrigated area (Fox, *Song of Songs*, 137).
94. The identity of the שושן is heavily debated. See §5.8 for further discussion.

נראה אם פרחה הגפן	to see if the vine has budded,
פתח הסמדר	[if] the blossom has opened,
הנצו הרמונים	[if] the pomegranates have bloomed.
שם אתן את־דדי לך:	There I will give you my love.
כרמי שלי לפני	8:12 My vineyard is my very own,
האלף לך שלמה	the thousand [shekels] belong to you, Solomon,
ומאתים לנטרים את־פריו:	two hundred are for the guards of its fruit.
היושבת בגנים	8:13 O you who dwells in the gardens,
חברים מקשיבים לקולך	[my] companions are listening for your voice,
השמיעיני:	let me hear it!

Source: Vineyard/Garden
Target: Woman's Body
Mapping: Secluded Privacy, Spring-Like Prosperity, Sensual Pleasures

Similar to the mountain imagery in the previous example, gardens and vineyards are also employed in the Hebrew Bible as physical places and metaphorical symbols. Often found adjacent to palaces or temples, they were well-watered spaces (Ezek 19:10; Isa 58:11), set apart for the cultivation of various fruits and flora (Eccl 12:5; 1 Kgs 21:12). A fertile garden signaled God's blessing, while its absence was linked to judgment (Isa 5:1–7; Amos 9:14). Such horticultural imagery is also a repeated theme in the love language of the Song of Songs (1:6; 2:15; 4:12–13, 16–5:1; 6:2, 11; 7:13; 8:12–13). Why? What exactly is this garden of love? Is it a person, a place, or both? If both are invoked, what are the attributes shared between the literal and figurative domains? What about the popular theory that the garden of love is an allusion to the garden of creation, redeeming the corruption of sexuality resulting from humanity's fall in Gen 2–3?[95]

4.4.1. Comparative Evidence

Horticultural imagery is also found in the love lyrics of surrounding cultures. In Egypt, the garden is often a place of rendezvous for lovers,

---

95. Ivory J. Cainion, "An Analogy of Song of Songs and Genesis Chapters Two and Three," *SJOT* 14 (2000): 219–60; F. W. Dobbs-Allsopp, "The Delight of Beauty and Song of Songs 4:1–7," *Int* 59 (2005): 276; Landy, *Paradoxes of Paradise*, 183; Trible, *God and the Rhetoric of Sexuality*, 144–65.

providing privacy and natural beauty to frame their amorous state of mind.⁹⁶ In Papyrus Harris, a girl details her journey to the "love garden" (*ddt*) to meet her lover, expressing her feelings of exaltation when they are together. Likely a play on words, the lovers meet in this "love garden" (*ddt*) for the purpose of lovemaking (*dd*).⁹⁷ Moreover, the garden also functions as a metaphor for the female body. Elsewhere in this collection, the boy exclaims, "How intoxicating are the plants of my wetland.... The lips of my beloved are the bud of a lotus, her breasts are mandrakes."⁹⁸ At times, the line between literal and metaphorical is blurred. The girl sings:

> I belong to you like a garden [ḫꜣ n(y) tꜣ]⁹⁹
> Which I have made to bloom
> With flowers and every sweet herb.
> Delightful is the canal there,
> Dug by your hand to refresh us in the breeze,
> A lovely place for strolling,
> Your hand holding mine.¹⁰⁰

Furthermore, the same dual metaphor is evident in the love songs from Mesopotamia.¹⁰¹ In Manchester Tammuz, lyrics centered on the marriage of Inanna and Dumuzi, the goddess proclaims her desire to be with her shepherd lover, "Me, the lady of heaven, let me go, let me go to the garden

---

96. Izak Cornelius, "The Garden in Iconography of the Ancient Near East: A Study of Selected Material from Egypt," *JSem* 1 (1989): 225. In Papyrus Westcar, Ubainer's wife meets a villager in a garden to dine, bathe, and take pleasure. See J. Hunt Cooke, "The Westcar Papyrus," *BW* 4 (1894): 50.

97. The Egyptian *dd* can mean "lovemaking" (Papyrus Harris 4.2–3) but can also refer to a garden (*WÄS*, "dd," 5:502; *GHb*, "dd," 1062; see tree determinative in Papyrus Anastasi III 2.5, 3.7).

98. Tobin, "Love Songs," 309.

99. The Egyptian term ḫꜣ n(y) tꜣ generally means "arable land," but it is best described here as a garden, in light of its variety of cultivated flowers (*WÄS*, "ḫꜣ-tꜣ," 3:220; *GHb*, "ḫꜣ-tꜣ," 622; Fox, *Song of Songs*, 28).

100. Tobin, "Love Songs," 316. The digging of a canal likely depicts intercourse.

101. For further examples of garden imagery in Mesopotamia, see Shalom M. Paul, "A Lover's Garden of Verse: Literal and Metaphorical Imagery in Ancient Near Eastern Love Poetry," in *Tehillah le-Moshe: Biblical and Judaic Studies in Honor of Moshe Greenberg*, ed. Mordechai Cogan, Barry L. Eichler, and Jeffrey H. Tigay (Winona Lake, IN: Eisenbrauns, 1997), 99–110.

[*ki-ri-ši*]! In the garden [*ki-ri-a*] dwells the man of my heart!"[102] Another lyric involving this pair of lovers tells how Dumuzi brought Inanna into his garden ($^{giš}kiri_6$-*ni-a*), where the couple made love in various positions among the different types of trees.[103]

In the later Akkadian love lyrics of Nabû and Tašmetu, the goddess similarly expresses her yearning to go to the garden with her lover, "Let me give you pleasure in the garden [*kirî*].... For what, for what are you adorned, my Tašmetu? So that I may [go] to the garden [*kirî*] with you, my Nabû" (r.15–18).[104] However, not only is the garden a popular locale for amorous encounters, the Mesopotamian lyrics also employ this motif as a metaphor for the female body.[105] In Gudea's Cylinder B, the goddess Baba, lying beside her husband, is described as a "beautiful fruit-bearing garden [$^{giš}kiri_6$-*nisi-ga kurun*$_3$]."[106] In another brief but erotic love song, Inanna's body is pictured as a garden watered by her lover:

> It sprouts, it sprouts, it is the lettuce he watered,
> In the garden [$^{giš}kiri_6$] of deep shade,
> bending down his neck, my darling of his mother,
> My one who fills the grain in their furrows with beauty, he watered,
> My apple tree bearing fruit at its top, it is the garden he watered.[107]

---

102. Alster, "Manchester Tammuz," 19.44–48.
103. Sefati, *Love Songs*, 321.
104. Nissinen, "Nabû and Tašmetu," 590. For a similar lyric about Banitu and her consort, see Karlheinz Deller, "ST 366: Deutungversuch 1982," *Assur* 3 (1982): 141.
105. Gwendolyn Leick, *Sex and Eroticism in Mesopotamian Literature* (New York: Routledge, 1994), 53. Cooper compares Ludingira's portrait of his mother, "a garden of delight," to Song 4:12–15 (Jerrold S. Cooper, "New Cuneiform Parallels to the Song of Songs," *JBL* 90 [1971]: 161–62).
106. Sefati, *Love Songs*, 34.
107. Alster, "Marriage and Love," 21. "Lettuce stands for [her] pubic hair ... and [the] apple tree is a metaphor for the male member." See Jacobsen, *Harps*, 94; see also Brigitte Groneberg, "Searching for Akkadian Lyrics: From Old Babylonian to the 'Liederkatalog' KAR 158," *JCS* 55 (2003): 67. Besnier concludes that gardens in Mesopotamian lyrics imply a delightful but sterile love (erotic pleasure over procreation), while agricultural imagery signifies a fruitful union (Marie-Françoise Besnier, "Temptation's Garden: The Gardener, a Mediator Who Plays an Ambiguous Part," in Parpola and Whiting, *Sex and Gender in the Ancient Near East*, 66). One of the Inanna-Dumuzi love songs (DI P) may present opposing evidence, though its fragmentary nature prevents certainty. Inanna sings a song of praise for her nakedness, asking who will plow her field (vulva). After a textual break, assumed to include the couple's sexual union,

Though not as common, the garden motif is also found in Greco-Roman lyrics, describing both the person and place of love. In retaliation for his lover's infidelity, Propertius depicts a garden setting for his sexual exploits, "I decided to beguile the night by inviting these [women] and add new experiences to my amorous ventures. A couch for three was set out in a garden, screened from view" (*El.* 4.8.33–36 [Goold]). Archilochus, a seventh-century BCE Greek poet, applied this image to the female body:

> Whenever [it] has become dark,
> You and I will deliberate on these matters with heaven's help.
> I shall do as you bid me.
> [You arouse in me?] a strong [desire?].
> But, my dear, do not begrudge my …
> Under the coping and the gate.
> For I shall steer towards the grassy garden;
> Be sure now of this.[108]

Likewise, love literature from ancient India also depicts the rendezvous of lovers in a garden. Noting a host of examples, Mariaselvam concludes, "The majority of night visits from the hero to the heroine take place in the garden near the house of the girl." However, in contrast to the above comparative evidence, the Tamil lyrics offer no examples in which the beloved's body is likened to a field, grove, or garden.[109]

As evident from the preceding survey, the garden motif is widespread across time and culture. Michael Sells notes the presence of this topos in Arab lyrics prior to the rise of Islam. In the ode of Ántara, a bedouin warrior and poet of the sixth century CE, this motif is used to praise the beauty of his beloved 'Abla, "Her mouth sweet to the kiss, sweet to the taste, as if

---

the poet depicts the resultant awakening of fertility in nature, compared to a "blossoming garden" (Sefati, *Love Songs*, 218–35).

108. Archilocus, frag. 196a (Gerber). See also Anselm C. Hagedorn, "Of Foxes and Vineyards: Greek Perspectives on the Song of Songs, *VT* 53 (2003): 344–48. The Greek κῆπος and Latin *hortus* "enclosed garden" are used as sexual metaphors for one's genitalia (LSJ, s.v. "κῆπος"; *OLD*, s.v. "hortus"). Also, in a Roman inscription, Hadrian alludes to the "flowering garden of Narcissus," a place for homosexual trysts. See James Davidson, *The Greeks and Greek Love: A Bold New Exploration of the Ancient World* (New York: Random House, 2009), 16–17, 48.

109. Mariaselvam, *Ancient Tamil Love Poems*, 164, 210–11.

a draft of musk from a spiceman's pouch, announced the wet gleam of her inner teeth, fragrant as an untouched garden."[110]

This imagery is also attested in medieval Hebrew and Arabic poetry, as well as the love songs of twentieth-century Arab bedouins.[111] Dalman and Stephan record examples in which the garden is invoked as a metaphor for the person and place of love. The man once exclaims, "Let us be drunk in the garden of your caressing." Elsewhere, this image clearly refers to the maiden's body, "Visit me, O you with the radiant face, and heal me from my miseries. Then I shall uncover your breast and see a garden—what a fine one too."[112] Again, the line between literal and figurative is often blurred, "Look at (my) Sweetness in the garden, she sways like a branch of the willow; as I stretched out my hand after the pomegranates, she said crossly, (they are) not ripe, O light of the eye!"[113] Similarly, in one medieval Provençal poem, the man laments the coming of dawn and wishes to stay in the garden, enjoying the presence and passion of his beloved, "May it please God the night would never wane, nor my love separate from me. Fair sweet love, let us renew delight, in the garden where birds sing."[114]

Garden imagery is also found in the writings of Shakespeare. After falling in love at their initial meeting, Romeo scales the Capulet's wall to enter Juliet's garden, where the lovers confess their undying love (*Romeo and Juliet* 2.1). In the passionate opening of *Venus and Adonis*, Adonis compares his beloved's cheeks to "a garden full of flowers" (65). In "The Seeds of Love," an anonymous English folk song, the poet also describes the planting of her flower garden but laments its deflowering by a courting

---

110. Michael A. Sells, "Guises of the Ghūl: Dissembling Simile and Semantic Overflow in Classical Arabic Nasīb," in *Reorientations/Arabic and Persian Poetry*, ed. Suzanne Stetkevych (Bloomington: Indiana University Press, 1994), 135.

111. Masha Itzhaki, *Toward the Garden Beds: Hebrew Garden Poems in Medieval Spain* [Hebrew] (Tel-Aviv: Notza ve'Keset, 1988); Henri Peres, *La poesie andaluse en Arabe calssique au XIe siècle* (Paris: Maisonneuve, 1953). The "garden" is adapted in medieval religious literature. See Helen Phillips, "Gardens of Love and the Garden of the Fall," in *A Walk in the Garden: Biblical, Iconographical, and Literary Images of Eden*, ed. Paul Morris and Deborah Sawyer, JSOTSup 136 (Sheffield: JSOT Press, 1992), 205–19.

112. Stephan, "Modern Palestinian Parallels," 215, 250.

113. Dalman, *Palästinischer Diwan*, 250.

114. Anne L. Klinck, *An Anthology of Ancient and Medieval Woman's Song* (New York: Palgrave Macmillan, 2004), 73.

suitor.[115] Finally, the garden motif has continued in contemporary Western culture.[116] In modern America, this iconic imagery is best captured in the advertisement for sexual stimulants in which aging lovers are transported from everyday scenes to a garden setting to ready them for love.

While such imagery would be especially vivid for an agrarian society in an arid region, the widespread distribution of this amorous metaphor, as demonstrated by the brief survey above, suggests that the garden is best explained as a commonality of human experience used to depict the place where lovers meet and symbolize the beloved's body.[117]

However, in contrast to the garden motif, a near universal variant of the BODY AS LANDSCAPE metaphor, the phrase "to go [down] to the garden" in Song 6:2, 11 may be a stock phrase shared across the Near East that poets employed as a mixed metaphor for the person and place for love.[118] In Egypt's Papyrus Harris, the girl describes her journey to the "love garden" (*ddt*) to meet her man, referring to a physical place. But she then depicts her arms as full of persea fruit and her hair laden with balm. In addition to the play on *dd* "lovemaking," the likeness of the girl's breasts to persea fruit and the link between balm and lovemaking in the Turin Love Song suggests the Egyptian poet uses garden imagery to blur the line between person and place.[119] Not only is the garden a rendezvous for lovers, but the beloved's body, with its sensual pleasure, is also the place for love!

A similar practice is found in Mesopotamia. In the love lyrics of Nabû and Tashmetu, the goddess repeatedly asks her lover to go to the garden (r.15–32).[120] Since the annual cultic ritual of Nabû and Tashmetu, detailed elsewhere but undoubtedly reflected in these lyrics, concludes with the gods' entrance into a physical garden, these lines initially appear to describe the locale for lovers.[121] Yet, since the ritual begins with the lovers' entrance and erotic encounter in their bedroom (r.9–14), Tashmetu's request to go the garden suggests that the garden may also be a metaphor for the female

---

115. Atkins, *Sex in Literature*, 3:236–37.

116. See Robert Haas and Stephen Mitchell, *Into the Garden: A Wedding Anthology of Poetry and Prose on Love and Marriage* (New York: HarperCollins, 1994).

117. On the vividness of this imagery in an arid region, see Mirko Novák, "The Artificial Paradise: Programme and Ideology of Royal Gardens," in Parpola and Whiting, *Sex and Gender*, 443.

118. Fox, *Song of Songs*, 44–51.

119. Westenholz, "Metaphoric Language in the Poetry of Love," 382.

120. Nissinen, "Nabû and Tašmetu," 590–91.

121. Eiko Matsushima, "Rituel Hiérogramique de Nabû," *ASJ* 9 (1987): 131–75.

body. Her desire to see the plucking of fruit and hear the twittering of birds may also support the dual nature of the garden motif. Noting the parallel to the Song, Nissinen concludes, "The garden is not only the place where erotic encounters take place, it is a multi-layered metaphor for luxury, love-making, a woman, and her genitals."[122]

Another example is found in an Old Akkadian incantation.[123] This love charm begins as Ea, the god of wisdom and incantations, is invoked, a magic aromatic is sought, and control is asserted over a desired woman (1–16).[124] Then, with vegetal metaphors, the speaker describes his approach toward the woman, "I climbed into the garden of the moon/Sîn, I cut down poplar for her daylight" (17–20). While the man's ensuing command, "Seek me among the boxwoods" (21), suggests that this garden is a place, the preceding line, "I have seized your vagina full of wetness" (16), implies a dual literal-figurative referent.[125] This amorous incantation combines the man's imagined physical approach to his object of desire in a literal garden with an anticipated sexual advance into her figurative garden.[126]

---

122. Nissinen, "Nabû and Tašmetu," 617–18.

123. Joan Westenholz and Aage Westenholz, "Help for Rejected Suitors: The Old Akkadian Love Incantation MAD V 8," *Or* 46 (1977): 198–213. The motif of "going to the garden" may also be present in other Mesopotamian lyrics, but their fragmentary nature or uncertain context prevents a conclusion. Inanna's repeated request (DI R) to go to the garden to meet her lover suggests a physical location, but the following lines are fragmentary (Sefati, *Love Songs*, 238–40). Likewise, when Shulgi invited "his fair sister" to his garden, apparently to enliven his barren lands, the literal referent seems clear enough. Yet, since sexual relations between the god-king and goddess were thought to bring agricultural fertility, a dual referent for the garden imagery is possible. Again, the fragmentary nature of the text prevents certainty. See Samuel N. Kramer, "Inanna and Šulgi: A Sumerian Fertility Song," *Iraq* 31 (1969): 18–23. KAR 158 contains a similar incipit, "she seeks your ripe garden of pleasures" (vii:26; see also lines 28, 35), but the lack of context prevents distinguishing a precise referent (Wasserman, *Akkadian Love Literature*, 220).

124. While the description of those who obtain this magic aromatic also uses garden imagery, two beautiful "blossoming maidens went down to the garden, went down to the garden," the fragmentary context prevents a precise understanding.

125. Thorkild Jacobsen favors a euphemism, equating Sîn's garden to the crescent-shaped pubic triangle ("Two Bal-Bal-e Dialogues," in Marks and Good, *Love and Death in the Ancient Near East*, 63).

126. Paul also recognizes that the phrase "to go down to the garden" functions as a metaphor for the place and act of lovemaking, but he does not recognize its use as a

This common theme may also be implicit in the literature from Ugarit. In both the Nikkal Hymn (*KTU* 1.24 1–15) and the Tale of Aqhat (*KTU* 1.17 ii.24–47), the Kothirāt, daughters of Hilal, are connected to conception and fertility. In the former, this group is described as "ones who go down among the nut trees" (40–45). Such horticultural imagery may describe a physical place, but the consistent connection of these characters to fecundity implies a further sexual referent. After Yariḫ's earlier promise, "I will make her fields into vineyards and her field of love into orchards" (22–23), perhaps the invocation of the Kothirāt is Yariḫ's attempt to enhance Nikkal's fertility, thus ensuring abundant progeny.

4.4.2. Meaning in the Song

In light of other agricultural, sexual metaphors in the Hebrew Bible (Prov 5:15–19; Sir 6:19), it is not surprising that garden-vineyard imagery is thus employed in the Song's amorous lyrics. The poet uses horticultural images for the physical place where lovers meet as well as a metaphorical symbol of the beloved's body, at times blurring the two spheres together.

In 1:6, the poet employs the term *vineyard* as a physical place *and* a metaphorical symbol, preparing the reader for the dual nature of such imagery. Lamenting that her brothers forced her to work outdoors, resulting in dark skin, the final line, "My own vineyard I have not kept," is best related to the maiden's inability to care for her appearance, not a loss of virginity.[127] Connected to 1:6 by the repeating phrase "my own vineyard" (כרמי שלי), 8:12 is also best understood as a metaphor for the beloved's body, whose exclusive ownership is contrasted with vineyards leased out by King Solomon. Vineyard may also be a figure for the lovers' bodies in 2:15, but the meaning of this verse is much debated.[128] In 4:12–5:1, the

---

literary device that blurs the literal and metaphoric distinction between the place and person of love (Paul, "Lover's Garden," 104).

127. Some scholars suggest that the vineyard is a euphemism for the female pudenda, suggesting she had not "kept" her virginity. Keel argues that the maiden was forced to care for the vineyards as punishment for her promiscuity (Keel, *Song of Songs*, 49–50). Yet would brothers punish their immoral sister by sending her to a place where lovers meet? Also, since this foists upon the woman a genital focus foreign to the Song, it is better to understand the vineyard as a general reference to her body.

128. Nearly every aspect of this verse is debated. Often taken as a warning against threats to their relationship or a playful request to catch a suitor, these options are out of place in this context. Since the preceding lyrics record the lover's request for

only extended metaphor in the Song, the lover compares his lady to a garden, stressing her exclusivity and exotic pleasures.[129]

Conversely, 7:13 appears to refer primarily to a physical place. The maiden invites her man to a tryst in the fields and vineyards, concluding with a promise, "There I will give you my love." Yet, the abrupt shift from countryside to doorway (7:12–14) and her allusion to the same "love fruits" found in her garden (4:13, 16) may signal a metaphoric undertone. Also, the beloved's epithet "one who dwells in gardens" in 8:13, suggests a physical locale, to which she invites her lover to indulge his passions.[130]

In contrast to these clear figures for the person and place of love, the precise referent of the garden imagery in 6:2 and 6:11 is more problematic. Following the woman's unsuccessful search for her lover (5:2–8) and the daughters' question regarding his location (6:1), 6:2 initially appears to describe a physical place. Yet, the presence of terms used metaphorically elsewhere (2:1, 16; 5:13) suggests that this garden may be a figure for the woman. Also, parallels between 6:11–12 and 7:12–14, especially if Tur-Sinai's emendation is accepted, suggest that 6:11 may also refer to the place of love, though a secondary metaphoric meaning is again possible.[131]

Yet, the lover's sudden shift from lost to found in 5:2–6:3 as well as the ambiguous imagery in 6:2, 11 is perplexing. Perhaps the poet intentionally blurs the line between the physical and figurative "garden of love." Seemingly with these passages in mind, Joan Westenholz and Aage Westenholz opine, "It is difficult to read the Song of Songs without sensing the distinction between the metaphorical and literal meanings of words vanish like smoke—the scents and colors of the land and its fruits and trees blend

---

his beloved to join him for a romp in nature (2:10–14) and the subsequent lines portray the passionate pair together (2:16–17), 2:15 should be read in a similar vein. The lovers' request demonstrates their desire to indulge their sexual passions in the place of love (vineyard) undisturbed by people or pressures (foxes). The concluding mention of the vineyards in blossom may also imply the lovers' physical readiness for love.

129. Although some seek to connect parts of the garden with parts of the maiden's body, this metaphor functions in general not specific terms.

130. Every invitation to come away to a distant place (2:10, 17; 7:11–12; 8:14) functions also as an invitation to erotic exploration. See Erik Gray, *The Art of Love Poetry* (Oxford: Oxford University Press, 2018), 55.

131. Tur-Sinai suggested a redivision (6:12): שם תני מרך בת עמי־נדיב "There give to me your myrrh, O daughter of my princely people." See Natali H. Tur-Sinai, "Song of Songs," in *The Language and the Book* (Jerusalem: Bialik, 1951), 2:386.

with the description of the beloved's charms into an indissoluble whole."[132] Regarding the Song, Robert Alter similarly states:

> Poetic language and its most characteristic procedure, figuration, are manipulated as pleasurable substance: metaphor transforms the body into spices and perfumes, wine and luscious fruit, all of which figurative images blur into the actual setting in which the lovers enact their love, a natural setting replete with just those delectable things.[133]

Yet, the question remains as to why the garden is a near universal symbol and what attributes connect the literal and figurative garden of love? There are three main attributes shared between the physical garden and its metaphoric referent, the beloved's body, which shed light on the widespread attestation of this image. First, gardens are a place of secluded privacy. Surrounded by walls to prevent despoliation, gardens and vineyards were private places, away from ordinary life and the prying eyes of others (see Sus 19–21).[134] The Song's garden of love is portrayed as a private place, in space and ownership. This seclusion is shown by the garden's connection to the undisturbed love motif, the desire of lovers for time alone to indulge their passions (7:12–14; 8:14; see also 2:7; 3:5; 8:4). Similarly, the beloved's body is also characterized as a private place, exclusively controlled (4:12; 8:12) and requiring an invitation for entrance (4:16; 8:8–10, 13–14; see also Song Rab. 5:1).

Second, the garden is a symbol of spring-like prosperity. The Song's amorous lyrics compare a girl's readiness for love to a flourishing garden at the coming of spring. Spring represents the rebirth of nature and renewal of love. In Song 2:10–15, when the man invites his beloved to a tryst in

---

132. Westenholz and Westenholz, "Help for Rejected Suitors," 217.
133. Robert Alter, *The Art of Biblical Poetry* (New York: Basic Books, 2011), 254.
134. Kathryn L. Gleason, "Gardens in Preclassical Times," *OEANE* 2:383. Munro separates the function of the two horticultural images, labeling the garden a paradise of pleasure while the vineyard only concerns socioeconomic ownership (Munro, *Spikenard and Saffron*, 98–99). Yet, there does not appear to have been a strict division between a well-watered, protected plot for fruits and flora and a well-watered, protected plot for grape vines. Egyptian *k3mw* can designate a garden or vineyard (*WÄS*, "k3mw," 5:106; *GHb*, "k3mw," 947). A close connection is also implied by the Song's mixed metaphors, which depict vines in the midst of a garden (4:12–5:1; 6:11). The garden and vineyard are portrayed as private places of pleasure (6:11; 7:12–14; 8:13–14), whose fruit is connected to love's intoxicating effect (4:10; 5:1; 6:11; 7:13; 8:2).

nature, likening the budding of love to the budding of spring, they respond together, desiring to indulge their growing passion amid the garden blooms. In 6:11–12 and 7:12–14, springtime garden imagery depicts the place lovers meet, but the sexual undertone must not be missed.

Finally, gardens are filled with innumerable sensual pleasures. In the Song, the beauty of the setting is merely an extension of the beloved's beauty, and the sensory pleasures of the place mirror the pleasure the couple finds in their mutual love. Both the place and person of love contain beautiful sights, wonderful aromas, and intoxicating tastes (4:12–5:1). Regardless of time or place, any lover can identify with this imagery depicting the desire for privacy to enjoy the plentiful pleasures of love.

Therefore, Trible's theory that Gen 2–3 is the hermeneutical key to interpreting the Song's garden imagery is myopic. These passages depict similar sensual pleasures, but the Song does not raise creation-related questions nor seek to restore what was lost.[135] Also, there is no complex pattern or unique cultural element connecting the two texts. While Landy rightly notes that "understanding a text is always a work of comparison … with other texts in the same literary tradition and beyond," even opining that the Song "transcends simple categories," he overlooks the universal nature of the book's garden imagery.[136]

4.5. The Woman's Intoxicating Fruits (7:3a, 8–10; 8:2)

שררך אגן הסהר	7:3 Your navel[137] is a round crater—
אל־יחסר המזג	may it never lack mixed wine.
זאת קומתך דמתה לתמר	7:8 Your stature resembles a palm tree,
ושדיך לאשכלות:	and your breasts are like [its] clusters.[138]

---

135. Pablo R. Andiñach, "Clandestine Relationship: An Approach to the Song of Songs," in *Foster Biblical Scholarship: Essays in Honor of Kent Harold Richards*, ed. Frank Ames and Charles Miller (Atlanta: Society of Biblical Literature, 2010), 297. Any argument based on the shared term תשוקה (Gen 3:16; 4:7; Song 7:11) is speculative in light of its infrequent occurrence and highly debated meaning.

136. Landy, "Song of Songs and the Garden of Eden," 513–14.

137. Some contend that שר refers to the vulva, based on etymology (Arb. *sirr* "pudenda"), position (thigh-belly), and description (Pope, *Song of Songs*, 618). While שר describes the unbiblical cord in Ezek 16:4 (see also Prov 3:8), and the *waṣf* order is not always exact (7:4–5), an erotic double entendre is not impossible.

138. Although the word אשכול "cluster" often refers to grapes (Gen 40:10; Num

אמרתי אעלה בתמר	⁷:⁹ I long to climb the palm tree,
אחזה בסנסניו	[and] lay hold of its fruit clusters.¹³⁹
ויהיו שדיך כאשכלות הגפן	May your breasts be like clusters of the vine,
וריח אפך כתפוחים:	the scent of your breath like apples,
וחכך כיין הטוב	⁷:¹⁰ And your mouth like the best wine,
הולך לדודי למישרים	flowing smoothly for lovers,¹⁴⁰
דובב שפתי ישנים:	gliding¹⁴¹ over scarlet lips.¹⁴²
אנהגך אביאך	⁸:² I would lead you, bring you
אל־בית אמי תלמדני	to my mother's house, she who taught me,
אשקך מיין הרקח	I would give you spiced wine to drink,
מעסיס רמני:	the juice of my pomegranate.

Source: Palm Tree/Clusters, Grapes, Apples, Wine, Pomegranate Juice
Target: Woman's Body, Breasts, Mouth, Navel
Mapping: Height, Size, Sensual Intoxication

Of all the book's amorous lyrics, these metaphors are unmistakably erotic. On Song 7:8–10, Keel aptly concludes, "What the classic descriptive songs

---

13:23–24; Song 7:9), this term likely refers to dates, following the reference to the palm tree (7:8).

139. The term סנסנה, a *hapax legomenon* in the Hebrew Bible, is best related to the Akkadian *sissinnu*, a spadix or stalk to which dates are connected. See *CAD*, "sissinnu," 15:325–28; Immanuel Löw, *Aramäische Pflanzennamen* (Leipzig: Engelmann, 1881), 119. Positing that Hebrew *palpal* nouns share a common semantic characteristic, often referring to a round object occurring in multiples, Viezel contends that סנסנה in Song 7:9 describes a fruit-laden cluster of dates. Eran Viezel, "סַנְסִנָּיו (*sansinnāyw*; Song of Songs 7:9) and the *Palpal* Noun Pattern," *JBL* 133 (2014): 751–56. The target of the metaphor is unclear, but the surrounding context favors her breasts.

140. Since דודי designates the male (Song 1:13–14, 16; 2:3, 8–10, 16–17; 4:16; 5:2, 4–6, 8, 10, 16; 6:2–3; 7:11–14; 8:14), some posit an unmarked change of speaker in 7:10b. Yet in light of the continuous metaphor, דודי is better explained as an apocopated plural (Gordis, *Song of Songs*, 95; Exum, *Song of Songs*, 239).

141. In light of the participle הולך in the preceding line, the *hapax* דובב is best related to Aram. דוב "to flow," possibly reflecting a northern dialect in the Song (Noegel and Rendsburg, *Solomon's Vineyard*, 14).

142. Rather than the nonsensical phrase "lips of sleepers," the Greek and Syriac manuscripts read שפתי ושנים "lips and teeth," explained by a *yod-waw* confusion. The proposed reading שפתי שנים "scarlet lips" assumes simple dittography instead. See Keith Schoville, "The Impact of the Ras Shamra Texts on the Study of the Song of Songs" (PhD diss., University of Wisconsin-Madison, 1969), 99.

(4:6; 5:16; 7:2b, 5c [3b, 6c]) only suggest becomes the main point here."[143] In a fitting addendum to his third *waṣf* song, praising the beauty of his beloved from foot to head (7:2–7), the man depicts her as a palm tree with pendulous fruits, declaring his intent to climb the tree and consume her culinary delights (7:8–10). Likewise, in the other two images, the man likens her navel to a goblet, wishing it was ever full of wine (7:3), while the maiden compares her own breasts to pomegranates, longing for a private rendezvous with her lover to share her intoxicating pleasures (8:1–2). While much of its meaning is clearly stated, the extent and significance of this imagery requires investigation. Why does the man employ *these* culinary images? Are such vegetal metaphors found in other love lyrics, or are there aspects of this imagery unique to the Song?

4.5.1. Comparative Evidence

Date palm imagery is also found in Mesopotamian literature, though its meaning is debated. While Jacobsen connects Sumer's two iconic lovers to the date, Inanna "queen of date clusters" and Amaushumgalana (Dumuzi) "the great source of the date clusters," positing that their sacred marriage brought together two gods from the sphere of date growing in a fertility rite, other etymologies have been suggested for these names.[144] Simo Parpola proposed that the iconography of a stylized date palm, often flanking Ishtar, symbolized the queen of heaven as a bridge linking heaven and earth.[145] However, other scholars have proposed differing ideas on the identity and meaning of the sacred tree.[146] Finally, Ishtar is often compared to a date palm in Assyrian poetry. The love lyrics of Marduk and Zarpanitu praise the goddess as "a palm of carnelian," and Assurbanipal's

---

143. Keel, *Song of Songs*, 239.

144. Jacobsen, *Treasures of Darkness*, 17, 26; Adam Falkenstein, "Tammuz," *Compte rendu de la troisième Rencontre Assyriologique Internationale: organisée à Leiden du 28 juin au 4 juillet 1952 par le Nederlandsch Instituut voor het Nabije Oosten*, CRRAI 3 (Leiden: Nederlands Instituut voor het Nabije Oosten, 1954): 61–62; Carsten Wilcke, "Inanna/Ishtar," *RlA* 5:74–75.

145. Simo Parpola, *Assyrian Prophecies*, SAA 9 (Helsinki: Helsinki University Press, 1997), xxxiv. See also Alasdair Livingstone, *Court Poetry and Literary Miscellanea*, SAAS 3 (Helsinki: Helsinki University Press, 1989), 19.

146. Wilfred G. Lambert, "The Background of the Neo-Assyrian Sacred Tree," in Parpola and Whiting, *Sex and Gender*, 326.

Hymn to Ishtar addresses Ishtar as "palm tree, daughter of Nineveh, stag of the lands."[147] These images may underscore her beauty or glory, yet their precise meaning in these contexts is uncertain.

In contrast to these debated texts, the date palm and its fruit are clearly connected to love. In one of the Inanna-Dumuzi love songs (DI F[1]), dates are mentioned alongside apple trees as a background to the couple's rendezvous in the garden.[148] Ishtar is also described as "she who envelopes him (her lover) like a spadix with dates" (*TCL* 15 48 16.44; *CAD*, "sissinnu," 15:325–28). Similarly, in an Old Babylonian love song, the beloved's description of her own physical allures, concluding with an "open" invitation to her lover, mentions a bracelet with date spadix charms.[149] Mesopotamian lyrics also highlight the date palm's delightful smell and sweet fruit. Ludingira labels his mother "a sweet date from Dilmun" and "a palm tree, with a very sweet smell."[150]

While the palm tree metaphor is present in Mesopotamia, literary parallels from preserved Indian and Arabic love literature are closer to the imagery of the Hebrew Song. In the ancient Indian epic *Ramayana*, the beautiful Sita is praised, "Your delightful breasts, how round they are, so firm and gently heaving; how full and lovely, smooth as two palm fruits, with their nipples standing stiff."[151] One Tamil love lyric, spoken by a man's wife, similarly likens his mistress to a tall black palm, full of fruit.[152] The Kamasutra, an Indian treatise on sex from the early centuries CE, plays on the tree image, with the woman "climbing" and embracing her lover to prepare for lovemaking.[153] In Jayadeva's *Gīta Govinda*, a twelfth-century poem devoted to the love of Krishna for Rādhā, her girlfriend questions

---

147. Lambert, "Problem of Love Lyrics," 123; Livingstone, *Court Poetry*, 18.
148. Sefati, *Love Songs*, 321.
149. Westenholz, "Forgotten Love Song," 423.
150. Miguel Civil, "The 'Message of Lu-Dingir-Ra to His Mother' and a Group of Akkado-Hittite 'Proverbs,'" *JNES* 23 (1964): 5:39.
151. Vālmīki, *Rāmāyaṇa*, trans. Sheldon Pollock (Princeton: Princeton University Press, 1988), 3:180 (44:18–19). Many scholars speculated that kernels of the work were written earlier, but recent studies suggest it dates to the early centuries BCE.
152. Ramanujan, *Interior Landscape*, 88 (Kuṟ 293).
153. Vatsyayana, *The Complete Kama Sutra*, trans. Alain Danielou (Rochester, VT: Park Street, 1994), 109. Hunt believes both texts so tastefully deal with eros, that he labels Song of Songs as "the Hebrew *Kamasutra*" (Hunt, *Song of Songs*, vii).

why Rādhā withholds herself from her lover, "Your swollen breasts are riper than palm fruit. Why do you waste their rich flavor?"[154]

Arabic love lyrics from the centuries preceding Islam similarly describe the female lover as a palm tree, with her hair likened to its panicles and her legs to its trunk.[155] Later, in the Tale of Haddār, on the thirtieth of the Arabian Nights (tenth century CE), as the man prepared to chase and catch his beloved, "the girl threw off her chemise and drawers, appearing like a young palm tree which moves a little under the west wind."[156] Stephan's modern Palestinian poems also contain similar portraits. The lady's body is likened to a palm tree in the wind, with her legs as its stem.[157] In the closest parallel to Song 7:8a, one lover calls his beloved, "O you whose height is that of a palm tree in a serail."[158]

Based on such evidence, Pope labels the comparison of a tall, slender lady to a palm tree as "classic."[159] Wilhelm Rudolph similarly characterizes this image as "common in Near Eastern love poetry."[160] Likewise, Hunt concludes that "the palm tree as a symbol of fertility and beauty is well-attested in Mesopotamia, Egypt, and the Classical world."[161] However, the broad extent of this imagery must be questioned.

While there is no consensus on when the cultivation of the date palm (*bnr*) reached Egypt, evidence exists beginning in the Middle Kingdom (*ÄWb*, "bnr," 2:817).[162] Thus, the absence of the palm tree in the New Kingdom love lyrics is curious. The presence of other floral metaphors (persea and sycamore-fig) only highlights this omission. Keel presents iconogra-

---

154. Barbara Stoler Miller, ed., *Love Song of the Dark Lord* (New York: Columbia University Press, 1977), 109.

155. Jinbachian, "Arabian Odes," 137.

156. Mathers, *Book of the Thousand Nights*, 1:241.

157. Stephan, "Modern Palestinian Parallels," 257, 263. In medieval and modern Arab lyrics, the beloved's breasts are also compared to pomegranates. See Dalman, *Palästinischer Diwan*, 101; Enno Littman, *Neuarabische Volkspoesie* (Berlin: Weidmann, 1902), 124; Mathers, *Book of the Thousand Nights*, 1:51, 354; Stephan, "Modern Palestinian Parallels," 214, 237, 244, 274.

158. Stephan, "Modern Palestinian Parallels," 275.

159. Pope, *Song of Songs*, 633.

160. Wilhelm Rudolph, *Des Buch Ruth, das Hohe Lied, die Klagelieder*, KAT 17 (Gütersloh: Mohn, 1962), 175, my translation.

161. Hunt, *Song of Songs*, 133.

162. Renate Germer, *Flora des pharaonischen ägytpen*, DAIK 14 (Mainz: von Zabern, 1985), 233.

phy depicting a female alongside or in the form of a date palm, positing a theomorphism, but the meaning of these reliefs is debated. Even Keel implicitly acknowledges the foreign nature of this image, suggesting that its origin came "perhaps under Asiatic influence."[163]

In the classical world, scholars appeal to Homer's *Odyssey*, where a shipwrecked Odysseus likens his awe at the sight of Nausicaa, daughter of the king of Phaeacia, with his amazement before the palm tree by the altar of Apollo at Delos (6.162–163). Yet, Theophrastus reveals that the date palm was not indigenous to the northern Mediterranean (*Hist. plant.* 3.3.5), and Xenophon and Pliny, aware of this tree and its use in wine and medicine, link its presence to travel in Arabia (*Anab.* 1.5.10; *Nat.* 6.32). Thus, some question Homer's botanical identification, while others suggest that the palm tree at Delos was a literary symbol of rest. Just as Leto, mother to Apollo and Artemis, found rest and regeneration on this island, giving birth to her children beneath the palm tree, so Odysseus hoped Nausicaa would be a similar avenue of rest.[164] Regardless, this lone, enigmatic example should not be used to support the presence of the palm tree metaphor in classical literature.

In sum, the presence or absence of the palm tree image is best explained as a blend of cultivation and culture. First, the presence of date palm imagery in Hebrew, Mesopotamian, Indian, and Arabic love lyrics as well as its absence from Hellenistic, Ugaritic, and later European and Western poetry can be partially attributed to climate and cultivation. Since date palms require a warm, dry climate, with high temperatures and low air humidity, their cultivation is centered in the deserts south of the Mediterranean Sea and on the southern fringes of the Near East.[165] Therefore, most cultures where the date palm was grown shared this common metaphor for the female body. On the other hand, the absence of this image in Egypt's love lyrics, with their suitable climate and references to dates elsewhere in their literature, suggests that the likeness of the female figure to a palm tree also involves an element of cultural perception. Even in the above comparative evidence, each culture added unique features to this

---

163. Keel, *Song of Songs*, 243–49.

164. Frederick Ahl and Hannah Roisman, *The Odyssey Re-formed* (New York: Cornell University, 1996), 54; Alfred Heubeck, Stephanie West, and J. B. Hainsworth, *A Commentary on Homer's Odyssey* (Oxford: Clarendon, 1998), 1:304.

165. Zohary and Hopf, *Domestication of Plants in the Old World*, 165.

shared symbol, highlighting its sweet smell, smooth feel, or visual likeness to a palm tree blowing in the wind.

However, while many of the specific body images in Song 7:3, 9b–10, 8:2 are unique, the conceptual metaphor LOVE AS INTOXICATION is not. In Egypt's amorous lyrics, the couple's lovemaking often takes place amid and is compared to the inebriating effects of beer and wine. In the Turin Love Song, a tree invites two lovers to enjoy intoxicating drinks and intimate pleasures beneath the privacy of its shade.[166] Another lyric encourages the lover, "Supply her with song and dance, and wine and ale ... that you may intoxicate [tḫtḫ] her senses and complete her in the night."[167] In Papyrus Harris, the girl likens her suitor's love to the effects of a strong drug, and she begs him for more pleasures, "My heart is not yet done with your lovemaking, my (little) wolf cub! Your liquor is your lovemaking."[168] Intoxicated with her love, the boy needs nothing else, "I'll kiss her, her lips are parted—I am happy without beer. How the void has been filled!"[169] To him, her breasts are aphrodisiacs, and even her scent stimulates his senses, "[Breeze] brings you her fragrance: an inundating aroma that intoxicates [tḫw] those who are present."[170]

Mesopotamian literature also connects love and lovemaking to images of intoxication. Inanna welcomes her beloved groom into their bridal chamber with a cup of wine.[171] In one Sumerian song (DI B), Dumuzi calls Inanna, "my sappy vine," likening her sexual attractiveness to beer and liquor, concluding with an invitation to love.[172] Likewise, Shusin's beloved concubine labels herself a wine-maid, comparing her sexual pleasures to the sweet intoxication of beer: "Like her beer her vulva is sweet, how sweet is her beer! Like her mouth her vulva is sweet, how sweet is her beer!"[173] Finally, remedies found in Mesopotamian potency incantations are often topical, but those with oral concoctions include wine or beer as the carrier: "If a man's potency comes to an end in the month of Nisannu, you catch a male partridge, you pluck its wings, strangle it, flatten it, scatter salt (on

---

166. Fox, *Song of Songs*, 46–47.
167. Fox, *Song of Songs*, 69.
168. Fox, *Song of Songs*, 8–10.
169. Fox, *Song of Songs*, 33.
170. Fox, *Song of Songs*, 71.
171. Jacobsen, *Harps*, 18.
172. Sefati, "Oath of Chastity," 52.
173. Sefati, *Love Songs*, 346; Jacobsen, *Harps*, 96.

it), dry (it); you pound (it) up together with a mountain *dadānu*-plant, you give (it) to him to drink in a beer and then that man will get potency."[174]

Though not as frequent as one might expect from a culture that enthroned Dionysus/Bacchus as god of the grape harvest, wine, and winemaking, the motif of intoxicating love is still evident in Hellenistic poetry.[175] Anacreon, one of the earliest Greek poets (sixth century BCE) employs this motif to describe the extreme effects of love, "I climb up and dive from the Leucadian Cliff into the grey wave, drunk with love" (frag. 376 [Campbell]).[176] Similar to the Song's imagery (7:9b), Paulus Silentarius (sixth century CE) employs this motif to express his partiality for an older lover, "I prefer your wine to the juice of her youth. Your breasts, like heavy ripe clusters, are what I long to cup in my hands" (*Anth. Pal.* 5.258 [Paton]). Macedonius the Consul (sixth century CE) similarly likens his beloved to a vine, depicting their sex as "the vintage of love" (*Anth. Pal.* 5.227 [Paton]). Finally, the underlying parallel between love and wine is highlighted by words attributed to Antiphanes (fifth century BCE), "One may hide all else ... but not these two things—that he is drinking wine, and that he has fallen in love. Both of these betray him through his eyes and through his words" (Athenaeus, *Deipn.* 2.38c [Olson]).

Furthermore, a few examples are found in Indian and Arab culture. Despite concluding that the metaphoric depiction of sex as eating is uncommon in Tamil lyrics, Mariaselvam does note one poem in which the beloved is compared to a toddy pot and her sexuality to toddy (Naṟ. 295).[177] In Jayadeva's *Gīta Govinda*, Krishna likens his lady's mouth to a lotus filled with fermented honey, while Rādhā, in the midst of lovemaking, depicts her man as "madly drunk on love."[178] Paramānand (sixteenth century CE) similarly draws on the motif of love as intoxication, describing Krishna as "drunk like a bee" on the nectar of Rādhā's flower garden.[179] This imagery is also evident in medieval and modern Arab lyrics. Arberry, in his primer

---

174. Biggs, *ŠÀ.ZI.GA*, 56 (KUB 4 48 i.1–7).

175. See also Hagedorn, "Of Foxes and Vineyards," 349–51.

176. This likely alludes to the tradition that Sappho killed herself for love of Phaon by jumping from the Leucadian Cliffs (Ovid, *Her.* 15.171–172).

177. Mariaselvam, *Ancient Tamil Love Poems*, 225.

178. Jayadeva, *Gīta Govinda: Love Songs of Rādhā and Kṛṣṇa*, trans. Lee Siegel (New York: New York University Press, 2009), 6.4, 12.10, 21.6.

179. A. Whitney Sanford, *Singing Krishna: Sound Becomes Sight in Paramānand's Poetry* (Albany: State University of New York Press, 2008), 96.

on Arabic poetry, lists examples of the intoxication motif in the writings of Ibn al-Khaiyāṭ and Ibn al-Fāriḍ (eleventh–thirteenth century CE).[180] Similarly in *Arabian Nights*, one lover is portrayed as "drunken with love," while another describes his lady's body as "a sweet wine for my mouth."[181] Finally, Stephan notes an example from the bedouins, "Let us be drunk in the garden of [your] caressing."[182]

In addition, this motif continues in modern European and Western love lyrics. John Gower, a contemporary of Chaucer in fifteenth-century England, confessed in his *Confessio Amantis*, "I am drunk with love, and often I know not what I do.... When I am absent from my lady I am drunk with the thoughts of her, and when I am present, with looking upon her."[183] Likewise, in Shakespeare's *Two Noble Kinsmen*, the jailer's daughter, having become obsessed with a man far above her social status, was intoxicated with love, lacking sleep, eating nothing, and dreaming of a better world (4.3 1–8). Finally, in the nineteenth century, John Keats likens his lady's lips to sweet roses "steep'd in dew rich to intoxication."[184] But how does this comparative evidence align with the Song's metaphors?

4.5.2. Meaning in the Song

The array of verses with this metaphor is best divided into two categories, form and function. The poet opens with a visual comparison of the woman to a palm tree (7:8–9a), before shifting to her stimulating effect on her lover (7:3, 9b–10; 8:2).[185] The pictorial nature of this image is highlighted by its stated focus on the woman's stature (קומתך). As Moldenke notes, the date palm (*Phoenix dactylifera*), with its branchless tapering stem of eighty feet in height, would have stood out among other trees in Palestine.[186] Though the date palm (תמר) is a symbol of fertility (Exod

---

180. Arthur John Arberry, *Arabic Poetry: A Primer for Students* (New York: Cambridge University Press, 1965), 20, 116.
181. Mathers, *Book of the Thousand Nights*, 1:198, 615.
182. Stephan, "Modern Palestinian Parallels," 215.
183. George C. MacAulay, ed., *The English Works of John Gower* (London: Oxford University Press, 1900), 1:lxxvi.
184. Cook, *John Keats*, 15.
185. "Only when the poet has finished the visually oriented description and turns to his subjective experience does he leave the palm comparison and selects objects that seem better suited to clarify his sensations" (Gerleman, *Hohelied*, 202, my translation).
186. Moldenke and Moldenke, *Plants of the Bible*, 170.

15:27; Joel 1:12) and feasting (Lev 23:40), both biblical and extrabiblical Jewish literature employ this tree as a symbol of size (Ps 92:13, Sir 24:13–14).[187]

The male lover not only highlights the date palm's tall height but also its fruit clusters. Although some suggest that אשכלות "clusters" are grapes, their connection to the palm tree (7:8–9a) favors an implied reference to dates. Serving as an important food source, the date palm produces large hanging clusters, weighing thirty to fifty pounds.[188] Various ideas have been posited concerning the attribute(s) shared between this tree's fruit and the beloved's breasts: multiplicity, attraction, taste, shape, or size. Pope compared the physical shape of large date clusters to the polymastia of Artemis of Ephesus, but this idea seems to be based on an assumed cultic background rather than the text or context of the Song.[189]

Some suggest that both date clusters and the breasts of the woman are attractive and enticing, while others opine that the fruit's sweet taste is the basis of comparison.[190] However, the picture of the maiden's body as a tall, slender date palm suggests that this image also centers on form, likely the large size of her breasts. Describing her "abundant endowment with fruits," Keel comments, "Huge date clusters look particularly voluptuous on the tall, narrow trunks of palms."[191] Landy similarly states, "It is a comparison of height and slenderness combined with pendulous breasts, heavy with fruit."[192] The stress on size is also favored by the man's ear-

---

187. The name Tamar is often linked to beauty and sexuality (Gen 38; 2 Sam 13). Though secondary to the theme of intoxication, the link between height and female beauty is also found in Jewish, Mesopotamian, Greco-Roman, and European culture. In the Mishnah (m. Ned. 9:10), a hypothetical situation is imagined where a man vows not to marry an ugly woman (black/short) who turns out to be beautiful (white/tall). The antitheses link height and beauty. In recounting sacred marriage practice in Babylon, Herodotus claims that "fair and tall" ladies were chosen to fulfill their cultic obligation quickly, while ugly women waited years to do their duty (*Hist.* 1.199). In Homer's *Odyssey*, Athena enhanced Penelope's appearance, increasing her tall stature, white color, and regal appearance (*Od.* 18.195–196). Later, Shakespeare highlights this widely shared ideal, contrasting the beauty of Helena's tall height with Hermia's short stature (*A Midsummer Night's Dream* 3.2.297–303).

188. Moldenke and Moldenke, *Plants of the Bible*, 170.

189. Pope, *Song of Songs*, 634.

190. Bergant, *Song of Songs*, 89; Carr, *Song of Solomon*, 162; Hess, *Song of Songs*, 220; Hunt, *Song of Songs*, 96.

191. Keel, *Song of Songs*, 242.

192. Landy, *Paradoxes of Paradise*, 82.

lier portrayal of his beloved's breasts as "mountains of pleasure" (2:17; 4:6; 8:14), though the following verses (7:9b–10) hint at a secondary meaning.

With his intent to scale the palm tree and take hold of its fruit (7:9a), an obvious sexual euphemism, the man shifts the *sense* and significance of his imagery. Simon Lehrman jests that he now tells his beloved to what heights he will go to obtain her love.[193] After a visual focus on her tall height and large breasts, the lover wishes to experience his beloved, a veritable sensual overload—to "grasp" (אחז) her fruit clusters, smell her stimulating "scent" (ריח), and "taste" (שקה/חך/שפה) her intoxicating juices (7:9b–10; 8:2). As Dianne Bergant notes, "The woman's body is not desired by the man for its reproductive potential, but for the sensual satisfaction of lovemaking."[194] But why the culinary images of grapes, apples, and wine? Falk labels these verses "a free-flowing sequence of disconnected images."[195] Yet, are these images disconnected, or is there a unifying theme in the man's desire?

The presence of a unifying theme is supported both by the syntax and similes in 7:9–10. The opening verb-particle collocation יהיו־נא governs all three metaphors, with simple *waw*-conjunctions joining them together. Also, the parallel syntax and escalating senses suggest an integral relationship between the three wishes.[196]

In addition, the three culinary metaphors reiterate a conceptual metaphor found throughout the Song: LOVE AS INTOXICATION. With a variety of images, the poet repeatedly connects physical love to food and beverages thought to excite love. In fact, Hunt tallies thirty-eight examples of banqueting imagery, the majority of which are metaphors for sexual hunger.[197] Lovemaking is better than wine (1:2–4; 4:10), stimulated by raisin cakes, apples (2:5), and mandrakes (7:13), and pictured as entering a banquet house or garden to eat honey and drink wine (2:4; 5:1). The use of dates in winemaking suggests that this theme may also be implicit in the preceding image of the beloved as a palm tree (7:8).

---

193. Simon Lehrman, "Song of Songs," in *The Five Megilloth*, ed. Abraham Cohen (New York: Soncino, 1946), 27.

194. Bergant, *Song of Songs*, 89. See also Annette Schellenberg, "The Sensuality of Song of Songs: Another Criterion to Be Considered When Assessing (So-Called) Literal and Allegorical Interpretations of the Song," in Schellenberg and Schwienhorst-Schönberger *Interpreting the Song of Songs*, 113–18.

195. Falk, *Love Lyrics*, 128.

196. Hunt, *Song of Songs*, 314.

197. Hunt, *Song of Songs*, 179.

First, the lover wishes that his beloved's breasts were like clusters of the vine (7:9b). With this yearning, the lover shifts away from a visual focus on the date palm to an emphasis on tactile experience. As mentioned above, אשכול "clusters" frequently refers to grapes (Gen 40:10; Num 13:23–24; Deut 32:32; Isa 65:1; Mic 7:1). Moreover, in the Hebrew Bible, grapes are often connected to wine, winemaking, and intoxication (Gen 40:10–11; 49:11; Num 6:3; Deut 32:14; Amos 9:13; see also Sir 39:26). In fact, *HALOT* translates ענב as "wine-berry" (s.v. "ענב"). Similar to date clusters, scholars have suggested various attributes shared between the grape clusters and the women's breasts: size, touch, and taste.[198]

Each possibility could be supported from the context: the huge, hanging clusters of dates (7:8), the man's intent to take hold of the tree's fruit (7:9a), or the commonality of food consumption (7:8–10). Though eating obviously involves taste, the frequent association of grapes with wine, the Song's repeated banqueting imagery, and the reference to wine in the following verse (7:10) suggests that love's inebriating effect is the governing metaphor here.[199] Like the palm tree, the vine is a symbol of the beloved, whose fruit is the source of her lover's intoxication.[200]

Second, the man likens his beloved's breath to the fragrance of apples (7:9b). The term אף, normally meaning "nose," functions as a metonymy, substituting the organ for its function.[201] But why the תפוח? As shown in the earlier discussion of the man's delicious apple (2:3), the motif of apple as love fruit is attested in many cultures from antiquity to modern times. It was considered an aphrodisiac whose consumption would stir sexual excitement and enhance fertility. In fact, this motif is invoked twice by the

---

198. Size: Longman, *Song of Songs*, 198; Touch: Keil and Delitzsch, *Commentary on the Old Testament*, 6:593; Rudolph, *Hohe Lied*, 175; Taste: Carr, *Song of Solomon*, 162; Ginsburg, *Song of Songs*, 180. Positing both touch and taste as basis for the comparison, Walsh describes the maiden's breasts as "sweet, supple, ripening, what I desire to feel, to pluck" (Walsh, *Exquisite Desire*, 123).

199. Bergant, *Song of Songs*, 89; Exum, *Song of Songs*, 238; Hess, *Song of Songs*, 220; Keel, *Song of Songs*, 246.

200. Though Atkins agrees that the meaning of such imagery is found in the sense rather than the thing itself, he suggests richness and luxury as the basis of comparison (Atkins, *Sex in Literature*, 3:183).

201. While Mitchell Dahood connected אף to the Ugaritic *'appī dadi* "nipples of the breast" (*KTU* 1.23 24, 59, 61), the oddity of a nipple's scent as well as the contextual mention of the mouth favors a reference to her breath. See "Canticle 7,9 and UT 52,61: A Question of Method," *Bib* 57 (1976): 109–10.

Song's poet. The maiden asked for apples to refresh her energy in the midst of their lovemaking (2:4–6), and the apple tree is the place where the man was conceived and aroused to love (8:5). Also, the term ריח "scent" is used throughout the Song "to signify charms that excite love."[202] The woman praises her lover's fragrant cologne before asking to be brought to his bedroom chamber (1:3–4; see also 1:12). Likewise, after lauding the scent of her perfume and clothing, the man launches into a lyrical description of his beloved's garden and his enjoyment of its choice fruits (4:10–5:1; cf. 2:13; 7:14). Thus, despite the shift from taste to smell, the scent of apples continues the theme of intoxication.[203]

In the final three images, the man compares his lady's mouth to the finest wine (7:10) and her navel to a crater filled with mixed wine (7:3), while she likens her own breasts to pomegranates filled with spiced wine (8:2).[204] Despite the lack of clarity on their exact nuance, the terms יין הטוב "best/sweet wine," מזג "mixed wine," יין הרקח "spiced wine" and עסיס "pomegranate juice" share the idea of inebriation.[205] With חך "palate" as a metaphor for kisses, the man desires to drink deeply of his beloved's intoxicating pleasures (7:10). Likewise, the woman's wordplay in 8:1–2 (נשק/שקה) highlights her wish to make her lover drunk on her sensual delights. In 7:3, whether the intended meaning is navel or vulva (or both), the man similarly pictures her body as a source of intoxication.[206]

Thus, as evident from the above survey of biblical and extrabiblical literature, the metaphor of drunken love surpasses both time and geography. Such imagery is not specific to one culture or era. The desire to be raptured by romantic love is part and parcel of the human experience. In his work on metaphor and emotion, Zoltán Kövecses notes the primary nature of this metaphor, which he labels EMOTION IS RAPTURE.[207] However, each culture adds unique features to this near universal symbol, adopting and adapting it to fit their milieu. For example, in light of the

---

202. Robert and Tournay, *Cantique des Cantiques*, 273.

203. Exum, *Song of Songs*, 239; Keel, *Song of Songs*, 246–47.

204. "The reference to wine is reminiscent of the association between drink and lovemaking (1.2; 4.10) just as the spices which give it a special tang are reminiscent of the delights of her garden (4.14; 5.1)" (Munro, *Spikenard and Saffron*, 101).

205. Bergant, *Song of Songs*, 93; Exum, *Song of Songs*, 248; Keel, *Song of Songs*, 262.

206. James A. Loader, "Exegetical Erotica to Canticles 7.2–6," *JSem* 10 (2001): 105.

207. Zoltán Kövecses, *Metaphor and Emotion: Language, Culture, and Body in Human Feeling* (New York: Cambridge University Press, 2003), 74.

prevalence of cereals and relative scarcity of wine in Egypt and Mesopotamia, love lyrics from these cultures speak of inebriation by liquor and beer more than wine.[208] Similarly, the rarity of viticulture in India likely explains their metaphors involving fermented honey.[209] In the same way, the Hebrew poet transforms this universal metaphor into a unique word picture: the beloved is a grape vine, whose breasts, navel, and mouth drive the man into an intoxicated frenzy of sensual pleasure. The Song's imagery beautifully illustrates the sage's admonition in Proverbs that his son find joy in his wife, being "intoxicated" (שׁגה) in her sexual pleasures (5:19).

4.6. Summary

With a multitude of metaphors drawn from nature, the Song's poet describes both the form and function of the lovers' bodies. Playing on the BODY AS LANDSCAPE and LOVE AS INTOXICATION metaphors, the horticultural images picture the lady's body as a private place of pleasure (4:12–5:1), while the apple tree similarly depicts the man as a source of sexual delights (2:3). Moreover, using motifs of mountains, trees, and horses, the lover characterizes his beloved's body as isolated (2:17; 4:6; 8:14), intoxicating (7:8–10), and irresistible (1:9–10), yet the same figures also describe her tall height, large breasts, and jeweled adornment.

With these erotic euphemisms and double entendre, the Song's poet most often plays on shared tradition and near universal symbols. Dependency is possible with the Song's mare metaphor (1:9, Egypt) and the symbolism of the man as an apple tree (2:3, Mesopotamia).

In addition, these natural motifs also contribute to the continuing debate over the Song's literary unity. The recurrence of similar themes throughout the Song, such as the female body as a pleasure garden (1:6; 2:15; 4:12–13, 16–5:1; 6:2, 11; 7:13; 8:12–13) and love as intoxication (1:2–4; 2:4–5; 4:10–11; 5:1, 13; 6:2–3; 7:3, 8–10, 13; 8:1–2), provides a coherence

---

208. Marvin A. Powell, "Wine and the Vine in Ancient Mesopotamia: The Cuneiform Evidence," in *Origins and Ancient History of Wine*, ed. Patrick E. McGovern, Stuart J. Fleming, and Solomon H. Katz (Amsterdam: Gordon & Breach, 2000), 121; Leonard H. Lesko, "Egyptian Wine Production During the New Kingdom," in McGovern, *Origins and Ancient History of Wine*, 230.

209. Lallanji Gopal and V. C. Srivastava, eds., *History of Agriculture in India (up to c. 1200 AD)*, History of Science, Philosophy, and Culture in Indian Civilization 5.1 (New Delhi: Concept, 2008), 426.

not normally found in an anthology. Also, mention of the girl's brothers at the beginning (1:5–6) and end of the book (8:8–10) suggest an authorial aim to present a balanced, unified work. Now, having analyzed the Song's nature imagery, we turn to the three descriptive songs that more fully detail the beauty of the maiden's body (4:1–7, 6:4–7; 7:2–7).

5
Anatomy of a Rose: Praise for the Female Body

The Song's four *waṣfs* or "descriptive songs," three dedicated to the woman (4:1–7; 6:4–7; 7:2–7) and one to the man (5:10–16), also contain body imagery, but these poems are different in form and content than the metaphors in preceding chapters. First, the *waṣf*, a feature of Arabic poetry "characterized by the minute, thorough description of certain objects," is used to refer to poems recited in praise of the lovers' bodies.[1] The *waṣf* is a distinct literary form known from the ancient Near East, with examples in Mesopotamian sacred marriage rites, the love lyrics of New Kingdom Egypt, a hymn and epic from Ugarit, the poetry of Greece and Rome, and even the Dead Sea Scrolls.[2] This form is distinct in two ways: (1) sequence, from head-to-foot or vice-versa, and (2) list parallelism, in which a part of the body is identified, often in initial position, followed by the source to

---

1. Akiko Sumi, *Description in Classical Arabic Poetry: Waṣf, Ekphrasis, and Interarts Theory* (Leiden: Brill, 2004), 4. See also Herrmann, "Beschreibungsliedes," 176–96. Bernat suggests that four passages in the Hebrew Bible play on this genre. He applies the title "enemy-*waṣf*" to YHWH's description of Behemoth and Leviathan (Job 40–41) as well as the portrait of Goliath's armor (1 Sam 17), and he labels the portrait of the valiant wife (Prov 31:10–31) and the wicked woman (4Q184) as an "anti-*waṣf*" (Bernat, "Biblical *Waṣfs*," 328–32).

2. For examples from Mesopotamia, see Sefati, *Love Songs*, 249–50; Nissinen, "Nabû and Tašmetu," 589 (r.5–8); Livingstone, *Court Poetry*, §38 (r.9–17), §39 (1–18); Westenholz and Westenholz, "Help for Rejected Suitors," 215–16 (25–29). For Egyptian parallels, see Fox, *Song of Songs*, 269–71. From Ugarit, see Kirta's praise for Hurriya's beauty (*KTU* 1.14 iii.38–48) and Baal's enthronement (*KTU* 1.101.5–9). See also Andrew R. George, "The Gilgamesh Epic at Ugarit," *AuOr* 25 (2007): 242 (31–33). For similar lyrics in Greek literature, as well as a comparison of Sarai's portrait of beauty (1Q20 XX, 2–8) with Philodemus's praise of Flora (*Anth. Pal.* 5.132), see Cohen, "The Beauty of Flora and the Beauty of Sarai," 41–53. For Arabic examples, see Dalman, *Palästinischer Diwan*, 100–101; Saarisalo, "Songs of the Druzes," 40–51.

which it is compared, at times with expanded description.³ For example, the man opens his first hymn by praising his beloved's beauty, עֵינַיִךְ יוֹנִים מִבַּעַד לְצַמָּתֵךְ "Your eyes are doves behind your veil" (4:1).

In addition to its catalogue of body parts, the discrete nature of these poems is further highlighted by bracketed declarations of *beauty* (יפה). In the first song (4:1–7), the man begins with a double declaration, "Look at you, you are *beautiful*, my dear! Look at you, you are *beautiful*" (4:1a), and he closes with the summation, "All of you is *beautiful*, my dear" (4:7). He opens his second poem likening his beloved's *beauty* to two prominent cities (6:4) and closes with a comparison of her splendorous *beauty* to the heavenly luminaries (6:10). The final song commences with praise for the Shulamite's *beautiful*, sandaled feet (7:2) and finishes with the summary, "How *beautiful* you are and delightful, O love, with your delights" (7:7). The maiden similarly lauds her man's appearance as "outstanding among ten thousand" (5:10) and "choice as Lebanon's cedars" (5:15), concluding, "All of him is desirable" (5:16). We begin with what some consider the most beautiful and erotically charged part of the body, the eyes.

5.1. Messengers of Love (1:15; 4:1a; cf. 5:12)

הִנָּךְ יָפָה רַעְיָתִי	1:15 Look at you, you are beautiful, my dear!
הִנָּךְ יָפָה	Look at you, you are beautiful!
עֵינַיִךְ יוֹנִים	Your eyes are doves⁴
מִבַּעַד לְצַמָּתֵךְ	behind your veil.⁵
עֵינָיו כְּיוֹנִים	5:12 His eyes are like doves,
עַל־אֲפִיקֵי מָיִם	beside streams of water,
רֹחֲצוֹת בֶּחָלָב	bathed in milk,
יֹשְׁבוֹת עַל־מִלֵּאת׃	sitting by a brimming pool.⁶

---

3. Watson, *Classical Hebrew Poetry*, 353–56; Geller, *Early Biblical Poetry*, 35.

4. The Peshitta and Vulgate link this metaphor to the dove's eyes, but this is unlikely in light of the Song's other comparisons to animals in toto (4:1b–2, 5; 5:2).

5. Despite its limited occurrence (Isa 47:2; Song 4:1, 6:7), צמה likely refers to the veiling of one's face (*DJPA*, "צמצם," 466), as reflected in Symmachus (κάλυμμα).

6. Since the *piel* stem of מלא often describes mounting jewels (Exod 39:10; 1 Chr 29:2; Song 5:14), some suggest "fitly set" (NRSV). Yet, the parallel line (5:12b), as well as the versions (LXX, Vulgate) favor "pools" (see also *DJPA*, "מלי," 309). מלאת and אפיק play on עין "eye, spring," but these descriptions likely depict the doves, not the eyes. Tawil posits that "bathing in milk" refers to the whiteness of foaming waters. See Hayim Tawil, "Bathing in Milk (SoS 5:12): A New Look," *BM* 42 (1997): 390.

5. Anatomy of a Rose: Praise for the Female Body

Source: Doves
Target: Eyes
Mapping: Timidity, Distance, Messengers

Though the source and target in these verses are clearly stated, the *tertium comparationis* between the lovers' eyes and doves is anything but clear. A brief survey of scholarship reveals a new idea at nearly every turn: color, clarity, delicacy, radiance, shape, fidelity, timidity, movement, or some combination of these qualities. Since many of these proposed attributes are based on comparative evidence, each proposal will be examined together with its biblical and/or extrabiblical evidence.

The options listed above can be divided into two main categories: form and function. While some posit a physical similarity between the lovers' eyes and doves, others suggest that the basis for comparison lies in their common character or behavior. Certainly, the possibility of multivalence is acknowledged, but some ideas are more likely than others. First, a few scholars claim that the shared attribute in this metaphor is color. Krinetzki, based on the beloved's description "bathed in milk" (5:12), opines that both source and target are white in color, whereas G. Lloyd Carr suggests a deep, smoke-grey color.[7] Yet the rock dove (*Columba livia*), which best fits the biblical יונה (2:14; Jer 48:28), is blue-gray, while the eyes of most people in the Near East are dark.[8] For both lovers to share such a unique eye color is doubtful. Also, if a white variety of this bird was intended, in contrast to the black raven (5:11), why add "bathed in milk" (5:12)? Eye color seems unlikely as the primary meaning of this metaphor.

Moreover, other scholars contend that this metaphor was intended to convey the clarity or delicacy of the eyes. Dalman advocates the former, pointing to the lovers' *ungewöhnlich klare Augen*, while Fox and Exum adopt the latter, suggesting that the common denominator is their softness and gentleness.[9] While clarity is easily applied to the eyes, how does this quality translate to the dove? Soft and delicate may describe a bird's velvet touch or its tame behavior, but what exactly are soft eyes? In addition to its

---

7. Krinetzki, *Hohenlied*, 169; Carr, *Song of Solomon*, 86. See also Dobbs-Allsopp, "Delight of Beauty," 269.

8. Keel, *Song of Songs*, 69. See also Saarisalo, "Songs of the Druzes," 128.

9. Gustaf H. Dalman, *Arbeit und Sitte in Palästina* (Gütersloh: Bertelsmann, 1964), 264; Fox, *Song of Songs*, 106; Exum, *Song of Songs*, 112.

ambiguity, contrary evidence may also be found in one of the few evaluations of appearance in the Bible. Leah's inferiority to her sister's beauty is linked to her "soft [רך] eyes" (Gen 29:17).

Third, some scholars suggest that the intended meaning is the objects' brilliant radiance. Acknowledging the ambiguity of this image and scholars' divergent suggestions, Pope concludes that the most likely idea is a dove's glistening color.[10] While the rock dove is not strikingly brilliant, its iridescent neck could be the basis of comparison. A dove's neck is employed as a word picture to describe the iridescence of lapis lazuli in an Old Babylonian lexical list on stones (*zagingutukku*), while a semantically related term (*šitʾāru*) is used in praise of Ishtar's lustrous eyes.[11] This interpretation aligns well with the man's later description of the maiden's eyes. With one glimpse of her eye or one jewel of her necklace, the lover is captivated by her radiant glance (4:9; see also Prov 6:25). Yet the Song's imagery, in contrast to the above Akkadian example, does not specify the bird's neck as the source for the metaphor. Also, the occurrence of יונה elsewhere in the Song suggests a different significance.

Furthermore, many suggest that the beloved's eyes are likened to doves due to their similar shape. Yehuda Feliks, who has published widely on botany and zoology in the Hebrew Bible, paraphrases the metaphor, "The structure of your eyes is like the outline of a dove's body."[12] Based on Egyptian visual arts, Gillis Gerleman similarly suggests that the eye's contour has a strong resemblance to a bird's body.[13] Though Garrett labels this idea "garish and nonsensical," it is true to life and matches the visual focus in the context (הנה, 1:15; 4:1).[14] In fact, the subsequent metaphors depicting the woman's hair as a flock of goats (4:1c), and her teeth like freshly washed sheep (4:2) also describe their visual likeness with an animal metaphor. As parallels, Stephan and Aapeli Saarisalo point to praise for a lady's "almond-shaped eyes" among early twentieth-century

---

10. Pope, *Song of Songs*, 356. See also Ginsburg, *Song of Songs*, 169.

11. Benno Landsberger, ed., *The Series HAR-ra=ḫubullu: Tablets XVI, XVII, XIX and Related Texts*, MSL 10 (Rome: Pontifical Biblical Institute, 1970), 16 (59); François Thureau-Dangin, "Un hymne à Isztar de la haute époque babylonienne," *RA* 22 (1925): 170 (12).

12. Yehuda Feliks, *Song of Songs: Nature Epic and Allegory* (Jerusalem: Israel Society for Biblical Research, 1983), 51.

13. Gillis Gerleman, "Die Bildsprache des Hohenliedes und die Altägyptische Kunst," *ASTI* 1 (1962): 29.

14. Garrett and House, *Song of Songs/Lamentations*, 147.

Palestinian bedouin.[15] In the category of appearance, this idea is most likely, though the Song's recurrent dove imagery favors another primary meaning.

Shifting to the category of function, medieval Jewish sages contended that this enigmatic metaphor symbolizes fidelity or purity. For Rashi and Ibn Ezra (based on the Song of Songs Rabbah), the meaning of the beloved's likeness to a dove (1:15) is that after meeting her mate, she never leaves him to join with another.[16] Similar to the proposal of shape, such a natural insight on the dove's mating habits is true to reality. Yet how does this quality relate to eyes? Also, a focus on fidelity would be unique to the biblical portrait of a dove (see below) and out of place in the visual orientation of the context (1:15; 4:1–3; 5:10–12). This interpretation may have arisen from Jewish allegorical reading(s) of the Song (Ps 74:19).

In contrast to the above ideas, both biblical and extrabiblical evidence suggest that the attribute shared between the lovers' eyes and doves is a combination of timidity, distance, and movement. In the Hebrew Bible, the יוֹנָה "dove," an animal associated with sacrifice (Lev 1:14; Num 6:10) and mourning (Ezek 7:16; Nah 2:8), is often characterized as reticent, preferring to nest in the distant cliffs. Jeremiah applies this imagery to the people of Moab, encouraging them to seek shelter from judgment, like doves that dwell in the rocky ravines (48:28). The psalmist similarly desires to be a dove so that he might escape his present suffering and find rest and refuge in the wilderness (55:7). This theme is also found in the Song. When the lover calls his lady to a rendezvous in nature yet is stopped by the wall outside her home (2:8–17), he alludes to her distance and inaccessibility by picturing her as a timid dove, hiding in the rocky crags (2:14). In addition, this idea seems implicit when the man knocks on the door, calling to his dove, seeking to coax her to open to him (5:2).

Timidity and distance may also be implicit in the man's praise for the maiden's eyes (4:1). His desire to go to the mountain of myrrh (4:6), a

---

15. Saarisalo, "Songs of the Druzes," 128; Stephan, "Modern Palestinian Parallels," 207.

16. On the similarity of Rashi, Ibn Ezra, and Song of Songs Rabbah (as well as an anonymous medieval commentary) on this verse (1:15), see Sara Japhet and Barry Dov Walfish, *The Way of Lovers: The Oxford Anonymous Commentary on the Song of Songs* (Leiden: Brill, 2017), 9. The dove's monogamous nature was known earlier, as attested by Tertullian's (third century CE) commentary on Paul's instruction to virgins in the early Christian church (Tertullian, *Mon.* 8.70 [*ANF* 4:65]).

euphemism for her breasts, as well as his subsequent call for her to come to him from a distant locale (4:8), suggests separation, either literal or metaphorical. Therefore, the lover's portrait of his beloved's eyes as doves likely conveys her timidity or bashfulness about being with him.

If this implication is correct in the opening portrait (4:1b), the man's second song (6:4–7) may also play on the dove image. Since 4:1–3 and 6:4–7 mirror one another, with a declaration of beauty and identical praise for the lady's hair, teeth, and cheeks, one wonders if the reference to her eyes in 6:5a is related to its parallel in 4:1b. The lady's eyes, no longer timid doves (4:1), have transformed her lover into one who trembles (הרהיבני) like a frightened bird.[17] Additionally, distance may also be implicit in the lady's depiction of her beloved's eyes (5:12), as this portrait is intended to identify her "lost" lover (5:9).

Though the metaphor "eyes like doves" is unique to the Song, images of this timid bird appear elsewhere in ancient literature. In the Homeric *Hymn to Apollo*, Iris and Eileithyia are depicted as anxious doves, crossing to Delos to aid Leto in Apollo's birth (114). Elsewhere Homer compares Artemis's flight from Hera to a timid dove speeding toward a cavern of cliffs (*Il.* 21.493–495). Sennacherib, in recounting his victory over the Elamites, similarly likens this easily frightened bird to fleeing soldiers, "whose hearts were beating like a pursued young dove."[18] In the closest parallel from ancient Near Eastern love lyrics, an Akkadian songstress compares her beloved to a distant dove, whom she hopes to catch:

> I've sent my lover out of town, [to the steppe]
> So now my daddy's gone,
> I'll have to make do with my own "coo-coo"
> For my dove has flown away
> Some trapper must bring my stray lover home
> So you can make sweet cooing with me
> Or let it be the gardener-man
> To bring me (to your tree)

---

17. Since רהב occurs only four times in the Hebrew Bible (Ps 138:3; Prov 6:3; Isa 3:5), this suggested reading is based on the Syriac *rehēb* "to frighten" (*SyrLex*, s.v. "ܪܗܒ," 1439) and Akkadian *ra'ābu* "to (cause to) tremble" (*CAD*, "ra'ābu B," 14:2–3).

18. Daniel D. Luckenbill, *The Annals of Sennacherib*, OIP 2 (Chicago: University of Chicago Press, 1924), 47 (30); David Marcus, "Animal Similes in Assyrian Royal Inscriptions," *Or* 46 (1977): 96. See also Wilfred G. Lambert, *Babylonian Wisdom Literature* (Oxford: Clarendon, 1967), 192 (11).

I've got the coop ready for the young man,
I'll catch the love bird (in one snap)
Then, when I "coo"
I'll get a round "yes!" (from my trap).[19]

As in the previous poem, the biblical portrait of a dove emphasizes timidity as well as its quick flight, especially when returning home. In his prophecy about the future glory of Zion, Isaiah likens the nation's return from exile to doves flying to their cotes (60:8). Hosea combines both aspects of the dove imagery when he speaks about God's future restoration of Israel, "They will come trembling like birds from Egypt, like doves from the land of Assyria, and I will settle them in their homes, declares YHWH" (11:11). Thus, the lovers may also employ this motif as an expression of desire, hoping to be quickly reunited in the arms of their distant beloved.

Furthermore, based on Near Eastern iconographic evidence, Keel suggests that the dove invokes an established metaphor or stereotypical comparison.[20] As many scholars note, the dove is connected to the love goddess in the Mediterranean world.[21] For example, on the famous wall painting at Mari, a dove sits atop palm trees outside of Ishtar's temple. Likewise, a dove is also found above the entrance to Astarte's temple in Beth-Shean as well as a model shrine from Transjordan. Also, numerous Syrian seals depict a dove flying from the face of the goddess to her partner. Since the goddess is often shown exposing herself, this may denote her readiness for love.[22] In the Hellenistic world, Ovid describes Venus as riding on a chariot drawn by doves (*Metam.* 14.597), and Virgil's Aeneas received two doves from his divine mother in response to his prayer for her guidance (*Aen.* 6.190). Based on such examples, Keel suggests that the dove was a symbol of the goddess and a messenger of her love.[23] In further support of this thesis, Keel and Urs Winter present evidence from Egypt and Western Asia for the use of doves as messengers.[24] An inscrip-

---

19. Foster, *Before the Muses*, 165.
20. Keel, *Deine Blicke sind Tauben*, 53.
21. Exum, *Song of Songs*, 112; Keel, *Song of Songs*, 71; Müller, "Hohelied," 21.
22. Keel and Uehlinger, *Gods, Goddesses, and Images of God*, 29, 163.
23. Keel, *Song of Songs*, 70–73.
24. Othmar Keel and Urs Winter, *Vögel als Bote: Studien zu Ps 68, 12-14, Gen 8, 6-12, Koh 10, 20 und dem Aussenden von Botenvögeln in Ägypten*, OBO 14 (Göttingen: Vandenhoeck & Ruprecht; Fribourg: Presses Universitaires, 1977). In one Akka-

tion at Lagash depicts a pair of doves bringing news to parties of a border conflict.[25]

Moreover, a poetic portrayal of the couple's eyes as messengers of love also best explains the meaning of this metaphor in the Song.[26] In 1:15, the lover praises his beloved's beauty, describing her glances as an envoy of affection. Playing on this image, the woman likens their bedroom chamber to the abode of the dove, the lush foliage and lofty cedars, inviting her lover to her haunt for a rendezvous out in nature (1:16–17). The repetition of this image (4:1), with the contextual implication of distance, combines the dove's timid nature with its emissary function. The lover likens his beloved's eyes to doves behind her veil, stressing her reticence and visual communication of love. In 5:12, the maiden's description of the man's eyes likely emphasizes his affectionate glances, but his absence (5:8–9) hints at an implication of distance as well. Also, the dove's timid nature fits well in the context of the man's epithet for the maiden, "my dove" (2:14, 5:2), and its messenger function dovetails with the depiction of her glances (4:9; 6:5). Thus, utilizing the BODY AS LANDSCAPE metaphor, the Song's poet has adopted a shared symbol, the dove as a messenger of love, creating a unique image of the lovers' eyes to highlight the attributes of timidity, distance, and communication of affection.

---

dian lyric, the girl wishes to hear from her lover, "The bird *will make known*(?) the n[ews(?)]" (Wasserman, *Akkadian Love Literature*, 48).

25. Alasdair Livingstone, "On the Organized Release of Doves to Secure Compliance of a Higher Authority," in *Wisdom, Gods, and Literature: Studies in Assyriology in Honour of W. G. Lambert*, ed. Andrew R. George and Irving Finkel (Winona Lake, IN: Eisenbrauns, 2000), 383–84. A similar motif may also be present in the Genesis flood story, as Noah sends and receives the dove twice with news of the earth's condition (8:8–12).

26. See also Izaak J. de Hulster, "Iconography, Love Poetry, and Bible Translation: A Test Case with Song of Songs 7:2–6," in *Iconographic Exegesis of the Hebrew Bible/Old Testament: Introduction to Its Method and Practice*, ed. Izaak J. de Hulster, Brent A. Strawn, Ryan P. Bonfiglio (Göttingen: Vandenhoeck & Ruprecht, 2015), 318. Later, Achilles Tatius, a Greco-Roman writer, refers to the eye as "the ambassador of love" (*Leuc. Clit.* 1.9.6).

5.2. Large, Life-Giving Eyes (7:5)

עֵינַיִךְ בְּרֵכוֹת בְּחֶשְׁבּוֹן   7:5 Your eyes are the pools in Heshbon,
עַל־שַׁעַר בַּת־רַבִּים   near the gate of Bat-Rabbim.[27]

Source: Pools (in Heshbon)
Target: Eyes
Mapping: Size, Vitality

In addition to likening the lovers' eyes to doves (1:15; 4:1; 5:12), the Song's poet also compares the maiden's eyes to pools of water (7:5), likely playing on the dual meaning of עַיִן as "eye/spring." But is semantics the only basis of comparison? While Longman concludes that one cannot be more specific than a general adjective of beauty, many do not adopt this minimalist approach, instead positing a myriad of shared attributes: radiance, serenity, purity/clarity, size, and/or vitality.[28] Many of these attributes are based on comparative evidence, so each option will again be examined together with its biblical and/or extrabiblical evidence.

The most common proposals are twinkling and tranquility. Christian Ginsburg combines both attributes in this paraphrase, "Thine eyes ... are as bright and serene as the celebrated translucent pools of this city."[29] Such imagery is also found in other love lyrics. In his *Ars amatoria*, Ovid instructs a man to find the place his beloved longs to be touched, whereby "you will see her eyes shooting tremulous gleams, as the sun often glitters

---

27. Based on the parallel geographical terms "Heshbon" and "daughters of Rabbah" in Jer 49:3, Brenner posits that Song 7:5 should be read "Your eyes are pools in Heshbon, by the gate of Bat-Rabbah." She further suggests that this portrait is a parody, which was intended to invoke fear and loathing for the aberrant sexual practices of these nations. See Athalya Brenner, "A Note on Bat-Rabbim (Song of Songs VII 5)," *VT* 42 (1992): 113–15. While another geographic term would fit well in the context (7:5–6), even Brenner acknowledges that this emendation is conjectural, with no explanation of how such a reading arose. As such, Brenner's proposal is unlikely.

28. Longman, *Song of Songs*, 196. Radiance: Jens Eichner and Andreas Scherer, "Die 'Teiche' von Hesbon: Eine exegetisch-archäologische Glosse zu Cant 7,5bα," *BN* 109 (2001): 14; Keel, *Song of Songs*, 236; Murphy, *Song of Songs*, 186; Pope, *Song of Songs*, 625. Serenity: Ariel Bloch and Chana Bloch, *The Song of Songs: A New Translation with an Introduction and Commentary* (Los Angeles: University of California Press, 1995), 202; Falk, *Love Lyrics*, 41. Purity/Clarity: Murphy, *Song of Songs*, 186. Size: Garrett and House, *Song of Songs/Lamentations*, 241. Vitality: Hess, *Song of Songs*, 216.

29. Ginsburg, *Song of Songs*, 179.

in clear water" (*Ars.* 2.719–722 [Goold]). Likewise, Meleager highlights tranquility, praising Asclepias, who "with her eyes blue like a calm sea, convinces all to sail on the sea of love" (*Anth. Pal.* 5.156 [Paton]).

While such qualities are shared between pools of water and the human eye, the source of this image is not any pool, but ones located in Heshbon. Why does the Song's poet specify this location? Some suggest that the foreign cities listed in this verse (7:5) were viewed as regal and exotic, but this idea overlooks the fact that physical places in the Song often contain meaning.[30] Qedar is used for its etymological and cultural connection to darkness (1:5). Sharon is linked to flowers found in its plains/valleys (2:1). Tirzah and Jerusalem are icons of beauty (6:4), and Lebanon is associated with luxury and excellence (3:9; 4:11; 5:15). Thus, with numerous pools located in Israel, why does the Song's poet highlight Heshbon?

The city of Heshbon, 200 meters above ʿAin Ḥesbân, 19 kilometers south of Amman, and 8 kilometers northeast of Mount Nebo, is mentioned thirty-eight times in the Hebrew Bible. This city is most often connected to Israel's defeat of Sihon, the Amorite king (Num 21:21–30; Neh 9:22), and its subsequent tribal allotment (Josh 13:8–27; Judg 11:18–28), but later it also appears in oracles of judgment against the nations surrounding Israel (Isa 15–16; Jer 48–49). Although Gerleman concluded that "we must content ourselves with the fact that we know nothing of the places mentioned," recent excavations may shed some new light on the meaning of this metaphor.[31] On the southern edge of the site, a huge water reservoir was discovered, measuring 17.5 meters per side and 7 meters deep, with a capacity of 2.2 million liters, an estimated five times the amount that could have been collected in an average rainy season and well beyond the needs of the site's inhabitants.[32] Another massive reservoir, holding 1.8 million

---

30. On foreign cities as regal and exotic, see Keel, *Song of Songs*, 236.

31. Gerleman, *Hohelied*, 198, my translation.

32. Paul J. Ray Jr., *Tell Hesban and Vicinity in the Iron Age*, ed. Lawrence Geraty and Øystein S. LaBianca, Hesban 6 (Berrien Springs, MI: Andrews University Press, 2001), 99, 107. If the above historical identification is correct, the date of the reservoir could shed light on the Song's date of composition, at least for this individual poem. The reservoir was initially assigned to the Moabite phase, stratum 17, ninth–seventh centuries BCE, based on four sherds in its wall, but Sauer revised his conclusions, attributing the header-stretcher ashlars to royal construction, stratum 18, tenth century. See James A. Sauer, "The Pottery at Hesban and Its Relationship to the History of Jordan: An Interim Report," in *Hesban after Twenty-Five Years*, ed. David Merling and Lawrence Geraty (Berrien Springs, MI: Andrews University Press, 1993), 241–44.

liters, was recently uncovered nearby at Tell Jalul.³³ If these structures are the iconic pools to which the maiden's eyes are compared, the shared attribute is likely their size. Amy Gansell similarly notes the pattern of large eyes on Levantine ivories, while Jeremiah refers to the practice of enlarging the eyes with cosmetics (4:30).³⁴

Thus, like the large dimensions of these reservoirs, with their abundant water supply, the man praises his beloved's big eyes, desiring to drink deeply of her beauty. To her lover, the maiden's eyes were vast pools of desire, inviting him to quench his thirst on her gorgeous appearance.

In addition to large size, archaeology also suggests another basis for comparison: vitality. The location and construction of any settlement in the Near East hinged on its water supply. "Water is so basic to life that it is one of the most common metaphors in the Bible. Its necessity for the subsistence of humans and animals, and the limited sources available in biblical lands, make water and water conservation primary considerations in the daily life of Israel."³⁵ Illustrating this fact, Hezekiah commissioned a massive task, to redirect the Gihon Spring from outside Jerusalem's city walls through an underground tunnel to the Siloam Pool, to preserve this source of life in the face Assyria's invasion (2 Kgs 20:20). Thus, just as water was vital for life, the lover may describe his lady's big beautiful eyes as life-giving, invigorating him with the energy of life, like a refreshing natural spring to a tired traveler in the heat of summer.³⁶

Furthermore, these attributes of size and vitality align with a repeated theme in the female *waṣf* songs. The man not only praises his beloved's beautiful body, but he often reveals the effect her body has on him. Her eyes captivate and overwhelm him (4:9; 6:5), her navel prompts his longing to be drunk on love (7:2), and her hair captures him in its tresses (7:6). At the conclusion of this third hymn (7:8–10), the lover likens his lady's

---

33. Glenn Corbett et al., "Archaeology in Jordan, 2014 and 2015 Seasons," *AJA* 120 (2016): 648. This reservoir is also (tentatively) dated to the tenth century.

34. Amy R. Gansell, "The Iconography of Ideal Feminine Beauty Represented in the Hebrew Bible and Iron Age Levantine Ivory Sculpture," in *Image, Text, Exegesis: Iconography and Interpretation in the Hebrew Bible*, ed. Izaak J. de Hulster and Joel M. LeMon, LHBOTS 588 (London: Bloomsbury, 2014), 54.

35. King and Stager, *Life in Biblical Israel*, 122.

36. Eichner and Scherer, "Die 'Teiche' von Hesbon," 14. The motif of life-giving eyes is also found in a Mesopotamian prayer to Ishtar, "Wherever you look, the dying person gets well" (Erica Reiner and Hans G. Güterbock, "The Great Prayer to Ishtar and Its Two Versions from Boğazköy," *JCS* 21 [1967]: 261).

body to a palm tree, longing to partake of her intoxicating fruits. In this image, the man compares the maiden's lovely eyes to huge wellsprings of life, whose exhilarating waters he desperately longs to drink.

Although ambiguity prevents a precise identification, an archetypal attribute, such as radiance, may be intended, but this leaves little explanation for the geographic terms. Keel's theory that the site was selected because it was the capital of a foreign kingdom is inadequate.[37] In contrast, the huge reservoir uncovered at Tell Hesban (and its companion at Tell Jalul) may reveal the reality behind this comparison. Playing on the BODY AS LANDSCAPE motif, the poet crafts a unique image, highlighting the effect of the woman's eyes on the man. Like vast pools of water, her eyes invite him to drink deeply of her beauty, promising to sustain his life.

5.3. Dark, Flowing, (F)Locks (4:1c; 6:5c; 7:6; cf. 5:11b)

שערך כעדר העזים	4:1 Your hair is like a flock of goats,
שגלשו מהר גלעד:	that flows in waves down Mount Gilead.
ראשך עליך ככרמל	7:6 Your hair (crowns) you like crimson,[38]
ודלת ראשך כארגמן	your hair's hanging locks are like purple;
מלך אסור ברהטים:	the king is bound by (its) flowing tresses.[39]
קוצותיו תלתלים	5:11 His locks are curls,[40]
שחרות כעורב:	black as a raven.

Source: Goats, Crimson, Raven
Target: Hair
Mapping: Wavy, Rich (Color/Value)

In these verses (4:1c; 6:5b; 7:6; 5:11b), the lovers laud one another's beautiful hair. Indeed, hair is commonly cited as a token of beauty, for men and women, both inside and outside the pages of Scripture. In the Hebrew

---

37. Keel, *Song of Songs*, 236.
38. The debated translation of this phrase will be discussed below.
39. The term רהטים (Aram. "to run, flow") only occurs twice in the Hebrew Bible (Gen 30:38, "watering troughs). This term is nuanced here based on context.
40. While many scholars connect תלתלים to the Akkadian *taltallu* "palm frond" (LXX, Vulgate), this term, from תלה "to hang down," is used in Mishnaic Hebrew to describe curls (b. Naz. 4b; b. Git. 58a; b. Ned. 9b; see also Num. Rab. 10:7). See also Viezel, "סַנְסִנָּיו (*sansinnāyw*; Song of Songs 7:9) and the *Palpal* Noun Pattern," 752.

Bible, when Absalom's appearance is praised as matchless, the sole quality highlighted by the biblical author is his hair (2 Sam 14:25–26). In one of the additional psalms at Qumran, the superior appearance of David's brothers included their tall stature and beautiful hair (11Q5 XXVIII, 9–12). The splendor of a woman's hair is stressed in Isaiah's warning that the beautiful braids of Zion's daughters would be reduced to baldness in Judah's coming exile (Isa 3:24). In later literature, Sarai's lovely locks drew the attention of Pharaoh's servant (1Q20 XX, 3), while Susanna's accusers "ordered her to be unveiled that they might feast their eyes on her beauty" (Sus 32), perhaps alluding to her face and hair. Likewise, the writers of the New Testament label a woman's long hair a sign of her glory (1 Cor 11:15), though offering a caution for wives not to adorn their body or hair in an ostentatious or seductive manner (1 Tim 2:9; 1 Pet 3:3). Therefore, since a woman's hair can be sexually stimulating, the early Jewish rabbis commend the necessity of its covering (b. Ber. 24a).

5.3.1. Comparative Evidence

As in Jewish literature, Egyptian, Mesopotamian, Greco-Roman, Indian, Arab, and European works identify a woman's hair as a criterion of beauty, charged with seductive power. In Egypt's lyrics, the girl's hair is portrayed as bait to lure her lover and the rope used to catch him.[41] Like the Song's captured king (7:6), the Greek poet Paulus Silentarius also tells of a woman who used a single strand of her hair to bind her lover (*Anth. Pal.* 5.230).

One of the Sumerian love songs (DI C) describes how the goddess prepared for her lover's entrance, painting her eyes and fixing her hair.[42] In contrast, Juvenal, with a satire against declining feminine virtue in Rome (second century CE), laments that the "business of beautification,"

---

41. Fox, *Song of Songs*, 9, 73. In Tale of Two Brothers, Anubis's wife donned her wig before trying to seduce her brother-in-law. See Philippe Derchain, "La Perruque et le Cristal," *SAK* 2 (1975): 59–60. Though fragmentary, the Story of the Herdsman also seems to link a lady's hair to her allure, "The goddess approached him ... bare of her coverings and she was messing with her hair." See Hans Goedicke, "The Story of the Herdsman," *CdE* 45 (1970): 256–58. See also Saphinaz-Amal Naguib, "Hair in Ancient Egypt," *AcOr* 51 (1990): 17–18; Robbins, *Women in Ancient Egypt*, 185.

42. Jacobsen, *Harps*, 17. One love charm labels a lady's hair as "causing arousal." See Mark J. Geller, "Mesopotamian Love Magic: Discourse or Intercourse?," in Parpola and Whiting, *Sex and Gender*, 1:137 (9).

illustrated by a wife's effort on her hair, is deemed more important than her treatment of husband and household (*Sat.* 6.474–511).

Likewise, a Tamil lover describes his journey home to his lady, his heart melting with every thought of her dense black hair being braided and made up with flowers.[43] The Ode of Imr, a pre-Islamic Arab love lyric, similarly praises a woman's dark hair, while an early twentieth-century bedouin poem characterizes such dark locks as arresting.[44] In medieval Europe, Shakespeare repeatedly returns to the beauty of a woman's hair (*As You Like It* 3.5.47; *Two Gentlemen of Verona* 4.4.186; *Troilus and Cressida* 1.1.41; 4.5.33; *Sonnet* 6).[45] The icon of a lady's locks is highlighted in his satire on the perfect portrait of beauty (*Sonnet* 130).

Across time and geography, a woman's hair is viewed as a symbol of alluring beauty, yet ancient and modern love lyrics also suggest a preference for wavy locks. In ancient Egyptian art, a woman's hair/wig is often depicted with curls. One fragmentary relief shows an Egyptian stylist crimping strands of hair (*ANEP*, 77). In a similar portrait on the Turin Papyrus, a lady is pictured with wavy hair, holding a mirror and applying paint to her lips (*ANEP*, 78). Also, two shards from Deir el-Medina (thirteenth century BCE) picture an acrobat dancer and naked musician with long, luxurious, curly locks.[46] Dancing to music or mourning the dead, Egypt's women are often shown with curls (*ANEP*, 209, 638).[47] For example, a woman unearthed in the Amarna cemetery (fourteenth century BCE) wore "a very complex coiffure with approximately seventy extensions fastened in different layers and heights on the head."[48]

A similar preference for wavy hair, in men and women, is evident in Mesopotamia.[49] From Gudea of Lagash and early Sumerian rulers to later Assyrian, Babylonian, and Persian kings, male hair/beards are repeatedly

---

43. Attipat K. Ramanujan, *Poems of Love and War: From the Eight Anthologies and Ten Long Poems of Classical Tamil* (New York: Columbia University Press, 1985), 79.

44. Jinbachian, "Arabian Odes," 137; Dalman, *Palästinischer Diwan*, 260. See also Stephan, "Modern Palestinian Parallels," 228.

45. Sujata Iyengar, *Shakespeare's Medical Language: A Dictionary* (New York: Continuum, 2011), 158–59.

46. Keel, *Song of Songs*, figs. 78–79.

47. See also Fox, *Song of Songs*, 335–44; Arnold and Allen, *Royal Women*, fig. 118.

48. Barry Kemp, "Tell El-Amarna 2012–13," *JEA* 99 (2013): 19.

49. Amy R. Gansell, "Images and Conceptions of Ideal Feminine Beauty in Neo-Assyrian Royal Context, c. 883–627 BCE," in *Critical Approaches to Ancient Near Eastern Art*, ed. Brian Brown and Marian Feldman (Boston: de Gruyter, 2013), 392.

shown in dark, stylized curls (*ANEP*, 430–51, 462–63). In Mesopotamia, "men and women of special status kept their hair in curls" (*CAD*, "kezēru," 8:316). An Old Babylonian physiognomic text aptly captures this ideal, "If the hair on a man's shoulder is curled, women love him" (i 21–22).[50] Mesopotamian women are rarely shown in art, but extant evidence follows a similar pattern: "Hairstyles varied from simple, shoulder or waist-length curled hair, sometimes braided in plaits, to the elaborate styles of the Early Dynastic period when hair was plaited and piled on top of the head or confined by a net or scarf, covered by a headdress."[51] For example, a female devotee in Eshnunna, in a draped dress, is depicted with elaborate, braided coils.[52]

Moreover, the portrayal of men and women with curly locks is also attested in Greco-Roman, ancient Tamil, and modern Arab bedouin culture. In her survey of the archaeology of first-century Corinth, Cynthia Thompson shows coins, statues, and figurines depicting men and women with wavy hair. In the first two centuries CE, Greek upper-class women wore increasingly complex and higher braids that likely required the use of a curling iron and help from a slave.[53] Likewise, Mariaselvam notes numerous Tamil lyrics that praise a maiden's thick curls.[54] Later, in the *Gīta Govinda*, Krishna lauds his beloved's hair as "curling locks" that caress her moon-like face.[55] Yet the closest parallel to the Song's metaphor of color and movement is found in a modern Syrian wedding *waṣf*, "Her black hair like the seven nights, the like are not in the whole year; in waves it moves hither and thither, like the rope of her who draws water."[56]

Furthermore, Near Eastern literature also praises men and women for dark-colored hair. Egypt's Mutirdis, priestess of Hathor, is lauded for her

---

50. Franz Köcher and A. Leo Oppenheim, "The Old Babylonian Omen Text VAT 7525," *AfO* 18 (1957–1958): 63.

51. Piotr Bienkowski, "Hair Dressing," *DANE*, 137. See also Jutta Börker-Klähn, "Haartrachten," *RlA* 4:1–12 (pls. 1–30). A relief from Ashurbanipal's palace shows the king and his queen, along with female servants, styled with curls (*ANEP* 451).

52. Henri Frankfort, *Sculpture of the Third Millennium B.C. from Tell Asmar and Khafājah*, OIP 44 (Chicago: University of Chicago Press, 1939), pl. 74.

53. Cynthia L. Thompson, "Hairstyles, Head-Coverings, and St. Paul: Portraits from Roman Corinth," *BA* 51 (1988): 108–9.

54. Mariaselvam, *Ancient Tamil Love Poems*, 196. See also M. Vasuki, "Variety of Hair-Dos in Ancient Tamil Nadu," *JTamS* 9 (1976): 52–53.

55. Miller, *Love Song of the Dark Lord*, 99.

56. Keil and Delitzsch, *Commentary on the Old Testament*, 6:624–25.

hair, blacker than night and grapes on a riverbank.[57] Egyptian medicinal and magical texts abound with references to hair, showing how Egyptians strived to keep their hair healthy, plentiful, and black. To bring back one's dark hair, Papyrus Ebers suggests mixing the blood of a black ox with oil and smearing it on one's head.[58] Similar prescriptions are found in Mesopotamia.[59] Likewise, Tamil poets compare a woman's black hair to black sand or the dark feathers of a peacock, while the pre-Islamic Arab lyrics compare a lady's locks to dark clusters on a date palm.[60] Yet the preference for "yellow/golden" hair in Greek poetry, for Homer's heroes and heroines, reminds us that beauty is always influenced by culture.[61]

Thus, while the depiction of men and women with dark, curly locks is attested in the textual and material evidence throughout the Near East and beyond, one must be careful not to make broad conclusions. "Our sources provide limited information, [and] … considerable change can occur over time."[62] Indeed, the shifting trends of hair fashion in our own culture should give us pause. In addition, the Song's poet chose to deliver his praise in a culturally unique image, adapting the BODY AS LANDSCAPE metaphor to Palestine's agricultural setting. Rather than the sands of Egypt or the rivers of Mesopotamia, the beloved's hair is portrayed with a pastoral image, linked to Gilead, a place known for its pasture (Num 32:1).

5.3.2. Meaning in the Song

While the survey above suggests that dark, wavy hair is a widely shared symbol of beauty, the Song's praise for its lovers' tresses employs enigmatic metaphors that have raised questions for many readers. In her survey of problems posed by the book's body imagery, Black cites Song 4:1 as her hallmark example.[63] Likewise, due to the perplexing nature of this verse,

---

57. Fox, *Song of Songs*, 349.
58. Naguib, "Hair in Ancient Egypt," 7.
59. R. Campbell Thompson, "Assyrian Medical Texts," *PRSM* 12 (1924): 4.1, 5.1.
60. Mariaselvam, *Ancient Tamil Love Poems*, 196–97; Jinbachian, "Arabian Odes," 137.
61. Jax, *Weibliche Schönheit*, 10, 43, 72, 125, 168. See also Susan Stewart, *Cosmetics and Perfumes in the Roman World* (Gloucestershire: Tempus, 2007), 43–44.
62. King and Stager, *Life in Biblical Israel*, 282–83.
63. Black, *Artifice of Love*, 19. Keel suggests that this metaphor reveals her "wild, almost demonic, lust for life," but this appears to be another attempt to avoid the representational import of the Song's body imagery (Keel, *Song of Songs*, 141–42).

Soulen rejects any correspondence between the source and target of these images.⁶⁴ Indeed, these puzzling lyrics require further examination.

First, the lady's hair is likened to a flock of goats (4:1, 6:5). While the source and target are clear, the *tertium comparationis* remains problematic, mainly due to the enigmatic גלש. Numerous cognates have been suggested for the meaning of this biblical *hapax legomenon*. From a similar faunal description in Papyrus Lansing, Adolf Erman posited the Egyptian *kršw*, "skip, hop."⁶⁵ Accepted by a few scholars, consonant correspondence weighs against this theory, as Hebrew *g* does not shift to *k* in Egyptian or vice versa.⁶⁶ Gesenius connected this term to Arabic *jalasa* "sit, move down," but a closer option is found in Aramaic and Ugaritic.⁶⁷

In rabbinic literature, גלש often describes boiling water (b. Pes. 37b; Qoh. Rab. 8:17; Song Rab. 4:3f). Similarly, the texts from Ras Shamra use the cognate *glṯ* in connection with water. In the phrase *tglṯ thmt*, the primordial deep is described as roiling or agitating.⁶⁸ But how does nautical imagery relate to the Song's pastoral metaphor for the beloved's hair? Steven Tuell presents the best explanation, suggesting that both flocks and locks move downward in a rippling, wavelike motion.⁶⁹ Ginsburg aptly captures the sense: "Nothing could more beautifully express the curly hair of a woman, dangling down from the crown of her head, than the sight, at a distance, of a flock of goats running down from the summit of this verdant hill on a beautiful day."⁷⁰

In addition to its primary description of her wavy locks, the lover's metaphoric praise for his beloved's hair in Song 4:1 may also contain an

---

64. Soulen, "*Waṣfs* of the Song of Songs," 190.
65. Adolf Erman, "Hebräische GLŠ 'springen,'" *OLZ* 28 (1925): 5
66. Gerleman, *Hohelied*, 144; Garrett and House, *Song of Songs/Lamentations*, 188; Yoshiyuki Muchiki, *Egyptian Proper Names and Loanwords in North-West Semitic*, SBLDS 173 (Atlanta: Society of Biblical Literature, 1999), 263; Gábor Takács, *Etymological Dictionary of Egyptian*, HdO 48 (Leiden: Brill, 1999), 1:263.
67. Gesenius, *Handwörterbuch*, s.v. "גלש."
68. Charles Virolleaud, *Le Palais Royal d'Ugarit: Textes en cunéiformes alphabétiques des archives sud, sud-ouest et du petit palais*, Mission de Ras Shamra (Paris: Klincksieck, 1965), 1.5.
69. Steven S. Tuell, "A Riddle Resolved by an Enigma: Hebrew גלש and Ugaritic GLṮ," *JBL* 112 (1993): 103. This unique term may also have been chosen for its sound effect, sharing two consonants with Mount Gilead, the iconic place of lush pastures (Noegel and Rendsburg, *Solomon's Vineyard*, 86–87).
70. Ginsburg, *Song of Songs*, 154.

implicit depiction of its dark color, which is clearly stated in the parallel passages (5:11b, 7:6). As mentioned in the preceding discussion of the maiden's dark skin (1:5–6), most scholars agree that the hair of goats in Palestine was commonly black or dark-colored.[71] Still the case today, this conclusion may also be evident in the biblical narrative itself. After aiding David in his flight from her father, Michal put a statue in his bed, with a pillow of goat's hair at the head, to create a visual illusion (1 Sam 19:13). Since Palestinian men have dark hair, one may safely assume that the goat's hair would have been dark as well.[72] Therefore, the man may also depict the maiden's hair as dark in color, cascading down in waves onto her shoulders (4:1c).

In addition, Song 5:11b and 7:6 contain similar depictions of the lovers' dark, wavy hair, though with different figures and problems. The color of the man's hair is compared to a raven (5:11), while the maiden's is likened to crimson and purple (7:6). Both praise locks dark in color, yet how does the lady's depiction in 7:6 relate to her previous portrait in 4:1? How should one understand the likeness of her ראש to כרמל?

First, how should one understand the seeming paradox between the man's initial image of his maiden's hair as a flock of black-haired goats (4:1) and its likeness to purple in his later portrait (7:6)? In the Hebrew Bible, the term ארגמן is often used to describe textiles made from dyed wool (Ezek 27:16; 2 Chr 2:6; Song 3:10). The key to solving this dilemma is found in understanding the process that produced the purple dye. Derived from murex shellfish, this dye varies in shades from pale pink to dark violet and black purple, with the latter being most valuable, "Its highest glory consists in the color of congealed blood, blackish at first glance but gleaming when held up to the light" (Pliny, *Nat.* 9.62.135 [Rackman]). On this last phrase, Itamar Singer notes, "The shining iridescent quality of ancient purple explains the confusion in translating terms used by the ancients to designate different shades of scarlet, purple,

---

71. Bergant, *Song of Songs*, 44; Carr, *Song of Solomon*, 114; Exum, *Song of Songs*, 162; Falk, *Love Lyrics*, 29; Feliks, *Song of Songs*, 75; Fox, *Song of Songs*, 129; Garrett and House, *Song of Songs/Lamentations*, 188; Gerleman, *Hohelied*, 147; Ginsburg, *Song of Songs*, 154; Hess, *Song of Songs*, 129; Keel, *Song of Songs*, 142; Krinetzki, *Hohelied*, 135; Longman, *Song of Songs*, 144; Murphy, *Song of Songs*, 159; Pope, *Song of Songs*, 458; Robert and Tournay, *Cantique des Cantiques*, 160; Rudolph, *Hohe Lied*, 146.

72. As mentioned above for the juxtaposition of dove and raven (5:11–12), the black-haired goats (4:1) present a fitting contrast to the sheep's white wool (4:2).

5. Anatomy of a Rose: Praise for the Female Body 155

and crimson."⁷³ Thus, Song 4:1 and 7:6 are complementary, praise for the beloved's dark locks, highlighting their luminous sheen.

In addition to its rich color, ארגמן "purple" implies value. As noted above, the darker color was considered most prized. In fact, Akkadian and Ugaritic use this same term for "tribute" (*CAD*, "argamannu," 1.2:253; *DULAT*, s.v. "argmn"). This conflation of meaning is likely explained by the value of purple-dyed fabrics, frequently offered as tribute. The name of the item given became synonymous with the term itself.⁷⁴ This connotation of value is evident in Song 7:6, with the adjoining invocation of royalty, "The king is bound by [its] flowing tresses." Playing on the OBJECT OF LOVE IS A VALUABLE OBJECT metaphor, the beloved's dark, wavy hair is revered as a prized possession. The combination of color, sheen, and value is also found in Mesopotamia and Egypt, where the lover's hair is likened to dark, luminous lapis lazuli.⁷⁵

However, one question remains: what is the meaning of the man's comparison of the woman's ראש to כרמל (7:6a), and how does this metaphor relate to his previous praise? First, most scholars render the MT literally, as a wordplay on ראש "top, head," "Your head (crowns) you like Carmel" (NRSV). But how is the woman's head like a mountain? Commentators are divided on the meaning of such a metaphor. On one hand, Fox and Longman conclude that the basis of comparison is height.⁷⁶ Just as Mount Carmel was an imposing sight that dominated the landscape below (Jer 46:18), the woman stands tall and dignified. The prophet Amos used the height of Carmel similarly to stress the inescapability of Israel's coming judgment (9:3). The maiden's height is later emphasized in her likeness to a date palm (7:8–9), but there her stature is specifically invoked (קומה). If her height is also in view here, why mention her head? On the other hand, some scholars explain this mountain imagery as a metaphor of majesty.⁷⁷ As Carmel rises majestically above the landscape below, the woman's head crowns her body. Isaiah used Carmel as an image of splendor, into which

---

73. Itamar Singer, "Purple-Dyers at Lazpa," in *Anatolian Interfaces: Hittites, Greeks and Their Neighbours*, ed. Billy Jean Collins, Mary R. Bachvarova, and Ian C. Rutherford (Oxford: Oxbow Books, 2008), 25. See also Dina Frangié-Joly, "Perfume, Aromatics, and Purple Dye," *JEMAHS* 4 (2016): 51.

74. Singer, "Purple-Dyers at Lazpa," 23.

75. Tobin, "Love Songs," 323; George, "Gilgamesh Epic at Ugarit," 242.

76. Fox, *Song of Songs*, 160; Longman, *Song of Songs*, 196.

77. Murphy, *Song of Songs*, 186.

the barren desert will be transformed upon the return of the exiles (35:2). But how is the human head majestic?[78] In the end, these explanations do not adequately make sense of this enigmatic image.

There is a better explanation for this phrase, which respects the consonantal text, better fits the context, and avoids the problems noted above. Instead of rendering 7:6 as a comparison of the maiden's head to a mountain, the same terms are better understood as a description of her hair (ראש) like crimson (כרמיל).[79] In this view, 7:6a–b form a synonymous couplet, praising the lady's dark, luminous hair (דלת ראשך /ארגמן/כרמיל; ראשך). Interestingly, the other occurrences of כרמיל in the Hebrew Bible are also connected to ארגמן (2 Chr 2:6, 13; 3:14).[80]

Finally, the lover's locks are also described as curly, "black as a raven" (5:11b). While this is the sole raven metaphor in the Hebrew Bible, the poet clearly identifies the source and target of the image, as well as its mapping. In contrast to light-color of his lower body (5:14–15), the man's dark hair resembled a black raven. Yet, this use of a raven for color comparison is not unique. Mesopotamian physiognomic texts employ similar images, "If he has the head of a raven (meaning that) the hair of his head is black."[81] In Rome, the author and engineer Vitruvius (first century BCE) describes sheep as white, white-brown, grey, or "black as a raven" (*De arch.* 8.3.14).[82] Moreover, the raven metaphor is also found in Arabic literature (Lane, "غُرَابٌ," 631). Several pre-Islamic poets were known as the *ʿAghribat-al-*

---

78. Pope, *Song of Songs*, 194–95. See also Black, "Beauty or the Beast?," 312.

79. Ginsburg, *Song of Songs*, 179; Rudolph, *Hohe Lied*, 169.

80. The proposal that כרמיל is a janus double entendre, with "Carmel" linked to the previous places and "crimson" in parallel with purple in the next line, does not adequately explain the comparison between the maiden's head and Carmel. See Shalom M. Paul, "Polysemous Pivotal Punctuation: More Janus Double Entendres," in *Texts, Temples, and Traditions*, ed. Michael Fox et al. (Winona Lake, IN: Eisenbrauns, 1996), 369; Yakov Eidelkind, "Intended Lexical Ambiguity in the Song of Songs," *Babel und Bibel* 6 (2012): 351.

81. Fritz R. Kraus, *Text zur babylonische Physiognomatik*, AfOB 3 (Berlin: Weidner, 1939), 17 (12); Hermann Hunger, *Spätbabylonische Texte aus Uruk*, ADFU 9 (Berlin: Mann, 1976), 83 (4–5).

82. The closest parallel to the Song's imagery is found in the Anacreontea (first century BC–fifth century CE): "Paint my beloved Bathyllus according to my prescription: make his hair shine, dark beneath but with the ends highlighted by the sun; add curling locks falling freely in disorder" (*Lyra Graeca* 2:17 [Campbell]).

ʿArab "ravens of the Arabs" because of their dark complexion.⁸³ However, while the raven is used throughout the Near East and Mediterranean for color comparison, a certain element of culture is implicit. This cultural factor is evident in the absence of this metaphor in Egypt, likely due to their unique standard of blackness (*kmt*), the soil of the "Black Land."⁸⁴

Thus, in these verses (4:1c, 6:5b; 7:6; 5:11), the lovers craft elaborate figures in praise for one another's beautiful hair. In 4:1c, the man likens his lady's locks to a flock of goats, playing on their black color and wave-like movement. Later, with a comparison to the rich color of royalty (7:6), he highlights the dark, luminous sheen and prized value of his beloved's hair, which captures him in its tresses. The beloved also emphasizes similar qualities in her praise, comparing her lover's dark, curly locks to the color of a raven (5:11). With three complementary portraits, the Song's poet combines a universal symbol of beauty and seduction (7:6c) with various shared metaphors, showing preference for dark, shining curls (4:1c; 7:6; 5:11), at times packaged in a culturally specific image (4:1c).

5.4. Perfect Pair of Wooly Whites (4:2; 6:6)

שניך כעדר הקצובות	⁴:² Your teeth are like a flock of sheep ready to be shorn,⁸⁵
שעלו מן־הרחצה	which have come up from the washing place;
שכלם מתאימות	all of which have twins,
ושכלה אין בהם:	not one of which⁸⁶ is missing.

Source: Sheep
Target: Teeth
Mapping: White, Well-Aligned, Whole

---

83. Goldenberg, *Curse of Ham*, 340 n. 114.

84. Gay Robins, "Color Symbolism," *OEAE* 1:291. Yet, Egyptians did recognize the iconic color of the raven. In Papyrus Ebers, one of the remedies for preventing gray hair was applying a mixture of balsam and blood to one's head, specifically from the *g3bgw* "raven." See Cyril P. Bryan, *The Papyrus Ebers* (London: Bles, 1930), 154–55.

85. Though most translations render הרקובות as a completed action, "shorn sheep" (ESV, NIV, NRSV), an attributive participle is atemporal (Joüon §121i). Thus, logic suggests that the sheep are ready to be shorn, having been washed. From texts at Nuzi and Elephantine, washing preceded the shearing. See Jonas C. Greenfield, "'Le Bain des brebis': Another Example and a Query," *Or* 29 (1960): 98–101.

86. Health is highlighted by wordplay, שכלם/שכלה (Zhang, *Song of Songs*, 50).

Though the Hebrew Bible employs the term שן "tooth" metaphorically to depict the threat of an enemy (Job 29:17; Pss 57:5; 124:6; Prov 30:14), this verse clearly refers to physical characteristics of the maiden's teeth. The basis of comparison is clear even from a surface reading of the passage. Using the BODY AS LANDSCAPE metaphor, the lady's teeth are praised as white, well-aligned, and whole, just like a flock of sheep, complete in number, with their freshly washed wool glistening in the sun. But is this image unique or does it reflect a shared conception of wellness and beauty?

5.4.1. Comparative Evidence

In the Near East, teeth were valued for their function and appearance. According to biblical law, retribution (*lex talionis*) was prescribed for the loss or damage of another's teeth (Exod 21:23–24; Lev 24:20; Deut 19:21). Similar laws are also found in other Near Eastern legal codes (*ANET*, 163, 175, 189, 525). The value of teeth is also evident in various prescriptions and incantations for dental problems in ancient medical texts. Egypt's Papyrus Ebers outlines a dozen recipes for loose or aching teeth with the use of a topical treatment.[87] Similar prescriptions for dental diseases are also found in Assyria and Rome (Pliny, *Nat.* 22.21; 23.28, 36–37; 25.105).[88]

Moreover, since earliest times, teeth have been deemed an important element of beauty. Egypt's Mutirdis inscription (tenth–eighth century BCE) praised the priestess of Hathor for her hair, blacker than night, and teeth, whiter than bits of plaster, while Gilgamesh is similarly described with teeth "gleaming like the rising sun."[89] When Horace described an undesirable woman, he pointed to her wrinkled skin, white hair, and discolored teeth (*Carm.* 4.13). For this reason, Ovid cautioned women on the detriment of bad teeth, "If you have a tooth that is black, too large, or growing out of place, laughing will cost you" (*Ars.* 3:279–280 [Goold]).

Tamil poets also lauded beautiful teeth, likening their white brilliance to shiny pearls, jasmine petals, sprouts of rice, or new buds on a

---

87. F. Filce Leek, "The Practice of Dentistry in Ancient Egypt," *JEA* 53 (1967): 53.

88. R. Campbell Thompson, "Assyrian Medical Texts II," *PRSM* 19 (1925): 65–66; René Labat, *Traité akkadien de diagnostics et prognostics medicaux* (Leiden: Brill, 1951), 60 (r.36–39).

89. Fox, *Song of Songs*, 349; George, "Gilgamesh Epic at Ugarit," 242.

palm.[90] Similar to Song 4:1–2, one lover juxtaposes praise for his lady's long (dark) flowing hair with her white teeth coming up in a perfect line.[91] In the *Gīta Govinda*, Krishna likened Rādhā's teeth to the radiant light of the moon.[92] Medieval and modern Arab love lyrics likewise extol a woman's brilliant smile. In *Arabian Nights*, both lovers' teeth are often compared to the color of pearls.[93] Similar imagery is found in the lyrics of modern Arab bedouins. Overcome by his beloved's beauty, one man exclaimed, "For the whiteness of her teeth, I left my religion."[94] The importance of teeth for physical beauty continues in Western literature. Robert Herrick compared the teeth of his beloved Julia to Zenobia, the queen of Palmyra, an icon of beauty known for her bright eyes and pearly white teeth.[95]

While this survey suggests that white teeth were widely considered a symbol of wellness and beauty, customs from Africa and Asia remind us that beauty is culturally constructed. Fashionable women in medieval Japan blackened their teeth as a mark of beauty, while some Africans change the shape or remove parts of the teeth for ornamental purposes.[96] Even today, some African-Americans plate their teeth with gold for adornment.[97] Thus, white, well-matched teeth is a broadly shared icon of beauty, yet this portrait does not transcend the influence of culture.[98] Even the Song's poet delivers his praise in a culturally specific package (4:2). While odd to the modern reader, the image of washing and shearing sheep would have been perfectly natural in Israel's pastoral society.

---

90. Ramanujan, *Poems of Love and War*, 16, 65; Mariaselvam, *Ancient Tamil Love Poems*, 198, 289.

91. Mariaselvam, *Ancient Tamil Love Poems*, 294.

92. Miller, *Love Song of the Dark Lord*, 111.

93. Muhsin Mahdi, ed., *The Arabian Nights* (New York: Norton, 1990), 68, 165.

94. Saarisalo, "Songs of the Druzes," 14. See also Dalman, *Palästinischer Diwan*, 80, 112, 243; Stephan, "Modern Palestinian Parallels," 217, 254.

95. Frederic W. Moorman, ed., *The Poetical Works of Robert Herrick* (Oxford: Clarendon, 1915), 24.

96. Victoria Sherrow, "Teeth" in *For Appearance' Sake: The Historical Encyclopedia of Good Looks, Beauty, and Grooming* (Westport, CT: Oryx, 2001): 254.

97. Cecilia Conrad, *African Americans in the U.S. Economy* (Lanham, MD: Rowman & Littlefield, 2005), 255.

98. See also Richard Corson, *Fashions in Makeup, From Ancient to Modern Times*, 3rd ed. (London: Owen, 2003), 498.

5.5. Sexy, Scarlet Lips (4:3a)

כחוט השני שפתתיך	⁴:³ Your lips are like a scarlet thread,
ומדבריך נאוה	and your mouth is lovely.

Source: Scarlet Thread
Target: Lips
Mapping: Color/Value

After his praise for the maiden's white teeth (4:2), the lover continues his tribute with emphatic focus on her mouth (4:3). Again, the components and basis of this metaphor are clear, but the significance of scarlet lips and the extent of this image need further study. Later in the Song, the lady's scarlet lips appear in a scene of sexual arousal, as the lover wishes for her intoxicating fruits, "Your mouth is like the best wine, flowing smoothly for lovers, gliding over scarlet lips" (7:10).[99] However, the Song's poet more likely draws on the OBJECT OF LOVE IS A VALUABLE OBJECT metaphor here, as שני "scarlet" often conveys value and luxury (2 Sam 1:24; Prov 31:21), similar to the likeness of the woman's hair to crimson above (7:6). But why are scarlet lips valuable, and how widespread is their connection to beauty?

5.5.1. Comparative Evidence

Archaeological evidence from Egypt indicates that females used red color to enhance the beauty of their lips. The Turin Papyrus depicts a lady holding a mirror in her hand, applying paint to her lips (*ANEP*, 78). Also, on the famous bust of Nefertiti, the strong red color of the queen's lips suggests the use of cosmetics.[100] The use of lip cosmetics is further supported by burial

---

99. As discussed in §4.5, the reading שפתי שנים (7:10) assumes dittography. Scarlet is also associated with Rahab (Josh 2:18) and Tamar (Gen 38:28). Hagedorn posits that this image also stresses her thin lips (4:3), but the same phrase (חוט השני) is used to describe the rope by which the spies escaped from Rahab's house. See Anselm C. Hagedorn, "Die Frau des Hohenlieds zwischen babylonisch-assyrischer Morphoskopie und Jacques Lacan (Teil II)," *ZAW* 122 (2010): 600. Jacob connects red to evil, concluding that lip color is negative, both in Egypt and in the Hebrew Bible. Ronja Jacob, *Kosmetik im antiken Palästina*, AOAT 389 (Münster: Ugarit-Verlag, 2011), 83–84. However, as demonstrated below, such a conclusion is spurious.

100. Lise Manniche, *Sacred Luxuries: Fragrance, Aromatherapy, and Cosmetics in Ancient Egypt* (Ithaca: Cornell University Press, 1999), 138–40.

evidence. One female mummy from the Old Kingdom was entirely painted, with yellow skin, black hair and eyes, and red lips.[101] Also, small burial chests containing a woman's most intimate possessions usually included jewelry, braids of hair, perfume, razor, tweezers, and cosmetics.[102] Finally, the Middle Kingdom title *sšt n(y)t r.s* "painter of her mouth" also suggests that Egyptian women tinted their lips with red cosmetics to enhance their natural beauty.[103]

In contrast, knowledge of make-up practices in Mesopotamia and Israel is limited, mainly due to the lack of color representation. However, cosmetic palettes, juglets, and utensils from eighth- to seventh-century BCE Judah and the color pigments found in the royal cemetery at Ur suggest that cosmetics were used in these cultures as well. Woolley writes, "Every woman's grave in the old cemetery seems originally to have contained cosmetics.... In all these were found remains of the actual cosmetics used, paints or powders now reduced to paste."[104] Cosmetic use among Mesopotamian women may also be implicit in a hymn to Ishtar, "Adorned with attractiveness, cosmetics [*mi-qí-a-am*], and sexual appeal" (5–6).[105]

While there is no archaeological evidence for the existence of lipstick in Greco-Roman society, nearly one thousand years of Hellenistic literature abounds with praise for the heroine's red lips.[106] In the fragmentary poetry of Semonides (sixth–fifth centuries BCE), one maiden speaks from a στόματος πορφύρεος "crimson mouth" (*Lyra Graeca* 3:585). Catullus and Ovid similarly depict their beloved's lips as *purpŭra*: Acme

---

101. William S. Smith, *A History of Egyptian Sculpture and Painting in the Old Kingdom*, 2nd ed. (London: Oxford University Press, 1949), 24.

102. Geraldine Pinch, "Private Life in Ancient Egypt," *CANE* 1:367–68; Mikhal Dayagi-Mendels, *Perfumes and Cosmetics in the Ancient World* (Jerusalem: Israel Museum, 1993), 39.

103. Georges Posener, "'Maquilleuse' en Egyptien," *RdE* 21 (1969): 150; William A. Ward, *Essays on Feminine Titles of the Middle Kingdom and Related Subjects* (Beirut: American University of Beirut, 1986), 16–17.

104. Sir Leonard Woolley, *The Royal Cemetery: A Report on the Predynastic and Sargonid Graves Excavated between 1926 and 1931* (Philadelphia: University of Pennsylvania Museum, 1934), 245. Bimson later confirmed this conclusion. Mavis Bimson, "Cosmetic Pigments from the 'Royal Cemetery' at Ur," *Iraq* 42 (1980): 76. See also Edward Neufeld, "Hygiene Conditions in Ancient Israel," *BA* 34 (1971): 51

105. Thureau-Dangin, "Hymne à Isztar," 170.

106. On the lack of archaeological evidence, see Stewart, *Cosmetics and Perfumes in the Roman World*, 12.

kissed her beloved Septimus with a crimson mouth (*Poems* 45), while Ovid longed to bury his tongue between his beloved's wine-colored lips (*Am.* 3:14.23–24). Using the comparable term ῥόδεος "rose," Macedonius (sixth century CE) likens his lady's "rosy" lips to a fishhook from which he hangs (*Ant. Pal.* 5:247), while the rose-colored lips of his beloved nearly caused Dioscorides (second century BCE) to lose his sanity (*Ant. Pal.* 5:56).[107] Likely composed in Greek, Joseph and Aseneth preserves a similar image, "Her lips (were) like a rose of life coming out of its foliage" (18.9).

Such praise for a woman's red-colored lips is also attested in later Indian and Arabic love literature. In his comparative study, Mariaselvam lists numerous examples, likening the beloved's mouth to coral or the petals of a blossoming red flower.[108] Krishna similarly longs for Rādhā's sweet "red berry lips."[109] Likewise, the medieval *Arabian Nights* and modern Palestinian love lyrics compare the lady's lips to crimson-colored roses, wine, carnelian, flowering nutmeg, plums, and pomegranates.[110] Similar imagery is commonly found in Western love lyrics. Though Shakespeare ridiculed the Petrarchan portrait of lovely lips, "coral is far more red than my beloved's lips" (*Sonnet* 130), his other writings often compare the color of a woman's lips to coral, cherries, and roses (*The Taming of the Shrew* 1.1.172; *Titus Andronicus* 3.1 24; *Richard III* 1.1.94; 4.3.12; *The Rape of the Lucrece* 420; *Romeo and Juliet* 1.5.104; 2.1.18; 4.1.99). Philip Sidney similarly likens his lady's lips to "red porphyr," an igneous rock of purple-red color, derived from πορφύρεος mentioned above.[111]

This perception of beauty is reflected throughout the sixteenth through the nineteenth centuries: Thomas Campion praises his lady's kissable lips as "cherry-ripe," Thomas Carew labels the lips of his beloved as "coral," and for Herrick, rubies grow on Julia's lips.[112] Even among the anticosmetic sentiment of the Victorian Era, natural recipes were sought

---

107. Rufinus also praises his beloved's mouth as "more delightful than a purple [πορφύρεος] rose" (*Anth. Pal.* 5.48).

108. Mariaselvam, *Ancient Tamil Love Poems*, 197, 288–89.

109. Miller, *Love Song of the Dark Lord*, 85.

110. Mathers, *Book of the Thousand Nights*, 1:273, 295, 418, 486, 553, 625; Stephan, "Modern Palestinian Parallels," 201.

111. Albert C. Hamilton, *Sir Philip Sidney: A Study of His Life and Works* (Cambridge: Cambridge University Press, 1977), 84.

112. Moorman, *Robert Herrick*, 24; Thomas Carew, *The Poems of Thomas Carew* (New York: Scribners, 1899), 137; Lindley, *Thomas Campion*, 45–46. A modern exam-

to achieve the same red tint.¹¹³ Moreover, the high importance of lip color for feminine beauty in America was aptly seen during the Second World War. When certain materials used in the production of cosmetics were deemed of major importance to the war effort, the Cosmetics Industry Advisory Committee sponsored a survey of middle-class American women. Asking one group of two hundred women to classify the necessity of certain cosmetics, lipstick was identified as a "most important" item by nearly 92 percent of respondents, with only six individuals claiming they could easily do without it.¹¹⁴

Mabbuby Ogle opined that such detailed portraits of beauty, which often included high praise for a lady's red lips, should be traced back to classical literature, but the above survey suggests that this value of feminine beauty is better viewed as a commonality of human experience.¹¹⁵ Across both space and time, the beauty of a woman's lips is enhanced when its natural color is highlighted with a shade of red. Perhaps, the reason for this phenomenon involves the captivating and inviting nature of this color. Jerome sensed this allure and castigated against cosmetics, "What place have rouge and white lead on the face of a Christian woman.... They serve to inflame young men's passions, to stimulate lust, and to indicate an unchaste mind" (*Ep.* 54 [*NPNF* 2/6:104]). Thus, alongside other portraits of the maiden's mouth, overflowing with enticing and intoxicating joys (4:11; 7:10), this image of her sexy, scarlet lips is best read as captivating her lover's attention and inviting him to taste their unending pleasures.

5.6. Rouge Red Cheeks (4:3b; 6:7)

כפלח הרמון רקתך	⁴:³ Your cheek is like a pomegranate slice,
מבעד לצמתך:	behind your veil.

---

ple would be Snow White, with "lips blood red" (Grimm and Grimm, *Folk and Fairy Tales*, 1:170).

113. Corson, *Fashions in Makeup*, 383. Among the Puritans, where rouging the lips was not accepted, "the more daring women would rub snips of red ribbon on their mouths when no one was looking." See Jessica Pallingston, *Lipstick: A Celebration of the World's Favorite Cosmetic* (New York: St. Martin's, 1999), 13.

114. Melissa A. McEuen, *Making War, Making Women: Femininity and Duty on the American Home Front, 1941–1945* (Atlanta: University of Georgia Press, 2011), 46.

115. Mabbuby B. Ogle, "The Classical Origin and Tradition of Literary Conceits," *AJP* 34 (1913): 125–52.

Source: Pomegranate
Target: Cheeks
Mapping: Color, Pattern and/or Shape

In contrast to the previous praise for the maiden's teeth and lips (4:2–3a), the imagery in this verse is less clear. The main debate surrounds the metaphor's target, the part of the lady's body being lauded. The term רקה occurs in one other place in the Hebrew Bible. In Judg 4–5, the narrator states three times that Yael murdered Sisera, driving a peg into his רקה while he lay sleeping (4:21–22; 5:26). Traditionally, the term has been rendered "temple," connecting the adjective רק to the "thin" part of the skull. Yet, praise for the lady's temple seems strangely specific, particularly "behind her veil." Thus, some have suggested that רקה is better connected to רקק "to spit," continuing the description of her mouth. Keel suggests, "The inviting slit in the pomegranate, revealing dark red and bright red parts, seems most likely to refer to the beloved's open mouth, to her palate."[116] But what is so beautiful about one's oral cavity? A more visible area is likely in view. In contrast to לחי, the lower part of the cheek or jaw (1:10; Job 40:26; Judg 15:15), רקה may describe the temple and upper cheek.

From earliest record, this image has been connected to the maiden's cheeks. Jerome rendered רקה with *genae* "cheeks," while the LXX chose the term μῆλον "apple," a metaphor used by Greek poets for a woman's rosy cheeks.[117] Rashi similarly explains, "This is the upper part of the face, next to the eyes. In the language of the Talmud, it is called 'the pomegranate of the face' (b. Avod. Zar. 30b). It resembles the split half of a pomegranate from the outside, which is red and round."[118] While scant evidence prevents a definitive conclusion, studying ancient customs and literature may shed further light on the meaning of this enigmatic image.

---

116. Keel, *Song of Songs*, 146. See also Marc Rozelaar, "An Unrecognized Part of the Human Anatomy," *Judaism* 37 (1988): 99–100. Rozelaar bases his argument on sequence, but the varying order of the different *waṣfs* weakens this conclusion.

117. The reading preserved in 4Q106 (מזקנתך, "chin/cheeks") may indicate that scribes also struggled to identify this body part, yet the presence of the Masoretic reading in 4Q107 weighs against this isolated variant (Tov, "Canticles," 202).

118. Yaakov Y. H. Pupko, *Five Megilloth/Rashi*, trans. Avrohom Davis (New York: Metsudah, 2001), 41.

5.6.1. Comparative Evidence

Archaeological and textual evidence from antiquity shows that women often applied red color to their cheeks in order to achieve a more youthful and beautiful appearance. In Egypt, rouge was not only used to color a lady's lips but also her cheeks. In a tomb painting of Nefertiti, the queen is clearly shown with circles on her cheeks of a darker red hue than the shade of her complexion.[119] A Middle Kingdom funerary stela similarly shows a woman applying a substance to her cheek with a piece of cloth.[120] Cosmetic utensils found among burial goods stress the high importance of a lady's appearance, in the present life and the hereafter. The value of one's complexion is further demonstrated by the various skin remedies found in Papyrus Ebers. One mixture combined honey and red natron to beautify the skin.[121] Thus, evidence from Egypt implies that a beautiful female complexion was light in color, with a shade of red on the lips and cheeks.

As mentioned above, insight into cosmetic use in Mesopotamia is limited by the lack of color representation. Yet discovery of pigments in the royal cemetery at Ur supports the presence of this practice. In addition, various Sumerian-Akkadian lexical lists include terms that describe such a custom, "to paint/color the cheek" or "rouge for the face."[122] The Divine Love Lyrics describe Ishtar as "a palm of carnelian ... whose figure is red to a superlative degree and who is beautiful to a superlative degree."[123] Although the lack of context in these cases prevents a conclusion, the connection of color and beauty in the latter example may suggest that the goddess's reddish complexion enhanced her beauty. Later, Xenophon labeled

---

119. Manniche, *Sacred Luxuries*, 138. See also Alfred Lucas, "Cosmetics, Perfumes and Incense in Ancient Egypt," *JEA* 16 (1930): 44.

120. Iorweth E. S. Edwards, "A Toilet Scene on a Funerary Stela of the Middle Kingdom," *JEA* 23 (1937): 165, pl. 20.

121. Bryan, *Papyrus Ebers*, 158–61. See also Joseph and Aseneth 18.9.

122. Irving Finkel, ed., *The Series SIG7.ALAN=Nabnītu*, MSL 16 (Rome: Pontifical Biblical Institute, 1982), M:168–69; Miguel Civil, ed., *Ea A=nâqu, Aa A=nâqu, with Their Forerunners and Related Texts*, MSL 14 (Rome: Pontifical Biblical Institute, 1979), A VIII/4:23; Benno Landsberger and Richard Hallock, eds., *Old Babylonian Grammatical Texts*, MSL 4 (Rome: Pontifical Biblical Institute, 1956), III:178–79; Benno Landsberger, ed., *The Series HAR-ra=ḫubullu. Tablets VIII–XII*, MSL 7 (Rome: Pontifical Biblical Institute, 1959), XI:319.

123. Lambert, *Problem of Divine Love Lyrics*, 123.

rouge "a common Median fashion" (*Cyr.* 1.3.2) while Aelian likened the skin of Cyrus's concubine to red roses (*Var. hist.* 12.1).

The evidence from Syria-Palestine is similarly scant. In Ugaritic literature, both ʿAnat and Pughat are described as applying rouge to redden the color of their skin (*KTU* 1.3 iii.1–3; 1.19 iv.42–43).[124] Also, the discovery of cosmetic palettes/utensils from eighth–seventh century BCE Judah, as well as the red faces on some Judean pillar figures suggests the presence of this practice in ancient Israel as well.[125] Rabbinic sources later confirm the use of cosmetics, permitting a woman to apply rouge during a festival (b. Mo'ed Qat. 9b), but not on Sabbath (m. Shabb. 10:6), during menstruation (b. Shabb. 64b) or mourning (b. Ketub. 4b).

In contrast to the paucity of evidence in Mesopotamia and Palestine, the Hellenistic world abounds with descriptions and depictions of ladies with rosy cheeks, as well as material evidence for cosmetic practice. In Greco-Roman culture, the perfect female complexion was pale with a hint of pink, likened to "rose-petals floating on pure milk" (Propertius, *El.* 2.3.12), "tinted Lydian ivory," or "red as roses among lilies" (Ovid, *Am.* 2.5.35–40). To create this effect, rouge was applied against a fashionable pale foundation.[126] Ovid advises, "You know, too, how to gain a bright hue by applying powder: art gives complexion if real blood does not" (*Ars.* 3.206 [Goold]).[127] Similar to the Song's imagery, rosy cheeks were compared to various red-colored fruits (LSJ, s.v. "μῆλον (B)," II.2). Archaeological and pictorial evidence attest the use of facial cosmetics. In the Greco-Roman world, boxes (*pyxides*) have been found containing rouge, visually shown by the female rosy cheeks on the wall paintings at Thera.[128]

---

124. Mark Smith and Wayne T. Pitard, *The Ugaritic Baal Cycle: Introduction with Text, Translation, and Commentary of KTU/CAT 1.3–1.4*, VTSup 114 (Leiden: Brill, 2009), 215.

125. Henry O. Thompson, "Cosmetic Palettes," *Levant* 4 (1972): 148–50; Kletter, *Judean Pillar-Figurines*, 50.

126. Stewart, *Cosmetics and Perfumes in the Roman World*, 42.

127. The clearest evidence for this practice stems from its opponents. Xenophon characterized cosmetics as trickery (*Oec.* 10.1–8). Among the church fathers, Clement and Jerome conclude that no chaste woman ought to stain her cheeks or paint her eyes, while Tertullian and Cyprian called such practices sin, attributing their origin to Satan (Clement of Alexandria, *Paed.* 3.2; Jerome, *Ep.* 54.7, 107.5; Tertullian, *Cult. fem.* 2.3; Cyprian, *Hab. virg.* 14). On the demonic origin of cosmetics, see also 1 En. 8:1.

128. Robert Laffineur, "Dress, Hairstyle and Jewelry in the Thera Wall Paintings," in *The Wall Paintings of Thera: Proceedings of the First International Symposium*, ed.

5. Anatomy of a Rose: Praise for the Female Body

Across both time and geography, praise is continually lavished upon a lady's red-colored cheeks. Tamil love lyrics do not often refer to the cheeks, though one lover describes his lady's face as "vermilion like the moon."[129] In *Arabian Nights*, the beloved's cheeks are often compared to a rose, while Judah Ha-Levi, one of the greatest Hebrew poets, likened a women's red complexion to a ruby and the color of the rising sun.[130] Similarly, modern Arab bedouin love lyrics compare a lady's lovely cheeks to sparkling wine, a bed of roses, blossoming pomegranates, and apples.[131]

Likewise, Western poets also compare a woman's cheeks to flowers, fruits, and other things red in color. Sidney likened Stella's body to a building, "whose porches rich (which name of cheeks endure), marble mixed red and white do interlace."[132] Thomas Lodge, an English physician and poet, invented the image of blushing cloud to describe the beauty of his beloved's cheeks.[133] Inverting this frequent theme, Shakespeare jested, "I have seen roses damasked, red and white, but no such roses see I in her cheeks" (*Sonnet* 130). Even in Victorian England, when rouge was regarded as disreputable, women still sought a rosy glow by pinching their cheeks or applying natural remedies like berry juice or beetroot.[134]

5.6.2. Meaning in the Song

While linguistic uncertainty prevents a precise identification, the likeness of the maiden's רקה to a pomegranate, playing on the BODY AS LANDSCAPE theme, suggests that the metaphor centers on her red-colored cheeks. As the above evidence suggests, a woman's desire to beautify

---

Susan Sherratt (Piraeus: Thera Foundation, 2000), 2:900; Mireille M. Lee, *Body, Dress, and Identity in Ancient Greece* (New York: Cambridge University Press, 2015), 67. A similar box was found in Israel at Dan. See Avraham Biran, *Biblical Dan* (Jerusalem: Israel Exploration Society, 1994), color pl. 15.

129. Mariaselvam, *Ancient Tamil Love Poems*, 196, 269.

130. Mathers, *Book of the Thousand Nights*, 1:296, 347, 363, 528, 569, 613; Judah Ha-Levi, *Dīwān des Abū'l-Ḥasan Jehuda ha-Levi*, ed. Heinrich Brody (Farnsborough: Gregg, 1971), 2:20.

131. Dalman, *Palästinischer Diwan*, 12, 100, 223, 260–61; Littman, *Neuarabische Volkspoesie*, 104, 141; Saarisalo, "Songs of the Druzes," 56, 110; Stephan, "Modern Palestinian Parallels," 214, 221, 245, 262, 275.

132. Hamilton, *Sir Philip Sidney*, 84.

133. Thomas Lodge, *Rosalynd*, ed. Brian Nellist (Staffordshire: Ryburn, 1995), 70.

134. Corson, *Fashions in Makeup*, 380–82.

herself with red-tinted lips and cheeks appears to be unchanged from antiquity, spanning both time and culture. The lover's praise for his beloved (4:3) may not refer to lipstick and rouge, but the consistent use of cosmetics throughout time betrays a universal ideal of beauty: a desire to enhance the natural red color of lips and cheeks to engender a healthy, youthful, lively appearance.

The shared red color of cheeks and pomegranates is likely the primary meaning of the lover's metaphor in Song 4:3b, but why the mention of a veil? A literary curtain around the woman's face (4:1–3), the veil may contribute an added visual facet.[135] There are two possibilities, depending on one's vantage. First, if the pomegranate slice is viewed from the outside, the poet may be comparing the curved exterior of the fruit to the round cheeks of the maiden. As Rashi suggests, her cheek "resembles the split half of a pomegranate from the outside, which is red and round."[136] The placement of the veil may have attracted attention to the curvature of her cheeks. On the other hand, if the poet's perspective was the inside of the pomegranate, the resulting portrait changes. Viewed through her veil, the red coloring of her cheeks may have resembled the internal pattern of the pomegranate. Fox advocates this idea, "In a slice of pomegranate, the membranes separating the seeds form a webbing, which is suggested by the shadow the girl's veil casts on her cheek."[137] Thus, the lover's praise for his beloved's cheeks highlights their red color, whose presence under the veil may have stressed their round shape or their red and white pattern.

5.7. Tower-Like Neck and Nose (4:4; 7:5)

כמגדל דויד צוארך	4:4 Your neck is like the tower of David,
בנוי לתלפיות	built to the heights;[138]

---

135. James, *Landscapes*, 126. Similar to Rebekah's veil (צעיף, Gen 24:65), the maiden's head-covering (צמה) may mark her as a betrothed/married woman (4:9).

136. Pupko, *Metsudah Rashi*, 41.

137. Fox, *Song of Songs*, 130. See also Falk, *Love Lyrics*, 84.

138. The term תלפיות is a *hapax legomenon*, whose uncertain meaning has spurred debate from earliest record. LXX translators simply rendered the term as a proper name, though no such place is known in antiquity. The suburb of modern Jerusalem was so named only recently. Ibn Ezra divided the terms תל פיות, "to hang weapons," though פי refers only to the edge of the sword. Rashi and Rashbam related the term to אלף "to teach," explaining this tower as a model of beauty. Elision of *aleph* is not uncommon, but the final *yod* is difficult to explain. Many modern scholars adopt

5. Anatomy of a Rose: Praise for the Female Body

| אלף המגן תלוי עליו | a thousand shields hang on it, |
| כל שלטי הגבורים: | all the weaponry[139] of warriors. |

צוארך כמגדל השן	7:5 Your neck is like an ivory tower;
אפך כמגדל הלבנון	your nose is like the tower of Lebanon,
צופה פני דמשק:	looking toward Damascus.

Source: Tower
Target: Neck, Nose
Mapping: Size/Straightness, Ornamentation, Color, Strength/Peace?

Honeyman's theory that תלפיות derives from Aram. לפי "to arrange." Alexander M. Honeyman, "Two Contributions to Canaanite Toponymy," *JTS* 50 (1949): 51; Pope, *Song of Songs*, 465–68. Proponents could better explain תלפיות as a by-form of לוף/לפף "to wrap, join," known from other Semitic languages (CAD, "lapāpu," 9:82; *DJPA*, s.v. "לפף"; *SyrLex*, s.vv. "ܠܦܦ," "ܠܦܦ," 680, 695; Lane, "لف," 3011). While לפף is well-attested linguistically, the interpretive leap from "join" to "courses" is difficult. Based on two modern South Arabic languages, Rendsburg theorized that תלפיות derives from לפי "to climb easily," referring to height. Gary Rendsburg, "תַּלְפִּיּוֹת (Song 4:4)," *JNSL* 20 (1994): 13–19. Since Jibbāli and Mehri are spoken by residents of remote areas in Oman and Yemen, these groups likely resisted the spread of Arabic culture, possibly preserving the meaning of an otherwise unattested term. For further support, Rendsburg notes other Northwest Semitic terms with parallels preserved only in modern South Arabic languages. He posits that the poet may have used this rare term for alliteration with אלף, תלוי, and שלט in the next line.

139. The meaning of שלט, found seven times in the Hebrew Bible, is difficult to determine. Often translated "shields," this gloss does not adequately explain all the evidence. In Jer 51:11, "Sharpen the arrows, fill the השלטים," the context implies that שלט refers to a quiver. For additional support, Borger points to a relief and inscription in the tomb of a Persian military official. Aspathines, a dignitary of Darius, carries the king's bow case, which is described by the Akk. *šaltu* (CAD, "šaltu," 17.1:271–72) and written with the logogram for wooden objects. See Rykle Borger, "Die Waffenträger des Königs Darius: Ein Beitrag zur alttestamentlichen Exegese und zur semitischen Lexikographie," *VT* 22 (1972): 385–98. Michael Sokoloff also points to 11Q10 (11QtgJob) (39:23), where the Aram. שלט is used to render the Heb. אשפה "quiver" (*The Targum to Job From Qumran Cave XI*, BISNELC [Ramat-Gan: Bar-Ilan University, 1974], 156). In addition to Jer 51:11, the LXX translators also render שלט as φαρέτρας "quiver" in Ezek 27:11, while Symmachus and Josephus (*Ant.* 7.104) use this term in 2 Sam 8:7 as well. The quivers seized by David (2 Sam 8:7) may be the same ones later issued by Jehoiada to protect Josiah (1 Kgs 11:10). Yet, the LXX rendering of שלט in Song 4:4 as βολίς "arrow" as well as the use of this term in the War Scroll (1QM VI, 2) to describe a javelin-like weapon suggests that שלט may generally describe military equipment. Therefore, due to the ambiguity of this term, the translation "weaponry" adopted above is intentionally vague (Fox, *Song of Songs*, 131).

In the Hebrew Bible, the neck is a symbol of life and vitality, whose bondage implies slavery (Gen 27:40; Jer 27:2) and whose harm equals death (Josh 10:24; Isa 8:8). The outward posture of the neck is often used to indicate the inward orientation of the heart: the psalmist warns against speaking with "a haughty neck" (75:5), Isaiah protests proud women walking with "outstretched necks" (Isa 3:16), and the people of Israel, in times of rebellion, are often labeled "stiff-necked" (Exod 32:9; Jer 7:26).

Based on this evidence, Keel concludes that the maiden's neck is a symbol of her attitude: "The beloved's neck—her pride—is like 'the tower of David.' As a symbol of an old proud dynasty, the tower symbolizes her inviolability."[140] Yet in light of the Song's unique genre, should such figurative language be expected to follow the pattern? Song 4:1–7; 6:4–7; and 7:2–7 contain a litany of praise for physical beauty: big, beautiful eyes; dark, wavy locks; white, well-aligned teeth; scarlet lips; and rosy cheeks. Keel's functional explanation violates the context and ignores similar depictions of beauty in other Near Eastern and Mediterranean cultures.

5.7.1. Comparative Evidence

Egyptian and Greco-Roman portraits of female beauty praise a woman's tall, slender neck. Egypt's Chester Beatty Papyrus contains a descriptive song, similar in literary form, in which the lover praises his beloved's body, including her long neck.[141] This ideal is also captured in the famous bust of Nefertiti (*ANEP*, 404). Likewise, in the Hellenistic world, a slender, white neck was the icon of female beauty, while an ugly woman is described as "short of neck" (Semonides, frag. 7.75 [Gerber]).[142] Philodemus lauds the slender neck of his tan beauty (*Anth. Pal.* 5.132), and Rufinus lists a long neck among the traits fleeing from his unfaithful lover (*Anth. Pal.* 5.27).

The same image occurs in Arab and Western literature. Medieval and modern Arab lyrics liken a lady's long neck to an antelope, whose graceful white neck is outstretched when alert.[143] Seventeenth-century English poets similarly praise a lady's long neck. Lodge likens the neck of

---

140. Keel, *Song of Songs*, 147. See also Keel, *Deine Blicke sind Tauben*, 32–39.
141. Fox, *Song of Songs*, 52.
142. Jax, *Weibliche Schönheit*, 127. See also see Warren G. Moon, *Greek Vase-Painting in Midwestern Collections* (Chicago: Art Institute, 1979), 220–21.
143. Jinbachian, "Arabian Odes," 129; Dalman, *Palästinischer Diwan*, 101, 112.

fair Rosalynd to a stately tower, where love itself lies imprisoned.[144] From East to West, a woman's long neck is still considered an asset of beauty in modern times. In Myanmar, some women use coiled brass rings to enhance the neck's length, while Western culture praises such women for their "swan-neck."[145] If Rendsburg's derivation is correct, בנוי לתלפיות "built to the heights" aligns with this widely shared ideal.

Furthermore, playing on the BODY AS LANDSCAPE theme, the visual focus in this metaphor is enhanced by the imagery in its concluding lines: the woman's neck is likened to a tall tower, "decorated with shields and the weaponry of warriors." Ezekiel refers to this military practice as a picture of perfect beauty (27:10–11). Yet, as most scholars have noted, the shining shields likely depict the beloved's alluring neckwear, whose visual attraction was stressed earlier in the Song (1:10) and again later in this same chapter, "You have captured my heart, my sister, my bride … with one jewel of your necklace" (4:9).

The beauty of this accessory is also reflected in texts and pictures throughout the Near East. In Egypt, the broad collar (*wesekh*) is attested from earliest times, using beads of decreasing lengths to create a curve form.[146] Many women and musicians in banquet scenes are depicted wearing them.[147] Likewise, material and textual evidence from Mesopotamia attest a similar practice. From the tomb of queen Pu-abi at Ur, close-fitting collar necklaces as well as necklaces with beads of gold, silver, lapis lazuli, carnelian, and agate worn in multiples are found from the early third millennium.[148] Numerous pictorial examples have been noted where wide or multistrand necklaces climb a woman's long neck.[149] The closest parallel to the Song's imagery was found at Mari, an early second millennium

---

144. Lodge, *Rosalynd*, 70.
145. Sherrow, "Neck," in *For Appearance' Sake*, 205–6.
146. James F. Romano, "Jewelry and Personal Arts in Ancient Egypt," CANE 3:1607.
147. Fox, *Song of Songs*, 131 (figs. 2–5, 9).
148. Zainab Bahrani, "Jewelry and Personal Arts in Ancient Western Asia," CANE 3:1636. See also Gansell, "Ideal Feminine Beauty," 62.
149. George F. Dales, "Necklaces, Bands, and Belts on Mesopotamian Figures," RA 57 (1963): figs. 3, 8, 13, 15–16; Maxwell-Hyslop, *Western Asiatic Jewelry*, figs. 5, 7–8, 18b, 54, 56–58, 63, 157; pls. 27, 61, 163; Keel, *Deine Blicke sind Tauben*, pls. 2–3; Ilse Seibert, *Woman in the Ancient Near East*, trans. Marianne Herzfeld (Leipzig: Edition Leipzig, 1974), ills. 2, 20, 23, 27b–29, 31–32, 35, 37. The Sumerians also praise Inanna's neckwear (Sefati, *Love Songs*, 198, 202, 232, 291, 314, 321).

figurine in which the goddess wears a six-stranded necklace formed with stone rows of various sizes (*ANEP*, 516).[150]

Likewise, women also adorned themselves with necklaces in Hellenistic culture. In his study of Greco-Roman jewelry, Reynold Higgins highlights examples of neckwear with shield-like pendants from the mid-third millennium to the turn of the era.[151] Necklaces are similarly depicted as beauty aids in Arabic and Western love lyrics. In *Arabian Nights*, ladies dressing to meet their men adorn themselves with a gold collar or string of pearls. Arab bedouins labeled such neckwear as "the beauty of women."[152] In Shakespeare's *Winter's Tale*, a necklace is listed among gifts of love which a man ought to buy for his beloved (4.4.221–30), while Alfred Tennyson longed to be the lovely necklace on his lady's neck.[153]

5.7.2. Meaning in the Song

As the preceding survey has demonstrated, adorning the neck with chokers, beads, pendants and other neckwear has been popular across time and culture since antiquity. Perhaps, neckwear serves as an asset of beauty since its shiny ornaments attract the eyes and accentuate the neck. However, while neckwear is nearly universal, comparing the maiden's beaded necklace to a tower ornamented with shields seems to be a unique innovation. Also, the invocation of David adds cultural meaning, though the uncertain identity of this tower prevents a conclusion.[154] Thus, the poet again wraps a universal symbol of beauty in culturally specific trappings.

Although its visual nature is primary, some posit that this martial image of a tower with shields denotes inaccessibility and unassailable strength. As Garrett opines, "There is a kind of beauty associated with mil-

---

150. Isserlin attempted to illustrate the Song's imagery with a multistrand necklace from Cyprus (sixth century BCE), comparing its top layer to the shields depicted on the Assyrian relief of the siege of Lachish and the two bottom rows to bossed headers found in the Near East. See Benedikt S. J. Isserlin, "Song of Songs IV, 4: An Archaeological Note," *PEQ* 90 (1958): 59–61.

151. Reynold A. Higgins, *Greek and Roman Jewellery*, 2nd ed. (Berkeley: University of California Press, 1980), pls. 2, 5, 7, 15a, 26–28, 33b–35, 44, 49b.

152. Mathers, *Book of the Thousand Nights*, 112, 326; Saarisalo, "Songs of the Druzes," 16.

153. Arthur T. Quiller-Couch, ed., *The Oxford Book of English Verse 1250–1900* (Oxford: Clarendon, 1902), 828.

154. In addition, מגדל דויד "tower of David" may be a play on דוד "lover."

itary hardware, but it is a beauty that connotes strength. Applied to walls and towers, this language connotes impregnability."[155] Yet the lady is not entirely remote; her intimate physical portrait betrays that she is already accessible to her lover's gaze. In addition, "weapons hung upon walls are not in use, and not so threatening as brandished weapons."[156]

Perhaps this architectural imagery symbolizes both strength and peace, similar to the woman's self-portrait in 8:8–10. Responding to her brothers, the beloved depicts her body as an impregnable wall, yet she rejects their promised reward for the peace she finds in the eyes of her lover. Similarly, the lover here likens his lady's neck to a strong tower, whose weaponry may symbolize the security and peace that he finds in her.

A second passage continues the visual focus of this imagery with its depiction of the tower's color, "Your neck is an ivory tower" (7:5). Though some scholars avoid connecting this metaphor to the maiden's complexion in light of her lament over her dark skin (1:5–6), such a meaning is not impossible.[157] In the Song, where the woman sees mediocrity and inferiority, her lover recognizes surpassing beauty (2:1–2). Thus, the beloved's eyes may only see the effects of the sun, but in her lover's eyes, her skin tone matches the widely shared ideal of beauty discussed earlier (§3.1, above).

Moreover, in light of the similarities between 4:4 and 7:5a, Fox offers a different theory.[158] The poet's metaphor may depict a tower, not constructed from ivory, but decorated with ivory pieces. Just as the tower bedecked with shields likely refers to the woman's neckwear, this ivory tower may also refer to a necklace strung with pieces of ivory. Why ivory? Since ivory was considered a luxury item across the Near East, the poet likely plays on the OBJECT OF LOVE IS A VALUABLE OBJECT metaphor here.[159]

In addition, Song 7:5 not only opens but also closes with an architectural image: "Your nose is like the tower of Lebanon, looking toward Damascus." Even more than the above figures, the enigmatic nature of this picture has spawned much debate. Rashi concluded, "I cannot explain this [אַף] to mean a nose, neither with respect to the simple meaning nor in reference to its allegorical meaning, for what praise of beauty is there in a

---

155. Garrett and House, *Song of Songs/Lamentations*, 191.
156. Exum, *Song of Songs*, 165.
157. Bergant, *Song of Songs*, 85; Longman, *Song of Songs*, 195.
158. Fox, *Song of Songs*, 160.
159. For further discussion on ivory, see the metaphor for the man's loins (§6.3).

nose that is large and erect as a tower."[160] Moses Segal labeled the metaphor in 4:4, 7:5 as "grotesque description," which could only be rationalized as playful banter.[161] Due in part to this image, Pope transferred the entire Song into the divine realm, "If our lady is superhuman in nature and size, then the dismay about her towering or mountainous nose disappears."[162] Yet, is there another explanation for such imagery?

Indeed, the importance of a woman's nose in Near Eastern portraits of beauty is vividly illustrated in its removal as punishment for the adulterous wife, both in Egypt and Mesopotamia. According to the Greek historian Diodorus (first century BCE), Egyptian law specified that the husband of an adulterous woman "should have her nose cut off ... [that she] be deprived of that which contributes most to a woman's comeliness" (*Bib. hist.* 1.78.5 [Oldfather]). In one Mesopotamian incantation, the rejected lover cries out, "Cut down her haughty nose, place her nose under my foot."[163] In fact, Middle Assyrian law (§15) also allowed the man to cut off his wife's nose and emasculate her lover (*ANET*, 181). For Greco-Roman culture, a straight nose was considered beautiful. Catullus derides a girl with an ugly snub nose (*Poems* 41.3), while Xenophon's imitation of Socrates satirically contrasts a snub nose with an attractive straight one (*Symp.* 5.6). However, as shifting American trends show, different shapes and sizes of noses have been considered more or less desirable, and these standards vary with cultures and era.

Three main options have been presented for the meaning of this image. First, since לבנון "Lebanon" closely resembles לבנה "frankincense," some posit that the nose metaphor invokes scent. Earlier in the Song, the lover likened the smell of his lady's garments to the fragrance of Lebanon, possibly employing a similar wordplay (4:10). Only a few verses after this tower imagery, the man longs to smell the intoxicating scent of the maiden's breath (7:8). As Fox quips, "If the boy's cheeks are 'towers of perfumes' (5:13), the girl's nose can be a 'tower of frankincense.'"[164] Second, similarity between לבנון "Lebanon" and לבן "white" may suggest that color is the basis of comparison, though the earlier stress on the maiden's complexion with different metaphors (7:5a) makes this option less likely. Finally, the

---

160. Pupko, *Metsudah Rashi*, 84–85.
161. Segal, "Song of Songs," 480.
162. Pope, *Song of Songs*, 627.
163. Wasserman, *Akkadian Love Literature*, 262.
164. Fox, *Song of Songs*, 160.

5. Anatomy of a Rose: Praise for the Female Body

likeness of the woman's nose to a tower may stress its beautiful length and straightness, with proper scale taken from the context.¹⁶⁵ In light of the visual focus in the context (7:5ab), a comparison of size seems most likely, though a secondary meaning is also possible.¹⁶⁶

5.8. Passion-Provoking Breasts (4:5; 7:4; cf. 5:13b)

שני שדיך כשני עפרים	⁴:⁵ Your two breasts are like two fawns,
תאומי צביה	twins of a gazelle,
הרועים בשושנים:	grazing among the lotuses.¹⁶⁷
שפתותיו שושנים	⁵:¹³ His lips are lotuses,
נטפות מור עבר:	dripping liquid myrrh.

Source: Fawns, Lotuses
Target: Breasts, Lips
Mapping: Symmetry, Shape/Shade?, Sexual Passion, Sensual Intoxication

In the Hebrew Bible, the female breast pictures physical provision (Gen 49:25) and proves a girl's maturity and readiness for love (Ezek 16:7; Song 8:8–10). In addition, breasts are employed as an erotic symbol, depicting the sexual satisfaction that a woman brings to her lover (Ezek 23:3, 21; Hos 2:4). The majority of occurrences in the Song fit this latter category. The beloved's breasts are pictured as a private place of pleasure (2:17; 4:6; 8:14), a source of intoxicating delight for all senses (7:8–9; 8:1–2).

Among the parts of the beloved's body, her breasts occupy the pride of place in the Song, mentioned or described in nearly every chapter, ten times in 117 verses (1:13; 2:17; 4:5–6; 7:4, 8–9; 8:2, 8, 10, 14). While one can readily understand why the man is captivated by his beloved's breasts, the metaphor he uses in 4:5 is either too subtle or so culturally distant that we are left in some doubt as to precisely what he means by such a comparison. Ginsburg opined that this faunal image was an icon of supreme beauty, but

---

165. Landy, *Paradoxes of Paradise*, 86; Bergant, *Song of Songs*, 87.
166. James argues that these verses employ defensive imagery, even explaining the pools and gate (7:4) as "constructive projects supporting military endeavors" (James, "Battle of the Sexes," 110). A contentious tone seems unwarranted here.
167. Absent in 7:4, Pope suggests the allusion to lotus-eating (4:5) was mistakenly introduced (Pope, *Song of Songs*, 470). The presence of lotuses in 7:4 may be assumed from 7:3, which fits the poet's abbreviation of refrains in later chapters (7:11; 8:4).

this theory does not explain why such a metaphor is specifically connected to the maiden's breasts.[168] Could this image also be connected to other parts of her body? Bergant posits that both source and target were symbols of grace and beauty, connected to sexuality and fertility, of tawny color, soft yet firm, youthful, and playful.[169] While many of these shared traits are obvious through observation, Bergant does not explain what textual or cultural evidence favors such a meaning. What trait(s) connect the female breast to the offspring of a gazelle?

5.8.1. Comparative Evidence

In Near Eastern literature, the clearest parallel to the Song's faunal imagery is found in a series of Old Babylonian texts.[170] In the ŠÀ.ZI.GA potency incantations, the gazelle is often invoked as an example of sexual virility,

> [Incantation. Get excited! Get excited! Get an erection! Get an erection! Get excited like a stag!] Get an erection [like a wild bull!] … [With the love-making of a mountain goat(?) six times], with the love-making of a stag [seven times], [With the love-making of a partridge(?)] twelve times make [love to me]! [Make love to me(?)]! [Make love to me] because I am young!… I am endowed with love, make love to [me]![171]

Another example may be evident in the Assyrian love lyrics of Nabû and Tašmetu. In the god's portrait of his beloved's body, her thighs are likened to a gazelle.[172] Amid other avenues of transportation (chariot, thighs, ankles, heels), this description likely highlights the beloved's speed in coming to her lover. However, falling between Tašmetu's expressed

---

168. Ginsburg, *Song of Songs*, 157.
169. Bergant, *Song of Songs*, 48. See also Landy, *Paradoxes of Paradise*, 76.
170. The gazelle as a symbol of female beauty is found in Arabic lyrics, though the focus is often on her eyes (Jinbachian, "Arabian Odes," 129; Mathers, *Book of the Thousand Nights*, 1:51; Dalman, *Palästinischer Diwan*, 218; Stephan, "Modern Palestinian Parallels," 238).
171. Biggs, *ŠÀ.ZI.GA*, 8 (1–8). The broken lines are restored based on numerous parallels in other incantations (incipit ii [13–15]; 5 [15]; 6 [1–2]; 7 [2–3]; 9 [3–8]; 12 [19]). Parts of the stag's body were viewed as sexual stimulants, mixed in potions to treat erectile dysfunction (Biggs, "The Babylonian Sexual Potency Texts," in Parpola and Whiting, *Sex and Gender*, 75–76).
172. Nissinen, "Nabû and Tašmetu," 589, 610–14.

desire to give her lover sexual pleasure (13–16) and her entrance into their bedroom chamber (r.9), the sexual nuance of this imagery should not be missed. In addition, Keel notes numerous examples in which the gazelle is depicted alongside the goddess of love in Near Eastern iconography. Two Syrian seals (eighteenth century BCE) depict a goddess with open garment beside copulating gazelles, while a pendant from Ras Shamra (fourteenth century BCE) shows a naked goddess with a gazelle in each hand.[173] Absent from Egyptian and Greek literature, the man's invocation of gazelles in praise of the maiden's breasts may derive from the East, though such parallels could also have arisen from natural observation.

5.8.2. Meaning in the Song

The Song's poet clearly draws on the BODY AS LANDSCAPE metaphor here. But how does the above comparative evidence help? First, the figure highlights the visual balance of the maiden's breasts. In addition to the dual form שדיך, the poet repeats שני "two," possibly for alliteration with שן "teeth" (4:2) and שני "scarlet" (4:3), and the fawns are specified as תאמם "twins." This emphasis on duality likely stresses symmetry, a trait that sociological and scientific studies often connect to beauty.[174] While asymmetrical breasts may be a universal fear of women, comparative literature is silent, perhaps due to a predominance of male authors.[175]

Second, the man's likeness of the maiden's breasts to two fawns may also highlight a similarity in shape and/or shade. Based on the specified position of the animals "grazing among the lotuses," some posit that this portrait is rightly viewed from behind. Like the juxtaposition of dark hair and white teeth/eyes (4:2–3a; 5:11–12), Budde opined that this figure compares two grazing fawns, their brown rear-ends visible amidst the surrounding white flowers, with the woman's breasts, whose dark nipples are surrounded by the light skin of her breasts.[176] Though this imagery aligns well with surrounding visual metaphors (4:2–4) and such praise matches the widely shared ideal of light-colored skin, (1:5–6), this theory

---

173. Keel, *Song of Songs*, figs. 45–47. Keel opines that the gazelle signifies fecundity, but attributes usually associated with fertility are described in erotic terms in the Song.

174. Geoffrey Cowley, "The Biology of Beauty," *Newsweek* 127.23 (1996): 60–67.

175. On the fear of asymmetrical breasts, see Sherrow, "Breasts," in *For Appearance' Sake*, 63.

176. Budde, "Hohelied," 21.

is dependent on the color of the enigmatic שושנים. Such a visual portrait is possible, but the ambiguous nature of the שושן prevents a conclusion. The meaning of שושן will be discussed in detail below.

Third, in addition to the visual basis of comparison noted above, a survey of faunal imagery in the Hebrew Bible reveals an added behavioral similarity. The closest parallel to the imagery in Song 4:5, 7:4 is found in Prov 5:18–19, "May your fountain be blessed, may you rejoice in your young wife—a love-doe, a graceful deer; may her breasts satisfy you at all times, may you be intoxicated with her love always." As in the Song, these verses also invoke faunal imagery in a portrait of passionate lovemaking. Though some render אילת אהבים as "lovely doe," other occurrences of אהב show that this term has a strong sexual nuance (Prov 7:18; Hos 8:9).[177]

Similar to the comparative evidence above, the Song's poet often links the gazelle with feelings of sexual desire. In the adjuration refrain (2:7; 3:5), gazelles and hinds are invoked in the maiden's warning not to disturb lovers in the midst of passion.[178] Later, the beloved describes herself as a garden of lotuses and her lover as a grazing gazelle (2:16; 6:2–3), inviting him to romp on her "cleft/spiced mountains" (2:17; 8:14). A variant on this latter refrain immediately follows the man's praise for the maiden's breasts (4:5). Having detailed his beloved's beauty in 4:1–5, his emotions are overwhelmed, and he stops, declaring his intention to spend the night enjoying her passion-provoking pleasures (4:6). Thus, the Song's poet likely employs the gazelle as a symbol of powerful sexual desire.

Finally, the sensuality of this imagery is also implicit in the invocation of the שושנים. The identity of this flower has been debated by botanists and biblical scholars, each trying to account for the biblical data and *realia*.[179] The term שושן occurs seventeen times in the Hebrew Bible, eight times in the Song. Its use can be divided in three categories, the others being cult

---

177. Michael V. Fox, *Proverbs 1–9: A New Translation with Introduction and Commentary*, AB 18A (New York: Doubleday, 2000), 202; Bruce K. Waltke, *The Book of Proverbs: Chapters 1–15*, NICOT (Grand Rapids: Eerdmans, 2004), 321–22.

178. Brian P. Gault, "An Admonition against 'Rousing Love': The Meaning of the Enigmatic Refrain in Song of Songs," *BBR* 20 (2010): 161–84.

179. Zohary and Feliks favor the white lily, Moldenke prefers the hyacinth, and Dalman posits a variety of iris (Dalman, *Arbeit und Sitte in Palästina*, 1.2:357; Feliks, *Song of Songs*, 28; Moldenke and Moldenke, *Plants of the Bible*, 114–16; Zohary, *Plants of the Bible*, 176–77). In light of this ambiguity, Löw concluded that שושן may have become a general floral term (Löw, *Flora der Juden*, 2:161). As a result, scholars similarly vary in their translation of this term.

5. Anatomy of a Rose: Praise for the Female Body 179

construction (1 Kgs 7:19, 22, 26) and hymnic superscriptions (Pss 45; 60; 69; 80). Though this term occurs in other Semitic languages (*CAD*, "šišnu," 17.3:126; *DNWSI*, "ššn¹," 1197; *DJPA*, "שושן," 543; *SyrLex*, "ܫܘܫܢܬܐ," 1539), שושן likely derives from Egyptian.¹⁸⁰ Since *sššn/sšn* clearly means "lotus" in Egyptian (*GHb*, "sššn," 834; *WÄS*, "sšn," 3:485–86), it most likely refers to the same flower in the Hebrew Bible.¹⁸¹ But why is the lotus invoked amidst the Song's breast imagery?

In Egyptian culture, the lotus was known for its narcotic properties.¹⁸² Iconography often depicts the lotus suspended over or wrapped around wine vessels in a fashion unlikely to exist in real life, and since

---

180. Kenneth A. Kitchen, "Lotuses and Lotuses, or … Poor Susan's Older Than We Thought," *VA* 3 (1987): 29–31; Muchiki, *Egyptian Proper Names and Loanwords in North-West Semitic*, 256. While the LXX and Vulgate render שושן as "lily" (κρίνον, *lilium*), Herodotus explains, "When the river is in spate, a large number of lilies grow in the water; the Egyptian name for this water lily is lotus" (*Hist.* 2.92 [Waterfield]).

181. While the superscriptions are enigmatic, the other references to the שושן are best linked to the lotus. First, the use of this flower in the ornamentation of Israel's temple (1 Kgs 7:19, 22, 26) is paralleled by similar objects in Egypt and Israel. Keel notes an Egyptian chalice in the form of a lotus blossom and scarabs from Beth-shan and Beth-shemesh depicting a man smelling a large lotus blossom (Keel, *Song of Songs*, 78–81). Hepper similarly points to the abundant use of the lotus in the tomb of Tutankhamen, atop columns on the Pharaoh's boat as well as the artificial capital on a papyrus burnisher. See F. Nigel Hepper, *Pharaoh's Flowers: The Botanical Treasures of Tutankhamun*, 2nd ed. (Chicago: KWS, 2009), 11–12. In fact, pollen from two species of the lotus was found in recent excavations near Jerusalem from the Persian period. See Dafna Langgut et al., "Fossil Pollen Reveals the Secrets of the Royal Persian Garden at Ramat Rahel, Jerusalem," *Palynology* 37 (2013): 126. But what about the Song? In 2:1–2, the maiden likens herself to "a crocus of Sharon, a lotus of the valleys," and her lover responds by praising her as "a lotus among thorns." The mention of the Sharon plain has caused some to assume that the flowers described here must be planted in soil, not based in water. Yet, prior to the Second Temple period, when the Romans cut outlets in its ridges, the Sharon was a swampy area, with dense forests and pastureland used for grazing. See Carl G. Rasmussen, *Zondervan Atlas of the Bible*, rev. ed. (Grand Rapids: Zondervan, 2010), 43. Therefore, the image of a lotus in the Sharon is logically consistent. If the Sharon was filled with marshes, with more lotuses than today, as Keel concludes, then the maiden's parallel statements portray modesty, one (crocus/lotus) among the many (Sharon/valleys) (Keel, *Song of Songs*, 78–80). See also W. Derek Suderman, "Modest or Magnificent? Lotus versus Lily in Canticles," *CBQ* 67 (2005): 49–53. Moreover, connecting the lotus to the Sharon pasturelands may also provide the background for the phrase "grazing among lotuses" (2:16; 6:2–3).

182. Manniche, *Sacred Luxuries*, 99.

the narcotic alkaloids were soluble in alcohol not water, the Egyptians likely noted the effect of their lotus-laced wine. Benson Harer also points out that the erotic Turin Papyrus consistently depicts a lotus above the head of the lady, even when her posture is upside down. "It seems likely that the woman is 'under the lotus,' meaning under the influence of the lotus to release her sexual inhibitions."[183] Like the origin of שׁוּשַׁן, the lotus imagery may derive from Egypt. Perhaps playing on the dual nature of the lotus as narcotic and food (Herodotus, *Hist*. 2.92), the Song invokes this flower amid the desire for intoxicating love (2:16–17; 6:2–3). Thus, the man's metaphor for his beloved's breasts may highlight their symmetry, but its link to floral and faunal images stresses sexual virility and sensual intoxication.

Following the lover's likeness of his beloved's breasts to fawns grazing among the lotuses (4:5, 7:4), an added erotic implication may be present when the woman identifies her man's lips as lotuses (5:13b).[184] Yet, there is also debate on the meaning of this metaphor. What is the basis for comparison between the man's lips and lotuses? Some posit smell, in connection with the spices mentioned in the previous line (5:13a), while others suggest color, shape, or both.[185] Though such physical traits are highlighted elsewhere in the lovers' praise, this flower is often connected to lovemaking (2:16–17; 4:6; 6:2–3; 8:14). The final line of the metaphor, "dripping liquid myrrh," further clarifies the poet's intended meaning. In the Song, myrrh is often connected to sexual desire. The lady likens her lover to a sachet of myrrh lying all night between her breasts (1:13), while the man metaphorically depicts his beloved's breast as a mountain of myrrh (4:6). When the man depicts the maiden's body as a garden filled with choice fruits and spices (4:12–15), myrrh appears in his poetic portrait of consummation (5:1). Finally, the woman's sexual desire is implicit when she rises to open the door to her lover, with "her hands dripping myrrh, her

---

183. W. Benson Harer, Jr., "Pharmacological and Biological Properties of the Egyptian Lotus," *JARCE* 22 (1985): 53–54. In an overly anatomical reading of the Song's erotic metaphor, Case misses the link between lotus and intoxication (M. L. Case, "Cunning Linguists: Oral Sex in the Song of Songs," *VT* 67 [2017]: 175).

184. Fox, *Song of Songs*, 131.

185. Smell: Bergant, *Song of Songs*, 71; Brenner, *Intercourse of Knowledge*, 47; Feliks, *Song of Songs*, 95; Color: Bloch and Bloch, *Song of Songs*, 87; Ginsburg, *Song of Songs*, 169; Landy, *Paradoxes of Paradise*, 77; Pope, *Song of Songs*, 541; Walsh, *Exquisite Desire*, 64; Shape: Gerleman, *Hohelied*, 175; Murphy, *Song of Songs*, 172.

fingers with liquid myrrh" (5:5). Thus, the man's lips are clearly viewed as a source of stimulating, sensual pleasure.

Moreover, references to the lips, tongue, and mouth are often linked to images of sensual stimulation and intoxication. In the Song's opening lines, the lady twice praises her man's lovemaking as more intoxicating than wine (1:2–4; 4:10). Likewise, the man compares his beloved's breath to apples and her mouth to the best wine (7:9–10). Similar to 5:13b, the lover refers to his lady's lips, "which drip nectar, with honey and milk under [her] tongue" (4:11). Concluding her *waṣf*, the woman exclaims, "His mouth is sweet, and he is altogether desirable" (5:16). Thus, drawing on metaphor LOVE AS INTOXICATION, the lady's comparison of her lover's lips to lotuses (5:13b), similar to his depiction of her breasts (4:5), is best read as a play on the intoxicating effect of the lotus. Both lovers envision the other's body as a stimulant that intoxicates the senses. They desire to be drunk with love, imbibing deeply of their lover's sexual pleasures.

5.9. Shapely, Superior Stomach (7:3b)

| בטנך ערמת חטים | 7:3 Your belly is a heap of wheat, |
| סוגה בשושנים: | encircled[186] with lotuses. |

Source: Heap, Wheat, Lotus
Target: Belly
Mapping: Shape, Shade, Sexual Satisfaction, Superior Beauty

In contrast to his first two poems of praise for the maiden's beauty (4:1–7; 6:4–7), the man changes direction in the final song, beginning at her sandaled feet and ending with her hair (7:2–7). After praising her feet, thighs, and navel (7:2–3a), the lover centers on his beloved's belly (7:3b). Scholars are generally agreed on the translation of this verse, though the same cannot be said for its interpretation. One scholar explicitly leaves its meaning to one's "personal preference."[187] Comparative data is limited, but the interpretation of this image need not be left to subjectivity.

---

186. A *hapax legomenon* in the Bible, סוג "to fence in" is found in other Semitic languages (*DJPA*, s.v. "סוג"; *SyrLex*, "ܣܘܓ," 975; Lane, "سوج," 1459), as well as the rabbinic desire to "make a fence" around Torah (m. Avot 1:1).

187. Stoop-van Paridon, *Song of Songs*, 370.

5.9.1. Comparative Evidence

The term ערמה "heap" is often used by biblical writers to describe a pile of grain (Ruth 3:7; Jer 50:26; Neh 13:15) or other produce (2 Chr 31:6), by definition stressing a curved shape. But is the heap big or small? Ginsburg opined that women of substance were prized in Israelite culture: "Corpulency was deemed essential to an Eastern beauty."[188] Yet, this idea does not match textual and material evidence from the Near East. Female pictorial evidence is scant in Palestine, but slender women are shown on two Megiddo ivories, a pendant from Beth-Shean, and many "Astarte-type" fertility plaques (*ANEP*, 70, 126, 464, 478). On the Levantine ivories, "the hourglass shape of these [female] bodies highlights small waists and slightly protruding bellies."[189] Robins notes a similar ideal in Egyptian art: "The slender-bodied woman is predominant, despite the fact that between puberty and menopause most Egyptian women probably spent much of their time in one stage or another of pregnancy."[190]

In addition, Mesopotamian women (other than fertility figurines) are also shown with a slender figure (*ANEP*, 22, 144, 167, 451, 510, 525, 632), while Hellenistic, Indian, and Arab lyrics laud a woman's slender body and curved belly.[191] The Roman era Greek poet Achilles Tatius praises Europa for her "deep-set navel, the long slight curve of the belly, the narrow waist, broadening down to the loins" (*Leuc. Clit.* 1.11; see also Ovid, *Am.* 1.5).

5.9.2. Meaning in the Song

Thus, in light of the widely shared ideal of slender beauty, the Song's unique metaphor likely refers to the maiden's gently curving belly. Yet the imagery of wheat likely depicts her skin color as well. As Delitzsch opines, "The comparison refers to the beautiful appearance of the roundness, but at the same time, also the flesh-color shining through the dress."[192] While color

---

188. Ginsburg, *Song of Songs*, 178.
189. Gansell, "Ideal Feminine Beauty," 54.
190. Robins, *Women in Ancient Egypt*, 80. For an example, see Arnold and Allen, *Royal Women*, figs. 21–22.
191. Mariaselvam, *Ancient Tamil Love Poems*, 201, 304; Jax, *Weibliche Schönheit*, 63; Jinbachian, "Arabian Odes," 137; Stephan, "Modern Palestinian Parallels," 220.
192. Keil and Delitzsch, *Commentary on the Old Testament*, 6:589. Rejecting this color portrait, Loader adopts an ultraerotic reading, linking בטן to the womb and

5. Anatomy of a Rose: Praise for the Female Body

is only implicit in the likeness to wheat, this basis for comparison is supported by the recurring emphasis on complexion and color in the Song. The maiden laments her dark skin (1:5–6) but praises the ruddy complexion of her lover (5:10). The man ignores his beloved's self-deprecation, lauding her ivory tone (7:5). Also, the lover frequently invokes color in his praise, highlighting his lady's dark, wavy locks (4:1; 6:5; 7:6), white teeth (4:2, 6:6), scarlet lips (4:3), rosy cheeks (4:3, 6:7), and white neck (7:5). Thus, drawing on the BODY AS LANDSCAPE theme, this metaphor likely highlights the curved shape and tawny color of her belly.

However, similar to some of the Song's previous imagery, the poet's likeness of the lady's belly to a heap of wheat pushes past the visual plane.[193] In the Hebrew Bible, wheat is a sign of divine blessing and symbol of agricultural abundance (Deut 8:8, 32:4; Joel 1:11; Hos 14:8; 2 Chr 2:14). For this reason, some scholars conclude that this imagery stresses her sexual fertility, with בטן referring to the lady's womb.[194] Yet fertility is foreign to the theme of the Song. Sexuality is celebrated, not for its utility as a means of procreation, but for the joy and pleasure of the act itself. Also, the imagery in the context focuses on the lady's external beauty and allure (7:2–10), not her potential fertility. So, why the agricultural imagery?

References to physical food in the Song are often metaphors for sexual desire (1:2–4; 2:3–5; 4:10–5:1; 7:8–10, 13; 8:1–2). Following this poem, the lover likens his beloved's body to a palm tree with pendulous fruits (7:8–10). Yet, the man does not speak out of physical hunger, but out of his overwhelming sexual desire. This idea is further supported by the imagery of wine in the opening lines of this verse (7:3a).[195] Thus, the images of wine and wheat do not refer to sexual fertility or physical hunger but are expres-

---

ערמה to the genitals around which hair grows like lilies (Loader, "Exegetical Erotica," 105–6). Yet this rendering turns euphemism into voyeurism. In contrast, "the Song keeps us out of the garden of eroticism. It renders our looking less voyeuristic, and our pleasure more aesthetic than erotic by clothing the lovers' bodies with metaphors, which never quite give access to the body described" (Exum, *Song of Songs*, 24).

193. Based on its use to describe a pile of threshed grain (Ruth 3:7), some scholars posit that ערמה "heap" also highlights the softness of her belly (Bloch and Bloch, *Song of Songs*, 201; Exum, *Song of Songs*, 234). Yet the application of this term to produce and rubbish (2 Chr 31:6; Neh 3:34) suggests that ערמה only describes the shape, with no implication regarding the nature of the product being collected.

194. Bergant, *Song of Songs*, 84; Hess, *Song of Songs*, 214; Keel, *Deine Blicke sind Tauben*, 74–77; Loader, "Exegetical Erotica," 105; Murphy, *Song of Songs*, 186.

195. The wine and wheat imagery may also be connected by unique terminology,

sions of passionate desire. The man views his beloved's body as a source of sexual satisfaction. Ironically, instead of being a symbol of want, craving the sustenance of physical food, the maiden's belly is portrayed as a feast to satisfy the man's sexual hunger.

However, the final phrase remains a question. Why does the man refer to a circle of lotuses? Is it merely a stylistic flourish or an important part of the visual metaphor? There is no other reference in ancient sources to wheat surrounded by lotuses, so the interpreter is left to infer its meaning based on the context of the Song.[196] First, Pope connected this imagery to a decorated belt worn between the waist and hips, often seen on Mesopotamian figurines, highlighting the female pubic region.[197] However, the lotuses surrounding the heap of wheat are a figure for the belly, not the waist. For this reason, others have suggested that the flowers refer to a garment or garland that partially covers the belly.[198] While possible, there are better explanations.

Second, another possibility is found in similar imagery from *Arabian Nights*. "On a certain night when they lay side by side drunken with wine and unfulfilled desire, Ghānim slipped his hand below the girl's chemise and, stroking her belly down until he reached her navel, began to play with the petals of the flesh he found there."[199] As pictured in this portrait, the lotus may refer to the petals of flesh on the lady's navel. While the navel is referred to in the opening lines of this verse (7:3a), the lotus is more naturally connected to the adjacent portrait of her belly.

Finally, many modern scholars connect this figure to an ancient practice of surrounding harvested grain with thorns for protection against thievery, often alluding to Boaz lying at the end of the grain heap (Ruth 3:7).[200] While the scene at the threshing floor may illustrate the practice of protecting grain, there is no mention of thorns. Also, the reference to lotuses rather than thorns is explained as more appropriate to the Song's maiden. But why? The appeal to such a cultural practice of encircling piles of wheat with thorns can be traced back as far as Rashbam, though this

---

מזג "spiced wine" and סוג "to fence in," possibly used for their alliteration (Noegel and Rendsburg, *Solomon's Vineyard*, 103).

196. Murphy, *Song of Songs*, 181.
197. Pope, *Song of Songs*, 622. See Dales, "Necklaces, Bands, and Belts," 37–40.
198. Murphy, *Song of Songs*, 182; Stoop-van Paridon, *Song of Songs*, 371.
199. Mathers, *Book of the Thousand Nights*, 329.
200. Exum, *Song of Songs*, 234; Fox, *Song of Songs*, 159; Keel, *Song of Songs*, 235.

custom may ultimately stem from the biblical text itself.[201] Thorns were used to keep valuables in and keep unwanted visitors out (Hos 2:8). In fact, Israel's law refers to the practice of surrounding fields with thorn bushes for this purpose (Exod 22:5). But how does this practice relate to the lover's poetic language. Exum suggests that a fence of lotuses may imply the beloved's lack of protection and sexual openness to her lover.[202] Yet, the imagery of the lotus may recall the man's earlier praise, likening his lady to a lotus among thorns (2:2).[203] Thus, the customary fence of thorns may have been altered as veiled reference to the maiden's superior beauty. The visual nature of other body images in the context weighs against such a functional explanation, but the poet's parenthetical comment in 7:3a may allow room such a unique allusion.

5.10. Sculpted Hips/Thighs (7:2b)

חמוקי ירכיך כמו חלאים 7:2 The curves of your hips/thighs are like gems,
מעשה ידי אמן׃   the handiwork of an artisan.[204]

Source: Gems
Target: Hips/Thighs
Mapping: Sculpted (Round) Shape

In comparison with preceding images, even those debated by scholars, the meaning of this verse is more tenuous—source, target, and mapping. Therefore, more space will be devoted to determining the possible meaning(s) of the terms before moving to comparative literature.

---

201. Yaakov Thompson, "The Commentary of Samuel Ben Meir on the Song of Songs" (PhD diss., Jewish Theological Seminary of America, 1988), 286. See also Denis Buzy, "Le Cantique des Cantiques," in *La Sainte Bible* (Paris: Letouzey, 1951), 6:349; Dalman, *Arbeit und Sitte in Palästina*, 1.2:359.

202. Exum, *Song of Songs*, 234.

203. Gary A. Long, "Simile, Metaphor, and the Song of Songs" (PhD diss., University of Chicago, 1993), 266–67.

204. Although the term אמן is a *hapax legomenon* in the Hebrew Bible, the meaning "artisan, craftsman" is clear based on widespread attestation across the Semitic languages: Akkadian (*CAD*, "ummânu," 20:111, 2a), Aramaic, (*DJPA*, s.v. "אומן"; *DJBA*, "אומנא," 90; *SyrLex*, "ܐܘܡܢܐ," 17; *MdD*, "'umana," 344), Nabataean, Punic, and Palmyrene (*DNWSI*, "'mn²," 71).

5.10.1. Meaning in the Song

The enigma begins with identifying the highlighted part of the maiden's body. Though the term ירך is not uncommon in the Hebrew Bible, it lacks precision. It can refer to the upper part of the thigh, covered by priestly undergarments (Exod 28:42); the hip, whose dislocation affected Jacob's ability to walk (Gen 32:26); the area of the genitals, touched while swearing an oath (Gen 42:2, 47:29); or the side of one's body, where a sword is strapped for battle (Exod 32:27; Song 3:8). This term is also used as spatial metaphor to describe the side of a building or piece of furniture (Exod 40:22; Lev 1:11). Thus, the poet's terminology is unclear, whether the man's praise centers on his beloved's thighs or hips.

Second, the praiseworthy trait of the maiden's thighs/hips is also tentative. The term חמוק is a *hapax legomenon* in the Hebrew Bible. The rendering found in most commentaries, also reflected above, is based on a related form חמק, which occurs only twice (Song 5:6; Jer 31:22). Since both of these passages appear to describe a turning motion, scholars infer that the man lauds the rounded shape of her thighs/hips. Yet, there is no cognate evidence to support this gloss. Pope's claim that חמק is used in postbiblical Hebrew to describe a wheel is mistaken.[205]

Also, Pope's assertion that כלילא "crown" in Targum Canticles 7:2 "approximates this sense" is also misguided. Linking Hebrew terms to the Targum's midrashic translation is notoriously difficult, but the construct חמוקי ירכיך best corresponds to נפקי ירכיהון, with the later mention of the crown being an added literary detail. The wide variation in the versions suggests that the meaning of the term may have been lost.[206]

Finally, the maiden's thighs/hips are likened to חלאים, another term of debated meaning. Despite only three occurrences in the Hebrew Bible, ḥly is a common Arabic root used to describe a woman's adornment (*HALOT*,

---

205. Pope, *Song of Songs*, 615. The mistake was fixed in a later printing of *Yalkut Shimoni*. See Nathan ben Jehiel, ʿ*Arukh ha-Shalem*, ed. Alexander Kohut (New York: Pardes, 1955), 3:432.

206. Old Greek ῥυθμοί and Syriac ṣur, "shape, form" (LSJ, s.v. "ῥυθμός"; SyrLex, "ܝܘ 1," 1282), Symmachus σύνδεσμοι "joints" and Vulgate *iuncturae* (LSJ, s.v. "σύνδεσμος"; OLD, s.v. "iunctura"), and Old Latin *moduli* "measures" (*OLD*, s.v. "modulus"). Origen's rendering *ambitus* "round shape," from one schooled in Hebrew by Jewish rabbis, may suggest that all knowledge was not lost. See Fridericus Fields, ed., *Origenis Hexaplorum quae supersunt* (Hildesheim: Olms, 1964), 2:421.

"I חֲלִי" 318; Lane, "حَلْيٌ," 634–35). Thus, most translators identify this term as a type of feminine ornament. Since the other biblical passages (Prov 25:12; Hos 2:15) place חלי in parallel with נזם "ring," some view this term similarly as a round piece of jewelry.[207] However, in contrast to the prevailing practice of rendering this term generally, greater specificity is possible. Both the Latin (*monilia*) and targumic (זהרון) traditions interpret חלי as a reference to precious stones. While these translators may have also struggled to understand this term, Aramaic and Akkadian cognates further support a connection to gemstones. In Mandaic, the term חאלים refers to jewels, often found in parallel to pearls (*MdD*, "halia," 121). Also, the Akkadian *ḫulalu* and *ḫaltu* refer to precious stones used in rituals (*CAD*, "ḫaltu," "ḫulālu A," 6:53, 226–27). Thus, using the OBJECT OF LOVE IS A VALUABLE OBJECT metaphor, the lover appears to liken his lady's thighs/hips to gemstones, stressing their sculpted shape.

5.10.2. Comparative Evidence

Praise for female thighs and hips is also found in other cultures. In Egypt, the girl invites her lover to caress her thighs, personifying them as a powerful entity that binds him.[208] Egyptian art accentuated a woman's curves, consistently depicting female figures in diaphanous garments, whose tight fabric highlighted the shape of her thighs and hips.[209]

Mesopotamian lyrics most often refer to a woman's thighs/hips in the context of physical love. On his beloved Inanna, Ishmedagan boasted, "With her thighs she has caused me amorous delight."[210] Westenholz notes a similar expression from an Old Babylonian love song, as the woman describes her sexual charms, concluding with this *open* invitation to love, "Enter, I have opened (my) thighs."[211] The portrait of female beauty in Greco-Roman and Indian culture also lauded a female's thighs/hips, particularly ones of large size (Philodemus, *Anth. Pal.* 5.132; [Lucian], *Am.*

---

207. Murphy, *Song of Songs*, 181.
208. Fox, *Song of Songs*, 7, 52, 73.
209. Manniche, *Sexual Life in Ancient Egypt*, 41; Robbins, *Women in Ancient Egypt*, 181–82.
210. Sefati, *Love Songs*, 37. For a similar example, see Åke W. Sjöberg, "Miscellaneous Sumerian Texts, II," *JCS* 29 (1977): 23 (10′).
211. Westenholz, "A Forgotten Love Song," 423.

14).²¹² India's *Gīta Govinda* praised Rādhā's broad hips as voluptuous.²¹³ Yet, the closest parallel to the Song's imagery is found in medieval and modern Arab love lyrics. In *Arabian Nights*, a woman's lovely curves are often praised, once likened to molded marble.²¹⁴ Dalman similarly notes a bedouin lyric where the lady's hips are compared to jewels.²¹⁵ While the meaning and distribution of the Song's imagery cannot be firmly established, the ancients widely considered a woman's slender curves part of her beauty.

5.11. Miss Universe (6:4, 10; cf. 5:15)

יפה את רעיתי כתרצה	⁶:⁴ My dear, you are beautiful as Tirzah
נאוה כירושלם	lovely as Jerusalem,
אימה כנדגלות:	awesome²¹⁶ as the most outstanding sights.²¹⁷

---

212. For the Greeks, narrow hips were a detriment, likely due to fertility concerns (Jax, *Weibliche Schönheit*, 79–80). As an example, Lee points to the Archaic *korai*, whose "small breasts and gently swelling hips suggest a youthful, fertile body" (Lee, *Body, Dress, and Identity in Ancient Greece*, 45). Europa is similarly depicted, "with a narrow waist, broadening down to the loins" (*Leuc. Clit.* 1.11).

213. Miller, *Love Song of the Dark Lord*, 35, 118.

214. Mathers, *Book of the Thousand Nights*, 237, 354, 476.

215. Dalman, *Palästinischer Diwan*, 125.

216. Since אימה/אים "terror, terrifying" most often depicts a negative emotional response (Hab 1:7; Exod 15:16; Josh 2:9; Job 39:20; Ps 88:16), and the context mixes praise and fear (6:4–10), the term "awesome" was intentionally chosen to convey the lover's sense of wonder and his implicit anxiety. Goitein's rendering "splendid" misses both ideas and does not fit the context. Shlomo D. Goitein, "*Ayumma Kannidgalot* [Song of Songs VI.10]: 'Splendid Like the Brilliant Stars,'" *JSS* 10 (1965): 220–21.

217. The meaning of נדגלות is a *crux interpretum*. The root דגל occurs four times in the Song (2:4; 5:10; 6:4, 10). Elsewhere, it is linked to Israel's cult arrangement, describing the visible sign for each tribe around the tent of meeting (Num 2:2; 10:14). Thus, many render this term consistently as "banner" (Garrett and House, *Song of Songs/Lamentations*, 228; Ginsburg, *Song of Songs*, 172; Keel, *Song of Songs*, 215; Longman, *Song of Songs*, 180). However, military imagery seems foreign to a *waṣf* song. In contrast, Gordis posited that this root is better tied to the Akkadian *dagâlu* "to look with astonishment" (Robert Gordis, "The Root דגל in the Song of Songs," *JBL* 88 [1969]: 203–4; Gary A. Long, "A Lover, Cities, and Heavenly Bodies: Co-Text and the Translation of Two Similes in Canticles [6:4c; 6:10d]," *JBL* 115 [1996]: 703–9). This meaning aligns well with 5:10, where the woman exalts her man as "outstanding (visible) among ten thousand." In 2:4, the poet extends this term's semantic range, adding a sense of volition, "He brought me to the house of wine, and his intent toward me

5. Anatomy of a Rose: Praise for the Female Body

מי־זאת הנשקפה כמו־שחר	6:10 Who is this peering down like the dawn,[218]
יפה כלבנה	beautiful as the moon,
ברה כחמה	radiant as the sun,[219]
אימה כנדגלות:	awesome as the most outstanding sights.

| מראהו כלבנון | 5:15 His appearance is like Lebanon, |
| בחור כארזים: | choice as its cedars. |

Source: Prominent Places, Heavenly Luminaries
Target: Physical Appearance
Mapping: Supreme Beauty

As mentioned at the opening of this chapter, the Song's four *waṣfs* are bracketed by assertions of beauty (4:1, 7; 5:10, 15–16; 6:4, 10; 7:2, 7). In three of these verses, the lover's physical appearance is praised with comparisons to prominent earthly locales and heavenly luminaries.

5.11.1. Comparative Evidence

While some have viewed the astral imagery in 6:10 as a description of deity, the likeness of feminine beauty to the heavenly luminaries is nearly universal, using a commonality of human experience to express the infatuation known to every lover.[220] In an Egyptian *waṣf*, the girl's matchless physical beauty is compared to Sothis (Sirius), the star whose rising signaled the

---

was lovemaking" (Pope, *Song of Songs*, 375–77). In the two passages above, contextual praise for the woman's physical beauty also supports a visual meaning. Like דגול in 5:10, נדגלות is best explained as outstanding sights. In this case, the article marks the superlative, indicating the climax of a progression (GKC §133g; Joüon §141j). Rendsburg attributes the use of this rare term to alliteration with ירד לגנו "he went down to his garden" (6:2) and אל־גנת אגוז ירדתי "I went down to the nut grove" (6:11), though the intervening break between 6:2 and 6:4 is problematic (Noegel and Rendsburg, *Solomon's Vineyard*, 100).

218. The "woman at the window" motif is also found in Mesopotamian literature and art (Held, "Faithful Lover in an Old Babylonian Dialogue," 8 [iii.18]; Lapinkivi, *Sumerian Sacred Marriage*, 233–40; Nissinen, "Nabû and Tašmetu," 602–3).

219. The word pair לבנה "white"/חמה "heat" are rare poetic terms used to describe the heavenly luminaries (Job 30:28; Isa 24:23; 30:26). These terms could also be implicit praise for the maiden's color, white and shining (see also 5:10). Rendsburg posits that לבנה reveals a northern dialect, though Isaiah's use of this term (30:26) to address Jerusalem is problematic (Noegel and Rendsburg, *Solomon's Vineyard*, 44).

220. For likening to deity, see Keel, *Song of Songs*, 220; Müller, "Hohelied," 67.

inundation of the Nile.²²¹ Similarly, in Joseph and Aseneth, the splendor of Aseneth's face is likened to the sun and her eyes to a rising morning star (18.9). The same language is found in two Mesopotamian hymns to Inanna, whose beauty and arrival is compared to the moon, "How she carried (her) beauty—like the rising moonlight" (*ANET*, 582 [Kramer]).²²² Similarly, Nana "is like the new moon to look upon, her wondrous features full of brilliance."²²³ Also, Ludingira likens his mother's beauty to a "bright light on the horizon … a morning star (shining) at noon."²²⁴ Finally, in a rare example of secular love lyrics, *KAR* 158 contains one astral image, "My beloved is a constellation which brightens an eclipse" (vii:45).²²⁵

Moreover, comparing matchless feminine beauty to the heavenly luminaries is also evident in Greco-Roman and Indian love literature. Alcman likened Agido's beauty to the stars (P. Louvre 3320 frag. 1.39–43), while Sappho links the radiance of Anactoria to the moon, "She stands out among Lydian women like the rosy-fingered moon around sunset, surpassing all the stars" (*Lyra Graeca* 96 [Campbell]; see also *Homeric Hymn to Aphrodite*, 90). Theocritus similarly compares Helen's perfect face to the rising dawn (*Id.* 18.26–28).²²⁶ Mariaselvam also notes examples in the Tamil love lyrics, where a beloved's beautiful appearance is likened to the moon and stars.²²⁷

The common use of such astral imagery in the hyperbolic praise of *waṣf* songs underlies the satire found in one Indian lyric:

> He came close, to look closer at my brow, my hands, my eyes, my walk, my speech, and said, searching for metaphors: "Amazed, it grows small, but it isn't the crescent. Unspotted, it isn't the moon. Like bamboo, yet it

---

221. Fox, *Song of Songs*, 52, 56.

222. Daniel D. Reisman, "Iddin-Dagan's Sacred Marriage Hymn," *JCS* 10 (1973): 189 (111).

223. Foster, *Before the Muses*, 89. Dumuzi's radiant appearance is also likened to the moon on his wedding day (Sefati, *Love Songs*, 292 [ii.20]).

224. Civil, "Message of Lu-Dingir-Ra," 3:22–23.

225. Groneberg, "Searching for Akkadian Lyrics," 67. Grammar and lack of context prevents gender identification, but the predominance of male authored lyrics in this catalog favors a feminine object.

226. Horace also applies astral imagery to the male appearance, describing one man as "more beautiful than a star" (*Carm.* 3.9 [Rudd]).

227. Mariaselvam, *Ancient Tamil Love Poems*, 196.

isn't on a hill. Lotuses, yet there's no pool. Walk mincing, yet no peacock. The words languish, yet you're not a parrot."[228]

While this motif is clearly evident in the above cultures, examples are even more abundant in both medieval and modern Arabic love lyrics. In *Arabian Nights*, the beloved's beauty surpasses the sun, moon, and stars. In fact, the heavenly luminaries draw their light from her, "She comes, a torch in the shadows, and it is day; her light more brightly lights the dawn. Sun leaps out from her beauty and moons are born in the smiling of her eyes."[229] Her fair face could be confused for the radiant sun, "When she raised her veil, the jeweler thought the sun had been brought into his house."[230] Compared to other women, her beauty is like the full moon surrounded by the light of tiny stars, "a fairer thing than any I had set eyes on in the world."[231]

Stephan, Dalman, and Saarisalo record similar praise in the love lyrics of twentieth-century Arab bedouins. "She stood opposite me and deprived me of reason; she is like Pleiades in the sky on high."[232] The beloved's face and brow are like the moon, the moon fades in the light of her smile, and her breasts eclipse the sun, "Her breast, why need I describe it, my mind could not grasp it.... Seven stars shine in it and rise from among its veins. If she does not cover it, it will veil the shining sun."[233] Her beauty is the envy of men and angels, an object of worship to the stars.[234] One wedding lyric likens the groom to the moon and his bride to the morning light, "in beauty, they say, she surpasses all."[235]

Likewise, the expression of superior female beauty by comparison to the celestial bodies was a stock theme in Petrarchan style. Sidney described Stella's beauty as residing in her eyes, whose beams shine as stars from the night sky, a theme on which Shakespeare plays in his satirical *Sonnet* 130, "My mistress' eyes are nothing like the sun."[236] Yet, even the master playwright incorporated astral imagery in the romance of *Romeo and Juliet*.

---

228. Ramanujan, *Poems of Love and War*, 197.
229. Mathers, *Book of the Thousand Nights*, 4.
230. Mathers, *Book of the Thousand Nights*, 631.
231. Mathers, *Book of the Thousand Nights*, 207.
232. Stephan, "Modern Palestinian Parallels," 211.
233. Saarisalo, "Songs of the Druzes," 48, 56.
234. Saarisalo, "Songs of the Druzes," 6, 58.
235. Dalman, *Palästinischer Diwan*, 193. Stephan records examples where celestial imagery is applied to the man (Stephan, "Modern Palestinian Parallels," 227).
236. Hamilton, *Sir Philip Sidney*, 89.

The beloved Juliet is the sun, whose light is fairer than the moon, with eyes that could replace the brightest stars, and cheeks even brighter (2.1.45–65). Similarly, Marlowe's Faustus praises Helen as "fairer than the evening's air, clad in the beauty of a thousand stars: brighter than flaming Jupiter … more lovely than the monarch of the sky."[237] Henry Wadsworth Longfellow, the nineteenth-century American poet, also employed this motif to praise his beloved's beautiful eyes and hair.[238] Thus, playing on the OBJECT OF LOVE IS A VALUABLE OBJECT metaphor, the Song's celestial imagery, an archetypal symbol of iconic beauty, climaxes the lover's praise for his matchless maiden (6:8–10).

5.11.2. Meaning in the Song

Song 6:4 and 6:10 form an *inclusio* around the man's second song, highlighted by the repetition of אימה כנדגלות "awesome as the most outstanding sights," while 5:15 concludes the woman's portrait of her man. The general idea in these verses is clear, but the details raise questions.[239]

First, why does the lover liken his lady to cities? In our culture, such a comparison seems strange, even offensive. In fact, Thomas Cheyne preferred to emend the MT, labeling it "hardly defensible," since "fair women would not be compared to cities."[240] Yet biblical authors commonly personify cities as young women (Isa 37:22, Lam 1:1).[241] Thus, if cities can be compared to women, why could women not be compared to cities?[242] Indeed, the poet's fondness for the city metaphor is evident in the lady's self-description as a defensive wall flanked with towers (8:10).

Second, why were *these* places chosen to describe the lovers? The selection of Jerusalem seems easy to explain. As the political and religious capital of the Southern Kingdom, Jerusalem is often depicted as an icon of beauty. The psalmist labels Zion as "the perfection of beauty" and "joy

---

237. Gill, *Complete Works of Christopher Marlowe*, 2:42 (xii:94–98).
238. Henry W. Longfellow, *Poetical Works* (London: Cassell, 1891), 21, 44.
239. Tsumura explains 5:15b as a single metaphor in vertical parallelism, line b explains line a. David T. Tsumura, "Metaphor, Grammar, and Parallelism in Song of Songs" (paper presented at the Annual Meeting of the Society of Biblical Literature, Atlanta, GA, 21 November 2010), 7–8.
240. Thomas K. Cheyne, "Canticles," in *Encyclopedia Biblica* 1:692.
241. James, "Battle of the Sexes," 111.
242. Keel, *Song of Songs*, 212–13.

of all the earth" (Pss 48:3; 50:2). In contrast, Tirzah is more problematic. Though this city appears to have functioned as the capital of the Northern Kingdom before Omri (1 Kgs 15:33; 16:8), its mention in the biblical record is minimal. Why choose an obscure city as a metaphor for iconic beauty? These two royal cities may have been linked as a merism for the entire land of Israel, but the poet more likely plays on the root meaning of Tirzah, from רצה "to take pleasure in, be pleasing." The ancient versions detected the secondary meaning but missed the wordplay with parallel place names.

Similarly, the source of the woman's metaphor, Lebanon, also evokes images of superior beauty. In the Song's 117 verses, Lebanon is invoked 6 times (3:9; 4:8, 11, 15; 5:15; 7:5), often as a distant source of opulence. As mentioned earlier (8:8–10), Lebanese cedar was considered a luxury item, imported for royal projects (1 Kgs 6:18). This implicit metaphor of excellence is made explicit with בחור "choice." Like Lebanon, with its superior, towering cedars, the lady's preeminent lover stands head and shoulders above his peers. In response to the question of Zion's daughters, "Why is your lover better than others?" (5:8), the maiden opens with her claim that he is "outstanding among ten thousand" (5:10) and closes by comparing him to the iconic cedars of Lebanon (5:15). However, this metaphor appears to be unique, with no evidence in other cultures.

5.12. Summary

Therefore, with three lyric portraits distinguished by vertical sequence, list parallelism and bracketed assertions (4:1–7; 6:4–7; 7:2–7), the Song's poet praises the woman's outstanding physical beauty. Though the function of her bodily members is mentioned, with eyes depicted as messengers of love (1:15; 4:1) and breasts as symbols of sexual passion and sensual intoxication (4:5; 7:4), their visual form is primary. The man lauds the maiden's matchless splendor (6:4, 10), from her big beautiful eyes (7:5), dark, wavy locks (4:1), scarlet lips/cheeks (4:3), and white teeth (4:2) to her straight nose (7:5), tall, beaded neck (4:4; 7:5), shapely stomach (7:3), and sculpted thighs (7:2). Aside from Heshbon's pools (7:5) and perhaps the Egyptian lotus (4:5, 7:3), the female *waṣf* songs are mainly built on shared cultural ideals and universal archetypes, using three common conceptual metaphors (BODY AS LANDSCAPE, LOVE AS INTOXICATION, OBJECT OF LOVE IS A VALUABLE OBJECT). Yet the Song's poet did not simply import well-known tropes but often wrapped shared symbols in cultural trappings to create unique metaphors. For example, when the lovers laud one another's beautiful hair, the Song's poet plays on an archetypal symbol of beauty and seduction (7:6c) and incorporates the shared Near Eastern preference for dark, shining curls (4:1c; 7:6a–b; 5:11), yet with the mention of goats grazing on Gilead, cultural data is combined with unique innovation.

In addition, the above lyrics also provide support for the Song's literary unity. Numerous physical characteristics are repeatedly praised: light complexion (1:5–6; 7:5), affectionate eyes (1:15, 4:1; 5:12), dark curls (4:1; 5:11; 7:6), jeweled neck (1:10–11; 4:4, 9), and large female breasts (2:17; 4:6; 7:8; 8:14). Shared structural features in the Song's body imagery also suggest a unified composition. As mentioned above, the three female *waṣf* songs share a similar literary form (4:1–7; 6:4–7; 7:2–7), with bracketed assertions of highest praise, a sequential list of physical description, and the resulting effects of such beauty on the gazing lover. This pattern of physical beauty and its amorous effect is found throughout the Song (1:15–17; 4:1–7, 9–5:1; 5:10–6:3; 6:4–12; 7:2–10). Now, having examined the man's praise for his maiden's body, we turn to the lady's ode to her lover (5:10–16).

6
Outstanding among Ten Thousand: An Ode to the Male Body

Similar to the lover's poems of praise for her beauty (4:1–7; 6:4–7; 7:2–7), the woman's ode to her man (5:10–16) is also distinguished by its literary form, with the same sequence (head-toe) and list parallelism. Likewise, these lyrics are set apart from the context by bracketed declarations of highest praise. The man is lauded as "outstanding among ten thousand" (5:10) and "like Lebanon, choice as its cedars" (5:15). In addition, parallels extend to the content of the lyrics as well. Just as the lover filled his praise with figures of flora and fauna, so the woman also draws on nature metaphors: "black as a raven" (5:11), "eyes like doves" (5:12), "cheeks like garden beds of spice" (5:13), and "lips like lotuses" (5:13).

However, the woman's portrait of her lover also contains important differences. The man's appearance is given only seven verses (5:10–16), in contrast to three songs dedicated to the woman, further supporting the Song's emphasis on the female. She is not only the dominant speaker, but more focus is placed on her physical body. Yet, the most significant difference in the man's likeness is the shift in metaphoric domain. While the woman's *waṣf* songs are packed with figures drawn from agriculture and architecture, the man's physique is predominantly depicted with images of precious metals and gems: gold, alabaster, ivory, topaz, and lapis lazuli. For this reason, some scholars describe the man as a statue, drawing parallels to Near Eastern portraits of divine statuary.[1] Yet, such an allusion seems unlikely in a context devoid of cultic references, with no mention in the Song of persons, places, or paraphernalia used in religious worship.[2]

---

1. Bernat, "Biblical *Waṣfs*," 329; Murphy, *Song of Songs*, 172; Nissinen, "Nabû and Tašmetu," 613; Pope, *Song of Songs*, 539; Ringgren, "Hohe Lied," 25.

2. Hamilton contends that statue imagery would be fit for a king, but not a

Rather, the key to unlocking these metaphors is found in the context. In contrast to the visual focus in the man's praise for his beloved (4:1, 7; 6:4, 9–10; 7:2, 7), these lyrics were intended to answer another question, "Why is your lover better than any other?" (5:9). Physical characteristics are included, but the primary purpose of this portrait is to praise the man's superiority, not to depict his *exact* likeness. What could be better than images of precious metals and gems? Having covered a few images in the previous chapter, let's look at the remaining metaphors for the male body.

6.1. Gold Standard (5:11a, 14a, 15a)

ראשו כתם פז	[11] His head is gold, pure gold[3]
ידיו גלילי זהב ממלאים בתרשיש	[14] His arms are rods[4] of gold, inlaid with golden topaz;[5]
שוקיו עמודי שש מיסדים על־אדני־פז	[15] His legs are pillars of alabaster,[6] set on bases of pure gold;

Source: Gold, Topaz, Alabaster; Rods, Pillars, Bases
Target: Head, Arms, Legs, Feet
Mapping: Superior Beauty/Value, Color/Sheen, Strength

---

common man. Mark W. Hamilton, *The Body Royal: The Societal Poetics of Kingship in Ancient Israel*, BibInt 78 (Leiden, Brill, 2005), 57. Yet, royal and courtly imagery is used to describe the lovers throughout the Song (1:4, 12; 3:6–11; 6:8–9; 7:5; 8:11–12).

3. Each found only nine times in the Hebrew Bible, mainly in late poetry, כתם and פז appear to describe superior quality gold. Often linked to Ophir, an unidentified site known for its gold (Job 28:16; Ps 45:10; Isa 13:12), כתם is also modified by adjectives of purity (Job 28:19; Lam 4:1) or connected to related terms to form a superlative (Job 31:24; Prov 25:12; Dan 10:5). Likewise, פז is also juxtaposed to similar terms, a climax in poetic parallelism (Job 28:17; Ps 19:11; Prov 8:19).

4. Derived from גלל "to roll," the rare term גליל is best explained as a cylinder shape, used to describe a door hinge (1 Kgs 6:34) or a rod/ring for curtains (Esth 1:6).

5. Though the exact identity of this gem is unknown, the name תרשיש is likely derived from Tartessos, a site on Iberia's southern coast at the mouth of the Guadalquivir River. Since Spain was known for its deposits of chrysolite (Pliny, *Nat.* 37.43), תרשיש may describe Spanish topaz or chrysolite, an identification supported by the LXX rendering χρυσόλιθος. See Benjamin J. Noonan, *Non-Semitic Loanwords in the Hebrew Bible: A Lexicon of Language Contact*, LSAWS 14 (Winona Lake, IN: Eisenbrauns, 2019), 228–29.

6. Found only twice in the Hebrew Bible (Esth 1:6), the term שש is likely an Egyptian loanword referring to alabaster (see *šś* in *ÄWb* 2:2480; *GHb*, 901; and *WÄS* 4:540).

With over four hundred references in the Hebrew Bible, gold was the most valuable metal in Israel during the biblical period.[7] From the tabernacle to Solomon's temple (Exod 25; 1 Kgs 6; 2 Kgs 24), gold was used to fashion items of importance, notably jewelry (Gen 24:22; Ezek 16:12; Job 42:11). As Benjamin Kedar-Kopfstein aptly summarizes, "It was the most precious of gifts (Gen 24:53; 1 Kgs 10:2), the currency of political bribery (1 Kgs 15:19), tribute levied for an offense (2 Kgs 18:14), and coveted booty (Josh 7:21)."[8] Yet, with no native supply in Palestine, gold was a luxury import, obtained from Egypt or Arabia (Exod 11:2; 1 Kgs 10:2; Ezek 27:22).

In light of its monetary value, gold was also used as a metaphor for great worth. Whether wisdom (Job 28:12–19) or a wise wife (Sir 7:18), when a person or thing is compared to gold, the high esteem of both source and target is in view. There is no better example than David's praise for YHWH's laws, "More desired are they than gold, even much fine gold, sweeter also than honey and the honeycomb" (Ps 19:11; see also 119:127). Thus, gold became a standard of value and beauty (Isa 13:12; Prov 11:22).

6.1.1. Comparative Evidence

The immense value of gold was not unique to Israel. Other Near Eastern cultures also refer to this precious metal as a concrete object and metaphoric symbol. In Egypt, the worth of gold is evident by its abundant presence in pharaonic tombs. An iconic example is the gold-laced tomb of Tutankhamun. When Carter stepped through its door, he looked in awe at "wonderful things," "everywhere the glint of gold."[9] The kings of Assyria and Mitanni attest to Egypt's vast supply of this asset in the Amarna letters (EA 16:13–14; 19:59–60). Gold is also used as a literary figure of worth. One hymn lauds the supreme status of Amun-Re, "His bones are made of silver, his flesh of gold."[10] Likewise, in a *waṣf* of love, the boy praises his beloved, "Her arms surpass gold" (*g3bwt.s ḥr itit nbw*). As Fox notes, gold was a cliché for superior beauty and value in Egypt.[11]

---

7. King and Stager, *Life in Biblical Israel*, 169.

8. Benjamin Kedar-Kopfstein, "זָהָב," *TDOT* 4:38.

9. Howard Carter and Arthur C. Mace, *The Tomb of Tut-ankh-Amen: Discovered by the Late Earl of Carnarvon and Howard Carter* (New York: Doran, 1923), 38.

10. Jan Assmann, *Ägyptische Hymnen und Gebete: Übersetzt, kommentiert und eingeleitet*, 2nd ed., OBO Sonderband 2 (Fribourg: Presses Universitaires; Göttingen: Vandenhoeck & Ruprecht, 1999), 311.

11. Fox, *Song of Songs*, 270.

Moreover, this dual significance of gold is also found in Mesopotamia. In a third-millennium BCE cemetery at Ur, Woolley notes the plentiful presence of this precious metal among the grave goods.[12] In addition, the Mesopotamian annals often refer to gold in the construction of royal and cultic statuary.[13] As a metaphor of value, the warrior-king Ninurta hoped that the truth stone, used as a weight on scales, would aid in just judgment, and to the wise, it would be as precious as gold.[14] Also, in an enigmatic cultic commentary, one of the Assyrian deities is personified, and his body parts are equated with the choicest elements of nature, his sperm like gold.[15] Likewise, Ludingira praises the choice beauty and worth of his mother, describing her as "bright gold (and) silver" (28–30).[16] Lastly, *KAR* 158 compares one lover's look to the most precious of metals, "Your love is obsidian, your smile is gold" (*ṣīḫātuka lu ḫurāṣu*, vii.43–44).[17]

Greco-Roman literature also refers to gold as a physical commodity and literary symbol, both implying value and beauty. As in Near Eastern cultures, the value of gold in Greece is evident from its cultic use. The second-century CE geographer Pausanias refers to images of Artemis and Dionysus in Corinth as overlaid with gold (*Descr.* 2.2.6).[18] On the beauty of gold, Plato states, "Even what before appeared ugly will appear beautiful when adorned with gold" (*Hipp. maj.* 289e [Fowler]). Roman writers also use gold as a symbol of worth and splendor. In his *Ars amatoria*, Ovid advises men anxious to keep their mistress to ensure the woman knows they are enamored with her beauty, "Let her be to you more precious than gold itself" (*Ars* 2.299 [Goold]). Finally, Horace labels the alluring beauty and sexual delights of a flirtatious woman as "golden charms" (*Carm.* 1.5 [Rudd]). Yet, unlike Mesopotamian and Egyptian lyrics, Greco-Roman literature does not equate the body or any of its parts to gold.

---

12. Woolley, *Royal Cemetery*, 292.

13. R. Campbell Thompson, *The Prisms of Esarhaddon and of Ashurbanipal Found at Nineveh, 1927–28* (London: British Museum, 1931), 33 (iii.49–iv.3); Donald J. Wiseman, "A New Stela of Aššurnaṣirpal II," *Iraq* 14 (1952): 34 (75–77); Stephen Langdon, *Die neubabylonischen königsinschriften*, VAB 4 (Leipzig: Hinrichs, 1912), 126 (iii.6–7); 276 (iv.9–13).

14. Jacobsen, *Harps*, 261 (509).

15. Livingstone, *Court Poetry*, 37 (r.5); 38 (r.15); 39 (12).

16. Civil, "Message of Lu-Dingir-Ra," 3.

17. Black, "Babylonian Ballads," 29; Groneberg, "Searching for Akkadian Lyrics," 67; Wasserman, *Akkadian Love Literature*, 221.

18. See also Aristotle, *Rhet.* 1.7.15.

In contrast, Indian poets often compare a woman's body to gold. One lover lauded his lady's unrivaled, supreme beauty: "The entire world surrounded by vast oceans, the scarcely achievable precious land of the gods—these two are worth nothing, if weighed against the day, on which I clasp the upper arms of the young maid ... with a body like gold."[19] In fact, the female body is repeatedly described as a glistening statue in Tamil literature, fashioned by supreme beings (gods) with supreme materials (gold). However, as Mariaselvam notes, this imagery is exclusively applied to the woman, with no parallel examples involving the male body.[20]

In modern Arabic and Western love literature, gold continues to be employed as a literary symbol of value and beauty, applied to love and lovers. In Stephan's collection of twentieth-century bedouin lyrics, one woman declares, "My beloved is in his house, his price is gold."[21] Enno Littman notes a similar example of value and purity, "He is Egyptian gold, in which there is no kind of inauthenticity."[22] In the West, gold is also viewed as a valuable commodity, whose monetary value propels its use as literary symbol of great worth. For example, Robert Browning likened his mistress to pure gold to highlight her superior beauty.[23] In sum, though items of worth vary between cultures, gold has long been considered a standard of value and beauty, often applied to love and lovers across space and time.

6.1.2. Meaning in the Song

Likewise, the Song's poet repeatedly refers to gold as a metal and metaphor of value and beauty. Similar to the deluxe decoration on Egyptian horses, the lover praises his beloved's beautiful bangles, promising to make for her "ornaments of gold, studded with silver" (1:9–11). Later, the arrival of Solomon's wedding couch is detailed, constructed from cedar, scarlet, silver, and gold (3:10). Last, in the lady's ode to her lover's body (5:10–16), the man's head, arms, and feet are compared to gold. Like the bracketed shouts of highest praise, the poet here employs an *inclusio* with the rare term פז (5:11–15), praising her lover as superior to all others (5:9).

---

19. Mariaselvam, *Ancient Tamil Love Poems*, 293, see also 297–99.
20. Mariaselvam, *Ancient Tamil Love Poems*, 214.
21. Stephan, "Modern Palestinian Parallels," 252.
22. Littman, *Neuarabische Volkspoesie*, 104.
23. John Woolford and Daniel Karlin, eds, *Poems of Browning: Volume Two 1841-1846* (New York: Routledge, 2014), 335.

Furthermore, this metaphor of the man's supreme value, immediately following his opening portrait as "radiant and ruddy" (5:10) may also depict the golden color and/or sheen of his head, arms, and feet. Despite the lack of material evidence and limited iconography from ancient Palestine, extant depictions of Canaanite dress consistently show these three areas of the male body exposed to the sun, whether on plaques from Hazor (fifteenth century BCE) and Megiddo (twelfth century BCE), the Black Obelisk of Shalmaneser III (ninth century BCE), or a potsherd from Ramat Raḥel (ninth century BCE).[24]

In addition, the terms תרשיש "golden topaz" and שש "alabaster" may also emphasize color as well as value. "Alabaster pillars atop bases of gold" (5:15a) likely contrasts the man's light-colored thighs with his suntanned feet, while his "rods of gold inlaid with topaz" (5:14a) may imply a shift in color from the dark, upper part of his forearm to its lighter underside which is shielded from the sun. The significance of color is a consistent theme in the Song's *waṣfs* (4:1–3; 5:11–12; 6:4–7; 7:5–6).

Moreover, the value of these gems also seems clear. In the Hebrew Bible, topaz is found in the high priest's breastplate (Exod 28:20) and the heavenly visions of Ezekiel (1:16) and Daniel (10:6), while alabaster is linked to Persia's royal court (Esth 1:6). In Egypt, the significance of alabaster is evident from its place in a common offering formula, used from the Old Kingdom onward to secure for the deceased necessities for the afterlife.[25] Likewise, the beauty and sheen of alabaster fueled its use in the statuary of Mesopotamia and Greece, while the Greeks also used alabaster flasks to hold precious perfumes and ointments (LSJ, s.v. "ἀλάβαστος").[26] Medieval and modern Arab lyrics as well as Western love lyrics continue to use alabaster as a metaphor of color and value, likening female breasts, thighs, and face to this lightly colored and supremely valuable substance.[27]

---

24. King and Stager, *Life in Biblical Israel*, 259–71.

25. Robbins, *Women in Egypt*, 175. The sarcophagi of some important Egyptian figures were also constructed from alabaster. See Zahi Hawass, *Silent Images: Women in Pharaonic Egypt* (Cairo: American University in Cairo Press, 2008), 41; Edward F. Wente, Jr., "A Ghost Story," in *The Literature of Ancient Egypt: An Anthology of Stories, Instructions, and Poetry*, ed. William K. Simpson, 3rd ed. (New Haven: Yale University Press, 2003), 114.

26. Pausanias, *Descr.* 1.18.9; Sefati, *Love Songs*, 130 (32); J. V. Kinnier Wilson, "The Kurba'il Statue of Shalmaneser III," *Iraq* 24 (1962): 96 (35–41).

27. Mathers, *Book of the Thousand Nights*, 1:250, 509; Stephan, "Modern Palestinian Parallels," 220, 237; Hamilton, *Sir Philip Sidney*, 84.

Finally, the multiplication of architectural terms in 5:14–15 also implies strength.[28] On the heels of the organic imagery in 5:11b–13, the invocation of rods, pillars, and bases naturally stresses strength and security. עמוד and אדן are construction terms, most often connected to the tabernacle and temple (Exod 26:19–40:18 [51x]; 1 Kgs 7:15–22). Thus, in the woman's ode to her man, the widely shared metaphor of gold primarily symbolizes his superiority (5:9), illustrating the conceptual metaphor THE OBJECT OF LOVE IS A VALUABLE OBJECT. Yet, the specific body parts highlighted may also signal the golden color and sheen of his skin, while the building terms likely stress the lover's strength.

6.2. Seductive Scent (5:13a)

לחיו כערוגת הבשם	[13] His cheeks are like beds[29] of spice,[30]
מגדלות מרקחים	which produce[31] perfume;

Source: Spice
Target: Cheeks
Mapping: Scent

---

28. Sirach also links the body and building, stressing beauty and strength (26:18).

29. Though the MT reads ערוגת הבשם as a singular noun "bed of spice," the versions (Symmachus, Peshitta, Vulgate) render the term as plural, matching the plural referent "cheeks." In support for this revocalization, this same phrase is found in the plural only a few verses later as a metaphor for the woman's body (6:2). The only other occurrences of this noun in the Hebrew Bible are also plural (Ezek 17:7, 10).

30. Since men commonly wore beards (Lev 19:27; 2 Sam 10:4–5), some suggest ערוגת "garden beds" depicts a man's bearded cheeks (Ginsburg, *Song of Songs*, 169; Longman, *Song of Songs*, 172). Much of the body imagery is visual, but the meaning centers not on a concrete likeness but on a shared stimulation of the olfactory sense.

31. The MT reading מִגְדְּלוֹת "towers" of perfume creates dissonance with the context, requiring one to explain the significance of an architectural metaphor in the midst of botanical imagery. Though the rules of textual criticism favor the more difficult reading, the revocalization to מְגַדְּלוֹת "producing" is preferred, as supported by the versions (LXX, Vulgate, targum) and medieval Jewish commentators (Rashi, Rashbam). While Fox rightly asserts that the *piel* stem of גדל "to increase, produce" is most often used of the person or means which causes plants to grow (Isa 44:14; Ezek 31:4; Jonah 4:10; Ps 144:12), this argument does not allow for poetic license (Fox, *Song of Songs*, 148). The Song's poet commonly stretches semantic range and uses terms in foreign contexts to create new meaning. Also, the resulting syntactical structure is common in the Song's *waṣfs* (4:1–2, 4–5; 5:14; 6:5; 7:3–4), with the source and target followed by an adjectival phrase that further elucidates the metaphor's mapping (see 5:13b).

6.2.1. Comparative Evidence

Men and women in antiquity used scented oils to mask offensive odors and protect their skin from the dry heat and bright sun.[32] Material, pictorial, and textual evidence show the widespread use of perfumes in Egyptian culture. From the Old Kingdom onward, unguent jars were an essential part of grave goods.[33] Analysis of unguent from Tutankhamun's tomb has shown that this substance was made of animal fat and aromatic resin.[34] New Kingdom reliefs show servants placing unguent on the heads of men and women at banquets. While the reality of this topos is debated, the end result is clear: Egyptians applied a perfumed substance to their hair and body, notably on celebratory occasions.[35]

In addition, fragrance is also connected to love and lovemaking. As Lise Manniche notes, "Unguent was personal and intimate, something redolent of a sexual relationship between man and woman."[36] In the legend of Hatshepsut's birth, the queen's mother was awakened by Amun's fragrance, and as the mighty god impregnated her body, his scent inundated the entire palace.[37] In Egypt's love lyrics, the lovers prepare themselves for lovemaking by applying moringa oil and balsam; the boy's scent is compared to Punt, while the girl's aroma is deemed intoxicating.[38]

Though little is known of cosmetics in Mesopotamia, the presence and use of scented oils is clear. From medicine and magic to religion and cosmetics, Martin Levey suggests that "one of the most important chemical industries in Mesopotamia was the preparation of aromatic substances."[39]

---

32. Neufeld, "Hygiene Conditions," 57–58.
33. Lucas, "Cosmetics, Perfumes, and Incense in Ancient Egypt," 45–46.
34. Manniche, *Sacred Luxuries*, 86, 108.
35. Manniche, *Sacred Luxuries*, 94–95. See also Fox, *Song of Songs*, figs. 2–3; Corson, *Fashions in Makeup*, figs. 12–13. Gerleman and Keel suggest that Egypt's unguent cone is the reality behind the metaphor for the man's cheeks, yet this lacks evidence and is hardly flattering (Gerleman, *Hohelied*, 175; Keel, *Song of Songs*, 201). For Hawass, this motif reflects a real custom, while Manniche suggests it may be artistic convention (Hawass, *Silent Images*, 119; Manniche, *Sacred Luxuries*, 96).
36. Manniche, *Sacred Luxuries*, 92.
37. Breasted, *Ancient Records of Egypt*, 2:196.
38. Fox, *Song of Songs*, 17, 44, 71.
39. Martin Levey, *Chemicals and Chemical Technology in Ancient Mesopotamia*

In fact, multiple texts have been found from Assyria and Babylonia that detail the making of perfumes.[40] Later Roman writers also commonly attribute fine aromatics to Assyria (Horace, *Carm.* 2.11.16; Catullus, *Poems*, 68a.144; Virgil, *Ecl.* 4.25). Similarly, Herodotus noted the use of perfume in Babylon (*Hist.* 1.195), while Pliny mistakenly believed that Persia invented unguent, since they soaked themselves in it (*Nat.* 13.2).[41] Akin to Egypt's festive use of perfume, Esarhaddon and Nabonidus instructed servants to pour oil on the heads of banquet guests.[42]

Moreover, Mesopotamian literature also connects scent and sexuality. In the Sumerian poems of Inanna and Iddin-Dagan and Enlil and Sud, as well as an Old Babylonian love song, the couples' beds are anointed with incense to prepare for their sexual union.[43] Likewise, one Old Akkadian love incantation links aromatic oils and plants to the person and place of love.[44] Also, incense and oils were often present in rituals to restore sexual potency, perhaps suggesting the ancients believed fragrance affected fertility.[45] Regardless, the impact of scent upon sexual attraction is clear. In *KAR* 158, one lover exclaims, "Let me sing of your fragrance" (ii.33) while another compares her man's love to the scent of cedar (vii.21).[46]

The importance of scent and its connection to love is also found in Greco-Roman culture. According to Antiphanes, Greeks applied perfumes lavishly, even using different scents for different parts of the body (Athenaeus, *Deipn.* 15.40). In Greek myth, Aphrodite (for whom aphrodisiacs are named) drenched Paris with scent before setting him on his wedding bed (Homer, *Il.* 3:381) and gave Phaon a fragrance that made the women of

---

(New York: Elsevier, 1959), 132. "Sweet oil" was also exchanged between Near Eastern kings (EA 14:32; 25:4.51–55; 27.65; 31:35–36; 34:50–53).

40. Erich Ebeling, *Parfümrezepte und Kultische Texte aus Assur* (Rome: Pontifical Biblical Institute, 1950), iv.

41. Levey notes perfume and cosmetic containers found at Susa (Levey, *Chemicals and Chemical Technology*, fig. 35).

42. Rykle Borger, *Die Inschriften Asarhaddons Konigs von Assyrien*, AfOB 9 (Osnabrück: Biblio, 1956), 63 (23:53); Stephen Langdon, *Sumerian and Semitic Religious and Historical Texts*, OECI 1 (Oxford: Oxford University Press, 1923), 36 (29).

43. Miguel Civil, "Enlil and Ninlil: The Marriage of Sud," *JAOS* 103 (1983): 60 (148–49); Jacobsen, *Harps*, 122; Westenholz, "Forgotten Love Song," 423.

44. Westenholz and Westenholz, "Help for Rejected Suitors," 203.

45. Biggs, *ŠÀ.ZI.GA*, 1 (15–16, 18–19); 2 (9–11); 6 (14–17); 11 (20); 34 (3'–6').

46. Ebeling, *Hymnen-Katalog*, 14; Groneberg, "Searching for Akkadian Lyrics," 67.

Mytilene fall in love with him (Aelian, *Var. hist.* 12.18), while Hera applied scented oils to seduce Zeus (Homer, *Il.* 14.170–173).

Catullus similarly notes the allure of fine perfume, "I will tell you of a perfume, which Venus and Cupid gave to my love; when you smell it, you will pray to the deities to make of you only a nose" (Catullus, *Poems* 13.11–14 [Cornish]). In fact, our knowledge of perfume in antiquity is based mainly on three Greco-Roman writers: Dioscorides (*Mat. med.* 1.32–63), Theophrastus (*Sens.* 4–12), and Pliny (*Nat.* 13). In addition, thousands of perfume containers have survived from the Greek world.

Moreover, Indian and Arab cultures also link aroma and attraction. In Tamil love lyrics, lovers and their setting are redolent with fragrance.[47] One poem links the person and place of love by their scent: "That man is from the place where white reed flowers in cool groves tear at the pale threads of the mango tree growing in a dune, its thick branches reeking of the scent of lovers' bodies."[48] Likewise, in the pre-Islamic Arab love lyrics, ʿAntara ibn Shaddād writes, "At daybreak, while she was still asleep, her resting place effused the aroma of her body, as though it were sprinkled with musk."[49] Similarly, the beloved's body is likened to various fragrant flowers and spices in twentieth-century bedouin lyrics, twice compared to a container of perfume. One poem depicts the woman's perfume as a trap that ensnares her lover and a stimulant causing him to rush to her.[50]

Scented oils continued to be utilized in Western cultures to improve body aroma and attract those of the opposite sex. In Elizabethan England, perfumes were widely used by both men and women. James Graham marketed his "Celestial Bed," whose scented dome and perfumed sheets was said to revive and invigorate childless couples attempting to conceive. Yet this idea is also found in tribal cultures. In New Guinea, ginger leaves are thought to bring sexual allure to men who rub them on their hands and face, while Yanomamö men in the Amazon carry sachets of fragrant pow-

---

47. Martha Ann Selby, *Tamil Love Poetry: The Five Hundred Short Poems of the Ainkurunuru* (New York: Columbia University Press, 2011), 70, 74, 84, 97, 173, 176, 240, 348, 446; Ramanujan, *Interior Landscape*, 68, 92.

48. Selby, *Tamil Love Poetry*, 19.

49. Jinbachian, "Arabian Odes," 131. See also Mathers, *Book of the Thousand Nights*, 1:61, 99.

50. Dalman, *Palästinischer Diwan*, 260; Littman, *Neuarabische Volkspoesie*, 143; Stephan, "Modern Palestinian Parallels," 208, 214, 241, 243, 267.

ders to make women fall into their arms.[51] Thus, the link between scent and sexuality is widespread both in space and time.

6.2.2. Meaning in the Song

"Sense images of taste, smell and touch are rare in biblical poetry. But in the Song of Songs they are frequent: perfumes, aromas, balsam, incense.... It is an atmosphere of joys brought by the senses."[52] Just like a garden of aromatic plants producing sweet-smelling scents, the woman lauds the fragrance of her lover's cheeks. In the Hebrew Bible, scent is often connected to beauty. Before meeting Boaz, Naomi instructed Ruth to wash, anoint herself with perfume (סוּךְ), and put on her best clothes (3:3). Similarly, Esther and the maidens of the Persian royal harem, prior to their night with the king, received a year of cosmetic treatments (2:12). Likewise, Ps 45 describes Israel's king on his wedding day, anointed with fragrant myrrh, aloes, and cassia (45:9). Spices and perfume were valuable commodities, stockpiled alongside precious metals in the royal treasury (2 Chr 32:27) and dispensed from tiny juglets to ensure sparing use.

The Song's poet also highlights the scent of love, both for person and place.[53] In love's idyllic setting, a stimulating fragrance is key. For example, when the man comes to call on his beloved, inviting her to join him for a romp in nature, the fragrance of blooming flowers and blossoming vines is detailed (2:8–17). Later, the woman similarly beckons her man to a tryst in the countryside, connecting the scent of mandrakes to her stored-up, sexual desires (7:12–14). Scent and spice are linked to beauty and intimacy in the Song. In the book's body imagery, the beloved's perfume is elevated above any spice (4:10), her garments are likened to Lebanon (4:11), her breasts are described as "mountains of spice" (4:6; 8:14), and her body is a garden filled with sensual delights (4:12–5:1). In fact, the phrase "garden beds of spice" is used as metaphor for the female body (6:2), the place where

---

51. Mandy Aftel, *Essence and Alchemy: A Natural History of Perfume* (New York: North Point, 2001), 160–61.

52. Luis A. Schökel, *A Manual of Hebrew Poetics*, SubBi 11 (Rome: Pontifical Biblical Institute, 1988), 121.

53. Matthew Boersma rightly notes the poet's consistent use of scent as a sexual metaphor, particularly as description moves toward erogenous areas, though his erotic reading of the wedding procession (3:6–11) is unconvincing ("Scent in Song: Exploring Scented Symbols in the Song of Songs," *CBW* 31 [2011]: 80–94).

her lost lover has gone to graze. For the man, the opening poem praises his alluring fragrance, leading to his lady's request to be taken to his bedroom (1:3–4). Combining BODY AS LANDSCAPE and LOVE AS INTOXICATION, the man's perfumed cheeks likely describe his sexual allure, furthered by the allusion to his intoxicating love in the parallel line.

Thus, while the maiden's metaphor comparing her lover's cheeks to beds of spice is unique to the Hebrew Song (5:13), the underlying praise for his alluring fragrance plays on a near-universal element of embodied experience. As is evident from the preceding survey of scent across space and time, peoples throughout the world have used and continue to apply perfumed substances to improve their body aroma and entice members of the opposite sex. In fact, this link between scent and sexuality is affirmed by scientific and psychological studies. In his work on the significance of scent, D. Michael Stoddart points to the twentieth-century study of Austrian perfumer Paul Jellinek, who concluded that certain odors can induce an erotic response. This conclusion was based in part on psychoanalytic research showing the significance of body odor for sexual attraction.[54] Thus, after drawing parallels to the topos of perfume in Arab lyrics, Jinbachian notes the universal appeal of scent and its link to love, "One could say that perfumes and fragrances ... have a role to play in love poems in all literature."[55]

6.3. Value of Virility (5:14b)

מעיו עשת שן   [14] His loins are a piece of ivory,
ספירים: מעלפת   adorned with lapis-lazuli.[56]

Source: Ivory, Lapis Lazuli
Target: Male Loins
Mapping: Virility, Value, Color, Shape?

---

54. D. Michael Stoddart, *The Scented Ape: The Biology and Culture of Human Odour* (Cambridge: Cambridge University Press, 1990), 161; Paul Jellinek, *The Practice of Modern Perfumery* (London: Hill, 1954).

55. Jinbachian, "Arabian Odes," 130.

56. Though some connect ספיר to the English "sapphire," its association to gold dust (Job 28:6) better matches the appearance of lapis lazuli, whose dark blue color is speckled with yellow spots. Also, YHWH's throne (Ezek 1:26), similar to Baal's sky-palace (*KTU* 1.4.5.15–19) and the throne of Bel-Marduk, was constructed with this precious stone. See Alasdair Livingstone, *Mystical and Mythological Explanatory Works of Assyrian and Babylonian Scholars* (Winona Lake, IN: Eisenbrauns, 2007), 83.

In contrast to previous imagery, nearly every aspect of this metaphor is debated, from the part of the man's body being praised to the nature of the ivory object and the resulting basis for comparison. Thus, before surveying any comparative evidence, the components of this figure must be explored.

6.3.1. Meaning in the Song

First, where is the man's מעה? Though this term often refers to one's inner person, both physical organs (2 Sam 20:10; Ezek 7:19) and the seat of emotions (Ps 22:15; Isa 16:11), the nature of the woman's ode clearly implies an external referent. Daniel uses the corresponding Aramaic term to refer to the bronze torso on Nebuchadnezzar's statue, the region between his chest and thighs (2:32). For this reason, many conclude that this image describes the external appearance of the man's abdomen, "His belly [is] a tablet of ivory" (JPS). While "belly" is possible, why employ this unique term and not the more common בטן, as used later in the Song (7:3)?

In the Hebrew Bible, the term מעה is not only used of one's inner person, but it more commonly refers to the reproductive organs. With this term, the siring of heirs is attributed to both genders, through the female womb (Gen 25:23; Ruth 1:11) and the male loins (Gen 15:14; 2 Sam 7:12). In fact, the implicit sexual nature of this term is evident from its usage earlier in this chapter. When the lover knocked on his beloved's door, desiring an evening tryst, "[He] stuck his hand [ידו] through the hole and my מעה were stirred for him" (5:4). With the possible euphemisms behind יד and מעה, the lady likely depicts her lover's attempt to physically enter her bedroom as well as her own desire for his *membrum virile* to sexually enter her. In fact, a shared erotic allusion is further supported by the myrrh dripping from her fingers (5:5) and his lips (5:13), a spice commonly linked to intimacy (1:13, 4:6, 12–5:1). While the woman's portrait of her man may describe his ivory-like torso, an erotic allusion is likely present.

The second enigma involves the shape of the ivory object. Since עשת is found only here in the Hebrew Bible, its meaning is debated. Based on its usage in postbiblical literature, many posit that עשת depicts a flat block (*HALOT*, s.v. "אֶשֶׁת"), a visual portrait of his abdomen. The LXX supports this reading, "His belly is a tablet of ivory." Yet the Peshitta's generic rendering ʿbd "work" and the absence of any term in the Vulgate suggests this term was uncertain at an early period. Even in rabbinic literature, the shape of an עשת is not clear. The Tosefta applies this term to gold and silver from which the candlestick and priestly trumpets were made (t. Hul. 1.18–19). Yet, in Sifre Num. 160 (35:16–21), עשת is paired with גלומים, a rough, unshaped object, and contrasted with כלי, an object of definite shape.[57]

Thus, the question remains: Is עשת שן a worked bar/plaque of ivory, describing the man's flat abdomen, or does this phrase refer to a piece of unworked ivory (cf. Ezek 27:15), playing on the tusk-like shape of his *membrum virile*?[58] Like the dual sexual metaphor earlier in this chapter (5:4), the Song's poet may have chosen vague terms here to allow for both readings. For this reason, the above rendering is intentionally ambiguous. While "loins" can refer to the area of the body between the ribs and the hips, it often describes a man's genital region. Also, the term "piece" does not denote any specific shape, allowing for both a flat stomach and a tusk-like phallus.[59] Veiling such intimate matters in metaphor is a favorite technique employed by the Song's poet throughout the book (see 4:12–5:1).

6.3.2. Comparative Evidence

But how does this dual metaphor compare to the literature of other Near Eastern and Mediterranean cultures? Is it unique, borrowed, shared, or universal? First, the likeness of the lover's abdomen to an ivory tablet is unique in the literature of the Near East and eastern Mediterranean. The external appearance of a man's stomach is not a common theme in ancient literature. In contrast, phallic symbols are widely attested in the textual and material evidence of antiquity. In Egypt, the male member is commonly highlighted on human and divine figures. As the Egyptian god associated with fertility and male sexual potency, Min is often depicted holding his erect penis in his hand. In her exploration of sexuality in ancient Egypt, Manniche similarly notes numerous reliefs and sculptures as well as phallic amulets that emphasize the male *membrum virile*.[60] Moreover, in the

---

57. Menahem Kahana, *Sifre on Numbers: An Annotated Edition* (Jerusalem: Magnes, 2011), 88.

58. A collection of later midrashim compares עשת שן to a Torah scroll, possibly invoking a similar cylindrical shape. See Shim'on ha-Darshan, ed., *Yalkut Shimoni* (Jerusalem: Machon HaMeor, 2001), 10:671. Gordis cites an Akkadian cognate *išitu* "column," but *išdu* is a general foundation term (*Song of Songs*, 90; *CAD*, "išdu," 7:235).

59. Garrett, *Song of Songs/Lamentations*, 222–23.

60. Manniche, *Sexual Life in Ancient Egypt*, 102–10 (figs. 3, 17–22, 38–40, 43–44, 47–48, 50, 53, 71, 75).

Chester Beatty Papyrus, as the boy bends over in preparation for the couple's festivities, the girl spies his penis and praises its large size, "He grants (me) the hue of [his] loins; it is longer than it is broad" (*sw ini inw n(y) ḏrww.[i] iw qꜣ.f r ws ḥt.tw.f*).⁶¹

Although phallicism never flourished in Mesopotamia the way it did in pharaonic Egypt or classical antiquity, Mesopotamian literature and archaeology still suggest an emphasis on the male member.⁶² After initiating human sexual reproduction, Enki extols his *membrum virile*, "Let now my penis be praised."⁶³ In one of the Inanna-Dumuzi love songs (DI B), a woman responds to the praise-filled advances of her suitor, asking him to swear an oath of fidelity. Since the ritual involved touching her genitals, Jacobsen labeled the oath, "an erotic ploy," interpreting praise for the man's "apple tree" and "alabaster pillar" as indicative of his *growing* sexual excitement.⁶⁴ In an Old Babylonian catalog of incipits, the lover similarly wishes "Let me grow long for the girl!" The next line appears to be the girl's reaction, "It is so long, an elephant's seems smaller than yours."⁶⁵ Also, potency incantations portray a man's phallus as a source of sexual pleasure, with reproductive concerns curiously absent.⁶⁶ In such rituals, the desired erection of a man's member is compared to animals known for their virility, and prescribed remedies often involve sexually excited animals.⁶⁷ Finally, excavations at Ishtar's temple in Assur produced stone phalli with bored holes, possibly used as amulets, and erotic drinking scenes present at many Mesopotamian sites show women grabbing a beer straw in one hand while the other grasps her partner's erect penis as it penetrates her.⁶⁸

Phallic symbolism is also evident in two Ugaritic mythological texts. In the Baal Cycle, when 'Aṯirat comes to intercede before 'El, to request

---

61. Fox, *Song of Songs*, 74, 402. Fox refers to a papyrus in which a woman demands an ithyphallic man, "Come behind me with your love, your penis belongs to me" (21).
62. Leick, *Sex and Eroticism in Mesopotamian Literature*, 21.
63. Jacobsen, *Harps*, 166.
64. Jacobsen, "Two Bal-Bal-e Dialogues," 62; see §4.1, above, on the man's apple (2:3).
65. George, *Babylonian Literary Texts*, 738–9.
66. Biggs, *ŠÀ.ZI.GA*, 14 (11–12); 15 (15–16).
67. Biggs, *ŠÀ.ZI.GA*, animals: 1 (12–13); 2 (7–8); 3 (20–22); 5 (15–16); 6 (1–5); 7 (2–7); 8 (1–7); 9 (4–8); remedies: 19 (23–24); KUB 4 48 (ii 27–32; iii 1–10; iv 3–4).
68. Walter Andrae, *Die jüngeren Ischtar-Tempel in Assur*, WVDOG 58 (Osnabrück: Zeller, 1967), pl. 36; Julia Assante, "Sex, Magic, and the Luminal Body in the Erotic Art and Texts of the Old Babylonian Period," in Parpola and Whiting, *Sex and Gender*, 30–36.

that a house be built for the young Ba'lu, 'El seeks to revive his wife's sexual passions, "Does the phallus [*yadu*] of 'El the king excite you?" (*KTU* 1.4 iv.35–39). Also, in the birth narrative of Shahar and Shalim, 'El attempts to seduce two women to become his wife using the exploits of his *membrum virile*, whose growing length is compared to the seas (*KTU* 1.23 33–35).

In contrast, the meaning of the textual and material evidence from Greece and Rome is heavily disputed. Hellenistic culture prized the beauty of the body, particularly the youthful male body.[69] In fact, the final stage of classical education took place in the gymnasium, whose name is derived from γυμνός "naked" because the young men performed their exercises and competed in the nude (Plato, *Resp.* 5.452b). While Mireille Lee contends that such nakedness was confined to the sporting arena, Eva Keuls disagrees, "Athenian men habitually displayed their genitals, and their city was studded with statues of gods with phalluses happily erect."[70]

Indeed, from Dionysus and Hermes to Pan and Priapus, Greco-Roman gods were commonly depicted with an abnormally large penis. In addition to the phallic procession by ecstatic women and ithyphallic men in the festival of Dionysus (Herodotus, *Hist.* 2.48; Aristophanes, *Ach.* 241–279), the ordinary citizen would have been familiar with herms in the street. These slab statues of the god Hermes, having testicles and an erect penis midway down, were placed in front of private houses and in courtyards.[71] Furthermore, as seen on a famous fresco from Pompeii, visual depictions of Priapus also highlight the size of his *membrum virile*.[72]

Yet, the relatively small size of the penis possessed by gods and heroes on Greek statues has puzzled scholars. "To judge by illustrations and statuary, the ideal penis was small, thin, and had a pointed foreskin. The Greeks believed a dainty penis was not only more attractive but more serviceable in reproduction."[73] Aristophanes similarly states:

---

69. Ian Jenkins et al., *The Greek Body* (Los Angeles: Getty Publications, 2010), 31.

70. Lee, *Body, Dress, and Identity*, 179; Eva C. Keuls, *The Reign of the Phallus: Sexual Politics in Ancient Athens* (Berkeley: University of California Press, 1993), 2.

71. Keuls, *Reign of the Phallus*, 385.

72. Catherine Johns, *Sex or Symbol? Erotic Images of Greece and Rome* (New York: Routledge, 1982), 50. The eighty-poem Priapea praises the virility of Priapus's genitals. See Richard W. Hooper, *The Priapus Poems: Erotic Epigrams from Ancient Rome* (Chicago: University of Illinois Press, 1999).

73. Angus McLaren, *Impotence: A Cultural History* (Chicago: University of Chicago Press, 2008), 3–4. See also Kenneth J. Dover, *Greek Homosexuality* (Cambridge: Harvard University Press, 1989), 125–28.

If you follow my recommendations…, you will always have a rippling chest, radiant skin, broad shoulders, a wee tongue, a grand rump and a petite dick. But if you adopt current practices, you'll start by having a puny chest, pasty skin, narrow shoulders, a grand tongue, a wee rump, and a lengthy edict. (*Nub.* 1009–1019 [Henderson])

While the phallic symbolism widely attested in the Near East may be common to human experience, use of such imagery in art and literature is dependent on social mores. In the sexually inhibited cultures of Victorian England and Puritan America where sex was regarded as shameful, anything that might inflame sexual feeling was classified as obscene, and its public display was offensive. Clearly, a culture that finds undraped legs enticing would be disturbed by visual or verbal imagery of genitals.[74]

In addition to the symbolism of virility, the Song's poet likely invokes ivory for its color and value. While the elevation of light skin has been adequately discussed (1:5–6; 4:4; 6:7; 7:5), the value of ivory in antiquity deserves further exploration. From textual and material evidence in Palestine, ivory was an item of luxury. In the Hebrew Bible, שׁן "ivory" is often connected to wealth and royalty. This valuable commodity was imported (1 Kgs 10:22) and used in the construction of Solomon's throne (1 Kgs 10:18) and Ahab's palace (1 Kgs 22:39). In Amos's oracles against Israel, ivory is linked to the rich elite guilty of oppressing the poor for monetary gain (3:15, 6:4). In fact, many ivory artifacts in Palestinian excavations were discovered in royal settings. For example, the Omride palatial complex (ninth–eighth centuries BCE) at Samaria produced about twelve thousand pieces of ivory, and nearly four hundred were found at Megiddo in the Late Bronze Egyptian palace (mid-twelfth century BCE).[75]

Furthermore, ivory was not only a valuable commodity in Israel but throughout the Near East and eastern Mediterranean. Its widespread worth is attested by its frequent mention among gifts between dignitaries (EA 5:13; 14:3.75–4.18; 24:25.97; 31:37). An ivory pen case from Megiddo carved with a cartouche of Ramses III suggests that this material was

---

74. Johns, *Sex or Symbol*, 10.
75. Claudia E. Suter, "Luxury Goods in Ancient Israel: Questions of Consumption and Production," in *Proceedings of the 6th International Congress of the Archaeology of the Ancient Near East*, ed. Paolo Matthiae, Frances Pinnock, and Lorenzo Romano (Wiesbaden: Harrassowitz, 2010), 993; Gansell, "Ideal Feminine Beauty," 46–48.

prized in ancient Egypt.[76] In fact, Amenemhab tells of Thutmose III hunting elephants, while Hatshepsut, in her mortuary temple, commemorated a trading mission to Punt, whose purpose was to bring back exotic animals, precious metals, and luxury items such as gold, incense, and ivory.[77]

Likewise, the value of and demand for ivory in Mesopotamia is evident in the repeated reference to hunting elephants, from Tiglath-Pileser I to Assurnasirpal II (eleventh through ninth century BCE).[78] Ivory was used in royal construction and named among political tribute and booty.[79] Near Eastern love lyrics also use ivory as a motif of beauty, for men and women. Inanna praises her lover Dumuzi as "my ivory figurine," and Ludingira depicts his mother as a "perfect ivory figurine full of loveliness and attraction."[80]

Greek literature similarly depicts ivory as a luxury import, frequently linking this substance to divine statuary (Pausanias, *Descr.* 1.12.4; 5.12.3; Diodorus Siculus, *Bib. hist.* 16.2). In his *Description of Greece*, Pausanias describes various temple statues made from gold and ivory, highlighting its value and beauty: Athena at the Parthenon, Zeus in Athens, Aphrodite in Megara, and Dionysus at Sicyon (*Descr.* 1.24.5; 40.4; 43.6; 2.7.5).

In his detailed study on ivory in the Middle East, Richard Barnett includes artifacts from Egypt, Assyria, and Israel, but he also demonstrates the widespread appeal of this precious material with examples from cultures spanning space and time: Sumer, Ugarit, Phoenicia, Anatolia, Cyprus, Elam, Persia, Greece, Rome, and India.[81] However, the beauty of this substance may be universally recognized, but the high value of ivory was dependent on its limited supply. In antiquity, ivory was primarily obtained from elephants in the jungles of Africa and parts of central Asia, or the hippopotamus found in swampy areas around the Nile and a small

---

76. Gordon Loud, *The Megiddo Ivories*, OIP 52 (Chicago: University of Chicago Press, 1939), 9.

77. Breasted, *Ancient Records of Egypt*, 2:588; Robbins, *Women in Egypt*, 47–48.

78. Richard D. Barnett, *A Catalogue of the Nimrud Ivories with Other Ancient Near Eastern Ivories in the British Museum* (London: British Museum, 1957), 166.

79. Borger, *Inschriften Asarhaddons*, 48 (2:76); 61 (6:9); Luckenbill, *Annals of Sennacherib*, 34 (3:44), 60 (56), 96 (79); 100 (56); 106 (6:14); Hayim Tadmor, *The Inscriptions of Tiglath-Pileser III King of Assyria* (Jerusalem: Israel Academy of Sciences and Humanities, 1994), 54–57 (21:10, 25:1).

80. Sefati, *Love Songs*, 270; Nougayrol, "Signalement Lyrique," 315.

81. Richard D. Barnett, *Ancient Ivories in the Middle East*, Qedem 14 (Jerusalem: Hebrew University Press, 1982), pls. 1–76.

section of Syria-Palestine. Since there is no evidence of hippopotamuses in Mesopotamia and Iron Age Syro-Phoenician workshops lack this type of ivory, this animal may have been extinct early in the first millennium.[82] Thus, ivory was a luxury acquired through expeditions to foreign lands.

In addition, the maiden's value of her man's loins is further supported by the concluding reference to lapis lazuli. Though Goulder appeals to anatomy and Fox divorces lapis lazuli from the man entirely, a shared significance provides the best explanation.[83] Similar to ivory, the incredible worth of lapis lazuli was widely shared in antiquity. This gem was exported from mines in northeastern Afghanistan to the early civilizations of the Near East and Egypt.[84] In fact, some of the earliest evidence of lapis lazuli suggests a trade link. A Mesopotamian cylinder seal was found in a necklace of lapis lazuli beads from a Predynastic grave in Egypt.[85]

Moreover, this precious gem also appears in Near Eastern love lyrics as a metaphor of value. In Egypt's Chester Beatty Papyrus, the lover exclaims, "Her hair is true lapis lazuli" (*ḥsbdt mꜣꜥ šnw.s*).[86] Sumer's Inanna, Dumuzi, and Shusin were equated with lapis, while Ludingira's mother is depicted as a statue sitting on a pedestal made of this gem.[87] In Sumerian love lyrics (DI B), similar to the Song's imagery, Dumuzi's phallus is described as an alabaster pillar set in lapis lazuli.[88] Likewise, in Ugarit's Kirta Epic, Hurriya's eyes are compared to pure lapis (*KTU* 1.14 vi.23–31). Finally, in the lyrics of Nabû and Tashmetu, when Nabû likened his beloved's body to a tablet of lapis, Nissinen captures the import, "It is the most precious item he can think of to compare her with."[89]

Thus, while modern translations restrict this metaphor to the man's abdomen, the presence of sexual terms in the context, combined with the

---

82. Peter R. S. Moorey, *Ancient Mesopotamian Materials and Industries: The Archaeological Evidence* (Oxford: Clarendon, 1994), 115–27; Thomas R. Trautmann. *Elephants and Kings: An Environmental History* (Chicago: University of Chicago Press, 2015), 70–73.

83. Goulder, *Fourteen Songs*, 6; Fox, *Song of Songs*, 149.

84. Michael O'Donoghue, "Lapis Lazuli," in *Gems: Their Sources, Descriptions, and Identification*, ed. Michael O'Donoghue, 6th ed. (Oxford: Elsevier, 2006), 329–30.

85. Ian Shaw, "Minerals," *OEAE* 2:417.

86. Fox, *Song of Songs*, 52. Since *ḥsbd* "lapis lazuli" refers to blue, Robins links the color's importance to the gem's value (Robins, "Color Symbolism," 291–92).

87. Sefati, *Love Songs*, 198, 250, 270, 361; Civil, "Message of Lu-Dingir-Ra," 3:30.

88. Jacobsen, "Two Bal-Bal-e Dialogues," 62–63.

89. Nissinen, "Nabû and Tašmetu," 614.

widespread use of phallic symbols in antiquity, suggests that this metaphor also includes veiled praise for the man's virility. Also, ivory may stress the light color of his skin, but this precious material, drawing on THE OBJECT OF LOVE IS VALUABLE OBJECT metaphor, more likely highlights the value of the man's sexual prowess. For her, it is one of the things that make him "outstanding among ten thousand," superior to any other (5:8–9).

6.4. Summary

In contrast to the visual images of female beauty surveyed in previous chapters, the maiden's ode to her man mainly focuses on his superiority, both his value and his virility (5:10–16). Building on the conceptual metaphor THE OBJECT OF LOVE IS A VALUABLE OBJECT, the lady touts her lover's superiority from head to toe, with images of gold and ivory, topaz and lapis lazuli.[90] Regardless of time and culture, these gems and precious metals combine splendor and worth. Jewelry and gems contribute to one's physical beauty, but they also connote value, demonstrating the worth of the other.[91] To a lesser extent, these architectural metaphors also highlight the color of the lover's skin and the sturdiness of his strength.

In addition to his superiority, strength, and sexual virility, the woman praises her man's perfumed cheeks. Again, the Song's poet relies on shared culture and universal symbols, drawing on the metaphor LOVE AS INTOXICATION to highlight the man's sexual attraction. Finally, the man's *waṣf* follows the structure of the other descriptive songs, with bracketed praise, sequential description, and the resulting effect, offering further evidence for the Song's literary unity.

---

90. Zoltán Kövecses, *Metaphors of Anger, Pride, and Love: A Lexical Approach to the Structure of Concepts*, Pragmatics & Beyond 7.8 (Philadelphia: Benjamins, 1986), 74.
91. Westenholz, "Metaphoric Language in the Poetry of Love," 383–87.

7
Conclusions:
Method, Metaphor, Beauty, and Unity

In his ode "The Singing Slave-Girl of 'Amhamah," ninth-century Persian poet Ibn al-Rūmī speaks of the surpassing beauty of his beloved: "Many a man beguiled by her beauty has said: Describe her! I said: that is easy and difficult, all at once."[1] This lyric aptly illustrates the Song's body imagery, "impressive and intriguing, yet at the same time difficult and foreign," the most obscure aspect of the book for modern readers.[2] Yet, interpreting these metaphors is vital for understanding the Song.

For this reason, the purpose of the preceding study was to analyze the Song's body metaphors in light of comparative data from the ancient Near East to shed light on their meaning. Using a conceptual-comparative method, our interpretive process began with translating specified verses and identifying the metaphor's source and target. After locating similar imagery in Near Eastern literature and iconography, shared attributes were evaluated based on similarities and differences in language, geography, chronology, culture, and context. Finally, parallels were used to clarify the meaning of the Song's enigmatic figures. In addition, classical, medieval, and modern love lyrics were also included to explore the origin and distribution of these metaphors, whether uniquely crafted by the Hebrew poet, (in)directly borrowed from a foreign source, widely shared across the cultures of the Near East and eastern Mediterranean, or nearly universal symbols of attraction and *amore*.

---

1. Sumi, *Description in Classical Arabic Poetry*, 127.
2. Fox, *Song of Songs*, 328. Exum similarly states, "Striking and unusual metaphorical descriptions of the body are not at all uncommon in love poetry, though for some reason they seem to be a stumbling block for literal-minded commentators on the Bible's only love poem" (Exum, *Song of Songs*, 17).

In sum, the uniqueness of this study centers around four major themes: method, metaphor, beauty, and unity. First, let's revisit the methodology used to analyze the Song's body imagery.

7.1. Methodology

One significant contribution of this study is a new direction for studying the Song. As nineteenth and twentieth century scholars began to decipher the newly discovered literature of Mesopotamia and Egypt, they soon realized that the writings of ancient Israel and Judah preserved in the Hebrew Bible were not so unique. As a result, many began to suggest that the biblical writings were dependent on foreign cultural influences. For example, Friedrich Delitzsch, in his iconic lecture *Babel und Bibel*, claimed that aspects of Israelite culture and religion originated in Babylon.[3] Soon after, Meek posited that the Hebrew Song was originally part of the Mesopotamian Tammuz-Ishtar cult.[4] Though most scholars have rejected theories of the Song's cultic origin, some still advocate the link to Mesopotamia. In his comparison of the Hebrew Song to Akkadian love lyrics, Nissinen concludes, "All this [similarity] suggests that the affinity between the Song of Songs and the Mesopotamian love poetry is not merely due to a haphazard distribution of universal expressions but to the continuity of a common erotic-lyric tradition in which the idea and ritual practice of sacred marriage is an important constituent."[5]

Other scholars have suggested that Egypt's New Kingdom love lyrics are closer in genre and geography. In this vein, Fox concludes, "The love song genre certainly underwent many changes between its presumed Egyptian origins and the time when it reached Palestine, took root in Hebrew literature, grew in native forms, and blossomed as the Song of Songs."[6] Garrett similarly states, "The similarities are too close and too numerous

---

3. Friedrich Delitzsch, *Babel und Bibel: Ein Vortrage* (Leipzig: Hinrichs, 1903), 4–62.

4. Meek, "Canticles and Tammuz," 1–14. Kramer echoed, "The Song of Songs, or at least a good part of it, is a modified and conventionalized form of an ancient Hebrew liturgy celebrating the reunion and marriage of the sun-god with the mother-goddess, which had flourished in Mesopotamia from earliest days" (Samuel N. Kramer, *The Sacred Marriage Rite: Aspects of Faith, Myth, and Ritual in Ancient Sumer* [Bloomington: Indiana University Press, 1969], 89).

5. Nissinen, "Song of Songs and Sacred Marriage," 209.

6. Fox, *Song of Songs*, 191–93.

to be explained as anything other than the influence of the Egyptian songs on the Israelite poet."[7] On the book's body metaphors, Keel likewise posits that the Song's *waṣfs* were clearly of Egyptian origin.[8]

In contrast, based on the insight of cognitive linguistics that metaphor is shaped both by the body and culture, our study explored the extent of universal themes as well as culturally specific variations in the Song's body imagery.[9] We learned that underlying many of these metaphors are motifs shared across Near Eastern cultures or archetypal themes common to human love lyrics. While some scholars previously posited the presence of universal motifs, no systematic study had been done to validate this broad claim, specifically on the Song's body metaphors.[10]

In fact, Richard Hess intentionally excluded comparative evidence from his commentary, citing the lack of "exegetical payoff" due to the universal nature of love poetry.[11] However, we have shown that parallels from the literature and archaeology of other cultures are vitally important for interpretation. For example, many claim that the architectural images in Song 8:8–10 contrast the girl's purity (*wall*) and promiscuity (*door*). Yet, the door is a common symbol of separation between lovers in lyrics from the Near East and beyond. Thus, our exegesis and comparative analysis has shown that the architectural images in Song 8:9 are best understood as a synonymous couplet, stressing the brothers' reward (*silver/cedar*) for their sister's sexual purity (*wall/door*). Also, in contrast to an oft-cited idea that the Song's garden (4:12–5:1) alludes to Eden, offering a redemption of sexuality, parallels from antiquity to modernity show that such horticultural images play on an archetypal symbol of love, mixing the place and person of love to highlight the man's sensual delight in his beloved's body. Finally, whereas some scholars resort to interpretive gymnastics to explain the man's likeness of his maiden's head to Carmel (7:6), the comparative data suggest that this verse is best read as synonymous praise for her dark locks, a nearly universal symbol of beauty and seduction.

Nevertheless, using widely known motifs and symbols does not imply that the Hebrew poet(s) lacked creativity. Rather than simply a collection of the best lyrics of other cultures, the Song's metaphors are innovative.

---

7. Garrett and House, *Song of Songs/Lamentations*, 53.
8. Keel, *Song of Songs*, 20–24.
9. Gibbs, *Embodiment and Cognitive Science*, 13.
10. Exum, *Song of Songs*, 48; White, *Song of Songs*, 162.
11. Hess, *Song of Songs*, 26–27.

The maiden's comparison of her tan skin to dark tents (1:5–6) and her body to a fortified wall (8:8–10), or the man's likeness of his beloved's eyes to doves (1:15) or her hair to a flock of goats (4:1) appear to be uniquely crafted. Also, references to people and places, from Solomon to Sharon, show that Israel's poet wrapped shared motifs in cultural trappings.

Even metaphors indirectly borrowed from other cultures are packaged in a unique way. When the woman likens her lover's lips to the lotus, whose origin and symbolism can be traced to Egypt, she characterizes his body as her source of intoxication. Although desirable traits of beauty are widely shared, the Song's portraits are incomparable: "This rich, highly metaphorical way of writing about the female remained the pattern for later writers, but no other race has equaled the Semites in this field."[12]

7.2. Metaphors

The Song's body metaphors were divided into three main categories: self-description, sexual euphemism, and songs of description. First, the maiden issues a self-conscious yet self-confident declaration of beauty, playing on fair skin as a widely shared ideal (1:5–6). Using architectural images, shared symbols of separation between lovers, she also declares her own purity and reward (8:8–10). Second, with sexual euphemism and double-entendre from nature, the man invokes the archetypal garden, portraying his beloved's body as a private place (4:6) with sensual pleasures (4:12–5:1) and intoxicating delights (7:8–10; 8:2). In contrast, the woman's metaphor of her man, an apple tree with tasty sexual fruits (2:3), as well as the lover's likeness of his lady to a mare (1:9–10), likely draws on foreign cultures.

Finally, in the book's four *waṣf* songs, the poet again employs many widely shared or universal motifs, praising the lovers' affectionate eyes and dark curls (4:1; 5:12), the lady's white teeth (4:2), red lips and cheeks (4:3), tall neck (4:4), and shapely stomach and thighs (7:2–3), as well as the man's seductive scent (5:13). In addition, comparing the matchless beauty of one's lover to the heavenly luminaries (6:10), prominent places (5:15, 6:4), or precious stones/metals (5:11, 14–15) are also themes commonly found in love lyrics. Conversely, the allusions to the lotus as well as the reference to Heshbon's pools are indirectly drawn from other cultures.

---

12. Atkins, *Sex in Literature*, 1:177–79.

While both lovers laud one another, celebrating their mutual desire, their choice of lyrics displays an important difference. Combining two metaphors, BODY AS LANDSCAPE and LOVE AS INTOXICATION, the man repeatedly returns to the beauty of his beloved, using visual images to capture her physical attraction and its overwhelming effect. In contrast, with the OBJECT OF LOVE IS A VALUABLE OBJECT metaphor, the woman employs precious metals and gems to craft a vision of her lover's inestimable value. The Song's body metaphors are summarized in the table on pages 220–22:

7.3. Physical Beauty

In addition, our study has also shown that the Song's physical portraits depict the function and form of the lovers' bodies. Keel rightly stresses the dynamic implication of the Song's body imagery.[13] The woman's body is a wall of separation (8:10), a private garden and source of intoxicating delights (4:12–5:1; 7:8–10; 8:1–2). Her neck is an icon of strength (4:4; 7:5), her breasts are symbols of passion (4:5), and her belly/vulva produces sexual satisfaction (7:3). Similarly, the man's body also produces desirable fruit (2:3), with intoxicating lips, scented cheeks (5:13), and loins likened to the most valuable gems (5:14). Yet, Keel dubiously argues against any hint of physical beauty. The poet seamlessly weaves together form and function, at times mixing both into a single metaphor.

The value of beauty and its link to sexual attraction are timeless. "Like their non-Jewish neighbors, Jews in antiquity (regardless of place and time) thought that beauty was good."[14] Indeed, the authors of the Hebrew Bible often praise the beauty of its characters. Yet, the Song provides the most vivid physical portraits (4:1–7; 5:10–16; 6:4–7; 7:2–10). The female appearance receives the greater focus, with three poems dedicated to her beauty. After opening with summary statements of highest praise, the man sequentially details the maiden's body (4:1–5; 7:2–7), concluding with his mounting desire to experience her bodily pleasures (4:6; 7:8–10). In the eyes of Israel's poet(s), female beauty included the following traits:

fair complexion (1:5–6)
tall height (7:8)

---

13. Keel, *Deine Blicke sind Tauben*, 27.
14. Michael L. Satlow, *Jewish Marriage in Antiquity* (Princeton: Princeton University Press, 2001), 116.

Verses	Target	Source	Mapping	Relation	Form/Function	METAPHOR
1:5–6	Female Skin	Qedar/Solomon	Dark Beauty	Shared-Universal	Form	LANDSCAPE
8:8–10	Female Body, Breasts	Wall/Door, Towers	Purity, Reward	Shared-Universal	Function	LANDSCAPE
2:3	Male Body	Apple Tree, Fruit	Protection, Pleasure	Borrowed (East)	Function	LANDSCAPE, INTOXICATION
1:9	Female Cheeks, Beauty	Egyptian Mare	Distinction, Decoration, Attraction	Borrowed (Egypt)	Form, Function	VALUABLE OBJECT
2:17; 4:6; 8:14	Female Breasts	Mountains	Size/Shape, Seclusion	Shared	Form, Function	LANDSCAPE
4:12–5:1, etc.	Female Body	Vineyard/Garden	Privacy, Prosperity, Pleasure	Universal	Function	LANDSCAPE
7:8–10 8:2; 7:3	Female Body, Breasts, Mouth Navel	Palm Tree, Clusters; Grapes, Apple, Wine, Pomegranates	Height, Size, Intoxication	Shared, Universal	Form, Function	LANDSCAPE, INTOXICATION

7. Conclusions: Method, Metaphor, Beauty, and Unity

Verses	Target	Source	Mapping	Relation	Form/Function	Metaphor
1:15, 4:1; 5:12	Male/Female Eyes	Doves	Shape? Timid, Distance, Messengers	Shared	Form? Function	LANDSCAPE
7:5	Female Eyes	Pools in Heshbon	Size, Vitality	Borrowed (Heshbon)	Form, Function	LANDSCAPE
4:1, 6:5; 7:6; 5:11	Male/Female Hair	Goats, Crimson, Raven	Wavy, Dark, Rich	Shared, Universal	Form	LANDSCAPE, VALUABLE OBJECT
4:2, 6:6	Female Teeth	Sheep	White, Whole, Well-Aligned	Shared	Form	LANDSCAPE
4:3	Female Lips	Thread	Color	Universal	Form	VALUABLE OBJECT
4:3, 6:7	Female Cheeks	Pomegranate	Color, Pattern/Shape	Universal	Form	LANDSCAPE
4:4, 7:5	Female Neck, Nose	Tower	Size, Color, Ornament, Straight, Peace/Strength?	Shared, Universal, Borrowed (Lebanon)	Form, Function	LANDSCAPE, VALUABLE OBJECT

Verses	Target	Source	Mapping	Relation	Form/Function	Metaphor
4:5; 7:4; 5:13	Female Breasts; Male Lips	Fawns, Lotus	Symmetry, Shape/Shade, Sexual Passion, Sensual Intoxication	Universal, Borrowed (Egypt)	Form, Function	LANDSCAPE, INTOXICATION
7:3	Female Belly	Heap, Wheat, Lotus	Shape/Shade, Superior Beauty, Sexual Satisfaction	Shared	Form, Function	LANDSCAPE
7:2	Female Thighs/Hips	Gems	Shape?	Shared?	Form	VALUABLE OBJECT
6:4, 10; 5:15	Male/Female Form	Cities, Luminaries	Supreme Beauty	Universal	Form	VALUABLE OBJECT
5:11, 14–15	Male Head, Arms, Legs	Gold, Topaz, Alabaster; Rods, Pillars, Bases	Supreme Value, Color/Sheen, Strength	Universal, Shared	Form, Function	VALUABLE OBJECT
5:13	Male Cheeks	Spices	Scent	Universal	Function	LANDSCAPE, INTOXICATION
5:14	Male Loins	Ivory, Lapis Lazuli	Virility, Value, Color, Shape?	Shared	Form, Function	VALUABLE OBJECT

7. Conclusions: Method, Metaphor, Beauty, and Unity

slim figure (7:3, 8)
long, dark locks (4:1; 7:6)
big, beautiful (almond-shaped?) eyes (4:1; 7:5)
scarlet lips (4:3)
red, round cheeks (4:3)
white, well-aligned teeth (4:2)
straight nose (7:5)
tall, beaded neck (4:4; 7:5)
large breasts (2:17; 4:6; 7:8; 8:14)
shapely stomach (7:3)
sculpted thighs/hips (7:2)

Though the woman's ode to her man mainly stresses his superior value (5:10–16) with shouts of high praise (5:10, 16) and reference to precious materials (5:11, 14–15), she also details alluring aspects of his appearance:

radiant, ruddy tone (5:10)
dark, wavy locks (5:11)
almond-shaped eyes? (5:12)
golden face, arms, feet (5:11, 14–15)
fair loins and thighs (5:14–15)

As many have noted, the Song's body metaphors do not offer a full-color portrait of the lovers. However, while these lyrics may not include a complete description of the lovers' likeness, the Song offers isolated insights into the conception of beauty in ancient Israel.

7.4. Literary Unity

Finally, this study on the Song's body imagery contributes to the ongoing debate over the book's composition. Whether the Song is a collection of love lyrics or a unified work will continue to be debated by biblical scholars.[15] Indeed, abrupt shifts in scene, speaker, and subject matter as well as the lack of plot structure suggest an anthology. Yet other arguments can be made for the book's unity. In addition to the repeating refrains (2:7, 3:5,

---

15. See J. Cheryl Exum, "Unity, Date, Authorship, and the 'Wisdom' of the Song of Songs," in *Goochem in Mokum: Wisdom in Amsterdam*, ed. George Brooke and Pierre van Hecke (Leiden: Brill, 2016), 53–56.

8:4; 2:16, 6:3, 7:11) and cycles of escalating desire (1:2–2:7; 2:8–17; 3:1–5; 3:6–5:1; 5:2–7:10; 7:11–8:4), "unity is created by an artistic vision—in this case, a distinct and consistent attitude toward love—and by continuity of character portrayal, which leads us to posit the same protagonists throughout and see everything that happens as happening to them."[16]

One feature that supports a unified vision is the repetition of similar motifs. Nearly all the Song's body imagery is based on three metaphors: BODY AS LANDSCAPE, LOVE AS INTOXICATION, and THE OBJECT OF LOVE IS VALUABLE OBJECT. Both lovers employ agricultural and architectural imagery to depict their lover's body as a source of sensual pleasure and intoxicating delights as well as prominent places and precious gems to highlight their value and superiority. In addition, numerous physical traits are repeatedly praised: fair skin, affectionate eyes, dark curls, bejeweled neck, and large breasts.

Furthermore, shared structural features in the Song's body imagery also support the book's unity. The three main *waṣf* songs (4:1–7; 5:10–16; 7:2–7) follow a similar form, with bracketed assertions of highest praise, a sequential list of physical description, concluding with the overwhelming effects of such beauty on the gazing lover. Also, the appearance of the brothers in the girl's two poems of self-description (1:5–6; 8:8–10) forms an *inclusio* for the book. Thus, whether a single author or skillful redactor, the repeating motifs and shared structure support a unified artistic vision.

Indeed, the body imagery in the Song of Songs, with its captivating metaphors and controversial meaning, beautifully illustrates Saʿadia's iconic image for this important yet debated book: "the Song of Songs is comparable to a lock whose key has been lost [and] a jewel surpassing any valuation."[17] While most commentators address the meaning of these enigmatic images, some even noting the presence of universal motifs, a systematic study of the Song's body imagery has been lacking. Incorporating both exegetical and comparative data, the goal of this volume has been to elucidate the meaning of these metaphors and explore their possible origins. As a result, a new direction has been forged. Instead of attributing similarities between the Song and other Near Eastern love literature to dependency, we have shown that many of these images were part of a wider tradition shared between cultures or near universal symbols

---

16. Exum, *Song of Songs*, 34.
17. Saʿadia Ga'on, "Commentary on the Song of Songs," 26.

common to human love lyrics. Also, it has been demonstrated that the Song's body metaphors include description of both the function and form of the lovers' bodies, with isolated insights into the perception of beauty in ancient Israel. Finally, the repetition of similar motifs and structure within the Song's body imagery provides additional evidence for the Song's literary unity. Nonetheless, the elusive nature of the Song's lyrics suggests that this unique book will continue to spawn debate for decades to come. In the words of the early rabbis, "Turn it and turn it again for everything is in it; contemplate it and grow gray and old over it" (m. Avot 5:22).

Bibliography

Aaron, David. *Biblical Ambiguities: Metaphor, Semantics, and Divine Imagery*. Leiden: Brill, 2001.

Achilles Tatius. *Leucippe and Clitophon*. Translated by Stephen Gaselee. LCL. Cambridge: Harvard University Press, 1969.

Aftel, Mandy. *Essence and Alchemy: A Natural History of Perfume*. New York: North Point, 2001.

Ahl, Frederick, and Hannah Roisman. *The Odyssey Re-formed*. New York: Cornell University Press, 1996.

Albright, William F. *From the Stone Age to Christianity: Monotheism and the Historical Process*. 2nd ed. New York: Doubleday, 1957.

Alcman. *Partheneion*. In *Greek Lyric: Anacreon, Ancreontea, Choral Lyric from Olympus to Alcman*. Translated by David A. Campbell. LCL. Cambridge: Harvard University Press, 1988.

Alexander, Philip S. "The Song of Songs as Historical Allegory: Notes on the Development of an Exegetical Tradition." Pages 14–29 in *Targumic and Cognate Studies: Essays in Honour of Martin McNamara*. Edited by Kevin J. Cathcart and Michael Maher. JSOTSup 230. Sheffield: Sheffield Academic, 1996.

———. *The Targum of Canticles*. ArBib 17A. Collegeville, MN: Liturgical Press, 2003.

Alobaidi, Joseph. *Old Jewish Commentaries on the Song of Songs I: The Commentary of Yefet ben Eli*. BdH 9. New York: Lang, 2010.

Alster, Bendt. *Dumuzi's Dream: Aspects of Oral Poetry in a Sumerian Myth*. Mesopotamia 1. Copenhagen: Akademisk, 1972.

———. "Manchester Tammuz." *ASJ* 14 (1992): 1–47.

———. "Marriage and Love in the Sumerian Love Songs." Pages 15–27 in *The Tablet and the Scroll: Near Eastern Studies in Honor of William H. Hallo*. Edited by Mark E. Cohen, Daniel C. Snell, and David B. Weisberg. Bethesda, MD: CDL, 1993.

———. "Sumerian Love Songs." *RA* 79 (1985): 127–59.

Alter, Robert. *The Art of Biblical Poetry*. New York: Basic Books, 1985.
———. "The Song of Songs: An Ode to Intimacy." *BRev* 18.4 (2002): 24–32.
Anacreon. *Lyrca Graeca II*. In *Greek Lyric: Anacreon, Ancreontea, Choral Lyric from Olympus to Alcman*. Translated by David A. Campbell. LCL. Cambridge: Harvard University Press, 1988.
[Anacreon]. *Anacreontea*. In *Greek Lyric: Anacreon, Ancreontea, Choral Lyric from Olympus to Alcman*. Translated by David A. Campbell. LCL. Cambridge: Harvard University Press, 1988.
Andiñach, Pablo R. "Clandestine Relationship: An Approach to the Song of Songs." Pages 295–312 in *Foster Biblical Scholarship: Essays in Honor of Kent Harold Richards*. Edited by Frank R. Ames and Charles W. Miller. Atlanta: Society of Biblical Literature, 2010.
Andrae, Walter. *Die jüngeren Ischtar-Tempel in Assur*. WVDOG 58. Osnabrück: Zeller, 1967.
Arberry, Arthur John. *Arabic Poetry: A Primer for Students*. New York: Cambridge University Press, 1965.
Archilocus. *Greek Iambic Poetry*. Translated by Douglas A. Gerber. LCL. Cambridge: Harvard University Press, 1999.
Aristophanes. *Clouds*. Translated by Jeffrey Henderson. LCL. Cambridge: Harvard University Press, 1998.
Arnold, Dorothea, and James P. Allen, eds. *Royal Women of Amarna: Images of Beauty from Ancient Egypt*. New York: Metropolitan Museum of Art, 1996.
Asher-Greve, Julia M. "The Essential Body: Mesopotamian Conceptions of the Gendered Body." *G&H* 9 (1997): 432–61.
Asiedu, F. B. A. "The Song of Songs and the Ascent of the Soul: Ambrose, Augustine, and the Language of Mysticism." *VC* 55 (2001): 299–317.
Assante, Julia. "Sex, Magic, and the Liminal Body in the Erotic Art and Texts of the Old Babylonian Period." Pages 27–51 in *Sex and Gender in the Ancient Near East*. Edited by Simo Parpola and Robert M. Whiting. CRRAI 47. Helsinki: Neo-Assyrian Text Corpus Project, 2002.
Assmann, Jan. *Ägyptische Hymnen und Gebete: Übersetzt, kommentiert und eingeleitet*. 2nd ed. OBO Sonderband 2. Fribourg: Presses Universitaires; Göttingen: Vandenhoeck & Ruprecht, 1999.
Astell, Ann W. *The Song of Songs in the Middle Ages*. Ithaca, NY: Cornell University Press, 1990.
Athenaeus. *Deipnosophistae*. Translated by S. Douglas Olson. LCL. Cambridge: Harvard University Press, 2007.
Atkins, John. *Sex in Literature*. 4 vols. London: Calder, 1978.

Ausloos, Hans, and Bénédicte Lemmelijn. "Canticles as Allegory? Textual Criticism and Literary Criticism in Dialogue." Pages 35–48 in *Florilegium Lovaniense: Studies in Septuagint and Textual Criticism in Honour of Florentino García Martínez*. Edited by Hans Ausloos, Bénédicte Lemmelijn, and Marc Vervenne. BETL 224. Leuven: Peeters, 2008.

———. "Praising God or Singing of Love? From Theological to Erotic Allegorisation in the Interpretation of Canticles." *AcT* 30 (2010): 1–18.

Auwers, Jean-Marie. "Le traducteur grec a-t-il allégorisé ou érotisé le Cantique des cantiques?" Pages 161–68 in *XII Congress of the International Organization for Septuagint and Cognate Studies: Leiden, 2004*. Edited by Melvin Peters. SCS 54. Atlanta: Society of Biblical Literature, 2006.

Ayo, Nicholas. *Sacred Marriage: Wisdom of the Song of Songs*. New York: Continuum, 1997.

Bahrani, Zainab. "Jewelry and Personal Arts in Western Asia." *CANE* 3:1635–45.

———. *Women of Babylon: Gender and Representation in Mesopotamia*. New York: Routledge, 2001.

Baildam, John D. *Paradisal Love: Johann Gottfried Herder and the Song of Songs*. JSOTSup 298. Sheffield: Sheffield Academic, 1999.

Barbiero, Gianni. *Song of Songs: A Close Reading*. Translated by Michael Tait. VTSup 144. Leiden: Brill, 2011.

Barnett, Richard D. *Ancient Ivories in the Middle East*. Qedem 14. Jerusalem: Hebrew University Press, 1982.

———. *A Catalogue of the Nimrud Ivories with Other Ancient Near Eastern Ivories in the British Museum*. London: British Museum, 1957.

Baum, Guilielmus, Edouard Cunitz, and Edouard Reuss, eds. *Ioannis Calvini Opera quae supersunt omnia*. Braunschweig: Schwentschke, 1863.

Beazley, John D., and Bernard Ashmole. *Greek Sculpture and Painting: To the End of the Hellenistic Period*. Cambridge: Cambridge University Press, 1932.

Beentjes, Pancratius C. *The Book of Ben Sira in Hebrew: A Text Edition of All Extant Hebrew Manuscripts and a Synopsis of All Parallel Hebrew Ben Sira Texts*. VTSup 68. Leiden: Brill, 1997.

Ben Gershom, Levi. *Commentary on Song of Songs*. Translated by Menachem Kellner. YJS 28. New Haven: Yale University Press, 1998.

Bergant, Dianne. *The Song of Songs*. Berit Olam. Collegeville, MN: Liturgical Press, 2001.

Berlin, Adele. *Lamentations*. OTL. Louisville: Westminster John Knox, 2002.

Bernard of Clairvaux. *On Song of Songs*. Translated by Irene Edmonds. CS 40. Kalamazoo, MI: Cistercian, 1980.

Bernat, David. "Biblical Waṣfs Beyond Song of Songs." *JSOT* 28 (2004): 327–49.

Besnier, Marie-Françoise. "Temptation's Garden: The Gardener, a Mediator Who Plays an Ambiguous Part." Pages 59–70 in *Sex and Gender in the Ancient Near East*. Edited by Simo Parpola and Robert M. Whiting. CRRAI 47. Helsinki: Neo-Assyrian Text Corpus Project, 2002.

Bialik, Chaim N. *Shirot Bialik*. Edited by Steven Jacobs. Columbus: Alpha, 1987.

Bienkowski, Piotr. "Hair Dressing." *DANE*, 137.

Biggs, Robert D. "The Babylonian Sexual Potency Texts." Pages 71–78 in *Sex and Gender in the Ancient Near East*. Edited by Simo Parpola and Robert M. Whiting. CRRAI 47. Helsinki: Neo-Assyrian Text Corpus Project, 2002.

———. *ŠÀ.ZI.GA: Ancient Mesopotamian Potency Incantations*. TCS 2. Locust Valley, NY: Augustin, 1967.

Bimson, Mavis. "Cosmetic Pigments from the 'Royal Cemetery' at Ur." *Iraq* 42 (1980): 75–77.

Biran, Avraham. *Biblical Dan*. Jerusalem: Israel Exploration Society, 1994.

Black, Fiona C. *The Artifice of Love: Grotesque Bodies and the Song of Songs*. LHBOTS 392. New York: T&T Clark, 2009.

———. "Beauty or the Beast? The Grotesque Body in Song of Songs." *BibInt* 8 (2000): 302–23.

———. "Looking in through the Lattice: Feminist and Other Gender-Critical Readings of the Song of Songs." Pages 211–29 in *Feminist Interpretation of the Hebrew Bible in Retrospect: Biblical Books*. Edited by Susanne Scholz. Sheffield: Sheffield Phoenix, 2013.

Black, Jeremy A. "Babylonian Ballads: A New Genre." *JAOS* 103 (1983): 25–34.

Bloch, Ariel, and Chana Bloch. *The Song of Songs: A New Translation with an Introduction and Commentary*. Los Angeles: University of California Press, 1995.

Bloch, Chana. "Translating Eros." Pages 151–61 in *Scrolls of Love: Ruth and the Song of Songs*. Edited by Peter S. Hawkins and Lesleigh Cushing Stahlberg. New York: Fordham University Press, 2006.

Blondell, Ruby. *Helen of Troy: Beauty, Myth, Devastation*. Oxford: Oxford University Press, 2013.

Bodkin, Maud. *Archetypal Patterns in Poetry: Psychological Studies of Imagination*. London: Oxford University Press, 1934.
Boddy, Janice. "Body: Female, Egypt and Sudan." Pages 34–35 in vol. 3 of *Encyclopedia of Women and Islamic Cultures: Family, Body, Sexuality, and Health*. Edited by Suad Joseph. Leiden: Brill, 2006.
Boer, Roland. "Night Sprinkle(s): Pornography and the Song of Songs." Pages 53–70 in *Knockin' on Heaven's Door: The Bible and Popular Culture*. New York: Routledge, 1999.
Boersma, Matthew. "Scent in Song: Exploring Scented Symbols in the Song of Songs." *CBW* 31 (2011): 80–94.
Börker-Klähn, Jutta. "Haartrachten." *RlA* 4:1–12.
Borger, Rykle. *Die Inschriften Asarhaddons Konigs von Assyrien*. AfOB 9. Osnabrück: Biblio, 1956.
———. "Die Waffenträger des Königs Darius: Ein Beitrag zur alttestamentlichen Exegese und zur semitischen Lexikographie." *VT* 22 (1972): 385–98.
Bossuet, Jacques Benigne. "Praefatio in Canticum Canticorum." Pages 177–88 in *Libri Salomonis, proverbia, ecclesiastes, canticum canticorum, sapientia, ecclesiasticus*. Paris: Anisson, 1693.
Boyarin, Daniel. *Intertextuality and the Reading of Midrash*. ISBL. Bloomington: Indiana University Press, 1990.
Breasted, James H. *Ancient Records of Egypt*. 5 vols. Urbana: University of Illinois Press, 2001.
Brenner, Athalya. *Colour Terms in the Old Testament*. JSOTSup 21. Sheffield: JSOT Press, 1982.
———. "'Come Back, Come Back the Shulammite' (Song of Songs 7.1–10): A Parody of the *Waṣf* Genre." Pages 251–75 in *On Humour and the Comic in the Hebrew Bible*. Edited by Athalaya Brenner and Yehuda Radday. BLS 23. JSOTSup 92. Sheffield: Almond Press, 1990.
———. *I Am … Biblical Women Tell Their Own Stories*. Minneapolis: Fortress, 2005.
———. *Intercourse of Knowledge: On Gendering Desire and "Sexuality" in the Hebrew Bible*. BibInt 26. Leiden: Brill, 1997.
———. "My Beloved Is Fair and Ruddy: On Song of Songs 5:10–11." *BM* 89 (1982): 168–73.
———. "A Note on Bat-Rabbim (Song of Songs 7:5)." *VT* 42 (1992): 113–15.
———. "To See Is to Assume: Whose Love Is Celebrated in the Song of Songs?" *BibInt* 1 (1993): 265–84.
Bryan, Cyril P. *The Papyrus Ebers*. London: Bles, 1930.

Budde, D. Karl. "Das Hohelied." Pages ix–48 in *Die Fünf Megilloth*. Leipzig: Mohr, 1898.

Burchard, Christoph. *Gesammelte Studien zu Joseph und Aseneth: Berichtigt und ergänzt Herausgegeben*. SVTP 13. Leiden: Brill, 1996.

———. "Joseph and Aseneth." *OTP* 2:177–247.

———. "The Text of Joseph and Aseneth Reconsidered." *JSP* 6 (2005): 83–96.

Buzy, Denis. "Le Cantique des Cantiques." In *La Sainte Bible*. Paris: Letouzey, 1951.

Byrne, Ryan. "Lie Back and Think of Judah: The Reproductive Politics of Pillar Figurines." *NEA* 67 (2004): 137–51.

Cabanes, Augustin. *Erotikon: Being an Illustrated Treasury of Scientific Marvels of Human Sexuality*. New York: Book Awards, 1966.

Cainion, Ivory J. "An Analogy of the Song of Songs and Genesis Chapters Two and Three." *SJOT* 14 (2000): 219–60.

Caird, George B. *The Language and Imagery of the Bible*. Philadelphia: Westminster, 1980.

Campbell, Robert C. "Sonnet." *The Germ* 1 (1850): 68.

Canter, Howard V. "The Paraclausithyron as a Literary Theme." *AJP* 41 (1920): 355–68.

Cantrell, Deborah. *The Horsemen of Israel: Horses and Chariotry in Monarchic Israel*. HACL 1. Winona Lake, IN: Eisenbrauns, 2011.

Carew, Thomas. *The Poems of Thomas Carew*. New York: Scribners, 1899.

Carr, David M. "Gender and the Shaping of Desire in the Song of Songs and Its Interpretation." *JBL* 119 (2000): 233–48.

———. "The Song of Songs as a Microcosm of the Canonization and Decanonization Process." Pages 173–89 in *Canonization and Decanonization*. Edited by Arie van der Kooij and Karel van der Toorn. SHR 82. Leiden: Brill, 1998.

———. *Writing on the Tablet of the Heart: Origins of Scripture and Literature*. Oxford: Oxford University Press, 2005.

Carr, G. Lloyd. *Song of Solomon*. TOTC 17. Downers Grove, IL: InterVarsity Press, 1984.

Carter, Howard, and Arthur C. Mace. *The Tomb of Tut-ankh-Amen: Discovered by the Late Earl of Carnarvon and Howard Carter*. New York: Doran, 1923.

Carty, Jarrett A. "Martin Luther's Political Interpretation of the Song of Songs." *Review of Politics* 73 (2011): 449–67.

Case, M. L. "Cunning Linguists: Oral Sex in the Song of Songs." *VT* 67 (2017): 171–86.

Caston, R. Rothaus. "Love as Illness: Poets and Philosophers on Romantic Love." *CJ* 101 (2006): 271–98.
Catullus. *Poems*. Translated by Francis W. Cornish. LCL. Cambridge: Harvard University Press, 1913.
Chambers, Robert, ed. *The Life and Works of Robert Burns*. Edinburgh: Chambers, 1856.
Chanel, Coco. "Glory of the Sun Powder" advertisement. *Vogue* 22 (June 1929): 100.
Chave, Peter. "Towards a Not Too Rosy Picture of the Song of Songs." *Feminist Theology* 18 (1998): 41–53.
Cheyne, Thomas K. "Canticles." *Encyclopedia Biblica* 1:681–95.
Civil, Miguel, ed. *Ea A=nâqu, Aa A=nâqu, with Their Forerunners and Related Texts*. MSL 14. Rome: Pontificum Institutum Biblicum, 1979.
———. "Enlil and Ninlil: The Marriage of Sud." *JAOS* 103 (1983): 43–66.
———. "The 'Message of Lu-Dingir-Ra to His Mother' and a Group of Akkado-Hittite 'Proverbs.'" *JNES* 23 (1964): 1–11.
———. "Studies on Early Dynastic Lexicography III." *Or* 56 (1987): 233–44.
Clark, Elizabeth A. "Origen, the Jews, and the Song of Songs: Allegory and Polemic in Christian Antiquity." Pages 274–93 in *Perspectives on the Song of Songs*. Edited by Anselm C. Hagedorn. BZAW 346. New York: de Gruyter, 2005.
Clines, David J. A. "Why Is There a Song of Songs and What Does It Do to You If You Read It?" Pages 94–121 in *Interested Parties: The Ideology of Writers and Readers of the Hebrew Bible*. JSOTSup 205. Sheffield: Sheffield Academic, 1995.
Cohen, Gerson D. "The Songs of Songs and the Jewish Religious Mentality." Pages 3–17 in *Studies in the Variety of Rabbinic Cultures*. New York: Jewish Publication Society, 1991.
Cohen, Mordechai Z. *Opening the Gates of Interpretation: Maimonides' Biblical Hermeneutics in Light of His Geonic-Andalusian Heritage and Muslim Milieu*. Leiden: Brill, 2011.
Cohen, Shaye D. "The Beauty of Flora and the Beauty of Sarai." *Helios* 8.2 (1981): 41–53.
Conrad, Cecilia. *African Americans in the U.S. Economy*. Lanham, MD: Rowman & Littlefield, 2005.
Cook, Elizabeth, ed. *John Keats: The Major Works*. Oxford: Oxford University Press, 2001.
Cooke, J. Hunt. "The Westcar Papyrus." *BW* 4 (1894): 49–53.

Cooper, Jerrold S. "Gendered Sexuality in Sumerian Love Poetry." Pages 85–97 in *Sumerian Gods and Their Representation*. Edited by Irving J. Finkel and Mark J. Geller. CM 7. Groningen: Styx, 1997.

———. "New Cuneiform Parallels to the Song of Songs." *JBL* 90 (1971): 157–62.

Copley, Frank. *Exclusus Amator: A Study in Latin Love Poetry*. Baltimore: American Philological Society, 1956.

Corbett, Glenn, Donald R. Keller, Barbara A. Porter, and China P. Shelton. "Archaeology in Jordan, 2014 and 2015 Seasons." *AJA* 120 (2016): 631–72.

Cornelius, Izak. "The Garden in Iconography of the Ancient Near East: A Study of Selected Material from Egypt." *JSem* 1 (1989): 204–28.

Corson, Richard. *Fashions in Makeup: From Ancient to Modern Times*. 3rd ed. London: Owen, 2003.

Cowley, Geoffrey. "The Biology of Beauty." *Newsweek* 127.23 (1996): 60–67.

Dahood, Mitchell J. "Canticle 7,9 and UT 52,61: A Question of Method." *Bib* 57 (1976): 109–10.

———. *Psalms I (1–50)*. AB 16. Garden City, NY: Doubleday, 1966.

Dales, George F. "Necklaces, Bands, and Belts on Mesopotamian Figurines." *RA* 57 (1963): 21–40.

Dalman, Gustaf H. *Arbeit und Sitte in Palästina*. Gütersloh: Bertelsmann, 1964.

———. *Palästinischer Diwan: Als Beitrag zur Volkskunde Palästinas*. Leipzig: Hinrich, 1901.

Davidson, James. *The Greeks and Greek Love: A Bold New Exploration of the Ancient World*. New York: Random House, 2009.

Davis, Ellen F. *Proverbs, Ecclesiastes, and Song of Songs*. WesBibComp. Louisville: Westminster John Knox, 2000.

Dayagi-Mendels, Mikhal. *Perfumes and Cosmetics in the Ancient World*. Jerusalem: Israel Museum, 1993.

De Crom, Dries. *LXX Song of Songs and Descriptive Translation Studies*. De Septuaginta Investigationes 11. Göttingen: Vandenhoeck & Ruprecht, 2019.

Deller, Karlheinz. "ST 366: Deutungsversuch 1982." *Assur* 3 (1982): 139–53.

Delitzsch, Franz, and Carl F. Keil. *Commentary on the Old Testament*. 10 vols. Peabody, MA: Hendrickson, 2002.

Delitzsch, Friedrich. *Babel und Bibel: Ein Vortrage*. Leipzig: Hinrichs, 1903.

Derchain, Philippe. "Le Lotus, la mandragore, et le perséa." *CdE* 50 (1975): 65–86.

———. "La Perruque et le Cristal." *SAK* 2 (1975): 55–74.

Dezső, Tamás. "The Reconstruction of the Neo-Assyrian Army as Depicted on the Assyrian Palace Reliefs, 745–612 BC." *AAASH* 57 (2006): 87–130.

Dhorme, Édouard. *L'emploi métaphorique des noms de parties du corps en hébreu et en akkadien*. Paris: Gabalda, 1923.

Diodorus Siculus. *Library of History*. Translated by Charles H. Oldfather. LCL. Cambridge: Harvard University Press, 1933.

Dirksen, Piet B. *General Introduction and Megilloth*. BHQ 18. Stuttgart: Deutsche Bibelgesellschaft, 2004.

———. "Septuagint and Peshitta in the Apparatus to Canticles in *Biblia Hebraica Quinta*." Pages 15–31 in *Sôfer Mahîr: Essays in Honour of Adrian Schenker*. Edited by Yohanan A. P. Goldman, Arie van der Kooij, and Richard D. Weis. VTSup 110. Leiden: Brill, 2006.

Dobbs-Allsopp, F. W. "The Delight of Beauty and Song of Songs 4:1–7." *Int* 59 (2005): 260–77.

———. "'I Am Black *and* Beautiful': The Song, Cixous, and *Écriture Féminine*." Pages 128–40 in *Engaging the Bible in a Gendered World: An Introduction to Feminist Biblical Interpretation in Honor of Katherine Doob Sakenfeld*. Edited by Linda Day and Carolyn Pressler. Louisville: Westminster John Knox, 2006.

———. "Late Linguistic Features in the Song of Songs." Pages 27–77 in *Perspectives on the Song of Songs*. Edited by Anselm C. Hagedorn. BZAW 346. Berlin: de Gruyter, 2005.

Dorsey, David A. "Literary Structuring in the Song of Songs." *JSOT* 46 (1990): 81–96.

Dover, Kenneth J. *Greek Homosexuality*. Cambridge: Harvard University Press, 1989.

Downame, John, ed. *Annotations upon All the Books of the Old and New Testament*. 2nd ed. London: Legatt, 1651.

DuBois, Page. *Sowing the Body: Psychoanalysis and Ancient Representations of Women*. Women in Culture and Society. Chicago: University of Chicago Press, 1988.

Durling, Robert M., and Ronald L. Martinez. *Time and the Crystal: Studies in Dante's Rime Petrose*. Berkeley: University of California Press, 1990.

Ebeling, Erich. *Ein Hymnen-Katalog aus Assur*. Berlin, 1923.

———. *Parfümrezepte und Kultische Texte aus Assur*. Rome: Pontifical Biblical Institute, 1950.
Edwards, Iorweth E. S. "A Toilet Scene on a Funerary Stela of the Middle Kingdom." *JEA* 23 (1937): 165.
Eichner, Jens, and Andreas Scherer. "Die 'Teiche' von Hesbon: Eine exegetisch-archäologische Glosse zu Cant 7,5bα." *BN* 109 (2001): 10–14.
Eidelkind, Yakov. "Intended Lexical Ambiguity in the Song of Songs." *Babel und Bibel* 6 (2012): 326–68.
———. "Two Notes on Song 4:12." *Babel und Bibel* 3 (2006): 217–36.
Elgvin, Torleif. *The Literary Growth of the Song of Songs during the Hasmonean and Early-Herodian Periods*. CBET 89. Leuven: Peeters, 2018.
Elliott, M. Timothea. *The Literary Unity of the Canticle*. EUS 23. New York: Lang, 1989.
Emanatian, Michele. "Metaphor and the Expression of Emotion: The Value of Cross-Cultural Perspectives." *Metaphor and Symbolic Activity* 10 (1995): 163–82.
Emerton, John A. "The Teaching of Amenemope and Proverbs xxii 17–xxiv 22: Further Reflections on a Long-Standing Problem." *VT* 51 (2001): 431–65.
Eph'al, Israel. *The Ancient Arabs: Nomads on the Borders of the Fertile Crescent 9th–5th Centuries B.C.* Leiden: Brill, 1982.
Epstein, Isidore, ed. and trans. *Hebrew-English Edition of the Babylonian Talmud*. 18 vols. New York: Soncino, 1960–1994.
Erman, Adolf. "Hebräische *GLŠ* 'springen.'" *OLZ* 28 (1925): 5.
———. *The Literature of the Ancient Egyptians: Poems, Narratives, and Manuals of Instruction from the Third and Second Millennia B.C.* Translated by Aylward M. Blackman. London: Methuen, 1927.
Exum, J. Cheryl. "Asseverative *'al* in Canticles 1:6?" *Bib* 62 (1981): 416–19.
———. "Developing Strategies of Feminist Criticism/Developing Strategies for Commentating the Song of Songs." Pages 206–49 in *Auguries: The Jubilee Volume of the Sheffield Department of Biblical Studies*. Edited by David J. A. Clines and Stephen D. Moore. JSOTSup 269. Sheffield: Sheffield Academic, 1998.
———. "The Little Sister and Solomon's Vineyard: Song of Songs 8:8–12 as a Lovers' Dialogue." Pages 269–82 in *Seeking Out the Wisdom of the Ancients: Essays Offered to Honor Michael V. Fox on the Occasion of His Sixty-Fifth Birthday*. Edited by Ron L. Troxel, Kevin G. Friebel, and Dennis R. Magary. Winona Lake, IN: Eisenbrauns, 2005.

———. *Song of Songs: A Commentary*. OTL. Louisville: Westminster John Knox, 2005.

———. "Unity, Date, Authorship, and the 'Wisdom' of the Song of Songs." Pages 53–66 in *Goochem in Mokum: Wisdom in Amsterdam*. Edited by George Brooke and Pierre van Hecke. OTS 68. Leiden: Brill, 2016.

Falk, Marcia. *Love Lyrics from the Bible: A Translation and Literary Study of the Song of Songs*. BLS 4. Sheffield: Almond Press, 1982.

Falkenstein, Adam. "Tammuz." Pages 41–65 in *Compte rendu de la troisième Rencontre Assyriologique Internationale: Organisée à Leiden du 28 juin au 4 juillet 1952 par le Nederlandsch Instituut voor het Nabije Oosten*. CRRAI 3. Leiden: Nederlands Instituut voor het Nabije Oosten, 1954.

Faraone, Christopher. *Ancient Greek Love Magic*. Cambridge: Harvard University Press, 1999.

Feliks, Yehuda. *Fruit Trees in the Bible and Talmudic Literature* [Hebrew]. Jerusalem: Mass, 1994.

———. *Song of Songs: Nature Epic and Allegory*. Jerusalem: Israel Society for Biblical Research, 1983.

Fernández-Galiano, Manuel, Joseph Russo, and Alfred Heubeck. *A Commentary on Homer's Odyssey*. 3 vols. Oxford: Oxford University Press, 1991–1993.

Fields, Fridericus, ed. *Origenis Hexaplorum quae supersunt*. 2 vols. Hildesheim: Olms, 1964.

Finkel, Iriving, ed. *The Series SIG7.ALAN=Nabnītu*. MSL 16. Rome: Pontifical Biblical Institute, 1982.

Fisch, Harold. *Poetry with a Purpose: Biblical Poetics and Interpretation*. ISBL. Bloomington: Indiana University Press, 1990.

Fishbane, Michael. *Biblical Interpretation in Ancient Israel*. Oxford: Oxford University Press, 1985.

———. *Song of Songs: The Traditional Hebrew Text with the New JPS Translation*. JPS Bible Commentary. Philadelphia: Jewish Publication Society, 2015.

Fitzmyer, Joseph A. *The Genesis Apocryphon of Qumran Cave 1 (1Q20): A Commentary*. 3rd ed. BibOr 18b. Rome: Pontifical Biblical Institute, 2004.

Flint, Peter. "The Book of Canticles (Song of Songs) in the Dead Sea Scrolls." Pages 96–104 in *Perspectives on the Song of Songs*. Edited by Anselm C. Hagedorn. BZAW 346. Berlin: de Gruyter, 2005.

Folsom, Robert S. *Attic Black Figured Pottery*. Park Ridge, NJ: Noyes, 1975.

Foster, Benjamin O. "Notes on the Symbolism of the Apple in Classical Antiquity." *HSCP* 10 (1899): 39–55.
Foster, Benjamin R. *Before the Muses: An Anthology of Akkadian Literature*. 3rd ed. Bethesda, MD: CDL, 2005.
Fox, Michael V. "From Amenemope to Proverbs: Editorial Art in Proverbs 22,17–23,11." *ZAW* 126 (2014): 76–91.
———. *Proverbs 1–9: A New Translation with Introduction and Commentary*. AB 18A. New York: Doubleday, 2000.
———. *Proverbs 10–31: A New Translation with Introduction and Commentary*. AB 18B. New Haven: Yale University Press, 2009.
———. *The Song of Songs and the Ancient Egyptian Love Songs*. Madison: University of Wisconsin Press, 1985.
Frangié-Joly, Dina. "Perfume, Aromatics, and Purple Dye." *JEMAHS* 4 (2016): 36–56.
Frank, Daniel. "Karaite Exegesis." Pages 110–28 in *Hebrew Bible/Old Testament: History of Interpretation; The Middle Ages*. Edited by Magne Sæbø. Göttingen: Vandenhoeck & Ruprecht, 2000.
Frankfort, Henri. *Sculpture of the Third Millennium B.C. from Tell Asmar and Khafājah*. OIP 44. Chicago: University of Chicago Press, 1939.
Frazer, James G. *The Golden Bough: A Study in Magic and Religion*. 3rd ed. 12 vols. London: Macmillan, 1911–1915.
Friedman, Norman, and Richard Sugg. "Archetypes." *PEPP*, 76–79.
Frost, Peter. "Human Skin Color: A Possible Relationship between Its Sexual Dimorphism and Its Social Perception." *Perspectives in Biology and Medicine* 32 (1988): 38–58.
Frye, Northrup. *The Great Code: The Bible as Literature*. New York: Harcourt Brace Jovanovich, 1981.
Frymer-Kensky, Tikva. *In the Wake of the Goddesses: Women, Culture, and the Biblical Transformation of Pagan Myth*. New York: Free Press, 1992.
Gansell, Amy Rebecca. "The Iconography of Ideal Feminine Beauty Represented in the Hebrew Bible and Iron Age Levantine Ivory Sculpture." Pages 46–70 in *Image, Text, Exegesis: Iconography and Interpretation in the Hebrew Bible*. Edited by Izaak J. de Hulster and Joel M. LeMon. LHBOTS 588. London: Bloomsbury, 2014.
———. "Images and Conceptions of Ideal Feminine Beauty in Neo-Assyrian Royal Context, c. 883–627 BCE." Pages 391–420 in *Critical Approaches to Ancient Near Eastern Art*. Edited by Brian Brown and Marian Feldman. Boston: de Gruyter, 2013.

Garrett, Duane A. "Song of Songs." Pages 518–31 in vol. 5 of *Zondervan Illustrated Bible Background Commentary: Minor Prophets, Job, Psalms, Proverbs, Ecclesiastes, Song of Songs*. Edited by John H. Walton. Grand Rapids: Zondervan, 2009.

Garrett, Duane A., and Paul R. House. *Song of Songs/Lamentations*. WBC 23B. Nashville: Nelson, 2004.

Gault, Brian P. "An Admonition against 'Rousing Love': The Meaning of the Enigmatic Refrain in Song of Songs." *BBR* 20 (2010): 161–84.

———. "A 'Do Not Disturb' Sign? Reexamining the Adjuration Refrain in Song of Songs." *JSOT* 36 (2011): 93–104.

———. "The Fragments of Canticles at Qumran: Implications and Limitations for Interpretation." *RevQ* 95 (2010): 351–71.

Geeraerts, Dirk. *Theories of Lexical Semantics*. Oxford Linguistics. Oxford: Oxford University Press, 2009.

Gelb, Ignace J. "Sumerian and Akkadian Words for 'String of Fruit.'" Pages 67–82 in *Zikir Šumim: Assyriological Studies Presented to F. R. Kraus on the Occasion of His Seventieth Birthday*. Edited by Govert van Driel. Leiden: Brill, 1982.

Geller, Mark J. "Mesopotamian Love Magic: Discourse or Intercourse?" Pages 129–39 in *Sex and Gender in the Ancient Near East*. Edited by Simo Parpola and Robert M. Whiting. CRRAI 47. Helsinki: Neo-Assyrian Text Corpus Project, 2002.

Geller, Stephen A. *Parallelism in Early Biblical Poetry*. HSM 20. Missoula, MT: Scholars Press, 1979.

George, Andrew R. *Babylonian Literary Texts in the Schøyen Collection*. CUSAS 10. Bethesda, MD: CDL, 2009.

———. *The Epic of Gilgamesh: Introduction, Critical Edition, and Cuneiform Texts*. 2 vols. Oxford: Oxford University Press, 2003.

———. "The Gilgamesh Epic at Ugarit." *AuOr* 25 (2007): 237–54.

Gerber, Douglas. "The Female Breast in Greek Erotic Literature." *Arethusa* 11 (1978): 203–12.

Gerleman, Gillis. "Die Bildsprache des Hohenliedes und die Altägyptische Kunst." *ASTI* 1 (1962): 24–30.

———. *Ruth, Das Hohelied*. BKAT 18. Neukirchen-Vluyn: Neukirchener Verlag, 1965.

Germer, Renate. *Flora des pharaonischen ägypten*. DAIK 14. Mainz: von Zabern, 1985.

———. *Handbuch der altägyptischen Heilpflanzen*. Philippika 21. Wiesbaden: Harrassowitz, 2008.

Gesenius, Wilhelm. *Hebräisches und Aramäisches Handwörterbuch über das Alte Testament*. Edited by Herbert Donner. 18th ed. Berlin: Springer, 2013.

Gibbs, Raymond. *Embodiment and Cognitive Science*. Cambridge: Cambridge University Press, 2005.

———. *Metaphor Wars: Conceptual Metaphors in Human Life*. New York: Cambridge University Press, 2017.

Gill, Roma, ed. *The Complete Works of Christopher Marlowe*. 5 vols. Oxford: Clarendon, 1987.

Ginsburg, Christian D. *The Song of Songs and Coheleth*. New York: Ktav, 1970.

Gioia, Ted. *Love Songs: The Hidden History*. New York: Oxford University Press, 2015.

Gleason, Kathryn L. "Gardens in Preclassical Times." *OEANE* 2:383–85.

Goedicke, Hans. "The Story of the Herdsman." *CdE* 45 (1970): 244–66.

Goetze, Albrecht, and Selim J. Levy. "Fragment of the Gilgamesh Epic from Megiddo." *Atiqot* 2 (1959): 121–28.

Goitein, Shlomo D. "*Ayumma Kannidgalot* (Song of Songs VI.10): 'Splendid Like the Brilliant Stars.'" *JSS* 10 (1965): 220–21.

Goldenberg, David M. *The Curse of Ham: Race and Slavery in Early Judaism, Christianity, and Islam*. Princeton: Princeton University Press, 2003.

Gopal, Lallanji, and V. C. Srivastava, eds. *History of Agriculture in India (up to c. 1200 AD)*. History of Science, Philosophy, and Culture in Indian Civilization 5.1. New Delhi: Concept, 2008.

Gordis, Robert. "The Root דגל in the Song of Songs." *JBL* 88 (1969): 203–4.

———. *Song of Songs: A Study, Modern Translation, and Commentary*. New York: Jewish Theological Seminary of America, 1954.

Goshen-Gottstein, Moshe. "Philologische Miszellen zu den Qumrantexten." *RevQ* 2 (1959): 43–51.

Gould, George M., and Walter L. Pyle. *Anomalies and Curiosities of Medicine*. London: Saunders, 1901.

Goulder, Michael. *The Song of Fourteen Songs*. JSOTSup 36. Sheffield: JSOT Press, 1986.

Govárdhana. *Seven Hundred Elegant Verses*. Translated by Friedhelm Hardy. Clay Sanskrit Library. New York: New York University Press, 2009.

Grady, Joseph E. "Metaphor." Pages 188–213 in *The Oxford Handbook of Cognitive Linguistics*. Edited by Dirk Geeraerts and Hubert Cuyckens. Oxford: Oxford University Press, 2007.

Gray, Erik. *The Art of Love Poetry*. Oxford: Oxford University Press, 2018.

Greenfield, Jonas C. "'Le Bain des brebis': Another Example and a Query." *Or* 29 (1960): 98–102.

Greengus, Samuel. *Laws in the Bible and in Early Rabbinic Collections: The Legal Legacy of the Ancient Near East*. Eugene, OR: Wipf & Stock, 2011.

———. "Old Babylonian Marriage Ceremonies and Rites." *JCS* 20 (1966): 55–72.

———. "The Old Babylonian Marriage Contract." *JAOS* 89 (1969): 505–32.

———. "Some Issues Relating to the Comparability of Laws and the Coherence of the Legal Tradition." Pages 60–87 in *Theory and Method in Biblical and Cuneiform Law*. Edited by Bernard M. Levinson. JSOTSup 181. Sheffield: JSOT Press, 1994.

Gregory the Great. *On the Song of Songs*. Translated by Mark DelCogliano. CS 244. Collegeville, MN: Liturgical Press, 2012.

Griffiths, Paul J. *Song of Songs*. BTCB. Grand Rapids: Brazos, 2011.

Grimm, Jacob, and Wilhelm Grimm. *The Original Folk and Fairy Tales of the Brothers Grimm*. 2 vols. Princeton: Princeton University Press, 2014.

Groneberg, Brigitte. "Searching for Akkadian Lyrics: From Old Babylonian to the 'Liederkatalog' KAR 158." *JCS* 55 (2003): 55–74.

Grossberg, Daniel. "Humanity, Nature, and Love in Song of Songs." *Int* 59 (2005): 229–42.

Gunkel, Hermann. "The Influence of Babylonian Mythology upon the Biblical Creation Story." Pages 25–52 in *Creation in the Old Testament*. Edited by Bernard Anderson. IRT 6. Philadelphia: Fortress, 1984.

Haas, Robert, and Stephen Mitchell. *Into the Garden: A Wedding Anthology of Poetry and Prose on Love and Marriage*. New York: HarperCollins, 1994.

Hadley, Judith M. *The Cult of Asherah in Ancient Israel and Judah*. New York: Cambridge University Press, 2000.

Hagedorn, Anselm C. "Die Frau des Hohenlieds zwischen babylonisch-assyrischer Morphoskopie und Jacques Lacan (Teil II)." *ZAW* 122 (2010): 593–609.

———. "Of Foxes and Vineyards: Greek Perspectives on the Song of Songs." *VT* 53 (2003): 337–52.

Hallo, William W. "Biblical History in Its Near Eastern Setting: The Contextual Approach." Pages 1–26 in *Scripture in Context: Essays on the Comparative Method*. Edited by Carl D. Evans, William W. Hallo, and John B. White. PTMS 34. Pittsburgh: Pickwick, 1980.

———. "Compare and Contrast: The Contextual Approach to Biblical Literature." Pages 1–30 in *The Bible in the Light of Cuneiform Literature*. Edited by William W. Hallo, Bruce W. Jones, and Gerald L. Mattingly. Scripture in Context 3. New York: Mellen, 1990.

Hamilton, Albert C. *Sir Philip Sidney: A Study of His Life and Works*. Cambridge: Cambridge University Press, 1977.

Hamilton, Mark W. *The Body Royal: The Social Poetics of Kingship in Ancient Israel*. BibInt 78. Leiden: Brill, 2005.

Harer, W. Benson, Jr. "Pharmacological and Biological Properties of the Egyptian Lotus." *JARCE* 22 (1985): 49–54.

Hawass, Zahi. *Silent Images: Women in Pharaonic Egypt*. Cairo: American University in Cairo Press, 2008.

Hays, Christopher B. "Echoes of the Ancient Near East? Intertextuality and the Comparative Study of the Old Testament." Pages 20–43 in *Word Leaps the Gap: Essays on Scripture and Theology in Honor of Richard B. Hays*. Edited by J. Ross Wagner, C. Kavin Rowe, and A. Katherine Grieb. Grand Rapids, Eerdmans, 2008.

Heidel, Alexander. *The Babylonian Genesis*. 2nd ed. Chicago: University of Chicago Press, 1963.

Held, Moshe. "A Faithful Lover in an Old Babylonian Dialogue." *JCS* 15 (1961): 1–26.

Hendel, Ronald. "The Life of Metaphor in Song of Songs: Poetics, Canon, and the Cultural Bible." *Bib* 100 (2019): 60–83.

Hepper, F. Nigel. *Pharaoh's Flowers: The Botanical Treasures of Tutankhamun*. 2nd ed. Chicago: KWS, 2009.

Herrmann, Wolfram. "Gedanken zur Geschichte des altorientalischen Beschreibungsliedes." *ZAW* 75 (1963): 176–97.

Herodotus. *Histories*. Translated by Robin Waterfield. Oxford World's Classics. Oxford: Oxford University Press, 2008.

Hess, Richard S. *Song of Songs*. BCOTWP. Grand Rapids: Baker, 2005.

———. "Song of Songs: Not Just a Dirty Book." *BRev* 21.5 (2005): 31–40.

Heubeck, Alfred, Stephanie West, and J. B. Hainsworth. *A Commentary on Homer's Odyssey*. 2 vols. Oxford: Clarendon, 1998.

Hicks, R. Lansing. "The Door of Love." Pages 153–58 in *Love and Death in the Ancient Near East*. Edited by John H. Marks and Robert M. Good. Guilford, CT: Four Quarters, 1987.

Higgins, Reynold A. *Greek and Roman Jewelry*. 2nd ed. Berkeley: University of California Press, 1980.

Hirsch, Hans. "Die Inschriften der Könige von Agade." *AfO* 20 (1963): 1–82.

Hoch, James. E. *Semitic Words in Egyptian Texts of the New Kingdom and Third Intermediate Period.* Princeton: Princeton University Press, 1994.

Hoffmann, David Zvi, ed. *Midrash Tannaim zum Deuteronomium.* Berlin: Itzkowski, 1908.

Hoffmeier, James K. "The Arm of God Versus the Arm of Pharaoh." *Bib* 67 (1986): 378–87.

Homer. *Iliad.* Translated by Augustus T. Murray. 2nd ed. LCL. Cambridge: Harvard University Press, 1999.

———. *Odyssey.* Translated by Augustus T. Murray. 2nd ed. LCL. Cambridge: Harvard University Press, 1995.

Honeyman, Alexander M. "Two Contributions to Canaanite Toponymy." *JTS* 50 (1949): 50–52.

Hooper, Richard W. *The Priapus Poems: Erotic Epigrams from Ancient Rome.* Chicago: University of Illinois Press, 1999.

Hopf, Matthias, "The Song of Songs as a Hebrew 'Counterweight' to Hellenistic Drama." *JAJ* 8 (2017): 208–21.

Horace. *Odes and Epodes.* Translated by Niall Rudd. LCL. Cambridge: Harvard University Press, 2004.

Horowitz, Wayne, and Takayoshi Oshima, "Hazor 16: Another Administrative Docket from Hazor." *IEJ* 60 (2010): 129–32.

Horowitz, Wayne, Takayoshi Oshima, and Seth L. Sanders. *Cuneiform in Canaan: The Next Generation.* 2nd ed. University Park, PA: Eisenbrauns, 2018.

Hubbard, Robert L, Jr. "The Eyes Have It: Theological Reflections on Human Beauty." *Ex Auditu* 13 (1997): 57–72.

Hulster, Izaak J. de. "Iconography, Love Poetry, and Bible Translation: A Test Case with Song of Songs 7:2–6." Pages 313–28 in *Iconographic Exegesis of the Hebrew Bible/Old Testament: Introduction to Its Method and Practice.* Edited by Izaak J. de Hulster, Brent A. Strawn, and Ryan P. Bonfiglio. Göttingen: Vandenhoeck & Ruprecht, 2015.

———. "Illuminating Images: A Historical Position and Method for Iconographic Exegesis." Pages 139–62 in *Iconography and Biblical Studies: Proceedings of the Iconography Sessions at the Joint EABS/SBL Conference, 22–26 July 2007, Vienna, Austria.* Edited by Izaak J. de Hulster and Rüdiger Schmitt. AOAT 361. Münster: Ugarit-Verlag, 2009.

Hunger, Hermann. *Spätbabylonische Texte aus Uruk*. ADFU 9. Berlin: Mann, 1976.
Hunt, Patrick. *Poetry in the Song of Songs: A Literary Analysis*. StBibLit 96. New York: Lang, 2008.
Ilan, Tal. *Massekhet Taʿanit: Text, Translation and Commentary*. FCBT 2/9. Tübingen: Mohr Siebeck, 2007.
Isserlin, Benedikt S. J. "Song of Songs IV, 4: An Archaeological Note." *PEQ* 90 (1958): 59–61.
Itzhaki, Masha. *Toward the Garden Beds: Hebrew Garden Poems in Medieval Spain* [Hebrew]. Tel-Aviv: Notza ve'Keset, 1988.
Iyengar, Sujata. *Shakespeare's Medical Language: A Dictionary*. New York: Continuum, 2011.
Jacob, Ronja. *Kosmetik im antiken Palästina*. AOAT 389. Münster: Ugarit-Verlag, 2011.
Jacobsen, Thorkild. *The Harps That Once…: Sumerian Poetry in Translation*. New Haven: Yale University Press, 1987.
———. "Religious Drama in Ancient Mesopotamia." Pages 65–97 in *Unity and Diversity: Essays in the History, Literature and Religion of the Ancient Near East*. Edited by Hans Goedicke and J. J. M. Roberts. Baltimore: Johns Hopkins University Press, 1975.
———. *The Treasures of Darkness: A History of Mesopotamian Religion*. New Haven: Yale University Press, 1976.
———. "Two Bal-Bal-e Dialogues." Pages 57–63 in *Love and Death in the Ancient Near East*. Edited by John H. Marks and Robert M. Good. Guilford, CT: Four Quarters, 1987.
James, Elaine T. "Battle of the Sexes: Gender and the City in Song of Songs." *JSOT* 42 (2017): 93–116.
———. "A City Who Surrenders: Song 8:8–10." *VT* 67 (2017): 448–57.
———. *Landscapes of the Song of Songs: Poetry and Place*. Oxford: Oxford University Press, 2017.
Japhet, Sara. "Exegesis and Polemic in Rashbam's Commentary on the Song of Songs." Pages 182–95 in *Jewish Biblical Interpretation and Cultural Exchange: Comparative Exegesis in Context*. Edited by Natalie Dohrmann and David Stern. Jewish Culture and Contexts. Philadelphia: University of Pennsylvania Press, 2008.
———. "Rashi's Commentary on Song of Songs: The Revolution of Peshat and Its Aftermath." Pages 199–219 in *Mein Haus wird ein Bethaus für alle Völker genannt werden (Jes 56,7): Judentum seit der Zeit des Zweiten Tempels in Geschichte, Literatur und Kult; Festschrift für Thomas Willi*

zum 65. Geburtstag. Edited by Julia Männchen and Torsten Reiprich. Neukirchen-Vluyn: Neukirchener Verlag, 2007.

Japhet, Sara, and Barry Dov Walfish. *The Way of Lovers: The Oxford Anonymous Commentary on the Song of Songs*. Leiden: Brill, 2017.

Jax, Karl. *Die Weibliche Schönheit in der Griechischen Dichtung*. Innsbruck: Wagner, 1933.

Jayadeva. *Gīta Govinda: Love Songs of Rādhā and Kṛṣṇa*. Translated by Lee Siegel. New York: New York University Press, 2009.

Jellinek, Paul. *The Practice of Modern Perfumery*. London: Hill, 1954.

Jenkins, Ian, Dudley Hubbard, Stephen Dodd, and Victoria Turner. *The Greek Body*. Los Angeles: Getty Publications, 2010.

Jinbachian, Manuel M. "The Genre of Love Poetry in the Song of Songs and the Pre-Islamic Arabian Odes." *BT* 48 (1997): 123–37.

Johns, Catherine. *Sex or Symbol? Erotic Images of Greece and Rome*. New York: Routledge, 1982.

Joüon, Paul. *Le Cantique des Cantiques: Commentaire philologique et exégétique*. Paris: Beauchesne, 1909.

Judah Ha-Levi. *Dīwān des Abū'l-Ḥasan Jehuda ha-Levi*. Edited by Heinrich Brody. 4 vols. Farnsborough: Gregg, 1971.

Kahana, Menahem. *Sifre on Numbers: An Annotated Edition*. Jerusalem: Magnes, 2011.

Kaplan, Jonathan. *My Perfect One: Typology and Early Rabbinic Interpretation of Song of Songs*. Oxford: Oxford University Press, 2015.

———. "The Song of Songs from the Bible to the Mishnah." *HUCA* 81 (2010): 43–66.

Kasher, Aryeh. *Jews, Idumaeans, and Ancient Arabs: Relations of the Jews in Eretz-Israel with the Nations of the Frontier and the Desert during the Hellenistic and Roman Era (332 BCE–70 CE)*. TSAJ 18. Tübingen: Mohr, 1988.

Keel, Othmar. *Deine Blicke sind Tauben: Zur Metaphorik des Hohen Liedes*. SBS 114/115. Stuttgart: Katholisches Bibelwerk, 1984.

———. *The Song of Songs*. CC. Minneapolis: Fortress, 1994.

Keel, Othmar, and Christoph Uehlinger. *Gods, Goddesses, and Images of God*. Translated by Thomas H. Trapp. Minneapolis: Fortress, 1998.

Keel, Othmar, and Urs Winter. *Vögel als Boten: Studien zu Ps 68, 12-14, Gen 8, 6-12, Koh 10, 20 und dem Aussenden von Botenvögeln in Ägypten*. OBO 14. Göttingen: Vandenhoeck & Ruprecht; Fribourg: Presses Universitaires, 1977.

Keen, Karen R. "Song of Songs in the Eyes of Rashi and Nicholas of Lyra: Comparing Jewish and Christian Exegesis." *CBW* 35 (2015): 212–31.

Keimer, Ludwig. "La baie qui fait aimer, Mandragora officinarum L." *BIE* 32 (1951): 351.

Kelly, Joseph R. "Identifying Literary Allusions: Theory and the Criterion of Shared Language." Pages 22–40 in *Subtle Citation, Allusion, and Translation in the Hebrew Bible*. Edited by Ziony Zevit. Sheffield: Equinox, 2017.

Kemp, Barry, "Tell El-Amarna 2012–13." *JEA* 99 (2013): 1–34.

Keuls, Eva C. *The Reign of the Phallus: Sexual Politics in Ancient Athens*. Berkeley: University of California Press, 1993.

Kimelman, Reuven. "Rabbi Yohanan and Origen on the Song of Songs: A Third-Century Jewish-Christian Disputation." *HTR* 73 (1980): 567–95.

King, Helen. "Sowing the Field: Greek and Roman Sexology." Pages 29–46 in *Sexual Knowledge, Sexual Science: The History of Attitudes to Sexology*. Edited by Roy Porter and Mikulas Teich. Cambridge: Cambridge University Press, 1994.

King, Philip J., and Lawrence E. Stager. *Life in Biblical Israel*. Louisville: Westminster John Knox, 2001.

Kingsmill, Edmée. *The Song of Songs and the Eros of God: A Study in Biblical Intertextuality*. Oxford: Oxford University Press, 2009.

Kinnier Wilson, J. V. "The Kurba'il Statue of Shalmaneser III." *Iraq* 24 (1962): 90–115.

Kitchen, Kenneth A. "Lotuses and Lotuses, or … Poor Susan's Older Than We Thought." *VA* 3 (1987): 29–31.

Kitchen, Kenneth A., and Paul J. N. Lawrence. *Treaty, Law and Covenant in the Ancient Near East*. 3 vols. Wiesbaden: Harrassowitz, 2012.

Klein, Jacob. *Three Šulgi Hymns: Sumerian Royal Hymns Glorifying King Šulgi of Ur*. BISNELC. Ramat-Gan: Bar-Ilan University Press, 1981.

Klein, Jacob, et al. "Song of Songs" [Hebrew]. Pages 10–69 in *Megilloth*. Tel-Aviv: Davidson Atai, 1994.

Kletter, Raz. *The Judean Pillar-Figurines and the Archaeology of Asherah*. BAR 636. Oxford: Tempus Reparatum, 1996.

Klinck, Anne L. *An Anthology of Ancient and Medieval Woman's Song*. New York: Palgrave Macmillan, 2004.

Knauf, Ernst Axel. *Ismael: Untersuchungen zur Geschichte Palästinas und Nordarabiens im 1. Jahtausend v. Chr*. ADPV 7. Weisbaden: Harrassowitz, 1985.

Köcher, Franz, and A. Leo Oppenheim. "The Old Babylonian Omen Text VAT 7525." *AfO* 18 (1957–1958): 62–77.
Kotzé, Zacharias. "A Cognitive Linguistic Methodology for the Study of Metaphor in the Hebrew Bible." *JNSL* 31 (2005): 107–17.
Kövecses, Zoltán. *Metaphor: A Practical Introduction*. Oxford: Oxford University Press, 2002.
———. *Metaphor and Emotion: Language, Culture, and Body in Human Feeling*. New York: Cambridge University Press, 2003.
———. *Metaphors of Anger, Pride, and Love: A Lexical Approach to the Structure of Concepts*. Pragmatics & Beyond 7.8. Philadelphia: Benjamins, 1986.
Kozodoy, Maud. "Messianic Interpretation of the Song of Songs in Late-Medieval Iberia." Pages 117–47 in *The Hebrew Bible in Fifteenth-Century Spain: Exegesis, Literature, Philosophy and the Arts*. Edited by Jonathan Decter and Arturo Prats. Leiden: Brill, 2012.
Kramer, Samuel Noah. "The Biblical 'Song of Songs' and the Sumerian Love Songs." *Expedition* 5 (1962): 25–31.
———. "BM 23631: Bread for Enlil, Sex for Inanna." *Or* 54 (1985): 117–32.
———. "Inanna and Šulgi: A Sumerian Fertility Song." *Iraq* 31 (1969): 18–23.
———. *The Sacred Marriage Rite: Aspects of Faith, Myth, and Ritual in Ancient Sumer*. Bloomington: Indiana University Press, 1969.
Kraus, Fritz R. *Text zur babylonische Physiognomatik*. AfOB 3. Berlin: Weidner, 1939.
Krinetzki, Günter. "Die Erotische Psychologie des Hohen Liedes." *TQ* 150 (1970): 404–16.
———. *Kommentar zum Hohenlied: Bildsprache und Theologische Botschaft*. BBET 16. Frankfurt am Main: Lang, 1981.
Kugel, James. "Some Thoughts on Future Research into Biblical Style: Addenda to *The Idea of Biblical Poetry*." *JSOT* 28 (1984): 107–17.
Kynes, Will. "Beat Your Parodies into Swords and Your Parodied Books into Spears: A New Paradigm for Parody in the Hebrew Bible." *BibInt* 19 (2011): 276–310.
Labat, René. *Traité akkadien de diagnostics et prognostics medicaux*. Leiden: Brill, 1951.
Laffineur, Robert. "Dress, Hairstyle and Jewelry in the Thera Wall Paintings." Pages 890–906 in *The Wall Paintings of Thera: Proceedings of the First International Symposium*. Edited by Susan Sherratt. 3 vols. Athens: Thera Foundation, 2000.

Lakoff, George, and Mark Johnson. *Metaphors We Live By*. Chicago: University of Chicago Press, 1980.
Lam, Joseph. "Metaphor in Ugaritic Literary Texts." *JNES* 78 (2019): 37–57.
Lambert, Wilfred G. *Ancient Mesopotamian Religion and Mythology: Selected Essays*. Edited by Andrew George and Takayoshi Oshima. ORA 15. Tübingen: Mohr Siebeck, 2016.
———. *Babylonian Wisdom Literature*. Oxford: Clarendon, 1967.
———. "The Background of the Neo-Assyrian Sacred Tree." Pages 321–26 in *Sex and Gender in the Ancient Near East*. Edited by Simo Parpola and Robert M. Whiting. CRRAI 47. Helsinki: Neo-Assyrian Text Corpus Project, 2002.
———. "Devotion: The Languages of Religion and Love." Pages 25–39 in *Figurative Language in the Ancient Near East*. Edited by Murray Mindlin, Markham J. Geller, and John E. Wansbrough. London: University of London School of Oriental and African Studies, 1987.
———. "A New Look at the Babylonian Background of Genesis." *JTS* 16 (1965): 287–300.
———. "The Problem of Love Lyrics." Pages 98–135 in *Unity and Diversity: Essays in the History, Literature and Religion of the Ancient Near East*. Edited by Hans Goedicke and J. J. M. Roberts. Baltimore: Johns Hopkins University Press, 1975.
Landsberger, Benno, ed. *The Series HAR-ra=ḫubullu: Tablets VIII–XII*. MSL 7. Rome: Pontifical Biblical Institute, 1959.
———, ed. *The Series HAR-ra=ḫubullu: Tablets XVI, XVII, XIX and Related Texts*. MSL 10. Rome: Pontifical Biblical Institute, 1970.
Landsberger, Benno, and Richard Hallock, eds. *Old Babylonian Grammatical Texts*. MSL 4. Rome: Pontifical Biblical Institute, 1956.
Landy, Francis. *Paradoxes of Paradise: Identity and Difference in Song of Songs*. BLS 7. Sheffield: Almond Press, 1983.
———. "The Song of Songs and the Garden of Eden." *JBL* 98 (1979): 513–28.
Lane, Lauriat, Jr. "The Literary Archetype: Some Reconsiderations." *JAAC* 13 (1954): 226–32.
Langdon, Stephen. *Die neubabylonischen königsinschriften*. VAB 4. Leipzig: Hinrichs, 1912.
———. *Sumerian and Semitic Religious and Historical Texts*. OECI 1. Oxford: Oxford University Press, 1923.
Lange, Nicholas de. "From Eros to Pneuma: On the Greek Translation of Song of Songs." Pages 73–83 in *Eukarpa: Études sur la Bible et ses*

éxègetes en hommage à Gilles Dorival. Edited by Mireille Loubet and Didier Pralon. Paris: Cerf, 2011.
Langgut, Dafna, Yuval Gadot, Naomi Porat, and Oded Lipschits. "Fossil Pollen Reveals the Secrets of the Royal Persian Garden at Ramat Rahel, Jerusalem." *Palynology* 37 (2013): 115–29.
Lapinkivi, Pirjo. *The Sumerian Sacred Marriage in Light of Comparative Evidence*. SAAS 15. Helsinki: Neo-Assyrian Text Corpus Project, 2004.
Lee, Alvin A. "Archetypal Criticism." *ECLT*, 3–5.
Lee, Mireille M. *Body, Dress, and Identity in Ancient Greece*. New York: Cambridge University Press, 2015.
Leech, Geoffrey. *A Linguistic Guide to English Poetry*. London: Longman, 1969.
Leek, F. Filce. "The Practice of Dentistry in Ancient Egypt." *JEA* 53 (1967): 51–58.
Lehrman, Simon M. "The Song of Songs." Pages 1–32 in *The Five Megilloth*. Edited by Abraham Cohen. New York: Soncino, 1946.
Leick, Gwendolyn. *Sex and Eroticism in Mesopotamian Literature*. New York: Routledge, 1994.
Lemmelijn, Bénédicte. "Textual History of Canticles." Pages 322–26 in *Writings*. Vol. 1C of *Textual History of the Bible*. Edited by Armin Lange. Brill: Leiden, 2017.
LeMon, Joel M. *Yahweh's Winged Form in the Psalms*. OBO 242. Göttingen: Vandenhoeck & Ruprecht; Fribourg: Presses Universitaires, 2010.
Lesko, Leonard H. "Egyptian Wine Production During the New Kingdom." Pages 215–30 in *The Origins and Ancient History of Wine*. Edited by Patrick E. McGovern, Stuart J. Fleming, and Solomon H. Katz. Amsterdam: Gordon & Breach, 2000.
Levey, Martin. *Chemicals and Chemical Technology in Ancient Mesopotamia*. New York: Elsevier, 1959.
Levine, Étan. *Marital Relations in Ancient Judaism*. BZAR 10. Wiesbaden: Harrassowitz, 2009.
Levinson, Bernard M. "Esarhaddon's Succession Treaty as the Source for the Canon Formula in Deuteronomy 13:1." *JAOS* 130 (2010): 337–47.
Lieber, Laura. *A Vocabulary of Desire: Song of Songs in the Early Synagogue*. Leiden: Brill, 2014.
Linder, Sven. *Palästinische Volksgesänge*. UUA 5. Uppsula: Lundequistska, 1952.
Lindley, David. *Thomas Campion*. Medieval and Renaissance Authors 7. Leiden: Brill, 1986.

Littauer, Mary A., and Joost H. Crouwell. "Ancient Iranian Horse Helmets?" *IA* 19 (1984): 41–51.
Littlewood, Antony R. "The Symbolism of the Apple in Greek and Roman Literature." *HSCP* 72 (1968): 147–81.
Littman, Enno. *Neuarabische Volkspoesie*. Berlin: Weidmann, 1902.
Livingstone, Alasdair. *Court Poetry and Literary Miscellanea*. SAAS 3. Helsinki: Helsinki University Press, 1989.
———. *Mystical and Mythological Explanatory Works of Assyrian and Babylonian Scholars*. Winona Lake, IN: Eisenbrauns, 2007.
———. "On the Organized Release of Doves to Secure Compliance of a Higher Authority." Pages 375–87 in *Wisdom, Gods, and Literature: Studies in Assyriology in Honour of W. G. Lambert*. Edited by Andrew R. George, and Irving Finkel. Winona Lake, IN: Eisenbrauns, 2000.
Loader, James A. "Exegetical Erotica to Canticles 7:2–6." *JSem* 10 (2001): 98–111.
Lodge, Thomas. *Rosalynd*. Edited by Brian Nellist. Staffordshire: Ryburn, 1995.
Loewe, Raphael. "Apologetic Motifs in the Targum to the Song of Songs." Pages 159–96 in *Biblical Motifs: Origins and Transformations*. Edited by Alexander Altmann. Cambridge: Harvard University Press, 1966.
Long, Gary A. "A Lover, Cities, and Heavenly Bodies: Co-Text and the Translation of Two Similes in Canticles (6:4c; 6:10d)." *JBL* 115 (1996): 703–9.
———. "Simile, Metaphor, and the Song of Songs." PhD diss., University of Chicago, 1993.
Longfellow, Henry W. *Poetical Works*. London: Cassell, 1891.
Longman, Tremper. *Song of Songs*. NICOT. Grand Rapids: Eerdmans, 2001.
Loud, Gordon. *The Megiddo Ivories*. OIP 52. Chicago: University of Chicago Press, 1939.
Löw, Immanuel. *Aramäische Pflanzennamen*. Leipzig: Engelmann, 1881.
———. *Die flora der Juden*. Leipzig: Löwit, 1924.
Lowth, Robert. *Lectures on the Sacred Poetry of the Hebrews*. Translated by George Gregory. 4th ed. London: Kessinger, 1839.
Lubetski, Meir. "A Tale of a Seal." Pages 191–96 in *Shlomo: Studies in Epigraphy, Iconography, History and Archaeology in Honor of Shlomo Moussaieff*. Edited by Robert Deutsch. Tel-Aviv: Archaeological Center, 2003.

Lucas, Alfred. "Cosmetics, Perfumes and Incense in Ancient Egypt." *JEA* 16 (1930): 40–53.
Luckenbill, Daniel D. *The Annals of Sennacherib*. OIP 2. Chicago: University of Chicago Press, 1924.
Luther, Martin. *Lectures on Song of Solomon*. Translated by Ian Siggins. LW 15. St. Louis: Concordia, 1972.
Lyra, Nicholas de. *The Postilla on the Song of Songs*. Translated by James George Kiecker. Milwaukee: Marquette University Press, 1998.
Maalej, Zouheir, and Ning Yu. "Introduction: Embodiment via Body Parts." Pages 1–20 in *Embodiment via Body Parts: Studies from Various Languages and Cultures*. Edited by Zouheir Maalej and Ning Yu. Amsterdam: Benjamins, 2011.
MacAulay, George C., ed. *The English Works of John Gower*. London: Oxford University Press, 1900.
Macedonius. *Anthologia Palatina*. Translated by William R. Paton. Revised by Michael Tueller. LCL. Cambridge: Harvard University Press, 2014.
Machiela, Daniel A. *The Dead Sea Genesis Apocryphon: A New Text and Translation with Introduction and Special Treatment of Columns 13–17*. STDJ 79. Leiden: Brill, 2009.
Mahdi, Muhsin, ed. *The Arabian Nights*. New York: Norton, 1990.
Malul, Meir. *The Comparative Method in Ancient Near Eastern and Biblical Legal Studies*. AOAT 277. Kevelaer: Butzon & Bercker; Neukirchen-Vluyn: Neukirchener Verlag, 1990.
Manniche, Lise. *Sacred Luxuries: Fragrance, Aromatherapy, and Cosmetics in Ancient Egypt*. Ithaca, NY: Cornell University Press, 1999.
———. *Sexual Life in Ancient Egypt*. New York: Methuen, 1987.
Marcus, David. "Animal Similes in Assyrian Royal Inscriptions." *Or* 46 (1977): 86–106.
Mariaselvam, Abraham. *The Song of Songs and Ancient Tamil Love Poems*. AnBib 118. Rome: Pontifical Biblical Institute, 1989.
Maspero, M. Gaston. "Les Chants d'Amour du Papyrus de Turin et du Papyrus Harris No. 500." *JA* 8 (1883): 5–47.
Mathers, E. Powys, ed. *The Book of the Thousand Nights and One Night*. 4 vols. New York: Routledge, 1986.
Matsushima, Eiko. "Le Rituel Hiérogramique de Nabû." *ASJ* 9 (1987): 131–75.
Matter, E. Ann. "The Love of the Millennium: Medieval Christian Apocalyptic and the Song of Songs." Pages 228–43 in *Scrolls of Love: Ruth*

and the Song of Songs. Edited by Peter S. Hawkins and Lesleigh Cushing Stahlberg. New York: Fordham University Press, 2006.

———. *The Voice of My Beloved: The Song of Songs in Western Medieval Christianity*. Philadelphia: University of Pennsylvania Press, 1990.

Maxwell-Hyslop, K. Rachel. *Western Asiatic Jewelry*. London: Methuen, 1971.

Mazar, Eilat, Wayne Horowitz, Takayoshi Oshima, and Yuval Goren. "A Cuneiform Tablet from the Ophel in Jerusalem." *IEJ* 60 (2010): 4–21.

McCartney, Eugene Stock. "How the Apple Became a Token of Love." *TAPA* 56 (1925): 70–81.

McConvery, Brendan. "Hippolytus' Commentary on the Song of Songs and John 20: Intertextual Reading in Early Christianity." *ITQ* 71 (2006): 211–22.

McEuen, Melissa A. *Making War, Making Women: Femininity and Duty on the American Home Front, 1941–1945*. Athens: University of Georgia Press, 2011.

McKnight, Edgar. "Reader-Response Criticism." Pages 230–52 in *To Each Its Own Meaning: An Introduction to Biblical Criticisms and Their Applications*. Edited by Steven McKenzie and Stephen Haynes. 2nd ed. Louisville: Westminster John Knox, 1999.

McLaren, Angus. *Impotence: A Cultural History*. Chicago: University of Chicago Press, 2008.

Meek, Theophilus J. "Canticles and the Tammuz Cult." *AJSL* 39 (1922): 1–14.

———. "The Song of Songs." *IB* 5:91–148.

Melamed, Abraham. *The Image of the Black in Jewish Culture*. London: Curzon, 2003.

Meleager. *Anthologia Palatina*. Translated by William R. Paton. Revised by Michael Tueller. LCL. Cambridge: Harvard University Press, 2014.

Menn, Esther M. "Thwarted Metaphors: Complicating the Language of Desire in the Targum of the Song of Songs." *JSJ* 34 (2003): 237–73.

Meyers, Carol. "Gender Imagery in the Song of Songs." *HAR* 10 (1987): 209–23.

Middleton, J. Richard. *The Liberating Image: The Imago Dei in Genesis 1*. Grand Rapids: Brazos, 2005.

Miller, Barbara Stoler, ed. *Love Song of the Dark Lord*. New York: Columbia University Press, 1977.

Miller, Robert D. "The Song of Songs: A Plea for an Aesthetic Reading." *Sacra Scripta* 10 (2012): 113–19.

Mitchell, Christopher W. *Song of Songs*. ConcC. St. Louis: Concordia, 2002.
Moldenke, Harold N., and Alma L. Moldenke. *Plants of the Bible*. Waltham, MA: Chronica Botanica, 1952.
Moon, Warren G. *Greek Vase-Painting in Midwestern Collections*. Chicago: Art Institute, 1979.
Moorey, Peter R. S. *Ancient Mesopotamian Materials and Industries: The Archaeological Evidence*. Oxford: Clarendon, 1994.
Moorman, Frederic W., ed. *The Poetical Works of Robert Herrick*. Oxford: Clarendon, 1915.
Moran, William L. *The Amarna Letters*. Baltimore: Johns Hopkins University Press, 1992.
Morgenstern, Julius. "The Book of the Covenant: Part II." *HUCA* 7 (1930): 19–258.
Muchiki, Yoshiyuki. *Egyptian Proper Names and Loanwords in North-West Semitic*. SBLDS 173. Atlanta: Society of Biblical Literature, 1999.
Müller, Hans-Peter. "Das Hohelied." Pages 3–90 in *Das Hohelied, Klagelieder, Das Buch Ester*. 4th rev. ed. ATD 16.2. Göttingen: Vandenhoeck & Ruprecht, 1992.
Munro, Jill M. *Spikenard and Saffron: A Study in the Poetic Language of the Song of Songs*. JSOTSup 203. Sheffield: Sheffield Academic, 1995.
Muraoka, Takamitsu. *Emphatic Words and Structures in Biblical Hebrew*. Jerusalem: Magnes, 1985.
———. "Sir. 51, 13–30: An Erotic Hymn to Wisdom?" *JSJ* 10 (1979): 166–78.
Murphy, Roland E. *The Song of Songs: A Commentary*. Hermeneia. Minneapolis: Fortress, 1990.
———. *Wisdom Literature: Job, Proverbs, Ruth, Canticles, Ecclesiastes, Esther*. FOTL 13. Grand Rapids: Eerdmans, 1981.
Murray, Gilbert. *Classical Tradition in Poetry*. London: Milford, 1927.
Muscarella, Oscar White. *The Catalogue of Ivories from Hasanlu, Iran*. Philadelphia: University Museum, 1980.
Naguib, Saphinaz-Amal. "Hair in Ancient Egypt." *AcOr* 51 (1990): 7–26.
Nathan ben Jehiel. ʿ*Arukh ha-Shalem*. 8 vols. Edited by Alexander Kohut. New York: Pardes, 1955. [Hebrew]
Negev, Abraham. *Personal Names in the Nabatean Realm*. Qedem 32. Jerusalem: Hebrew University Press, 1991.
Neufeld, Edward. "Hygiene Conditions in Ancient Israel." *BA* 34 (1971): 41–66.
Neusner, Jacob. "Divine Love in Classical Judaism." *RRJ* 17 (2014): 121–44.

———. *Song of Songs Rabbah: An Analytical Translation*. BJS 197–198. 2 vols. Atlanta: Scholars Press, 1989.

Nissinen, Martti. "Akkadian Love Poetry and the Song of Songs: A Case of Cultural Interaction." Pages 145–70 in *Zwischen Zion und Zaphon: Studien im Gedenken an den Theologen Oswald Loretz*. Edited by Ludger Hiepel and Marie-Theres Wacker. AOAT 438. Münster: Ugarit-Verlag, 2016.

———. "Akkadian Rituals and Poetry of Divine Love." Pages 93–136 in *Mythology and Mythologies: Methodological Approaches to Intercultural Influences*. Edited by Robert M. Whiting. MSym 2. Helsinki: Neo-Assyrian Text Corpus Project, 2001.

———. "Love Lyrics of Nabû and Tašmetu: An Assyrian Song of Songs?" Pages 585–634 in *"Und Mose schrieb dieses Lied auf": Studien zum Alten Testament und zum Alten Orient; Festschrift für Oswald Loretz zur Vollendung seines 70. Lebensjahres mit Beiträgen von Freunden, Schülern und Kollegen*. Edited by Manfried Dietrich and Ingo Kottsieper. AOAT 250. Münster: Ugarit-Verlag, 1998.

———. "Song of Songs and Sacred Marriage." Pages 173–218 in *Sacred Marriages: The Divine Human Sexual Metaphor from Sumer to Early Christianity*. Edited by Martti Nissinen and Risto Uro. Winona Lake, IN: Eisenbrauns, 2008.

Noegel, Scott B., and Gary A. Rendsburg. *Solomon's Vineyard: Literary and Linguistic Studies in the Song of Songs*. AIL 1. Atlanta: Society of Biblical Literature, 2009.

Noonan, Benjamin J. "Did Nehemiah Own Tyrian Goods? Trade Between Judea and Phoenicia During the Achaemenid Period." *JBL* 130 (2011): 281–98.

———. *Non-Semitic Loanwords in the Hebrew Bible: A Lexicon of Language Contact*. LSAWS 14. University Park, PA: Eisenbrauns, 2019.

Norris, Richard A., Jr., ed. *The Song of Songs: Interpreted by Early Christian and Medieval Commentators*. CB 1. Grand Rapids: Eerdmans, 2003.

Nougayrol, Jean. "Signalement Lyrique (RS 25.421)." *Ugaritica* 5 (1968): 310–19.

Novák, Mirko. "The Artificial Paradise: Programme and Ideology of Royal Gardens." Pages 443–60 in *Sex and Gender in the Ancient Near East*. Edited by Simo Parpola and Robert M. Whiting. CRRAI 47. Helsinki: Neo-Assyrian Text Corpus Project, 2002.

Nunnally, Wave E. "Early Jewish Interpretation, Use, and Canonization of

Song of Songs." *The History of Interpretation of Song of Songs*. Edited by Paul Raabe. Downers Grove, IL: InterVarsity Press, forthcoming.

O'Donoghue, Michael. "Lapis Lazuli." Pages 329–31 in *Gems: Their Sources, Descriptions, and Identification*. Edited by Michael O'Donoghue. 6th ed. Oxford: Elsevier, 2006.

Ogle, Mabbuby B. "The Classical Origin and Tradition of Literary Conceits." *AJP* 34 (1913): 125–52.

Opificius, Ruth. *Das altbabylonische Terrakottarelief*. UAVA 2. Berlin: de Gruyter, 1961.

Origen. *The Song of Songs Commentary and Homilies*. Translated by Ruth P. Lawson. ACW 26. New York: Paulist, 1957.

Ovid. *Ars amatoria*. Translated by John H. Mozley. Revised by George P. Goold. LCL. Cambridge: Harvard University Press, 2014.

———. *Remedia Amoris*. Translated by John H. Mozley. Revised by George P. Goold. LCL. Cambridge: Harvard University Press, 2014.

Pallingston, Jessica. *Lipstick: A Celebration of the World's Favorite Cosmetic*. New York: St. Martin's, 1999.

Pardes, Ilana. "'I Am a Wall, and My Breasts like Towers': The Song of Songs and the Question of Canonization." Pages 118–43 in *Countertraditions in the Bible: A Feminist Approach*. Cambridge: Harvard University Press, 1992.

Parpola, Simo. *Assyrian Prophecies*. SAA 9. Helsinki: Helsinki University Press, 1997.

Paul, Shalom M. "A Lover's Garden of Verse: Literal and Metaphorical Imagery in Ancient Near Eastern Love Poetry." Pages 99–110 in *Tehillah le-Moshe: Biblical and Judaic Studies in Honor of Moshe Greenberg*. Edited by Mordechai Cogan, Barry L. Eichler, and Jeffrey H. Tigay. Winona Lake, IN: Eisenbrauns, 1997.

———. "Polysemous Pivotal Punctuation: More Janus Double Entendres." Pages 369–74 in *Texts, Temples, and Traditions*. Edited by Michael V. Fox, Victor Avigdor Hurowitz, Avi Hurvitz, Michael L. Klein, Baruch J. Schwartz, and Nili Shupak. Winona Lake, IN: Eisenbrauns, 1996.

———. "The Shared Legacy of Sexual Metaphors and Euphemisms in Mesopotamian and Biblical Literature." Pages 299–314 in *Sex and Gender in the Ancient Near East*. Edited by Simo Parpola and Robert M. Whiting. CRRAI 47. Helsinki: Neo-Assyrian Text Corpus Project, 2002.

Percy, Thomas. *Reliques of Ancient English Poetry*. 3 vols. New York: Dutton, 1910.

Peres, Henri. *La poesie andalouse en Arabe classique au XIe siècle*. Paris: Maisonneuve, 1953.
Phillips, Helen. "Gardens of Love and the Garden of the Fall." Pages 205–19 in *A Walk in the Garden: Biblical, Iconographical, and Literary Images of Eden*. Edited by Paul Morris and Deborah Sawyer. JSOTSup 136. Sheffield: JSOT Press, 1992.
Philonenko, Marc. *Joseph et Aséneth: Introduction, Texte critique, Traduction, et Notes*. Leiden: Brill, 1968.
Pinch, Geraldine. "Private Life in Ancient Egypt." *CANE* 1:363–81.
Plato. *Greater Hippias*. Translated by Harold N. Fowler. LCL. Cambridge: Harvard University Press, 1926.
Pope, Marvin H. "A Mare in Pharaoh's Chariotry." *BASOR* 200 (1970): 56–61.
———. *Song of Songs: A New Translation with Introduction and Commentary*. AB 7C. Garden City, NY: Doubleday, 1977.
Porteous, J. Douglas. "Bodyscape: The Body-Landscape Metaphor." *Canadian Geographer* 30 (1986): 2–12.
Posener, Georges. "'Maquilleuse' en Egyptien." *RdE* 21 (1969): 150–51.
Postgate, J. Nicholas. "Notes on Fruit in the Cuneiform Sources." *BSA* 3 (1987): 115–44.
Powell, Marvin A. "Wine and the Vine in Ancient Mesopotamia: The Cuneiform Evidence." Pages 97–121 in *The Origins and Ancient History of Wine*. Edited by Patrick E. McGovern, Stuart J. Fleming, and Solomon H. Katz. Amsterdam: Gordon & Breach, 2000.
Propertius. *Elegies*. Edited and translated by George P. Goold. LCL. Cambridge: Harvard University Press, 1990.
Provan, Iain. *Ecclesiastes/Song of Songs*. NIVAC. Grand Rapids: Zondervan, 2001.
Pruss, Alexander. "The Use of Nude Female Figurines." Pages 537–45 in *Sex and Gender in the Ancient Near East*. Edited by Simo Parpola and Robert M. Whiting. CRRAI 47. Helsinki: Neo-Assyrian Text Corpus Project, 2002.
Puech, Émile. "Le *Cantique des Cantiques* dans les Manuscrits de Qumran: 4Q106, 4Q107, 4Q108 et 6Q6." *RB* 123 (2016): 29–53.
Pupko, Yaakov Y. H. *Five Megilloth/Rashi*. Translated by Avrohom Davis. New York: Metsudah, 2001.
Quiller-Couch, Arthur T., ed. *The Oxford Book of English Verse 1250–1900*. Oxford: Clarendon, 1902.
Rabin, Chaim. "The Song of Songs and Tamil Poetry." *SR* 3 (1973): 205–19.

Ramanujan, Attipat K., ed. and trans. *The Interior Landscape: Love Poems from a Classical Tamil Anthology*. Bloomington: Indiana University Press, 1967.

———. *Poems of Love and War: From the Eight Anthologies and Ten Long Poems of Classical Tamil*. New York: Columbia University Press, 1985.

Rasmussen, Carl G. *Zondervan Atlas of the Bible*. Rev. ed. Grand Rapids: Zondervan, 2010.

Ratzaby, Yehudah. "A Motif in Hebrew Love Poetry: In Praise of the Apple." *Ariel* 40 (1976): 14–24.

Ray, Paul J., Jr. *Tell Hesban and Vicinity in the Iron Age*. Edited by Lawrence T. Geraty and Øystein S. LaBianca. Hesban 6. Berrien Springs, MI: Andrews University Press, 2001.

Reiner, Erica. "A Sumero-Akkadian Hymn of Nanâ." *JNES* 33 (1974): 221–36.

Reiner, Erica, and Hans G. Güterbock. "The Great Prayer to Ishtar and Its Two Versions from Boğazköy." *JCS* 21 (1967): 255–66.

Reisman, Daniel. "Iddin-Dagan's Sacred Marriage Hymn." *JCS* 25 (1973): 185–202.

Renan, Ernest. *Le Cantique des Cantiques*. Paris: Lévy, 1860.

Rendsburg, Gary. "תַּלְפִּיּוֹת (Song 4:4)." *JNSL* 20 (1994): 13–19.

Richards, Ivor A. *The Philosophy of Rhetoric*. Oxford: Oxford University Press, 1936.

Ricks, Christopher, ed. *The Oxford Book of English Verse*. Oxford: Oxford University Press, 1999.

Riley, James Whitcomb. *The Complete Poetical Works of James Whitcomb Riley*. Bloomington: Indiana University Press, 1993.

Ringgren, Helmer. "Das Hohe Lied." Pages 3–38 in *Das Hohe Lied, Klagelieder, Das Buch Esther*. ATD 16.2. Göttingen: Vandenhoeck & Ruprecht, 1958.

———. "The Marriage Metaphor in Israelite Religion." Pages 421–28 in *Ancient Israelite Religion: Essays in Honor of Frank Moore Cross*. Edited by Patrick D. Miller, Paul D. Hanson, and S. Dean MacBride Jr. Philadelphia: Fortress, 1987.

Robert, André, and Robert Tournay. *Le Cantique des Cantiques: Traduction et Commentaire*. EBib. Paris: Gabalda, 1963.

Robins, Gay. "Color Symbolism." *OEAE* 1:291–94.

———. "Gender Roles." *OEAE* 2:12–16.

———. *Women in Ancient Egypt*. Rev. ed. London: British Museum, 2008.

Romano, James F. "Jewelry and Personal Arts in Ancient Egypt." *CANE* 3:1605–21.
Rowley, Harold H. "The Interpretation of the Song of Songs." *JTS* 38 (1937): 337–63.
———. "The Interpretation of the Song of Songs." Pages 197–245 in *The Servant of the Lord and Other Essays*. 2nd ed. Oxford: Blackwell, 1965.
———. "The Song of Songs: An Examination of a Recent Theory." *JRAS* 2 (1938): 251–76.
Rozelaar, Marc. "An Unrecognized Part of the Human Anatomy." *Judaism* 37 (1988): 97–101.
Rudolph, Wilhelm. *Des Buch Ruth, das Hohe Lied, die Klagelieder*. KAT 17. Gütersloh: Mohn, 1962.
Ruffle, John. "The Teaching of Amenemope and Its Connection with the Book of Proverbs." *TynBul* 28 (1977): 29–68.
Rufinus. *Anthologia Palatina*. Translated by William R. Paton. Revised by Michael Tueller. LCL. Cambridge: Harvard University Press, 2014.
Ryken, Leland. *How to Read the Bible as Literature*. Grand Rapids: Zondervan, 1984.
Saʿadia Gaʾon. "Commentary on the Song of Songs." in *Sefer* Geʾon *ha-Geʾonim*, Edited by Solomon A. Wertheimer. Jerusalem, 1925.
———. "Commentary on the Song of Songs." In *Five Scrolls*. Edited by Joseph Qafikh. Jerusalem: Society for the Preservation of Yemenite Manuscripts, 1962.
Saarisalo, Aapeli. "Songs of the Druzes." *StOr* 4 (1932): 2–144.
Sandmel, Samuel. "Parallelomania." *JBL* 81 (1962): 1–13.
Sanford, A. Whitney. *Singing Krishna: Sound Becomes Sight in Paramānand's Poetry*. Albany: State University of New York Press, 2008.
Sappho. *Greek Lyric*. Translated by David A. Campbell. LCL. Cambridge: Harvard University Press, 1982.
Sasson, Jack M. "A Major Contribution to Song of Songs Scholarship." *JAOS* 107 (1987): 733–39.
Sasson, Victor. "King Solomon and the Dark Lady in the Song of Songs." *VT* 39 (1989): 407–14.
Satlow, Michael L. *Jewish Marriage in Antiquity*. Princeton: Princeton University Press, 2001.
Sauer, James A. "The Pottery at Hesban and Its Relationship to the History of Jordan: An Interim Report." Pages 225–81 in *Hesban after Twenty-Five Years*. Edited by David Merling and Lawrence T. Geraty. Berrien Springs, MI: Andrews University Press, 1994.

Schechter, Solomon. "Agadath Shir Hashirim." *JQR* 6 (1896): 672–97.

———. "A Further Fragment of Ben Sira: Prefatory Note." *JQR* 12 (1900): 456–65.

Schellenberg, Annette. "The Sensuality of the Song of Songs: Another Criterion to Be Considered When Assessing (So-Called) Literal and Allegorical Interpretations of the Song." Pages 103–29 in *Interpreting the Song of Songs—Literal or Allegorical*. Edited by Annette Schellenberg and Ludger Schwienhorst-Schönberger. BTS 26. Leuven: Peeters, 2016.

Scheper, George L. "Reformation Attitudes toward Allegory and the Song of Songs." *PMLA* 89 (1974): 551–62.

Schoenbaum, Samuel. "Shakespeare's Dark Lady: A Question of Identity." Pages 221–39 in *Shakespeare's Styles: Essays in Honour of Kenneth Muir*. Edited by Philip Edwards, Inga-Stina Ewbank, and G. K. Hunter. Cambridge: Cambridge University Press, 2004.

Schökel, Luis A. *A Manual of Hebrew Poetics*. SubBi 11. Rome: Pontifical Biblical Institute, 1988.

Schoville, Keith. "The Impact of the Ras Shamra Texts on the Study of the Song of Songs." PhD diss., University of Wisconsin-Madison, 1969.

———. "חומה." *NIDOTTE* 2:49–50.

Schroer, Silvia, and Thomas Staubli. *Body Symbolism in the Bible*. Collegeville, MN: Liturgical Press, 2001.

Schwab, George, "Waṣf." Pages 835–42 in *Dictionary of the Old Testament: Wisdom, Poetry, and Writings*. Edited by Tremper Longman III and Peter Enns. Downers Grove, IL: InterVarsity Press, 2008.

Schwienhorst-Schönberger, Ludger. "The Song of Songs as Allegory: Methodological and Hermeneutical Considerations." Pages 1–50 in *Interpreting the Song of Songs—Literal or Allegorical*. Edited by Annette Schellenberg and Ludger Schwienhorst-Schönberger. BTS 26. Leuven: Peeters, 2016.

Scurlock, Joanne. "Medicine and Healing Magic." Pages 101–43 in *Women in the Ancient Near East: A Sourcebook*. Edited by Mark Chavalas. New York: Routledge, 2014.

Sefati, Yitschak. *Love Songs in Sumerian Literature: Critical Edition of the Dumuzi-Inanna Songs*. BISNELC. Ramat-Gan: Bar-Ilan University, 1998.

———. "An Oath of Chastity in a Sumerian Love Song (SRT 31)?" Pages 45–63 in *Bar-Ilan Studies in Assyriology: Dedicated to Pinhas Artzi*. Edited by Jacob Klein. Ramat-Gan: Bar-Ilan University, 1990.

Seibert, Ilse. *Woman in the Ancient Near East*. Translated by Marianne Herzfeld. Leipzig: Edition Leipzig, 1974.

Segal, Moses H. "The Song of Songs." *VT* 12 (1962): 470–90.

Selby, Martha Ann. *Tamil Love Poetry: The Five Hundred Short Poems of the Ainkurunuru*. New York: Columbia University Press, 2011.

Sells, Michael A. "Guises of the Ghūl: Dissembling Simile and Semantic Overflow in the Classical Arabic Nasīb." Pages 130–64 in *Reorientations/Arabic and Persian Poetry*. Edited by Suzanne Stetkevych. Bloomington: Indiana University Press, 1994.

Semonides. *Greek Iambic Poetry*. Translated by Douglas A. Gerber. LCL. Cambridge: Harvard University Press, 1999.

Shaw, Ian. "Minerals." *OEAE* 2:415–19.

Sherrow, Victoria, ed. *For Appearance' Sake: The Historical Encyclopedia of Good Looks, Beauty, and Grooming*. Westport, CT: Oryx, 2001.

Shimʿon ha-Darshan, ed. *Yalkut Shimoni*. Jerusalem: Machon HaMeor, 2001. [Hebrew]

Shuve, Karl. *The Song of Songs and the Fashioning of Identity in Early Latin Christianity*. Oxford: Oxford University Press, 2016.

Siegfried, D. Carl. *Prediger und Hohelied*. HKAT 3/2. Göttingen: Vandenhoeck & Ruprecht, 1898.

Silentarius, Paulus. *Anthologia Palatina*. Translated by William R. Paton. Revised by Michael Tueller. LCL. Cambridge: Harvard University Press, 2014.

Singer, Itamar. "Purple-Dyers at Lazpa." Pages 21–43 in *Anatolian Interfaces: Hittites, Greeks and Their Neighbours*. Edited by Billie Jean Collins, Mary R. Bachvarova, and Ian C. Rutherford. Oxford: Oxbow Books, 2008.

Sinha, Chris. "The Cost of Renovating the Property: A Reply to Marina Rakova." *Cognitive Linguistics* 13 (2002): 271–76.

Sjöberg, Åke. "Miscellaneous Sumerian Texts, II." *JCS* 29 (1977): 3–45.

Smith, Mark S., and Wayne T. Pitard. *The Ugaritic Baal Cycle: Introduction with Text, Translation, and Commentary of KTU/CAT 1.3–1.4*. VTSup 114. Leiden: Brill, 2009.

Smith, Wilfred Cantwell. *What Is Scripture? A Comparative Approach*. Minneapolis: Fortress, 1993.

Smith, William S. *A History of Egyptian Sculpture and Painting in the Old Kingdom*. 2nd ed. London: Oxford University Press, 1949.

Smith, Yancy. *The Mystery of Anointing: Hippolytus' Commentary on the Song of Songs in Social and Critical Contexts; Texts, Translations, and*

Comprehensive Study. Gorgias Dissertation 62. Piscataway, NJ: Gorgias, 2015.
Sokoloff, Michael. *The Targum to Job from Qumran Cave XI*. BISNELC. Ramat-Gan: Bar-Ilan University, 1974.
Soulen, Richard N. "The *Waṣfs* of the Song of Songs and Hermeneutic." *JBL* 86 (1967): 183–90.
Sowden, Lewis. "Theatre: Origins." *EncJud* 19:669–71.
Spengler, Robert N., Farhod Maksudov, Elissa Bullion, Ann Merkle, Taylor Hermes, and Michael Frachetti. "Arboreal Crops on the Medieval Silk Road: Archaeobotanical Studies at Tashbulak." *PLoS ONE* 13 (2018): 1–16.
Stager, Lawrence E. "Key Passages." *ErIsr* 27 (2003): 240–45.
Steele, Valerie. *The Corset: A Cultural History*. New Haven: Yale University Press, 2003.
Steinert, Ulrike. "Concepts of the Female Body in Mesopotamian Gynecological Texts." Pages 275–357 in *The Comparable Body: Analogy and Metaphor in Ancient Mesopotamia, Egyptian, and Greco-Roman Medicine*. Edited by John Z. Wee. Studies in Ancient Medicine 49. Leiden: Brill, 2017.
Stephan, Stephan H. "Modern Palestinian Parallels to the Song of Songs." *JPOS* 2 (1922): 199–278.
Stern, David. "Ancient Jewish Interpretation of the Song of Songs in a Comparative Context." Pages 87–107 in *Jewish Biblical Interpretation and Cultural Exchange: Comparative Exegesis in Context*. Edited by Natalie Dohrmann and David Stern. Philadelphia: University of Pennsylvania Press, 2008.
Stewart, Susan. *Cosmetics and Perfumes in the Roman World*. Gloucestershire: Tempus, 2007.
Stoddart, D. Michael. *The Scented Ape: The Biology and Culture of Human Odour*. Cambridge: Cambridge University Press, 1990.
Stol, Marten. *Women in the Ancient Near East*. Berlin: de Gruyter, 2016.
Stone, Michael. "The Interpretation of Song of Songs in 4 Ezra." *JSJ* 38 (2007): 226–33.
Stoop-van Paridon, Petronella W. T. *The Song of Songs: A Philological Analysis of the Hebrew Book*. ANESSup 17. Leuven: Peeters, 2005.
Strack, Hermann L., and Günter Stemberger. *Introduction to the Talmud and Midrash*. Translated by Markus Bockmuehl. 2nd ed. Minneapolis: Fortress, 1996.

Strawn, Brent A. "'With a Strong Hand and an Outstretched Arm': On the Meaning(s) of the Exodus Tradition(s)." Pages 103–16 in *Iconographic Exegesis of the Hebrew Bible/Old Testament: An Introduction to Its Method and Practice*. Edited by Izaak J. de Hulster, Brent A. Strawn, and Ryan P. Bonfiglio. Göttingen: Vandenhoeck & Ruprecht, 2015.

Subramoniam, V. I. "The Dating of Sangam." Pages 75–86 in *Proceedings of the Third International Conference Seminar of Tamil Studies, Paris—July 1970*. Pondicherry: Institut Français d'Indologie, 1973.

Suderman, W. Derek. "Modest or Magnificent? Lotus versus Lily in Canticles." *CBQ* 67 (2005): 42–58.

Sumi, Akiko. *Description in Classical Arabic Poetry: Waṣf, Ekphrasis, and Interarts Theory*. Leiden: Brill, 2004.

Suter, Claudia E. "Luxury Goods in Ancient Israel: Questions of Consumption and Production." Pages 993–1002 in *Proceedings of the 6th International Congress of the Archaeology of the Ancient Near East*. Edited by Paolo Matthiae, Frances Pinnock, and Lorenzo Romano. Wiesbaden: Harrassowitz, 2010.

Tadmor, Hayim. *The Inscriptions of Tiglath-Pileser III King of Assyria*. Jerusalem: Israel Academy of Sciences and Humanities, 1994.

Takács, Gábor. *Etymological Dictionary of Egyptian*. 3 vols. HdO 48. Leiden: Brill, 1999–2001.

Tawil, Hayim. "Bathing in Milk (SoS 5:12): A New Look." *BM* 42 (1997): 387–92.

———. "Two Biblical Architectural Images in Light of Cuneiform Sources (Lexicographical Note X)." *BASOR* 341 (2006): 37–52.

Theocritus. *Idylls*. Translated by Neil Hopkinson. LCL. Cambridge: Harvard University Press, 2015.

Thompson, Cynthia L. "Hairstyles, Head-Coverings, and St. Paul: Portraits from Roman Corinth." *BA* 51 (1988): 99–115.

Thompson, Henry O. "Cosmetic Palettes." *Levant* 4 (1972): 148–50.

Thompson, R. Campbell. "Assyrian Medical Texts." *PRSM* 12 (1924): 1–34.

———. "Assyrian Medical Texts II." *PRSM* 19 (1925): 29–78.

———. *The Prisms of Esarhaddon and of Ashurbanipal Found at Nineveh, 1927–28*. London: British Museum, 1931.

Thompson, Yaakov. "The Commentary of Samuel Ben Meir on the Song of Songs." PhD diss., Jewish Theological Seminary of America, 1988.

Thomson, William M. *The Land and the Book*. New York: Harper, 1859.

Thöne, Yvonne S. "Female Humanimality: Animal Imagery in Song of Songs and Ancient Near Eastern Iconography." *JSem* 25 (2016): 389–408.
Thureau-Dangin, François. "Un hymne à Isztar de la haute époque babylonienne." *RA* 22 (1925): 169–77.
Tibullus. *Elegies*. Translated by John P. Postgate. LCL. Cambridge: Harvard University Press, 1913.
Tigay, Jeffrey H. *The Evolution of the Gilgamesh Epic*. Philadelphia: University of Pennsylvania Press, 1982.
Tilford, Nicole L. *Sensing World, Sensing Wisdom: The Cognitive Foundation of Biblical Metaphor*. AIL 31. Atlanta: SBL Press, 2017.
Tobin, Vincent A. "Love Songs and the Song of the Harper." Pages 307–34 in *The Literature of Ancient Egypt: An Anthology of Stories, Instructions, Stelae, Autobiographies, and Poetry*. Edited by William K. Simpson. 3rd ed. New Haven: Yale University Press, 2003.
Topsfield, Leslie T. *Troubadours and Love*. New York: Cambridge University Press, 1975.
Tov, Emanuel. "Canticles." Pages 195–219 + pls. xxiv–xxv in *Qumran Cave 4.XI: Psalms to Chronicles*. Edited by Eugene Ulrich, et al. DJD XVI. Oxford: Clarendon, 2000.
———. "Three Manuscripts (Abbreviated Texts?) of Canticles from Qumran Cave 4." *JJS* 46 (1995): 88–111.
Trautmann, Thomas R. *Elephants and Kings: An Environmental History*. Chicago: University of Chicago Press, 2015.
Treat, Jay Curry. "Aquila, Field, and the Song of Songs." Pages 136–76 in *Origen's Hexapla and Fragments*. Edited by Alison Salveson. TSAJ 58. Tübingen: Mohr Siebeck, 1998.
———. "Lost Keys: Text and Interpretation in Old Greek Song of Songs and Its Earliest Manuscript Witnesses." PhD diss., University of Pennsylvania, 1996.
Trible, Phyllis. *God and the Rhetoric of Sexuality*. OBT. Philadelphia: Fortress, 1978.
Tsumura, David T. "Metaphor, Grammar, and Parallelism in Song of Songs." Paper presented at the Annual Meeting of the Society of Biblical Literature. Atlanta, GA, 21 Nov 2010.
Tuell, Steven S. "A Riddle Resolved by an Enigma: Hebrew גלש and Ugaritic *GLṮ*." *JBL* 112 (1993): 99–104.
Tur-Sinai, Naftali H. "Song of Songs." Pages 351–88 in vol. 2 of *The Language and the Book*. Jerusalem: Bialik, 1951.

Turner, Denys. *Eros and Allegory: Medieval Exegesis of the Song of Songs.* CS 156. Kalamazoo, MI: Cistercian, 1995.
Ullmann, Stephen. *Language and Style.* New York: Barnes & Noble, 1966.
Ulrich, Eugene. *The Dead Sea Scrolls and the Developmental Composition of the Bible.* VTSup 169. Leiden: Brill, 2015.
Ussishkin, David. *The Renewed Archaeological Excavations at Lachish (1973-1994).* 5 vols. Tel Aviv: Emery and Claire Yass Publications in Archaeology, 2004.
Vālmīki. *Rāmāyaṇa.* Translated by Sheldon Pollock. Princeton: Princeton University Press, 1988.
Vasuki, M. "Variety of Hair-Dos in Ancient Tamil Nadu." *JTamS* 9 (1976): 50–58.
Vatsyayana. *The Complete Kama Sutra.* Translated by Alain Danielou. Rochester, VT: Park Street, 1994.
Verde, Danilo, and Pierre Van Hecke. "The Belligerent Woman in Song 1,9." *Bib* 98 (2017): 208–26.
Vico, Giambattista. *New Science: Principles of the New Science Concerning the Common Nature of Nations.* Translated by David Marsh. 3rd ed. New York: Penguin, 1999.
Viezel, Eran. "סַנְסִנָּיו (*sansinnāyw*; Song of Songs 7:9) and the *Palpal* Noun Pattern." *JBL* 133 (2014): 751–56.
Virgil. *Eclogues.* Translated by H. Rushton Fairclough. LCL. Cambridge: Harvard University Press, 1916.
Virolleaud, Charles. *Le Palais Royal d'Ugarit: Textes en cunéiformes alphabétiques des archives sud, sud-ouest et du petit palais.* Mission de Ras Shamra. Paris: Klincksieck, 1965.
Viviers, Hendrik. "The Rhetoricity of the 'Body' in the Song of Songs." Pages 237–54 in *Rhetorical Criticism and the Bible.* Edited by Stanley Porter and Dennis Stamps. JSNTSup 195. Sheffield: Sheffield Academic, 2002.
Wabyanga, Robert K. "Songs of Songs 1:5–7: An Africana Reading." *JTSA* 150 (2014): 128–47.
Wacks, David A. "Between Secular and Sacred: The Song of Songs in the Work of Abraham Ibn Ezra." Pages 47–58 in *Wine, Women and Song: Hebrew and Arabic Literature of Medieval Iberia.* Edited by Michelle M. Hamilton, Sarah J. Portnoy, and David A. Wacks. Newark: de la Cuesta, 2004.
Walsh, Carey Ellen. *Exquisite Desire: Religion, the Erotic, and the Song of Songs.* Minneapolis: Fortress, 2000.

Waltke, Bruce K. *The Book of Proverbs: Chapters 1–15*. NICOT. Grand Rapids: Eerdmans, 2004.

———. *The Book of Proverbs: Chapters 15–31*. NICOT. Grand Rapids: Eerdmans, 2005.

Walton, John H. *Ancient Near Eastern Thought and the Old Testament: Introducing the Conceptual World of the Hebrew Bible*. 2nd ed. Grand Rapids: Baker, 2018.

Ward, William A. *Essays on Feminine Titles of the Middle Kingdom and Related Subjects*. Beirut: American University of Beirut, 1986.

Wasserman, Nathan. *Akkadian Love Literature of the Third and Second Millennium BCE*. LAOS 4. Weisbaden: Harrassowitz, 2016.

———. "Piercing the Eyes: An Old Babylonian Love Incantation and the Preparation of Kohl." *BO* 72 (2015): 601–12.

Watson, Wilfred G. E. *Classical Hebrew Poetry: A Guide to Its Techniques*. 2nd ed. JSOTSup 26. Sheffield: Sheffield Academic, 1995.

———. "Some Ancient Near Eastern Parallels to the Song of Songs." Pages 253–71 in *Words Remembered, Texts Renewed: Essays in Honour of John F. A. Sawyer*. Edited by Jon Davies, Graham Harvey, and Wilfred G. E. Watson. JSOTSup 195. Sheffield: Sheffield Academic, 1995.

Weems, Renita J. "The Song of Songs." *NIB* 5:363–434.

Weinfeld, Moshe. "Traces of Assyrian Treaty Formulae in Deuteronomy." *Bib* 46 (1965): 417–27.

Wellhausen, Julius. *Prolegomena to the History of Israel*. Edinburgh: Black, 1885.

Wells, Bruce. "The Covenant Code and Near Eastern Legal Traditions." *Maarav* 13 (2006): 85–118.

Wente, Edward F., Jr. "A Ghost Story." Pages 112–15 in *The Literature of Ancient Egypt: An Anthology of Stories, Instructions, and Poetry*. Edited by William K. Simpson. 3rd ed. New Haven: Yale University Press, 2003.

Westbrook, Raymond. "What is the Covenant Code?" Pages 15–36 in *Theory and Method in Biblical and Cuneiform Law*. Edited by Bernard M. Levinson. JSOTSup 181. Sheffield: Sheffield Academic, 1994.

Westbrook, Raymond, and Bruce Wells. *Everyday Law in Biblical Israel: An Introduction*. Louisville: Westminster John Knox, 2009.

Westenholz, Joan G. "A Forgotten Love Song." Pages 415–25 in *Language, Literature, and History: Philological and Historical Studies Presented to Erica Reiner*. Edited by Francesca Rochberg-Halton. AOS 67. New Haven: American Oriental Society, 1987.

———. "The Good Shepherd." Pages 281–310 in *Schools of Oriental Studies and the Development of Modern Historiography: Proceedings of the Fourth Annual Symposium of the Assyrian and Babylonian Intellectual Heritage Project; Held in Ravenna, Italy, October 13–17, 2001*. Edited by Antonio Panaino and Andrea Piras. MSym 4. Milan: Università di Bologna & Islao, 2004.

———. "Love Lyrics from the Ancient Near East." *CANE* 4:2471–84.

———. "Metaphorical Language in the Poetry of Love in the Ancient Near East." Pages 381–87 in *La circulation des biens, des personnes et des idées dans le Proche-Orient ancien*. Edited by Dominique Charpin and Francis Joannès. Paris: Editions Recherche sur les civilisations, 1992.

Westenholz, Joan, and Aage Westenholz. "Help for Rejected Suitors: The Old Akkadian Love Incantation MAD V 8." *Or* 46 (1977): 198–219.

Wetzstein, Johann G. "Die syrische Dreschtafel." *ZfE* 5 (1873): 270–302.

Whedbee, J. William. "Paradox and Parody in the Song of Solomon: Towards a Comic Reading of the Most Sublime Song." Pages 266–78 in *A Feminist Companion to the Song of Songs*. Edited by Athalaya Brenner. FCB 1. Sheffield: Sheffield Academic, 1993.

White, John B. *A Study of the Language of Love in the Song of Songs and Ancient Egyptian Poetry*. SBLDS 38. Missoula, MT: Scholars Press, 1978.

Whitesell, Connie J. "Behold, Thou Art Fair, My Beloved." *Parab* 20 (1995): 92–99.

Wilcke, Carsten. "Inanna/Ishtar." *RlA* 5:74–87.

Winter, Urs. *Frau und Göttin: Exegetische und ikonographitche Studien zum weiblichen Gottesbild im Alten Israel und in dessen Umwelt*. OBO 53. Fribourg: Universitätsverlag; Göttingen: Vandenhoeck & Ruprecht, 1983.

Wiseman, Donald J. "A New Stela of Aššur-naṣir-pal II." *Iraq* 14 (1952): 24–44.

Wolff, Hans W. *Anthropology of the Old Testament*. Translated by Margaret Kohl. London: SCM, 1974.

Woolford, John, and Daniel Karlin, eds. *Poems of Browning: Volume Two 1841–1846*. New York: Routledge, 2014.

Woolley, Leonard. *The Royal Cemetery: A Report on the Predynastic and Sargonid Graves Excavated between 1926 and 1931*. Philadelphia: University of Pennsylvania Museum, 1934.

Wright, David P. *Inventing God's Law: How the Covenant Code of the Bible Used and Revised the Laws of Hammurabi*. Oxford: Oxford University Press, 2009.

Yadin, Yigael. *The Scroll of the War of the Sons of Light against the Sons of Darkness*. Oxford: Oxford University Press, 1962.

Younger, K. Lawson, Jr. "The Contextual Method." Pages xxxv–xlii in *The Context of Scripture: Vol. 3 Canonical Compositions, Monumental Inscriptions and Archival Documents from the Biblical World*. Edited by William W. Hallo and K. Lawson Younger Jr. Leiden: Brill, 2003.

Yu, Ning. "Metaphor from Body and Culture." Pages 247–61 in *The Cambridge Handbook of Metaphor and Thought*. Edited by Raymond Gibbs. Cambridge: Cambridge University Press, 2008.

———. "The Relationship between Metaphor, Body, and Culture." Pages 387–408 in *Body, Language, and Mind: Sociocultural Situatedness*. Edited by Roslyn M. Frank, René Dirven, Tom Ziemke, and Enrique Bernárdez. 2 vols. Berlin: de Gruyter, 2007.

Zevit, Ziony. *The Religions of Ancient Israel: A Synthesis of Parallactic Approaches*. London: Continuum, 2001.

Zhang, Sarah. *I, You, and the Word 'God': Finding Meaning in the Song of Songs*. Siphrut 20. Winona Lake, IN: Eisenbrauns, 2016.

Zlotowitz, Meir and Nosson Scherman. *Song of Songs*. ArtScroll Tanach Series 26. New York: Mesorah, 1977.

Zohary, Daniel, and Maria Hopf. *Domestication of Plants in the Old World*. 3rd ed. Oxford: Oxford University Press, 2000.

Zohary, Michael. *Plants of the Bible*. New York: Cambridge University Press, 1982.

Zvelebil, Kamil. *The Smile of Murugan on Tamil Literature of South India*. Leiden: Brill, 1973.

Zwan, Pieter van der. "Beneath the Body of the Text: Body-Images in the Song of Songs." *JSem* 26 (2017): 611–31.

———. "Psychological Approaches to Song of Songs." *JSem* 25 (2016): 658–72.

Ancient Sources Index

Hebrew Bible/Old Testament

Genesis

1:1–2:3	48
2–3	19, 112, 122
3:8	103
3:16	122
4:7	122
8:8–12	144
10:19	75
12:11	61
12:14	33
15:14	207
24:16	33
24:22	197
24:50	81
24:53	197
24:65	168
25:13	69
25:23	207
27:40	170
29:9–14	39
29:17	33, 140
30:38	148
32:26	186
34:25–29	81
38	131
38:28	160
39:6	33
40:10	122, 133
40:11	133
42:2	186
47:29	186
49:11	133
49:25	105, 175

Exodus

2:15–22	39
3:19	49
6:6	49
11:2	197
13:16	49
14:23	101
15:1	101
15:4	98
15:16	188
15:27	131
21:1–22:19	52
21:23–24	158
22:16–17	81
22:25	185
25	197
26:19–40:18	201
27:8	83
28:20	200
28:42	186
31:18	83
32:4	83
32:9	170
32:15	83
32:27	186
34:1	83
39:10	138
40:22	186

Leviticus

1:11	186
1:14	141
13:49	69
19:27	201
23:40	131

Leviticus (cont.)		5:28	98
24:20	158	6:2	105
		9:7–20	17
Numbers		11:18–28	146
2:2	188	15:15	164
5:11–31	21		
6:3	133	Ruth	
6:10	141	1:11	207
10:14	188	3:3	205
13:23–24	123, 133	3:7	182–84
21:21–30	146		
31:10	82	1 Samuel	
32:1	152	5:11	69
		14:22	105
Deuteronomy		16:12	33, 60–61
3:5	75	17	137
4:34	49	17:42	61
5:15	49	19:13	154
6:21	49	25:3	33
7:8	49	25:16	75
7:19	49	25:39	81
8:8	183		
9:9	83	2 Samuel	
9:26	49	1:24	160
11:2	49	2:18	104
19:21	158	5:2	39
20:7	81	5:11	84
22:13–27	81, 84	7:2	71
26:8	49	7:12	207
32:4	183	8:7	169
32:14	133	10:4–5	201
32:32	133	11:1	83
33:29	9	11:2	33
		13	131
Joshua		13:1	33
2:9	188	13:16–19	75
2:18	37, 160	13:23–33	81
7:21	197	14:25	33, 149
10:24	170	14:27	33
13:8–27	146	20:10	207
15:9–11	105		
15:53	90	1 Kings	
		1:5	98
Judges		3:1	75
4–5	164	6	197

Reference	Page
6:18	193
6:34	196
7:1–12	71
7:15	83
7:15–22	201
7:19	179
7:22	179
7:26	179
8:9	83
10:2	197
10:18	211
10:22	211
10:26–29	84, 98, 102
11:10	169
14:23	106
15:19	197
15:33	193
16:8	193
21:12	112
22:39	211

2 Kings

Reference	Page
5:9	98
6:18	84
18:14	197
19:23	83
20:20	147
23:6	106
24	197

1 Chronicles

Reference	Page
1:29	69
12:9	104

2 Chronicles

Reference	Page
2:6	154
2:14	183
31:6	182–83

Nehemiah

Reference	Page
3:34	183
9:22	146
13:15	182

Esther

Reference	Page
1:6	196, 200
2:7	33
2:12–15	97, 205

Job

Reference	Page
3:12	105
9:19	82
9:30	60
15:15	60
24:9	106
28:6	206
28:12–19	197
28:16	196
28:17	196
28:19	196
29:17	158
30:28–30	60–61, 189
31:24	196
39:20	188
40–41	137
40:17	83
40:26	164
42:11	197

Psalms

Reference	Page
11:1	105
17:8	90
19:11	196–97
22:10	106
22:15	207
23:1	39
29:5	83
45	179, 205
45:10	196
48:3	193
50:2	193
55:7	141
57:5	158
60	179
69	179
74:19	6, 141
80	179
80:11	83
88:16	188

Psalms (cont.)		1:7–8	38–39, 55, 67, 106
92:13	84, 131	1:8	68
102:12	104	1:8–10	68
119:127	197	1:9	11–12, 42, 98–102, 135, 220
120:5	70	1:9–10	33, 97–99, 135, 218
124:6	158	1:9–11	199
138:3	142	1:10	97, 101–2, 164, 171
139:5	83	1:10–11	99–101, 194
139:14	83	1:12	134, 196
144:12	201	1:13	18, 104, 106, 175, 180, 207
		1:13–14	123
Proverbs		1:15	15, 37, 68, 138–41, 144–45, 193–94, 218, 221
3:8	122		
5:15–19	104, 119, 178	1:15–16	37, 89
5:19	135	1:15–17	194
6:3	142	1:16	123
6:25	140	1:16–17	55, 106, 144
7:18	178	1:17	57, 84
8:19	196	2:1	68, 73, 120, 146
11:22	197	2:1–2	89, 139, 173
22:17–23:11	48	2:2	9, 68, 89, 100, 185
23:5	48	2:2–3	90
25:11	90	2:3	9, 14, 33, 41–42, 57, 89, 91, 94–97, 123, 133, 135, 209, 218, 219–20
25:12	187, 196		
25:21	82		
30:14	158	2:3–5	183
31:10–31	20, 137	2:4	97, 132, 188
31:21	160	2:4–6	134–35
		2:5	57, 91, 132
Ecclesiastes		2:7	24, 55, 104, 106, 121, 178, 223
12:4	75	2:8–9	37, 98, 104
12:5	112	2:8–10	123
		2:8–13	25
Song of Songs		2:8–17	75, 86, 103, 141, 205, 224
1:2	5, 13, 41–42, 68, 134	2:9	75, 80, 104
1:2–4	67, 72, 132, 135, 181, 183	2:10	68, 120
1:2–2:7	86, 224	2:10–13	55, 57, 105–6, 110
1:3–4	134, 206	2:10–14	120
1:4	55, 106, 196	2:10–15	121
1:5	17, 24, 37, 66–69, 71, 73, 146	2:13–14	68
1:5–6	33, 41, 59–60, 62, 67, 81, 87, 136, 154, 173, 177, 183, 194, 211, 218–20, 224	2:13	134
		2:14	37, 139, 141, 144
		2:15	33, 110–12, 119, 120, 135
1:6	21, 25, 33, 59, 68–69, 71–72, 110, 112, 119, 135	2:16	97, 120, 178–79, 224
		2:16–17	41, 120, 123, 180

Ancient Sources Index 273

2:17　7, 33, 101–5, 110, 120, 132, 135, 175, 178, 194, 220, 223
3:1–5　18, 86, 224
3:3　37
3:4　15, 25, 55
3:4–5　106
3:5　24, 55, 104, 121, 178, 223
3:6–8　3
3:6–11　25, 196, 205
3:6–5:1　86, 224
3:7　16
3:9　146, 193
3:10　154, 199
3:11　37
4:1　2, 10, 36–37, 138, 140–42, 144–45, 148, 152–55, 157, 183, 189, 193–94, 196, 218, 221, 223
4:1–2　138, 159, 201
4:1–3　3, 141–42, 168, 200
4:1–5　3, 23, 104, 178, 219
4:1–7　10, 14–15, 18, 20, 33, 37, 41, 51, 68, 101, 103, 136–38, 170, 181, 193–95, 219, 224
4:2　24, 36, 140, 154, 157, 159–60, 177, 183, 193, 218, 221, 223
4:2–3　164, 177
4:2–4　177
4:3　7, 37, 160, 163, 168, 177, 183, 193, 218, 221, 223
4:4　2, 7, 19, 168–69, 173–74, 193–94, 218–19, 223
4:4–5　201
4:4–7　3
4:5　3, 12, 80, 104, 106, 138, 175, 178, 180–81, 193, 219, 221–22
4:5–6　175
4:6　7, 33, 101–5, 110, 124, 132, 135, 141, 175, 178, 180, 194, 205, 207, 218–20, 223
4:7　37, 138, 189, 196
4:8　99, 142, 193
4:8–6:10　3
4:9　37, 100, 140, 144, 147, 168, 171, 194
4:9–10　50

4:9–5:2　80, 194
4:10　5, 41–42, 121, 132, 134, 174, 181, 205
4:10–11　135
4:10–5:1　134, 183
4:11　41, 97, 146, 163, 181, 193, 205
4:12　50, 76, 80, 111, 121
4:12–13　33, 110, 112, 135
4:12–15　114, 180
4:12–5:1　16, 19, 41–42, 57, 86, 101, 119, 121–22, 135, 205, 207–8, 217–20
4:13　41, 111, 120
4:14　134
4:14–5:1　3
4:14–5:5　104
4:15　41, 193
4:16　41, 55, 97, 106, 111, 120–21, 123
4:16–5:1　110, 112, 135
5:1　41, 50, 111, 121, 132, 134–35, 180
5:1–7　17, 112
5:2　68, 75, 80, 123, 138, 141, 144
5:2–3　15, 99
5:2–8　3, 18, 55, 75, 86, 106, 120
5:2–6:3　120
5:2–7:10　86, 224
5:4　207–8
5:4–5　57
5:4–6　123
5:5　181, 207
5:6　186
5:7　75
5:7–8　21
5:8　57, 123, 193
5:8–9　144, 214
5:9　68, 142, 196, 199, 201
5:10　9, 60–61, 123, 138, 183, 188–89, 193, 195, 200, 223
5:10–12　141
5:10–16　18, 20, 34–35, 51, 137, 194–95, 199, 214, 219, 223–24
5:10–6:3　194
5:11　2, 10, 42, 139, 148, 154, 156–57, 194–96, 218, 221–23

Song of Songs (cont.)
- 5:11–12   154, 177, 200
- 5:11–13   201
- 5:11–15   199
- 5:12   2, 138–39, 142, 144–45, 195, 218, 221, 223
- 5:13   2, 120, 135, 174–75, 180–81, 195, 201, 206-7, 218–19, 222
- 5:13–15   41–42
- 5:14   138, 196, 200–1, 206, 219, 222
- 5:14–15   42, 156, 201, 218, 222–23
- 5:15   84, 138, 146, 188–89, 192–93, 195–96, 200, 218, 222
- 5:15–16   189
- 5:16   123–24, 138, 181, 223
- 6:1   68, 120
- 6:1–2   18
- 6:2   10–11, 33, 110–12, 117, 120, 135, 189, 201, 205
- 6:2–3   57, 97, 123, 135, 178–80
- 6:2–7   41
- 6:3   224
- 6:4   42, 138, 146, 188–89, 192–93, 196, 218
- 6:4–7   3, 10, 18, 20, 34, 51, 68, 101, 136–37, 142, 170, 181, 193–95, 200, 219, 222
- 6:4–10   188
- 6:4–12   194
- 6:5   2, 24, 37, 101, 141–42, 144, 147–48, 153, 157, 183, 201, 221
- 6:6   157, 183, 221
- 6:7   138, 163, 183, 211, 221
- 6:8–9   100, 196
- 6:8–10   18, 192
- 6:9   68
- 6:9–10   68, 196
- 6:10   7, 37, 42, 138, 188–89, 192, 218
- 6:10–12   41
- 6:11   24, 33, 110–12, 117, 120–21, 135, 189
- 6:11–12   55, 57, 97, 120, 122
- 7:1   37, 68, 73
- 7:1–10   20, 101
- 7:2   2, 9–10, 21, 124, 138, 147, 185, 189, 193, 196, 222–23
- 7:2–3   181, 218
- 7:2–7   3, 10, 16, 18, 20, 24, 34, 51, 68, 124, 136–37, 170, 181, 193–95, 219, 224
- 7:2–10   183, 194, 219
- 7:3–4   201
- 7:3–6   41
- 7:3   41, 97, 122, 124, 128, 130, 134–35, 175, 181, 183–85, 193, 207, 219–20, 222–23
- 7:4   2, 18, 37, 104, 106, 175, 178, 180, 193, 222
- 7:4–5   19, 122
- 7:5   37, 68, 145–46, 168–69, 173–75, 183, 193–94, 196, 211, 219, 221, 223
- 7:5–6   200
- 7:6   24, 124, 147–49, 154–57, 160, 183, 194, 217, 221, 223
- 7:7   138, 189, 196
- 7:7–9   97
- 7:8   122, 126, 132–33, 174, 194, 219, 223
- 7:8–9   41, 80, 130–31, 155, 175
- 7:8–10   22, 24, 33, 41–42, 122–24, 133, 135, 147, 183, 218–20
- 7:8–14   57
- 7:9   18, 91, 106, 123, 129, 132–33
- 7:9–10   128, 132, 181
- 7:10   41, 123, 133–34, 160, 163
- 7:11   122, 175, 224
- 7:11–12   120
- 7:11–13   55, 106
- 7:11–14   24, 123
- 7:11–8:4   86, 224
- 7:12–13   97
- 7:12–14   41, 57, 120–22, 205
- 7:13   33, 37, 110–12, 120–21, 132, 135, 183
- 7:14   41, 134
- 8:1–2   33, 49, 55, 86, 105–6, 124, 134–35, 175, 183, 219
- 8:1–3   26

Ancient Sources Index 275

8:1–4	49, 106	32:4	60
8:1	49	32:12	106
8:2	15, 41–42, 49, 97, 106, 121–23, 128, 130, 132, 134, 175, 218, 220	35:2	155–56
		37:22	192
8:4	24, 55, 121, 175, 224	40:11	39
8:5	91, 134	42:11	70
8:5–14	103	44:14	201
8:6	69	47:2	138
8:6–7	86	54:2	71
8:7	86	54:10	105
8:8	81, 85, 99, 175	58:11	112
8:8–9	80–81, 85	59:11	6
8:8–10	21, 26, 33, 41, 59, 73, 76, 80, 86–87, 105–6, 121, 136, 173, 175, 193, 217–18, 220, 224	60:7	70
		60:8	143
		60:16	106
8:9	75–76, 82–84, 217	65:1	133
8:9–10	41, 85	66:11	106
8:10	2, 10, 19, 85–86, 175, 192, 219		
8:11–12	196	**Jeremiah**	
8:12	112, 119, 121	2:10	70
8:12–13	33, 42, 110, 112, 135	4:20	71
8:12–14	41	4:30	147
8:13	105–6, 110, 112, 120	5:8	98
8:13–14	121	6:4	104
8:14	7, 33, 55. 98, 101–5, 110, 120–21, 123, 132, 135, 175, 178, 180, 194, 205, 220, 223	7:26	170
		10:20	71
		22:7	84
		22:14–15	84
Isaiah		27:2	170
1:18	60	31:22	186
3:5	142	46:18	155
3:16	170	48–49	146
3:24	149	48:28	139, 141
4:6	90	49:3	145
5:1–7	17, 112	49:28–29	70
8:8	170	50:6	105
9:10	84	50:26	182
13:12	196–97	51:11	169
15–16	146		
16:11	207	**Lamentations**	
18:4	60	1:1	97, 192
21:16–17	70	2:7	75
24:23	189	4:1	196
28:19	106	4:3	106
30:26	189	4:7–8	60, 66

Lamentations (cont.)		9:14	106
5:10	61	10:6	49
		11:11	143
Ezekiel		14:6	6
1:16	200	14:8	90, 183
1:26	206		
7:16	141	Joel	
7:19	207	1:11	183
8:1–18	27	1:12	90, 131
8:14	26	2:16	106
16	17		
16:4	122	Amos	
16:7–8	81, 106, 175	2:9	84
16:12	197	3:15	211
17:7	201	6:4	211
17:10	201	9:3	155
17:22–24	83	9:13	133
19:10	112	9:14	112
20:33–34	49		
23:2	98	Jonah	
23:3	106, 175	4:6	90
23:21	106, 175	4:10	201
27:5	83		
27:10–11	169, 171	Micah	
27:15	208	5:3	39
27:16	154	7:1	133
27:21	70		
27:22	197	Nahum	
31:3–5	84, 201	2:8	141
38:11	75		
		Habakkuk	
Daniel		1:7	188
2:32	207	3:7	71
7:9	10		
10:5	196	Zechariah	
10:6	200	2:9	75
		4:7	105
Hosea			
1–3	17	Malachi	
2:4	106, 175	1:6	82
2:8	185		
2:15	187	Ancient Near Eastern Texts	
2:21	81		
5:13	49	Akkadian	
8:9	178	Babylonian Ballad	77, 198

Ancient Sources Index

Cultic Commentary	198	Where Has My Lover Gone?	95, 142–43
Divine Love Lyrics	65–66, 165		
Faithful Lover	50, 189	Egyptian	
Forgotten Love Song	108, 125, 187, 203	Cairo Love Songs	
Help for Rejected Suitors	118, 137, 203	no. 21a	137
		no. 20g	128
Hymn to Ištar	140, 161	no. 21a–g	49
Middle Assyrian Song List		Deir el-Medina	
ii	203	no. 54	28
vii	13, 118, 190, 198, 203	Mutirdis inscription	28, 151–52, 158
Mystical Miscellanea	137, 198	Papyrus Ebers	152, 157–58, 165
Nabû and Tashmetu		Papyrus Harris	
13–16	177	no. 1	128, 187
r.5	176	no. 3	28, 94, 109, 113, 128, 149
r.5–8	51, 137	no. 4	128, 113
r.8	213	no. 7	76
r.9	177	no. 8	94, 117
r.9–14	117	no. 9	202
r.15–18	114	no. 14	55
r.15–32	117	no. 18	113
r.18	55	Papyrus Chester Beatty	
r.20	95	no. 31	7, 28, 51, 62, 109, 155, 170, 187, 189–90, 197, 213
Rites of Egašankalamma	137, 198	no. 38	98, 104
ŠÀ.ZI.GA Incantations		no. 41	128
1	203, 209	no. 42	128, 202
2	203, 209	no. 43	149, 187
3	209	no. 45	209
5	176, 209	no. 46	76
6	176, 203, 209	no. 47	76
7	176, 209	Turin Love Songs	
8	176, 209	no. 28	28, 94, 109, 117, 128, 202
9	176, 209	no. 30	28
11	203		
12	176	Sumerian	
14	209	Gudea Cylinder B	114
15	209	Manchester Tammuz	113–14
19	209	Šulgi Hymns	
21	104	A	98
24	104	D	95
26	104	X	108
34	203	Z	118
70	92	Sumerian Love Songs	
74	92	DI B	95, 128, 209, 213
Schøyen Collection	51, 209		

Sumerian Love Songs (cont.)

DI C	66, 128, 149
DI D	55
DI E	94–95, 114, 171
DI F	55
DI H	55
DI I	171, 213
DI P	114–15, 171
DI R	118
DI T	137, 213
DI V	39
DI Y	76–77, 212–13
DI C^1	77, 171, 190
DI E^1	171
DI F^1	55, 114, 125
Dumuzi's Dream	108
Enki and Ninhursag	77, 91–92, 209
Enlil and Ninlil	203
Išmedagan A	187
Šušin A	128
Šušin C	213

West-Semitic
  Amarna Letters

5	211
14	203, 211
16	197
19	197
24	211
25	203
27	203
31	203, 211
34	203
286–288	49

  Aqhat Epic

1.17	55, 119
1.18	50
1.19	166

  Baal Cycle

1.3	166
1.4	206, 210
1.101	137

  Kirta Epic

1.14	137, 213

  Nikkal Hymn

1.24	55, 119

  Shahar and Shalim

1.23	133, 210

Deuterocanonical Books

Tobit

6:12	33
7:16	6
8:4	6

Judith

8:7	33

Sirach

6:19	119
7:18	197
24:13–14	131
25:17	61
26:18	201
39:26	133
51:13–30	4

Susanna

2	33
19–21	121
32	149

Old Testament Pseudepigrapha

1 Enoch

8:1	166

4 Ezra

4:37	6
5:24–26	6

Joseph and Aseneth

8.5	7
18.9	6–8, 162, 165, 190
19.5	7

Jubilees

27:14	6
27:17	6

Ancient Sources Index

Dead Sea Scrolls

1Q20
  XX, 2–8 — 4, 137
  XX, 3 — 149

1QM
  VI, 2 — 169

1QS
  VI, 11 — 97

4Q106 — 3–4, 164

4Q107 — 3–4, 164

4Q108 — 3–4

4Q184
  1 12–14 — 4, 137

6Q6 — 3

11Q5
  XXI, 11–18 — 4
  XXVIII, 9–12 — 149

11Q10 — 169

CD
  XIV, 11 — 97
  XXVIII, 9–12 — 149

Early Jewish Writings

Josephus, *Jewish Antiquities*
  7.104 — 169

New Testament

1 Corinthians
  11:15 — 149

1 Timothy
  2:9 — 149

1 Peter
  3:3 — 149

Revelation
  1:8 — 15

Greco-Roman Literature

Achilles Tatius, *Leucippe and Clitophon*
  1.9.6 — 144
  1.11 — 182, 188

Aelian, *Nature of Animals*
  6.48 — 99

Aelian, *Varia historia*
  12.1 — 166
  12.18 — 204

Alcman, *Partheneion*
  1.44–57 — 99, 190

Apollodorus, *Library*
  3.9.2 — 92

Aristophanes, *Clouds*
  1009–1019 — 210–11

Aristophanes, *Acharnians*
  241–279 — 210

Aristotle, *Rhetoric*
  1.7.15 — 198

Athenaeus, *Deipnosophistae*
  2.38c — 129
  15.40 — 203

Anthologia Palatina
  5.27 — 170
  5.48 — 162
  5.56 — 162
  5.103 — 78
  5.132 — 63, 137, 170, 187
  5.156 — 146

Anthologia Palatina (cont.)
5.172	56
5.189	78
5.213	78
5.227	129
5.230	149
5.247	162
5.258	129

Clement of Alexandria, *Christ the Educator*
3.2	166

Cyprian, *Dress of Virgins*
14	166

Diodorus, *Bibliotheca historica*
1.78.5	174
16.2	212

Dioscorides, *De materia medica*
1.32–63	204

Herodotus, *Histories*
1.195	203
1.199	131
2.48	210
2.92	179–80
3.85–86	101

Hippolytus, *On Song of Songs*
3.3–4	13

Homer, *Hymn to Aphrodite*
90	190

Homer, *Hymn to Apollo*
114	142

Homer, *Iliad*
1.55–56	63
3.381	203
14.170–173	204
21.493–495	142

Homer, *Odyssey*
5.225–227	55–56
6.162–163	127
18.195–196	131
23.239–259	56

Horace, *Odes*
1.5	198
2.4.4	63
2.11.16	203
3.9	190
3.11.9–12	99
4.13	158

Jerome, *Adversus Jovinianum*
1.30	16

Jerome, *Adversus Rufinum*
2.14	13

Jerome, *Epistles*
54	163, 166
107	3, 166

Juvenal, *Satires*
6.474–511	150

[Lucian], *Amores*
14	187

Martial, *Epigram*
14.134	109

Origen, *Commentary on the Song*
Prologue	3, 13, 24
3.71	14

Ovid, *Amores*
1.5	182
2.5.35–40	166
14.23–24	162
21.103–128	92

Ovid, *Ars amatoria*
1.723–729	64

2.523–534	78	4.8.33–36	115
2.719–722	145–46		
3.206	166	Plato, *Republic*	
3:279–280	158	5.452b	210

Ovid, *Heroides* Tertullian, *Apparel of Women*
15.171–172	129	2.3	166
16.251–252	63		
20.120	63	Tertullian, *Monogamy*	
		8.70	141

Ovid, *Metamorphoses*
14.597	143	Theocritus, *Idylls*	
		3.10–11	92
Ovid, *Remedia amoris*		3.40–42	92
337	109	10.27–28	63
		18.26–28	190
Pausanias, *Description of Greece*		18.30–31	99
1.12.4	212		
1.18.9	200	Theophrastus, *De sensu*	
1.24.5	212	4–12	204
1.40.4	212		
1.43.6	212	Theophrastus, *Historia plantarum*	
2.2.6	198	3.3.5	127
2.7.5	212		
5.12.3	212	Tibullus, *Elegies*	
		1.2.5–9	78
Plato, *Greater Hippias*			
289e	198	Virgil, *Aeneid*	
		6.190	143
Pliny, *Natural History*			
6.32	127	Virgil, *Eclogae*	
9.62.135	154	2.17–18	63
13.2	203–4	3.64–65	92
22.21	158	4.25	203
23.28	158	10.37–41	63
23.36–37	158		
25.105	158	Vitruvius, *De architectura*	
37.43	196	8.3.14	156

Propertius, *Elegies* Xenophon, *Anabasis*
1.3.24	92	1.5.10	127
1.16	78		
2.3.10	63–64	Xenophon, *Cyropaedia*	
2.3.12	166	1.3.2	166
4.7.15–20	56		

Xenophon, *Oeconomicus*		7b	84
10.1–8	166	Mo'ed Qatan	
Xenophon, *Symposium*		9b	166
5.6	174	Nazir	
Mishnah		4b	148
Avot		Nedarim	
1:1	181	9b	148
5:22	225	Pesachim	
Nedarim		37b	153
9:10	62, 131	87a	10
Shabbat		Sanhedrin	
10:6	166	101a	1
Yadayim		Shabbat	
3:5	1, 8	64b	166
Tosefta		Ta'anit	
		23b	62
Hullin		Rabbinic Works	
1.18–19	208		
Sanhedrin		'Abot de Rabbi Nathan	
12:10	1, 8	A:4	1
Babylonian Talmud		Aggadath Shir Hashirim	
		22	1
Avodah Zarah			
30b	164	Exodus Rabbah	
Berakot		23:14	101
24a	9, 149	Genesis Rabbah	
Gittim		40:4	61
58a	148	Mekilta le-Devarim	9
Hagigah		Numbers Rabbah	
14a	10	10:7	148
Ketubboth		Qoheleth Rabbah	
4b	166	8:17	153

Sifre Numbers
    160   208

Song of Songs Rabbah
    1:6   62
    1:9   101
    1:15   141
    4:3   153
    5:1   121
    6:2   10

Modern Authors Index

Aaron, David 44, 227
Aftel, Mandy 205, 227
Ahl, Frederick 127, 227
Albright, William F. 47, 227
Alexander, Philip S. 9–10, 12, 62, 91, 227
Allen, James P 109, 150, 182, 228
Alobaidi, Joseph 11, 227
Alster, Bendt 27, 77, 92, 94–95, 108, 114, 227
Alter, Robert 86, 121, 228
Andiñach, Pablo R. 122, 228
Andrae, Walter 209, 228
Arberry, Arthur John 129–30, 228
Arnold, Dorothea 109, 150, 182, 228
Asher-Greve, Julia M. 42, 228
Ashmole, Bernard 63, 229
Asiedu, F. B. A. 15, 228
Assante, Julia 209, 228
Assmann, Jan 197, 228
Astell, Ann W. 16, 228
Atkins, John 57, 92, 117, 133, 228
Ausloos, Hans 2, 5, 229
Auwers, Jean-Marie 5, 229
Ayo, Nicholas 37, 229
Bahrani, Zainab 65, 171, 229
Baildam, John D. 25, 229
Barbiero, Gianni 4, 229
Barnett, Richard D. 212, 229
Beazley, John D. 63, 229
Beentjes, Pancratius C. 61, 229
Bergant, Dianne 59, 85–86, 131–34, 154, 173, 175–76, 180, 183, 229
Berlin, Adele 60, 229
Bernat, David 4, 137, 195, 230

Besnier, Marie-Françoise 114, 230
Bienkowski, Piotr 151, 230
Bialik, Chaim 93, 230
Biggs, Robert D. 92, 104, 129, 176, 203, 209, 230
Bimson, Mavis 161, 230
Biran, Avraham 167, 230
Black, Fiona C. 19–20, 22, 57, 152, 156, 230
Black, Jeremy A. 77, 198, 230
Bloch, Ariel 145, 180, 183, 230
Bloch, Chana 57, 145, 180, 183, 230
Blondell, Ruby 100, 230
Bodkin, Maud 53, 231
Boddy, Janice 110, 231
Boer, Roland 23, 231
Boersma, Matthew 205, 231
Börker-Klähn, Jutta 151, 231
Borger, Rykle 169, 203, 212, 231
Boyarin, Daniel 50, 231
Breasted, James H. 93, 100, 202, 212, 231
Brenner, Athalya 18, 20–21, 33, 59–61, 69, 145, 180, 231
Bryan, Cyril P. 157, 231
Budde, D. Karl 25, 177, 232
Bullion, Elissa 261
Burchard, Christoph 7, 232
Buzy, Denis 185, 232
Byrne, Ryan 106–7, 232
Cabanes, Augustin 110, 232
Cainion, Ivory J. 112, 232
Caird, George B. 34, 232
Canter, Howard V. 77–78, 232
Cantrell, Deborah 99, 101, 232

Carr, David M. 13, 18, 30, 232
Carr, G. Lloyd 96, 131, 133, 139, 154, 232
Carter, Howard 197, 232
Carty, Jarrett A. 17, 232
Case, M. L. 180, 232
Caston, R. Rothaus 57, 233
Chave, Peter 21, 233
Cheyne, Thomas K. 192, 233
Civil, Miguel 95, 125, 165, 190, 198, 203, 213, 233
Clark, Elizabeth A. 13, 233
Clines, David J. A. 19, 22–23, 233, 236
Cohen, Gerson D. 8, 233
Cohen, Mordechai Z. 12, 233
Cohen, Shaye D. 4, 43, 51, 137, 233
Conrad, Cecilia 159, 233
Cook, Elizabeth 93, 130, 233
Cooke, J. Hunt 113, 233
Cooper, Jerrold S. 27, 114, 234
Copley, Frank 78, 234
Corbett, Glenn 147, 234
Cornelius, Izak 113, 234
Corson, Richard 159, 163, 167, 202, 234
Cowley, Geoffrey 177, 234
Crouwell, Joost H. 99, 250
Dahood, Mitchell J. 69, 133, 234
Dales, George 171, 184, 234
Dalman, Gustaf H. 26, 64, 93, 116, 126, 137, 139, 150, 159, 167, 170, 176, 178, 185, 188, 191, 204, 234
Davidson, James 115, 234
Davis, Ellen F. 23, 234
Dayagi-Mendels, Mikhal 161, 234
De Crom, Dries 5, 234
Deller, Karlheinz 114, 234
Delitzsch, Franz 25, 104, 133, 151, 182, 234
Delitzsch, Friedrich 216, 234
Derchain, Philippe 94, 149, 235
Dezső, Tamás 99, 235
Dhorme, Édouard 40, 235
Dirksen, Piet B. 5, 235
Dobbs-Allsopp, F. W. 67, 76, 112, 139, 235

Dodd, Stephen 245
Dorsey, David A. 86, 235
Dover, Kenneth J. 210, 235
DuBois, Page 42, 235
Durling, Robert M. 56, 235
Ebeling, Erich 26, 203, 235–36
Edwards, Iorweth E. S. 165, 236
Eichner, Jens 145, 147, 236
Eidelkind, Yakov 76, 111, 156, 236
Elgvin, Torleif 4, 236
Elliott, M. Timothea 59, 81, 86, 90, 236
Emanatian, Michele 41, 236
Emerton, John A. 48, 236
Eph'al, Israel 70, 236
Epstein, Isidore 10, 236
Erman, Adolf 28, 153, 236
Exum, J. Cheryl 17, 19, 21–22, 30, 67–69, 71–72, 81, 83–86, 91, 103, 123, 133–34, 139, 143, 154, 173, 183–85, 215, 217, 223–24, 236–37
Falk, Marcia 35, 43–44, 67–68, 81, 91, 132, 145, 154, 168, 237
Falkenstein, Adam 124, 237
Faraone, Christopher 92, 237
Feliks, Yehuda 91, 140, 154, 178, 180, 237
Fernández-Galiano, Manuel 63, 237
Fields, Fridericus 186, 237
Finkel, Iriving 28, 144, 165, 234, 237, 250
Fisch, Harold 9, 237
Fishbane, Michael 2, 8, 12, 50, 73–74, 89–90, 237
Fitzmyer, Joseph A. 61, 237
Flint, Peter 3–4, 237
Folsom, Robert S. 63, 237
Foster, Benjamin O. 92, 95, 238
Foster, Benjamin R. 95, 143, 190, 238
Fox, Michael V. 28–29, 36, 43, 48–51, 55, 69, 71–72, 76, 81, 94, 98, 100–101, 104, 111, 113, 117, 128, 137, 139, 149–50, 152, 154–56, 158, 168–71, 173–74, 178, 180, 184, 187, 190, 197, 201–2, 209, 213, 215–16, 236, 239, 255
Frachetti, Michael 261

Frangié-Joly, Dina	155, 238	Grady, Joseph E.	40, 47, 240
Frank, Daniel	11, 238	Gray, Erik	120, 241
Frankfort, Henri	151, 238	Greenfield, Jonas C.	157, 241
Frazer, James G.	46, 238	Greengus, Samuel	52, 77, 241
Friedman, Norman	53–54, 238	Griffiths, Paul J.	16, 241
Frost, Peter	65, 238	Grimm, Jacob	65, 163, 241
Frye, Northrup	53, 238	Grimm, Wilhelm	65, 163, 241
Frymer-Kensky, Tikva	107, 238	Groneberg, Brigitte	114, 190, 198, 203, 241
Gadot, Yuval	249		
Gansell, Amy Rebecca	147, 150, 171, 182, 211, 238	Grossberg, Daniel	89, 241
		Gunkel, Hermann	48, 241
Garrett, Duane A.	24, 29, 80, 94, 101, 140, 145, 153–54, 172–73, 188, 208, 216–17, 239	Güterbock, Hans G.	147, 257
		Haas, Robert	117, 241
		Hadley, Judith M.	106, 241
Gault, Brian P.	4, 55, 178, 239	Hagedorn, Anselm C.	3, 13, 76, 115, 129, 160, 233, 235, 237, 241
Geeraerts, Dirk	40, 239–40		
Gelb, Ignace J.	96, 239	Hainsworth, J. B.	127, 237
Geller, Mark J.	28, 66, 149, 234, 239, 248	Hallo, William W.	44, 241–42
Geller, Stephen A.	36, 138, 239	Hallock, Richard	165, 248
George, Andrew R.	28, 51, 95, 137, 144, 155, 158, 209, 239, 248, 250	Hamilton, Albert C.	162, 167, 191, 200, 242
Gerber, Douglas	7, 61, 92, 109, 115, 170, 228, 239, 260	Hamilton, Mark W.	195–96, 242
		Harer, W. Benson, Jr.	180, 242
Gerleman, Gillis	28, 72, 98, 130, 140, 146, 153–54, 180, 202, 239	Hawass, Zahi	200, 202, 242
		Hays, Christopher B.	50, 242
Germer, Renate	94, 126, 239	Heidel, Alexander	48, 242
Gibbs, Raymond	40, 42, 217, 240, 267	Held, Moshe	50, 189, 242
Gill, Roma	56, 192, 240	Hendel, Ronald	2, 242
Ginsburg, Christian D.	2, 17, 21, 24, 73, 91, 133, 140, 145, 153–54, 156, 175–76, 180, 182, 188, 201, 240	Hepper, F. Nigel	179, 242
		Hermes, Taylor	261
		Herrmann, Wolfram	51, 137, 242
Gioia, Ted	54, 57, 79, 240	Hess, Richard S.	21, 81, 91, 103, 131, 133, 145, 154, 183, 217, 242
Gleason, Kathryn L.	121, 240		
Goedicke, Hans	65–66, 77, 149, 240, 244, 248	Heubeck, Alfred	63, 127, 237
		Hicks, R. Lansing	74, 80–1, 83, 242
Goetze, Albrecht	46, 240	Higgins, Reynold A.	172, 242
Goitein, Shlomo D.	188, 240	Hirsch, Hans	84, 243
Goldenberg, David M.	64, 157, 240	Hoch, James. E.	93–94, 243
Gopal, Lallanji	135, 240	Hoffmann, David Zvi	9, 243
Gordis, Robert	80, 91, 100, 123, 188, 208, 240	Hoffmeier, James K.	49, 243
		Honeyman, Alexander M.	169, 243
Goren, Yuval	252	Hooper, Richard W.	210, 243
Goshen-Gottstein, Moshe	4, 240	Hopf, Matthias	24, 243
Gould, George M.	110, 240	Hopf, Maria	91, 127, 267
Goulder, Michael	24, 68, 98, 213, 240	Horowitz, Wayne	29, 46, 243, 252

House, Paul R.   24, 29, 80, 94, 101, 140, 145, 153–54, 173, 188, 217, 239
Hubbard, Dudley   245
Hubbard, Robert L, Jr.   33, 243
Hulster, Izaak J. de   45, 49, 144, 147, 243, 262
Hunger, Hermann   156, 244
Hunt, Patrick   37, 125–26, 131–32, 244
Ilan, Tal   62, 244
Isserlin, Benedikt S. J.   172, 244
Itzhaki, Masha   116, 244
Iyengar, Sujata   150, 244
Jacob, Ronja   160, 244
Jacobsen, Thorkild   77, 92, 94–95, 108, 114, 118, 124, 128, 149, 198, 203, 209, 213, 244
James, Elaine T.   41, 75, 84, 168, 175, 192, 244
Japhet, Sara   10–11, 141, 244–45
Jax, Karl   63, 109, 152, 170, 182, 188, 245
Jellinek, Paul   206, 245
Jenkins, Ian   210, 245
Jinbachian, Manuel M.   42, 64, 126, 150, 152, 170, 176, 182, 204, 206, 245
Johns, Catherine   210, 245
Johnson, Mark   40–41, 248
Joüon, Paul   4, 12, 97, 157, 189, 245
Kahana, Menahem   208, 245
Kaplan, Jonathan   6, 9, 245
Karlin, Daniel   199, 266
Kasher, Aryeh   72, 245
Keel, Othmar   2, 5, 17, 28–29, 36–39, 67, 69, 82, 91, 103–6, 119, 123–24, 126–27, 131, 133–34, 139, 143, 145–46, 148, 150, 152, 154, 164, 170–71, 177, 179, 183–84, 188–89, 192, 202, 217, 219, 245
Keen, Karen R.   16, 246
Keil, Carl F.   25, 104, 133, 151, 182, 234
Keimer, Ludwig   94, 246
Keller, Donald R.   147, 234
Kelly, Joseph R.   47, 246
Kemp, Barry   150, 246
Keuls, Eva C.   210, 246

Kimelman, Reuven   13, 246
King, Helen   42, 246
King, Philip J.   83, 147, 152, 197, 200, 246
Kingsmill, Edmée   12, 96, 246
Kinnier Wilson, J. V.   200, 246
Kitchen, Kenneth A.   48, 179, 246
Klein, Jacob   70, 95, 98, 108, 246, 259
Kletter, Raz   106–7, 166, 246
Klinck, Anne L.   116, 246
Knauf, Ernst Axel   72, 246
Köcher, Franz   151, 247
Kotzé, Zacharias   44, 247
Kövecses, Zoltán   34, 134, 214, 247
Kozodoy, Maud   10, 247
Kramer, Samuel Noah   26, 108, 118, 190, 216, 247
Kraus, Fritz R.   156, 247
Krinetzki, Günter   18–19, 139, 154, 247
Kugel, James   82, 247
Kynes, Will   21, 247
Labat, René   158, 247
Laffineur, Robert   166, 247
Lakoff, George   40–41, 248
Lam, Joseph   86, 248
Lambert, Wilfred G.   28, 48, 65–66, 124–25, 142, 165, 248
Landsberger, Benno   140, 165, 248
Landy, Francis   19, 81, 86–87, 96–97, 112, 122, 131, 175–76, 180, 248
Lane, Lauriat, Jr.   53, 248
Langdon, Stephen   198, 203, 248
Lange, Nicholas de   5, 248
Langgut, Dafna   179, 249
Lapinkivi, Pirjo   26, 189, 249
Lawrence, Paul J. N.   48, 249
Lee, Alvin A.   54, 249
Lee, Mireille M.   167, 249
Leech, Geoffrey   34, 249
Leek, F. Filce   158, 249
Lehrman, Simon M.   132, 249
Leick, Gwendolyn   114, 209, 249
Lemmelijn, Bénédicte   2, 5, 229, 249
LeMon, Joel M.   38, 44, 147, 238, 249
Lesko, Leonard H.   135, 249

Levey, Martin	202–3, 249	McCartney, Eugene Stock	94, 252
Levine, Étan	84, 249	McConvery, Brendan	13, 252
Levinson, Bernard M.	48, 52, 241, 249, 265	McEuen, Melissa A.	163, 252
		McKnight, Edgar	18, 252
Levy, Selim J.	46, 240	McLaren, Angus	210, 252
Lieber, Laura	10, 249	Meek, Theophilus J.	26–27, 100, 216, 252
Linder, Sven	64, 249		
Lindley, David	79, 162, 249	Melamed, Abraham	73, 252
Lipschits, Oded	249	Menn, Esther M.	10, 252
Littauer, Mary A.	99, 250	Merkle, Ann	261
Littlewood, Antony R.	92, 94, 250	Meyers, Carol	19–21, 252
Littman, Enno	126, 167, 199, 204, 250	Middleton, J. Richard	50, 252
Livingstone, Alasdair	124–25, 137, 144, 198, 206, 250	Miller, Barbara Stoler	126, 151, 159, 162, 188, 252
Loader, James A.	134, 182–83, 250	Miller, Robert D.	35, 252
Loewe, Raphael	9, 250	Mitchell, Christopher W.	16, 253
Long, Gary A.	185, 188, 250	Mitchell, Stephen	117, 241
Longman, Tremper	51, 73, 85–86, 133, 145, 154–55, 173, 188, 201, 250, 259	Moldenke, Alma L.	90–91, 130–31, 178, 253
Loud, Gordon	212, 250	Moldenke, Harold N.	90–91, 130–31, 178, 253
Löw, Immanuel	93, 123, 178, 250		
Lubetski, Meir	69, 250	Moon, Warren G.	170, 253
Lucas, Alfred	165, 202, 251	Moorey, Peter R. S.	213, 253
Luckenbill, Daniel D.	142, 212, 251	Moran, William L.	46, 253
Maalej, Zouheir	42–43, 251	Morgenstern, Julius	52, 253
Machiela, Daniel A.	61, 251	Muchiki, Yoshiyuki	153, 179, 253
Mahdi, Muhsin	159, 251	Müller, Hans-Peter	74, 143, 189, 253
Maksudov, Farhod	261	Munro, Jill M.	37, 96, 121, 134, 253
Malul, Meir	47, 49, 251	Muraoka, Takamitsu	4, 69, 253
Manniche, Lise	109, 160, 165, 179, 187, 202, 208, 251	Murphy, Roland E.	49, 81, 86, 96, 100–1, 145, 154–55, 180, 183–84, 187, 195, 253
Marcus, David	142, 251		
Mariaselvam, Abraham	55, 66, 108, 115, 129, 151–52, 159, 162, 167, 182, 190, 199, 251	Murray, Gilbert	53, 253
		Muscarella, Oscar White	99, 253
		Naguib, Saphinaz-Amal	149, 152, 253
Martinez, Ronald L.	56, 235	Negev, Abraham	72, 253
Maspero, M. Gaston	28–29, 251	Neufeld, Edward	161, 202, 253
Mathers, E. Powys	64, 126, 130, 162, 167, 172, 176, 184, 188, 191, 200, 204, 251	Neusner, Jacob	8–10, 62, 101, 253–54
		Nissinen, Martti	26–27, 30, 50–51, 55, 93, 95, 104, 114, 117–18, 137, 176, 189, 195, 213, 216, 254
Matsushima, Eiko	117, 251		
Matter, E. Ann	13, 15, 251–52	Noegel, Scott B.	23, 59, 123, 153, 184, 189, 254
Maxwell-Hyslop, K. Rachel	97, 171, 252		
Mazar, Eilat	29, 46, 252	Noonan, Benjamin J.	46, 196, 254
Mace, Arthur C.	197, 232	Norris, Richard A., Jr.	14–16, 62, 254

Nougayrol, Jean   66, 212, 254
Novák, Mirko   117, 254
Nunnally, Wave E.   6–7, 254–55
O'Donoghue, Michael   213, 255
Ogle, Mabbuby B.   163, 255
Opificius, Ruth   107, 255
Oppenheim, A. Leo   151, 247
Oshima, Takayoshi   29, 46, 243, 252
Pallingston, Jessica   163, 255
Pardes, Ilana   21, 255
Parpola, Simo   41, 107, 114, 117, 124, 149, 176, 209, 228, 230, 239, 247–48, 254, 255–56
Paul, Shalom M.   41, 91, 113, 116, 118–19, 156, 255
Peres, Henri   116, 256
Phillips, Helen   116, 256
Philonenko, Marc   8, 256
Pinch, Geraldine   161, 256
Pitard, Wayne   166, 260
Pope, Marvin H.   2–3, 21, 55, 67, 69–72, 91, 93, 100–2, 122, 126, 131, 140, 145, 154, 156, 169, 174–75, 180, 184, 186, 189, 195, 256
Porat, Naomi   249
Porteous, J. Douglas   41, 256
Porter, Barbara A.   147, 234
Posener, Georges   161, 256
Postgate, J. Nicholas   96, 256
Powell, Marvin A.   135, 256
Provan, Iain   24, 256
Pruss, Alexander   107, 256
Puech, Émile   4, 256
Pupko, Yaakov   164, 168, 174, 256
Pyle, Walter L.   110, 240
Quiller-Couch, Arthur T.   172, 256
Rabin, Chaim   104, 256
Ramanujan, Attipat K.   79, 125, 150, 159, 191, 204, 257
Rasmussen, Carl G.   179, 257
Ratzaby, Yehudah   93, 257
Ray, Paul J., Jr.   146, 257
Reiner, Erica   107, 147, 257
Reisman, Daniel   190, 257
Renan, Ernest   25, 257
Rendsburg, Gary   23, 59, 123, 153, 169, 171, 184, 189, 254, 257
Ricks, Christopher   56, 257
Richards, Ivor A.   34, 257
Riley, James Whitcomb   56, 257
Ringgren, Helmer   26, 74, 99, 195, 257
Robert, André   12, 72, 134, 154, 257
Robins, Gay   62–63, 157, 182, 213, 257
Roisman, Hannah   127, 246
Romano, James F.   171, 258
Rowley, Harold H.   2, 17, 27, 258
Rozelaar, Marc   164, 258
Rudolph, Wilhelm   126, 133, 154, 156, 258
Ruffle, John   48, 258
Russo, Joseph   63, 237
Ryken, Leland   54, 258
Saarisalo, Aapeli   25, 64, 100, 137, 139–41, 159, 167, 172, 191, 258
Sanders, Seth L.   29, 243
Sandmel, Samuel   44, 258
Sanford, A. Whitney   129, 258
Sasson, Jack M.   30–31, 258
Sasson, Victor   69, 258
Satlow, Michael L.   219, 258
Sauer, James A.   146, 258
Schechter, Solomon   1, 61, 259
Schellenberg, Annette   12, 132, 259
Scheper, George L.   1, 259
Scherer, Andreas   145, 147, 236
Scherman, Nosson   12, 267
Schoenbaum, Samuel   65, 259
Schoville, Keith   75, 123, 259
Schökel, Luis A.   205, 259
Schroer, Silvia   36, 259
Schwab, George   51, 259
Schwienhorst-Schönberger, Ludger 12, 132, 259
Scurlock, Joanne   57, 259
Sefati, Yitschak   39, 50, 66, 76, 95, 114–15, 118, 125, 128, 137, 171, 187, 190, 200, 212–13, 259
Seibert, Ilse   171, 259
Segal, Moses H.   57, 174, 260
Selby, Martha Ann   204, 260

Sells, Michael A. 115–16, 260
Shaw, Ian 213, 260
Shelton, China P. 147, 234
Sherrow, Victoria 159, 171, 177, 260
Shuve, Karl 14, 260
Siegfried, D. Carl 25, 260
Singer, Itamar 154–55, 260
Sinha, Chris 43, 260
Sjöberg, Åke W. 187, 260
Smith, Mark S. 166, 260
Smith, Wilfred Cantwell 1, 260
Smith, William S. 161, 260
Smith, Yancy 13, 260
Sokoloff, Michael 169, 261
Soulen, Richard N. 35, 57, 153, 261
Sowden, Lewis 24, 261
Spengler, Robert N. 96, 261
Srivastava, V. C. 135, 240
Stager, Lawrence E. 75, 83, 147, 152, 197, 200, 246, 261
Staubli, Thomas 36, 259
Steele, Valerie 110, 261
Steinert, Ulrike 42, 261
Stemberger, Gunter 9, 261
Stephan, Stephan H. 25, 64, 72, 79, 93, 116, 126–27, 130, 140–41, 150, 159, 162, 167, 176, 182, 191, 199–200, 204, 261
Stern, David 11, 13, 244, 261
Stewart, Susan 152, 161, 166, 261
Stoddart, D. Michael 206, 261
Stol, Marten 81, 84, 261
Stone, Michael 6, 261
Stoop-van Paridon, Petronella W. T. 24, 100, 181, 184, 261
Strack, Hermann L. 9, 261
Strawn, Brent A. 49, 144, 243, 261–62
Subramoniam, V. I. 66, 262
Suderman, W. Derek 179, 262
Sugg, Richard 53–54, 238
Sumi, Akiko 137, 215, 262
Suter, Claudia E. 211, 262
Tadmor, Hayim 212, 262
Takács, Gábor 153, 262
Tawil, Hayim 74–75, 83, 138, 262

Thompson, Cynthia L. 151, 262
Thompson, Henry O. 166, 262
Thompson, R. Campbell 152, 158, 198, 262
Thompson, Yaakov 185, 262
Thomson, William M. 70, 262
Thöne, Yvonne S. 102, 262
Thureau-Dangin, François 140, 161, 262
Tigay, Jeffrey H. 29, 113, 255, 263
Tilford, Nicole L. 43, 263
Tobin, Vincent A. 7, 109, 113, 155, 263
Topsfield, Leslie T. 64, 263
Tournay, Robert 12, 72, 134, 154, 257
Tov, Emanuel 3, 164, 263
Trautmann, Thomas R. 213, 263
Treat, Jay Curry 5, 263
Trible, Phyllis 19, 21, 90, 112, 122, 263
Tsumura, David T. 192, 263
Tuell, Steven S. 153, 263
Tur-Sinai, Naftali H. 120, 263
Turner, Denys 15, 263
Turner, Victoria 245
Ullmann, Stephen 40, 263
Ussishkin, David 46, 264
Van Hecke, Pierre 102, 264
Vasuki, M. 151, 264
Verde, Danilo 102, 264
Viezel, Eran 123, 148, 264
Vico, Giambattista 40, 264
Virolleaud, Charles 153, 264
Viviers, Hendrik 57, 264
Wabyanga, Robert K. 73, 264
Wacks, David A. 11, 264
Walfish, Barry Dov 141, 245
Walsh, Carey Ellen 23, 133, 180, 264
Waltke, Bruce K. 48, 82, 178, 264
Walton, John H. 50–51, 101, 239, 265
Ward, William A. 161, 265
Wasserman, Nathan 26, 50, 77, 95, 108, 118, 144, 174, 198, 265
Watson, Wilfred G. E. 30, 34–35, 73, 138, 265
Weems, Renita J. 90, 98, 265
Weinfeld, Moshe 48, 265

Wellhausen, Julius	71–72, 265
Wells, Bruce	52, 265
Wente, Edward F., Jr.	200, 265
West, Stephanie	127, 237
Westbrook, Raymond	52, 265
Westenholz, Aage	118, 120–21, 203, 214, 266
Westenholz, Joan G.	6, 30, 39, 42, 50, 93, 108, 117–18, 120–21, 125, 137, 187, 203, 265–66
Wetzstein, Johann G.	25, 266
Whedbee, J. William	20–21, 266
White, John B.	30, 44, 54, 217, 241, 266
Whitesell, Connie J.	1, 266
Winter, Urs	107, 143, 245, 266
Wiseman, Donald J.	198, 266
Wolff, Hans W.	36–37, 266
Woolford, John	199, 266
Woolley, Leonard	161, 198, 266
Wright, David P.	52, 266
Yadin, Yigael	99, 266
Younger, K. Lawson, Jr.	44–46, 267
Yu, Ning	41–43, 47, 251, 267
Zevit, Ziony	47, 107, 246, 267
Zhang, Sarah	105, 157, 267
Zlotowitz, Meir	12, 267
Zohary, Daniel	91, 127, 267
Zohary, Michael	91, 178, 267
Zvelebil, Kamil	108, 267
Zwan, Pieter van der	18, 267